Jonathan Fenby has reported from France since 1965 for a wide variety of news organisations including Reuters, *The Economist*, *The Times*, the *Independent*, the *Guardian* and the *Observer*. He has also contributed to French publications such as *Libération*, *L'Express*, *Sud-Ouest* and *L'Évènement du Jeudi* as well as appearing on French radio and television. To his surprise, he was made a *Chevalier* of the French Order of Merit in 1990.

Married to a Frenchwoman, he feels as much at home in France as in England. Still, he worked for nine years in what used to be known as Fleet Street, as Assistant Editor of the *Independent*, Deputy Editor of the *Guardian* and Editor of the *Observer* before moving to Hong Kong, where he has edited the region's main English-language newspaper, the *South China Morning Post*, from 1995 to 2000, since when he has written widely for newspapers and magazines as well as broadcasting on France. He was made a Commander of the British Empire in 2000 for services to journalism. He is also the author of *Dealing With the Dragon: A Year in the New Hong Kong* (Little, Brown).

'Among the many virtues of *On the Brink* is its historical scrutiny of the prejudices that have clouded British views of the F-place . . . Packed with anecdote and detail, it is a thoughtful, strongly felt study of what Jonathan Fenby believes are France's ills . . . Many of his criticisms hit the mark'

The Economist

'Fenby's book is an admirable summary of many recent social, political and economic developments in France. It would make perfect reading for anyone who had overlooked news reports on the country since Mitterrand came to power, and neatly summarises many of the complex scandals that one is liable to lose sight of in Britain . . . By the end of *On the Brink* one has been wonderfully entertained . . . A witty and engaging confession of love–hate for a complex country'

ALAIN DE BOTTON in the *Spectator*

'Fenby is particularly good at chronicling the plethora of financial scandals which have beset France in recent years and in demonstrating the close connections between the State and the business community . . . Anyone interested in the recent history and politics of France will find Fenby's book informative and readable, packed as it is with a wealth of detail and gossipy anecdote'

JAMES F. MCMILLAN in the *Times Literary Supplement*

'Excellent . . . The contradictions [of modern France] are brilliantly teased out and wrestled with in this book: a book which seeks to be critical of France, sometimes very critical, but from the point of view of a friend and Francophile and long-term observer . . . Fenby [writes] with passion, and deserved anger, about the depths of political corruption revealed in recent years; about the collapse of Mitterrandism into empty arrogance and venality; and about the menace of the National Front. There are especially moving chapters on the hollowing-out of rural France and the empty lives, and extreme Islamic temptations, of the second-generation immigrant youth of the inner suburbs of French cities'

JOHN LICHFIELD in the *Independent on Sunday*

'A committed Francophile's lament for a country that manages to be at once infuriating and captivating, deeply uncertain of its future and breathtakingly arrogant about its past . . . Fenby's indictment of France is often sharp but never vicious, avoiding the caricature and exposing the cliché that so often taints British attitudes to France . . . We rattle along from sociology to history, business scandal to political corruption, Chirac to Cantona, and the whole is seasoned with good stories, winking asides and plenty of jokes . . . As with some of the best multi-course French meals, the reader is often left wanting more'

BEN MACINTYRE in *The Times*

'The analysis pulls no punches, drawing on a wide knowledge of French history and *belles-lettres* as well as on an abundance of examples and statistics which lift its argument to the level of a solid indictment . . . studded with flashes of wit'

VALERIE BRAUNSCHWIG in *Le Monde*

'Fenby's fine book explores the multi-faceted nature of [the French] crisis, from the decline of the baguette to widespread political corruption . . . Impressive'

ANAND MENON in the *London Review of Books*

'A gripping and enlightening read . . . An excellent survey of the state of modern France. Taking in all the major themes of French identity and exploring how they have been undermined – from agriculture to the motor industry, smoking to fashion – and with acute analysis of recent French political history, Fenby argues that France is a country without direction; a once-great power now unsure of itself and its place in the world . . . Whether you live in France, own French property, take holidays there, or just love the place, you should read this challenging study without delay'

Living France

ON THE BRINK

BRINK

*The Trouble
With France*

JONATHAN FENBY

A *Time Warner* Paperback

First published in Great Britain in 1998
by Little, Brown and Company
This edition published in 1999 by Warner Books
Reprinted in 1999, 2001
Reprinted by Time Warner Paperbacks in 2004

Material from Chapter 13, 'A French Life', first
appeared in different form in the *Guardian* 'Weekend'
magazine in 1995.

The moral right of the author has been asserted.

A CIP catalogue record for this book
is available from the British Library.

Map by Neil Hyslop

Typeset in Bembo by M Rules
Printed and bound in Great Britain by
Clays Ltd, St Ives plc

Time Warner Paperbacks
An imprint of
Time Warner Book Group UK
Brettenham House
Lancaster Place
London WC2E 7EN

www.twbg.co.uk

To the memory of
Alter and Fanny

CONTENTS

Contents

PREFACE

The first time I went to France, I didn't like it much. My god-mother had invited me to join her on holiday in Brittany to look after her children. I have two memories of the trip: daringly calling out '*Ah, les flics!*' at the police on the seafront, and trying to learn to sail on a boat with a grizzled Frenchman who kept yelling about '*le foc*' – the mizzen sail, not a Breton approximation of a four-letter swear-word.

Forty years later, I was sitting in my office by the harbour in Hong Kong, having edited the *South China Morning Post* through the territory's return to China. It had been a breathless summer, with no time to think of anything except work. One Wednesday in August, I was seized by a single thought. My wife was in France, taking the waters at an obscure spa in the wilds of the Cévennes. In three days' time, she and three of our closest friends would drive to a favourite restaurant and hotel in a medieval village by the Aveyron river. My diary was embarrassingly empty. So I booked a ticket for that night, flew to Paris, changed airports and boarded a little plane to the town of Rodez. Once there I hired a car, drove twenty miles, and was sitting in the garden by the river when they drove over the hump-backed bridge on Saturday afternoon.

France gets you that way. Its lure is the reason for this book. I had wanted to write an account of the state of France for some time; what got me started was the virulence and scale of the protests that were set off by President Chirac's decision to resume nuclear testing in the summer of 1995. Why, I wondered, did France arouse such strong emotions? What is it that is so unusual about this nation and its people? And then, looking at the morosity which spread across the country from the mid-1980s, how did one reconcile the superior sheen which France displays to the world with the realities of double-digit unemployment, a rampant extremist party of the far right and a people who reject the elite that has ruled them for decades? And then, for this new and extensively updated edition, there was the experience of the long collaboration between Jacques Chirac and the socialists, followed by the political earthquake of 2002.

Without a healthy France, there is no Europe. That is why the state of the land between the Atlantic and the Rhine, the Mediterranean and the Channel matters so much, and why its political, social and economic evolution at the start of the twenty-first century is of wider significance.

For a foreigner to try to grapple with such matters may seem arrogant. But I hope that three decades spent either living in France or watching it closely from abroad have enabled me to take the pulse of the nation, though I know that many friends living in Paris, the Berry or the Auvergne would disagree with my concerns about their country. My starting-point is certainly not that of a Francophobe; rather more that of a lover who entertains some fundamental worries about the object of his affection.

That affection comes from personal experience, encounters and observation as well as from my work as a journalist in France for Reuters, *The Economist*, *The Times*, the *Guardian*, the *Independent*, the *Observer* and other publications in Britain and the United States. I could never have undertaken this book, let alone finished it, without the help of my wife, who has given me roots-by-marriage in France and whose assistance has been as invaluable as it has been rigorous. Hundreds of people have contributed to my knowledge of France and given me material for this book. I owe a special debt to my colleagues in the French press and broadcasting; in particular to *L'Express*, *Le Monde*, *Libération*, *Le Figaro*, *Le Nouvel Observateur*, *Le Point* and RTL. I have indicated their specific contributions at various points in the text, but, beyond that, they have given me a far broader insight into France over the years as friends and colleagues.

Louis and Lya Wartski and their children have been an invaluable well on which to draw since the mid-1960s. Roger Galéron was a particularly moving witness of one day in 1942. The late André Passeron was my first and best guide to French politics, while Louis Marcerou opened windows on to France that I could never have found elsewhere. Paul Webster was an essential companion at historic moments in the 1990s as well as unearthing valuable material on the saga of François Mitterrand, which he generously made available.

I owe a special debt to the inhabitants of Mourjou and Calvinet in the Cantal, and in particular to our generous and ever-dependable host in the chestnut country, Peter Graham, whose sharp eye and broad knowledge contributed greatly to improving the book for this edition. Among the Anglo-New Zealand tribe to be found in those parts, Keith Walker, Brian Oatley, Peter and Win Campbell have provided information and food for thought over the years in the Place de l'Église. Ginette Vincendeau has been both a valuable source of material and a stimulating verbal sparring-partner. Bernard Edinger has always been there when facts needed to be checked or leads followed up, while Simon Caulkin, Jack Altman and David Lawday have been friendly sources of ideas through more years than any of us would like to acknowledge.

I would also like to thank the following, for their often unwitting contribution over the years: Jacques Attali; Raymond Barre; Jean-Philippe Béja; Pierre Bérégovoy; Luc and Annie Besnier; Jean-Louis Bianco; Géraud de Bonnafos; Sylvain Bourmeau; Denis and Geneviève Brulet; Claude Cheysson; Jacques Chirac; Mary Dejevsky; Roland Dumas; Albert Duroy; the Estienne family and others who stayed on in the village of Saint-André-de-Rosans; Nicole and Michèle Fagegaltier, and their father; Philippe and Claire Ferras; Anne Freyer; Marie-France Garaud; Valéry Giscard d'Estaing; Jacques and Annie Hudès; Denis Jeambar; Douglas Johnson; Serge July; Pascal Lamy; Jean-Marie Le Pen; Jean-Yves and Michèle Libeskind; John Lichfield; Gerald Long; Serge Marti; Dominique Moïsi; Christine Ockrent; Micheline Oerlemans; André Poitevin; Louis-Bernard Puech; Martine Schultz; Dominique Strauss-Kahn; Margie Sudre; the Vincendeau family and John Vinocur.

The chapter on the National Front draws, in part, on Alexander Fenby's thesis on the party, and Sara Fenby kept me up to date on the latest relevant French writings while I was on the other side of the world. In Hong Kong, Winnie Tam, Joseph Leung and other colleagues helped in producing the origianl manuscript, for which deep thanks to them.

Though our paths diverged, Faith Evans set the ball rolling, and Gillon Aitken gave valuable advice. Paul Theroux suggested a vital connection. Christopher Sinclair-Stevenson's enthusiasm made all the difference. I am grateful to Philippa Harrison, to Andrew Gordon for editing the original edition, and Tim Whiting for overseeing the volume of changes in this edition with calm efficiency, not to mention the long-suffering production department. But, in the end, it all comes down to Renée, without whom none of this would have been possible. That's why one flies from the other side of the world to sit by a river in the Rouergue.

July 2002

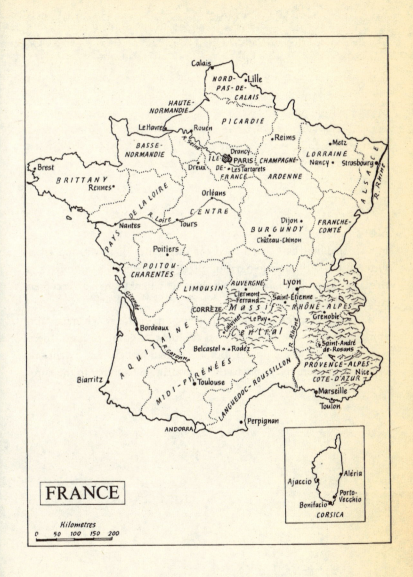

FRANCE

Kilometres
0   50   100   150   200

Note

French spellings have been used for the names of towns and cities throughout, although geographical or administrative regions (e.g. Brittany, Burgundy) take the English name where there is an accepted Anglicised version.

Because of movements in the currency market, French francs and euros have not been converted. At the time of going to press, there were 1.55 euros to the pound. Before the national currency went out of use, there were ten francs to the pound and 6.65 francs to the euro.

I

SOMETHING SPECIAL

France occupies an exclusive place in the world, and could accept nothing less. Its President declares it a beacon for the human race. The nation and its people may be loved or hated, but they can never be ignored, revelling in what they call *l'exception française*. France claims to have evolved a special economic and social model, midway between market capitalism and state control. It is the world's favourite holiday destination, and the proclaimed home of *Liberté, Égalité, Fraternité*. It gave the planet Joan of Arc and Charles de Gaulle, the Three Musketeers, Madame Bovary and Cyrano de Bergerac, Édith Piaf, Brigitte Bardot and Marcel Proust, the cinema, foie gras and the bidet, denim and champagne, the Statue of Liberty and the modern totalitarian revolution, liposuction and the vegetable mixer, the sardine can, the Impressionists, disposable razors, babies' feeding bottles, Louis Pasteur and Marie Curie, the World Cup football champions of 1998 and Grand Slam rugby winning teams.

France is central to Europe, and, it sincerely believes, to the globe as a whole. With one of the half-dozen biggest economies, nuclear weapons and a permanent seat on the United Nations Security Council, it claims to offer an alternative to the domination of Washington as shown most recently by its leadership of opposition to the war in Iraq which also put cross-Channel relations under severe strain. Since General de Gaulle restored the country's faith in itself after 1958, the national psyche has sprouted a self-confidence which is not always becoming, but which leaves no doubt that it offers the rest of the world something out of the ordinary.

Not for the French the small opt-outs or grey compromises which satisfy others; they wield vetoes and strut the stage with a panache rare in the twenty-first century. Their vision of history is unabashedly Francocentric. The supreme monarch, Louis XIV, didn't win many wars, but no European doubted that his Sun King court at Versailles was the centre of the Universe – and just imagine what would have happened if his successors hadn't made a hash of the Anglo-French wars of the mid-eighteenth century and had emerged dominant in North America. The most famous Corsican of all time may have ended up in poisoned exile on an island in the Atlantic, and become an overblown inspiration to dictators and press barons alike, but Bonaparte could still appear to Hegel as the master of the world, inspire an estimated 45,000 books and set Beethoven to write the 'Eroica' Symphony, even if the composer did withhold the dedication in what may have been the awakening of the Romantic movement to reality. Charles de Gaulle could be, in the words of an adviser to Franklin Roosevelt, 'one of the biggest sons-of-bitches that ever straddled a pot', yet his style of national leadership equalled Napoléon's in coining a new adjective for the world. Wherever they go, the French take their country with them – from Corsican restaurants in Indochina to their unrivalled network of *lycée* schools, which ensures that French children follow the central curriculum from Bonn to Beijing.

Lenin and Mao may have overthrown empires, but they were johnnies-come-lately in the revolutionary stakes. The uprising of 1789 set the template for getting rid of tyrants, and the national anthem still urges citizens to brandish their bloody banner against reaction. That being the case, the French are nurtured in the knowledge that they belong to the mother of modern republics, erected into a lay religion in the nineteenth century and epitomised in every mayor's office by the bust of the young woman Marianne, with her revolutionary headgear and exposed bosom. The fact that the bust is modelled on the most beautiful actress or model of the day helps: for the historian Emmanuel Le Roy Ladurie, it is enough that 'France is, first of all, a woman. A beautiful woman.'

The people of the country called the Hexagon – bounded by the Channel, the Atlantic, the Pyrenees, the Mediterranean, the Alps and the Rhine – feel they do not have to bother overmuch about what the rest of the world thinks of them; simply being French is enough. Traditionally, they have had little time for multiculturalism – foreigners and emigrants from other nations should count themselves lucky to be allowed inside the tent, and should conform to French ways and its culture. After all, which other nation can boast such a baker's dozen of writers as Rabelais, Molière, Corneille, Racine, Stendhal, Flaubert, Balzac, Hugo, Zola, Baudelaire, Proust and Dumas *père* and *fils*? Feydeau set the template for farce and, even if his creator originated from across the border in Belgium, Commissaire Maigret was quintessentially French. When it comes to painting, the list is equally impressive – from Poussin and De la Tour through Corot and Cézanne to the Impressionists and on to Matisse and Braque. Henri Cartier-Bresson and his peers are monuments of photography, and the whole world knows the Hunchback of Notre Dame, the horrors of Bluebeard, the adventure of *Around the World in Eighty Days*, the Cannes film festival and the Paris fashion shows.

It is not only that France feels no concern about standing apart: the urge to be different is, in the words of the commentator Dominique Moïsi, a fundamental part of national existence. As the novelist Julian Barnes puts it, the French embody 'otherness'. We are almost perfect, declared a Tourism Minister, though she also urged her compatriots to be more welcoming to visitors since 'even the most attractive girl needs a bit of make-up to seduce'. The French are conceited rather than vain, in a phrase used by the British politician, Roy Jenkins, about De Gaulle. Two centuries ago, Napoléon hit a note for the nation to live up to: 'My power depends on my glory, and my glories on the victories I have won. My power will fail if I do not feed it on new glories and new victories.' Or, as *le Général* remarked: 'The French need to be proud of France. Otherwise, they fall into mediocrity.'

This nation's special character looms far larger around the globe than any country containing only 1 per cent of the planet's population has the right to expect. Presidents of the Republic play on their double role as head of state and head of executive government to impress the world. As they travel abroad, they carry Europe 'on the soles of their shoes', one French minister declared. France was the last Western nation to test nuclear weapons, and one of the first to take serious action in Bosnia, where seventy of its soldiers died. In the post-colonial world, it maintains territories stretching from the North Atlantic to the South Seas, not to mention its shared suzerainty over the tiny tax haven of Andorra, high in the Pyrenees. Its natural position as the leader of Southern Europe puts it at the head of 175 million people from Portugal to Greece. Long after decolonialisation, Paris retained a *chasse gardée* in Africa, where rulers looked to the banks of the Seine for guidance and protection. France ranks ahead of Britain, Germany, Japan and the USA in the proportion of its gross national product devoted to overseas aid, and has produced a truly great humanitarian organisation in Médecins Sans Frontières.

Open the record book and the achievements come tumbling out. The French have unusually high life expectancy – an American scientist predicted that it would soon reach 85, and go to 100 by the next century. At the other end of the scale, Étienne Bacrot became the youngest-ever chess grandmaster at the age of fourteen. France has the world's largest opera house, one of Europe's most extensive and least crowded road networks, and as big a railway system as Britain and Italy put together. The French go to the cinema more than other mainland Europeans, and their film industry produces the most full-length features on the continent. They eat high levels of butter and eggs while maintaining a low rate of heart disease and – until recently at least – an obesity level one-fifth of that of Americans. A Europe-wide investigation reported that their children were the most healthy on the continent.

This country grows the most expensive potatoes on the planet, nurtured on seaweed and once sold for 3,000 francs a kilo. It is the world's biggest exporter of apples, and bred the first hybrid tea rose. France houses what may be the world's earliest work of art in the form of a 32,000-year-old cave painting, and the most ancient walnut, an 8-million-year-old fossil discovered in Burgundy in 1995. It produced the greatest court diarist in Saint-Simon, and witnessed the first parachute descent, two centuries ago from a balloon above the Parc Monceau in Paris – the intrepid jumper had prudently tried it on his dog beforehand. A French sailor was the first man to make a solo crossing of the Atlantic. A seventeenth-century prelate, Pierre de Fermat from Toulouse, set out the theorem which took three centuries to prove, Louis Braille enabled the blind to read, and another French man of science, Alfred Binet, invented the intelligence test. Baron Pierre de Coubertin launched the modern Olympics, and Jules Rimet organised the first football World Cup in 1930.

It was French agents who finally captured the terrorist Carlos the Jackal in the Sudan and took him back to Paris to spend the rest of his life in jail. A Frenchman holds the world record for the longest time spent under water without breathing; another set a speed-eating standard by consuming 267 large snails in 15 minutes. Their compatriots are both champion pet-owners (42 million household animals for 58 million people) and leading carnivores (just 1 per cent of the population is reckoned to be vegetarian). The Tour de France cycle race is watched by more on-the-spot spectators than any other annual sporting event on Earth, and is televised in 163 countries. France may have a weak national press, but Canal+ runs Europe's biggest cable television operation and *Elle* magazine claims to be the highest-selling international women's publication.

When it comes to literature, the French count the largest number of Nobel Prizes; their authors include one who wrote a whole book without using the letter 'e' and another who, suffering from 'locked-in syndrome' after a severe stroke, dictated a memoir by blinking his eye as an amanuensis read through the alphabet. For years, a literary programme went out in prime time on national television. Which other people could have prompted a 235-page academic treatise on their gestures, from the Phallic Forearm Jerk to the Ambiguous Gut-Punch? And a best-selling book of the late 1990s even claimed that Christ was buried in France.

The French Post Office set up the first on-line data network available to households throughout the nation, and French engineers helped to develop the supersonic airliner. A high-speed rail service has brought once distant regional centres into swift reach of Paris, making it easy for provincials to spend a day in the capital or Parisians to go to Lyons for lunch. After the government pressed Britain to build the Channel Tunnel link between the two countries, the comparative speed of trains on either side of the narrow sea reduced railway executives in England to making jokes about the virtue of giving travellers time to appreciate the Kent countryside.

The economy, which had once been the target of jibes about

soaring prices and feather-bedding, became an exemplar of anti-inflationary achievement during the 1990s, complete with a central bank which was finally given its independence of politicians and refused to be swayed from its path of rigour. Corporate dinosaurs were re-organised, and benefited to the full from the boom flowing from across the Atlantic at the end of the twentieth century. Productivity rose, and wage settlements were kept low. Services grew in importance to balance the decline of old industries. France became the second favourite location, after Britain, for foreign companies setting up in Europe, and the fourth biggest recipient of foreign investment in the world, as companies such as IBM, Motorola and FedEx developed their operations – and Toyota decided to build a 4-billion-franc plant in Valenciennes rather than across the Channel. A survey of international managers in 2002 showed it to be the preferred country as regards its quality of life, infrastructure and telecommunications and its scientific and technical excellence – and only marginally behind Germany in the quality of its workforce.

Governments of left and right brought down the budget deficit, and got public finances into healthier shape, resisting the devaluations that had punctuated modern French history at regular intervals. The strong franc was one of the lynchpins of the European common currency introduced at the turn of the century, and the initial decline of the euro against the dollar and sterling only served to boost French exports across the Atlantic. There were promises of tax cuts, and corporate chieftains became media stars as governments pursued privatisation of state assets.

French companies prospered and expanded across the globe while investors at home and abroad discovered the opportunities offered by under-valued shares on the Paris Bourse. Investment funds boomed, and French savers started to put their money into the stock market. As a result, the index more than tripled between the mid-1980s and the end of the century. A breed of modern-minded managers promised shareholder value, attracting foreign funds in their billions – non-French investors accounted for half the turnover on the stock market.

French enterprises became world leaders in products ranging from tyres to cosmetics and yoghurts. Électricité de France is by far Europe's biggest exporter of power. France is a major force in the

European Airbus consortium, whose development is being steered by a Frenchman. A hundred space rockets have been launched from French Guyana. Vivendi took over Universal Studios in Hollywood, and Renault taught the Japanese how to make cars at Nissan. British trains and electricity suppliers were run by companies from across the Channel. A French firm installed the world's largest flight kitchen at Hong Kong's new airport; another laid almost half the new telephone lines in China. From a country which seemed doomed always to lag behind Germany, France had built its economy into one of the world's success stories by the time the twenty-first century dawned. As we will see, maintaining such a position was to prove difficult on a number of fronts. But the way the Hexagon re-invented itself in industry, commerce and services was an undeniable achievement for a nation where business has never been regarded as particularly estimable.

If the business surge was new, France's appeal as a place to visit stretches back at least to the grand tourists of the eighteenth century. As the world's favourite holiday destination, the country attracts around 70 million visitors a year. The reasons are evident. Which other country can offer the châteaux of Versailles and the Loire, the walled city of Carcassonne and the papal palace of Avignon, the jewel church of Vézelay and the Romanesque beauties along the pilgrim trail towards Compostela, the hilltop fortresses of the doomed Cathar heretics in the Pyrenees, the cathedrals of Chartres, Reims or Albi, the central square of Nancy or the Dominican church and hidden medieval town-houses of Toulouse, the Spanish-accented charm and Fauvist colours of the anchovy port of Collioure on the Mediterranean and the turn-of-century elegance of Deauville on the Channel? From the rough beauty of the Cévennes and the towering peaks of the Alps to the lavender fields of the Drôme and the softness of Anjou, from the wild horses of the mountain plateaux of the Spanish border and the pink flamingos of the Camargue to the storks nesting on the rooftops of Alsace and the seagulls wheeling over the vast D-Day invasion beaches of Normandy – no country of comparable size, perhaps not even those of much greater size, can equal such variety of landscape and life.

Its capital offers an unparalleled range of architecture, history and personal memory, from the Roman relics of the Arènes de Lutèce to the Renaissance mansions of the Marais around the Place des Vosges, through Baron Haussmann's nineteenth-century construction of a city centre, and on to the legacy of steel, glass and concrete bequeathed by François Mitterrand. Its most popular attraction, the Centre Georges Pompidou in the Beaubourg district, lured five times as many visitors as originally planned, and had to close for two years to repair the resulting wear and tear. It has some of the most famous monuments and open spaces in the world – the Eiffel Tower, the Louvre, the Place de la Concorde, the Champs-Élysées and the Arc de Triomphe. It also has a uniquely private aspect with its courtyards, alleyways, hidden buildings and concierges who long ago learned that information was power. From China to Argentina, cities in search of glamour call themselves the 'Paris of the East' or the 'Paris of the Americas'. Though London's rebirth as the most lively city in the world hits magazine covers once a decade, it is Paris which clocks in with unbeatable regularity in the top league of the most beautiful and exciting capitals. Despite all those tales of outrageously priced cups of coffee on the Champs-Élysées, it is not among the most expensive to visit; and its famously abrupt inhabitants are as likely to be in a hurry as rude. In the summer of 2002, the Mayor put sand and grass on an expressway by the Seine – and attracted millions of visitors to his seaside in the city, or 'Paris-Plage' as it was known, complete with palm trees, deck chairs and volleyball courts.

For more than a century, the city was the magnet for art and writing and for political exiles, from White Russians fleeing Communism and Jews fleeing Hitler to the Duke and Duchess of Windsor in their memento-filled villa in the Bois de Boulogne. Reporting on the Dreyfus case for a Vienna newspaper set Theodor Herzl on the road to Zionism. The men who were to become Ho Chi Minh and Pol Pot studied Marxism and Leninism in France's capital. For decades, Paris was at the cutting-edge of modernity. One of the troop of foreign writers and artists who came to live there, Walter Benjamin, called it the capital of the nineteenth century; a bit later, another resident foreigner, Gertrude Stein, dubbed the city 'the place where the twentieth century was'. It was home to Picasso and Modigliani, and a last refuge for Oscar Wilde and Marlene Dietrich. Ernest Hemingway and Scott Fitzgerald sized up their penises in a Left Bank café lavatory. Paris and France adopted

Josephine Baker and Sidney Bechet. Jazz musicians fleeing American racism found a home from home in the Hôtel Louisiane on the Rue de Bucci. In different musical modes, Mstislav Rostropovich headed for Paris when he left the Soviet Union, and Jim Morrison's grave is a pilgrimage spot for Doors fans on the northern slopes of the city.

A Paris publisher was the first to print Joyce and Nabokov. George Gershwin sailed home in 1928 with a collection of Paris taxi-horns to use in *An American in Paris*. Eugène Ionesco and Samuel Beckett wrote in the language of their adopted country; asked why he lived in Paris, the Irish playwright replied: 'Well, you know, if I was in Dublin I would just be sitting around in a pub.' Cole Porter made April the city's month. Gene Kelly and Fred Astaire gave it the sheen of musical romance for cinema audiences around the globe. Humphrey Bogart comforted Ingrid Bergman in *Casablanca* by assuring her, 'We'll always have Paris.' Even Hitler had to admit that, while levelling London or Moscow would not have disturbed him, he would have been greatly pained to have had to destroy the capital of France.

Not to be outdone, other cities, towns and regions have attracted their stars, too. The still two-eared Van Gogh drew his inspiration from Provence. Salvador Dalí proclaimed Perpignan station to be the centre of the Universe. Medieval popes took up residence in Avignon. Deng Xiaoping worked in a provincial factory which branded him 'unsuitable for re-employment'. Chopin made beautiful music with George Sand in the dank flatlands of the centre. Robert Louis Stevenson trekked through the Cévennes on a donkey. Madonna named her daughter after the pilgrimage shrine of Lourdes, and Yul Brynner's ashes were laid to rest in a monastery in the Loire Valley. As for the Côte d'Azur, Scott Fitzgerald's 'pleasant shore of the Riviera' became such a mecca for the smart set of the 1920s that they could believe they had invented it; later, Somerset Maugham held lugubrious court in his villa at Cap Ferrat; and Graham Greene denounced the local political mafia as he saw out his last years in one of the less fashionable towns of the coastline.

For all the rivalry from across the Channel and from the New World, France's food still sets the international benchmark (despite such aberrations as *foie gras* sushi). The world pays ever-rising prices for great French wines, and downs 100 million bottles of Champagne a year. Though it is fashionable to decry French cooking for immobilism, and despite the popularity of lessons by Jamie Oliver and Delia Smith from across the Channel, the criticism is, for the most part, misplaced since it consists of taking France to task for not doing as others do – which is rather like attacking Chinese cuisine for not including *salade niçoise*. Plain steak and chips may be the favourite national dish, and some foreign food entrepreneurs may have attracted the smart set in Paris, but, as we will see, the allegation that French chefs have become stultified and boring simply ignores the widest-ranging gastronomy on Earth, and one which has a completely different dimension to all the seared seabass with Thai spices on a bed of curried Californian lettuce.

When a top French chef lays down his chopping-knife, it is news around the globe. No other country has as many different cheeses or wines; not to mention a 100-kilogram pumpkin grown by a gardener east of Paris, a 16-foot-wide quiche made from 1,928 eggs and the world's longest tripe sausage – all 150 feet of it. Champagne can legally come only from France. Smart eateries off the Champs-Élysées may adopt Americanised names, and you may stumble across a Tex-Mex restaurant on the Place de la Bastille, but French denotes quality eating around the globe: New York has Le Cirque, Los Angeles Ma Maison, London Le Gavroche and Tante Claire, and both Stockholm and Hanoi L'Opéra. Tokyo's Ginza shopping avenue is swamped with French outlets, and Japanese gourmets can spend a fortune eating the potato purée of three-star chef Joël Robuchon in a full-scale replica of a Loire Valley château constructed with stone imported from France. Across the sea from Japan, North Korea marked the elevation of a new Great Leader by ordering 66,000 bottles of French wine for the occasion, while China's biggest city has a Café de la Seine on the riverfront and a brasserie called Chamselisee (say it fast with a Shanghai accent and all becomes clear).

France may no longer produce the unchallenged leaders of world fashion – its top couture houses employ British, Italian and Russian designers to give them start-of-century edge – but these designers still want to work for the top houses in what, for the global imagination, remains the city that epitomises high style. Boutiques from Oslo to Osaka call themselves by French names in the quest for smartness. Rag-trade workshops around the world stitch in 'Arc de Triomphe' or 'Tour Eiffel' labels. At the top of the scale, it was Christian Dior who invented international haute couture, and his successor, Yves Saint-Laurent, who carried on the tradition – even if, as his lover and manager said, he was born with a nervous breakdown.

The great figures of French history have a global dimension. As well as the male political and military leaders already mentioned, Joan of Arc symbolises the defiant heroine, and Marie Curie the triumph of women in science while Brigitte Bardot was the most natural sex-symbol the cinema has known. Captain Dreyfus stands as an example of the way intolerance can make a victim of an upright man, and Zola's *J'accuse* in defence of him demonstrates the power of words. In another dimension, France's football team showed for four years how the game should be played, with its star, Zinedine Zidane, parading skills of a universal nature as he added to his national achievements by volleying Real Madrid to the top European club title while Arsène Wenger and Thierry Henri hoisted Arsenal to glory in England.

France fascinates, irritates and intrigues. It has a unique capacity to be brilliant one moment, self-destructive the next, mixing high rhetoric and partisan concern without a bat of the eyelid. Seeing itself as possessing a universal message for the planet, it could only be deeply resentful when the American way of democracy and markets stole the show. Even if they find it hard to define in practice, the French believe that they have a model to offer to the world. Their great solo artist of international politics of the post-war era, General de Gaulle, insisted on proclaiming his 'certain view of France', his conviction that the country must be 'dedicated to an exalted and exceptional destiny'. Others might use less sonorous words, but if anybody summed up France's view of itself, it was the man who saved his nation's honour twice in a lifetime.

The tone was set in 1940, when he insisted on his Free French command in London being the only Allied European force not to be integrated under the British. For more than a decade of the Cold War from 1958, Gaullist Paris presumed to act as a bridge between East and West and denounced the division of Europe. It insisted on freedom to target friend and foe alike with its nuclear force. In 1963, France vetoed Britain's entry into the European Common Market for the first time, mocking poor Prime Minister Macmillan from across the Channel. A little later, the General simply left the French chair at Common Market meetings empty for months when he didn't like the way the Community was going. His successors on left and right have pursued a policy which takes it for granted that Paris has a central role to play in the world. Its voice has to be heard on Europe, Africa and Asia. It loves to play host to international conferences, and staged the first of the meetings of world leaders that ballooned from an informal session on the island of Guadeloupe into the mammoth G8 sessions of later years.

Throughout, independence from Washington has been vital – De Gaulle was the first Western leader to attack the US over Vietnam, and took France out of the integrated military structure of the Nato alliance. More recently, Paris has differed sharply from Washington on the Israeli–Palestinian conflict, and made its major break with the Bush administration over the war against Iraq. Whatever the specific arguments about weapons inspection on that occasion, French policy was founded on a deep belief – shared by right and left – that it is the role of Paris to offer an alternative to what a Socialist Foreign Minister had referred to as the 'hyperpower' across the ocean, using the United Nations to leverage its own position. Having assured itself of German solidarity, France assumed that it could speak for Europe, and relations cooled with Britain, Spain and Italy when they decided to back Washington.

But there could be solidarity too – de Gaulle gave staunch backing to the United States in the Cuban missile crisis and Chirac was the first foreign head of state to visit the White House after 9/11. But, for France, the vital thing is that Washington should treat it seriously, take note of what it has to say, and not expect to be able to lay down the law to the world. There is no doubt that the idea of France being a power that is willing and able to dissent from the United States goes down well at home. An anti-globalisation group which made the US its prime target thrived at the start of the century, and a book saying the September 11 attacks were a put-up job by the Americans became an instant best-seller.

Under Presidents of right and left alike, the Gaullist heritage has been an enduring element in France's relations with the world. The repertoire has always ranged far and wide. In a single press conference, the founder of the Fifth Republic managed to dismiss Britain's application to join the Common Market, support a return to the Gold Standard, criticise the Israelis as 'an elite people, self-confident and dominating', and refer to Quebec as a sovereign state. Three decades later, the Socialist Foreign Minister, Hubert Védrine, insisted that 'France is a great country. She is not going to dissolve herself into a global magma, nor even a European one.' Paris sees the world as a multi-polar place where it will not be daunted by what Védrine termed the 'hyperpower' of the United States or constrained by its European partners. It insisted that it should take the lead role in deciding Western policy in Central Africa, that it would follow its own line on globalisation, and had the right to break international embargoes – all the while denying that any of this dented Western solidarity. To burnish its aura, France is particularly keen on its civil servants holding high international positions – asked about his country's appetite for top jobs, a Finance Minister likened it to taking both cheese and a dessert at dinner. What's wong with a healthy appetite?

Coherence, or rather lack of it, is not a problem. The first President of the left caused concern in Washington by taking Communists into his government, but then backed American missile policy in Europe. Jacques Chirac cancelled summits with France's closest partners for alleged lack of solidarity, but then announced a major military reorganisation which affected them without prior consultation. France signed up for the European common currency, but broke the rules to pursue tax cuts and increases in state spending. Though insisting on the right of nations to act independently when Washington is concerned, Chirac told Central European states which differed from Paris over Iraq that they should have shut up. Behind subjunctives and conditional tenses, the French can be 'masters of splendid ambiguity' as Britain's former Foreign Secretary, Douglas Hurd, noted. As Secretary of State, Madeleine Albright heard a French diplomat remarking on a proposed system for European organi-sations: 'It will work in practice, yes. But will it work in theory?'

'The French are by nature inclined to bully the weak and to fear the strong. Although they are boastful and vainglorious, as soon as an enterprise becomes difficult they abandon it; they are better at starting

things than following them through.' That was the judgement of
Marquis Tseng, the Chinese minister in Europe, who negotiated with
the French over Vietnam in 1881. Echoing the familiar description of
the French cavalry as being magnificent when it advances but ragged
in retreat, this is a verdict which many, including some friends of
France, would regard as an apposite piece of oriental wisdom. But
when I put the notion to a French professor, she gave me a Gallic
response from a 1930s film: 'The locomotive of your ignorance runs
on the rails of my indifference.' *Et schlack* – so there!

The international self-confidence is not hard to understand. All
over the world, traces of France pop up. Archaeologists reckon that
the greatest symbol of Britain's prehistoric past, the stone circle at
Stonehenge, was probably the work of invaders from Brittany. The
remains of a tenth-century monastery transposed from Saint-Michel-
de-Cuxa in the Pyrénées-Orientales department stand above the
Hudson River in New York; down below, the Statue of Liberty was
a gift from France, and the televisual *Friends* have a poster of a park in
northern Paris on their wall. The first crusaders were sent on their
way to the Holy Land by a papal proclamation in a field outside the
town of Clermont. Frederick the Great named his palace in Potsdam
Sanssouci, and his successors called their supreme military medal *Pour
le mérite*. Quebec remains a Francophone enclave, and Louisiana is
home to half a million Cajuns descended from French settlers ethni-
cally cleansed from Nova Scotia by the British, who keep the
language of the Hexagon alive on the bayous. Lenin had a French
mistress; Japan has its version of the Eiffel Tower. An Indochinese sect
counts Louis Pasteur and Victor Hugo among its saints, and
Cambodians smoke cigarettes named after the actor Alain Delon.
Schools on the resort island of Phuket in Thailand learn to play
pétanque, and Madame Mao (somehow 'Mrs Mao' doesn't sound
right) plotted the Cultural Revolution from a Shanghai villa modelled
on a Louis XIII manor house. Duke Ellington defined himself as a
drinker of Beaujolais; James Dean found solace in Saint-Exupéry's
Little Prince; and Ella Fitzgerald was once spotted reading a book by
Jean-Paul Sartre in her dressing-room.

This country invented the pressure cooker and the non-stick frying
pan which gave Ronald Reagan his Teflon nickname. Its fiction gave
the world the icons of Candide, Emma Bovary and les Misérables, as

well as providing Mozart with the *Marriage of Figaro*. Ferdinand de Lesseps would have added Panama to his canal at Suez if the terrain in Central America and corruption in Paris had not interceded. In more relaxed mode, the Club Méditerranée set the model for informal, all-inclusive holiday resorts, and it was a Parisian who commercialised the bikini swimsuit, employing a nude dancer to model it after the regular mannequins refused to wear it. Frenchmen invented the first non-iron pure cotton shirt and won the world's top mathematics prize for the seventh time in 2002. A muddy spring in the south discovered by Hannibal in 218 BC and rediscovered by a crippled Englishman twenty-one centuries later has become synonymous with fizzy water in countries where 'eau' means nothing.

Nicéphore Niepce invented photography in Burgundy, and, if they cannot claim the first motor-car, French manufacturers did make two landmark vehicles. In 1955 Citroën unveiled its DS (the initials sound like the French word for 'goddess') with front-wheel drive, disc brakes, spaceship looks and self-levelling suspension. Sixteen years earlier, the same firm had turned out one of the world's most practical conveyances, the Deux Chevaux, on the specification of being able to transport 2 people and 50 kilos of potatoes at 60 kilometres an hour on no more than 3 litres of petrol per 100 kilometres – the ability to carry eggs over a ploughed field without cracking them and to leave enough room for hats to be worn inside were added later. Despite their flapping canvas roofs and self-motivated folding windows, they were wonderful cars. A friend of ours had a thirty-year-old 2CV which had been driven to Kenya and back; it still sat for a week in the snow at Orléans railway station and started with one turn of the ignition – or three, at most. But the coming of the motorway and the desire for a car in which you could sit in comfort meant the end of Deux Chevaux production – in France, at least. Some years after manufacture stopped in France, Chrysler had one of the cars shipped across the Atlantic, took it to bits and used it as the model for a people's car for China, India and South America, made of plastic. A Citroën spokesman agreed that imitation was the sincerest form of flattery.

The Lumière brothers made the first moving picture. Marcel Carné's *Les Enfants du Paradis* regularly figures high in lists of the best films ever produced. One French author provided the inspiration for both *The Bridge on the River Kwai* and *Planet of the Apes*; two others served up the plot for *Vertigo*, and *films noirs* have become a Hollywood genre. French films have been a highly fruitful pillaging ground for a string of Hollywood vehicles for Arnold Schwarzenegger, Sharon Stone, Steve Martin and others. 'Another week, another Hollywood remake of a French movie,' as the *New Yorker* remarked. Although patriotic French *cinéastes* decry the process and insist that *Trois Hommes et un Couffin* is far superior to *Three Men and a Baby*, the studio bosses may not always be wrong in their remaking frenzy. French directors and actors do not, as a rule, work well in Hollywood. In France, Disney's cartoon version of *The Hunchback of Notre Dame* was a major hit, while France's biggest-ever home-grown success, *Les Visiteurs*, grossed just $36,732 across the Atlantic.

A pair of Frenchmen created the marathon musicals, *Les Misérables* and *Miss Saigon*; Claude François, a singer who subsequently electrocuted himself in his bath, wrote the music of 'My Way', while Gilbert Bécaud penned the song that became 'What Now, My Love?'. Though linguistic backwoodsmen are up in arms about the spread of the English language, French terms still permeate the globe: if anybody sat down to calculate whether more words of French origin are used in English than vice-versa, French would come off much better than its fearful defenders might think. Chic, after all, is smarter than smart. *Faute de mieux*, invitations in London or Hong Kong come marked RSVP or Pour Mémoire. Generals have *aides de camp*, newspapers call their foreign offices bureaux and America's greatest artistic gift to the world probably takes its name from the use of the chattering verb *jaser* by Creole speakers in New Orleans. Louis Pasteur, Joseph Guillotin and the Marquis de Sade bestowed their names on posterity. The caped cloaks of the Limousin region of France provided the synonym for motor-cars with hoods. Extreme patriots and opponents of women's rights take their label from an enthusiastic Napoleonic veteran, Nicolas Chauvin. Gymnasts somersault more easily thanks to the garment invented by the trapeze artist, Jules Léotard. Disciplinarians should flick their whips towards Colonel Martinet for the strict order he imposed on Louis XIV's infantry. Napoléon's name, albeit bereft of the acute accent, was used by Conan Doyle to describe his master criminal, and by the US Secret Service as its code-name for Frank Sinatra. The extremely grand Vicomte de Turenne, on the other hand, might be less than charmed to know that, outside the history class, his name is perpetuated by his habit of using his helmet as a soup bowl.

In filmdom, even producers like to be called *auteurs*. Gourmets eat in restaurants, tourists buy souvenirs, bourgeois folk gather at table for dinner, and may make a rendezvous at a café afterwards. Negligees and culottes may no longer be in style, but women wear brassieres everywhere except in France itself (where they prefer the *soutien-gorge*). Hotel concierges and waiters the world over address women as Madame. The French are even credited with things to which they would never wish to lay claim: such as the goo called French dressing across the Atlantic. As for French beans and French kisses, even the most ardent disciple of M. Chauvin would hardly pretend that they were exclusively national property.

At first sight, there is no end to the aura created by this nation, no reason to doubt its claims to enduring, special greatness. So long, that is, as you do not look too carefully in the mirror, or stray too close to the brink of the apparently settled plateau of national existence. Keep to the surface, and everything seems in order. Lift the curtain, and things become very different. '*Tout va très bien, Madame la Marquise,*' as the butler told his employer over the telephone in a famous French song. The château and the stables are burning down, your favourite mare is dead, your husband has killed himself, but, apart from that little matter, everything's all right, Ma'am: *Tout va très bien, tout . . . va . . . très . . . bien.*

No comparable country has undergone as many changes of regimes in the last two centuries. After the various phases of the Revolution of 1789 came the Napoleonic Empire, the Bourbon Restoration, the revolution of 1830 and the Orleanist Monarchy under the country's last king, the pear-shaped Louis-Philippe. He was overthrown by the Revolution of 1848 which brought in the Second Republic, only to be displaced by the Second Empire of Napoléon III. After he had been defeated by the Germans in 1870, the Third Republic lasted until 1940, to be replaced in the unoccupied zone of France by the Vichy administration of Marshal Pétain. Liberation brought the Fourth Republic which was succeeded by General de Gaulle's Fifth Republic in 1958. That makes ten different forms of government – or eleven if you include the Ancien Régime that crumbled after the storming of the Bastille – and takes no account of other deep shocks to the system such as the Dreyfus Affair or the student riots and strikes of 1968.

The latest system, the Gaullist Republic, was meant to introduce stability and firm leadership after the revolving-door coalition governments of the Fourth Republic. But, since the initial Gaullist dominance faded in the 1970s, France has experienced an electoral switchback unequalled elsewhere. In 1981, the left won the presidency, swiftly followed by victory at legislative elections called by the new Head of State. Since then, control of the National Assembly has changed hands at each successive poll. In 1986, the right came out on top, only to lose its majority two years later. After five years of Socialist government, the Gaullists and their allies won a crushing parliamentary majority in 1993, followed by the neo-Gaullist, Jacques Chirac, talking the presidency in 1995. Two years later, a rebellion against public sector reforms rammed through by Chirac's prime minister, Alain Juppé, gave a National Assembly majority to a left-wing coalition under the Socialist, Lionel Jospin, who had been beaten for the presidency in 1995, but now formed a government with the Greens and Communists.

If France prides itself on long-term planning for projects such as its high-speed train and telecommunications, its politics show the opposite tendency. "We have a culture not of dialogue but of confrontation," its President observed in 2004. Conflict and change have become ingrained. Since the system separates the function of the directly elected President and that of the Prime Minister, who is usually the head of the biggest group in parliament, the two can be from opposing parties, particularly before a new electoral calendar brought the two elections into synch in 2002. For nine of the years between 1986 and 2002, France was ruled by such *cohabitation,* which proved particularly uneasy for the five years during which Chirac and Jospin prepared their second presidential contest.

After each election, disappointment soon set in. When he became the first left-wing president of the Fifth Republic in 1981, François Mitterrand launched an ambitious programme of nationalisations, wage rises and plans to build Socialism in one country. After three devaluations and amid soaring inflation, the dream had to be abandoned and replaced by prolonged belt-tightening which sent unemployment soaring. Polls showed that people regarded eleven of the years between 1980 and 1995 as having been 'bad times'. The suicide rate rose to one of the highest among developed nations as 45 per cent of the French said they could see themselves falling into clinical depression. What Jacques Chirac called a 'social fracture' cut through the nation. The mood lightened as prosperity rose and unemployment fell at the turn of the century. But the President was assailed by allegations of scandal, and the Socialist government failed to connect with the nation's concerns, particularly about rising crime. The media was full of stories of violent robberies and street thefts, symbolised by the snatching of mobile telephones while their users were in mid-sentence. The prison population rose by 12 per cent in the first half of 2002, and Chirac seized on law and order as one of his main re-election campaign themes. But, as the poll approached, France appeared to have turned off politics, deeply fed up with the men and women playing the same old tunes. It is, however, a mistake to confound alienation with boredom. In one of the most famous headlines of the 1960s, *Le Monde* declared that France was bored; soon afterwards, students pulled up cobble stones on the Left Bank and Communist-led unions brought the country to a halt. As the novelist, Philippe Sollers, reflects, however passive they may appear at times, his compatriots have a taste for sudden outbursts – 'The French seem to be asleep, then they suddenly wake up, mobilise, agitate, demonstrate and then soon go back to sleep.'

Chirac and Jospin might have pondered that as they approached their second presidential encounter in 2002. Each of them assumed that the first round of voting, in which 16 candidates ran, would be a formality before they duelled in the decisive run-off two weeks later. Though opinion polls showed short-lived bursts of support for some minor candidates, the Socialist-Gaullist dominance of politics was assumed as a fact of life. What the pollsters and the political commentators did not appreciate was the extent to which voters rejected that dominance, and wanted to vent their anger against the system in what came to be known as an earthquake.

At 8 P.M. on 21 April , the faces of the two men who would confront one another for the presidency in the second round of voting appeared on televisions screens across the country. One was the incumbent who topped the poll, though with only just under 20 per cent – the lowest score ever recorded for a president running for re-election. Beside him on the television screen was not the face of Lionel Jospin, but that of a one-eyed ex-paratrooper who had been peddling extreme right-wing rhetoric for 45 years and had dismissed the Nazi gas chambers as a 'detail' of history. At 73, the National Front chief, Jean-Marie Le Pen, had finally achieved his ambition, finishing second to advance to the run-off after scoring strongly in areas of the country which felt neglected by the Parisian elite. If votes for another far right candidate were added in, 19 per cent had gone for parties that advocated expelling immigrants, restoring the death penalty in a draconian law-and-order programme, pulling out of the European Union and the euro currency system, and abolishing income tax.

The far right's score was bad enough, but was only part of a damning verdict on the political system and those at its apex. Nearly two-third of those who voted backed neither the President nor the Prime Minister. Almost 30 per cent of the electorate did not bother to vote – in all 51 per cent abstained, cast spoiled ballots or backed extremist parties, compared to 39 per cent at the previous presidential poll. Trotskyites took 11 per cent against 7 per cent for the main centrist and 3 per cent for the Communist partners in Jospin's coalition. A hunting and fishing candidate finished ahead of the leading free-market politician.

Despite his low score, the result was manna for Chirac. The shock of seeing Le Pen in the run-off meant that there would be a huge national movement of resistance to the far right – in one instance of his taste for conspiracy theories, the National Front leader even suggested that Chirac had engineered the outcome to save himself from having to face Jospin. The Socialists and their allies went into a state of serious depression, with their leader immediately announcing that he would withdraw from politics after the second round of the election on 5 May. Editorial writers lambasted the stupidity of left-wing voters who had dallied with the Trotskyites. A former Interior Minister, Jean-Pierre Chevènement, who had resigned in protest at concessions to autonomists in Corsica and ran as an independent candidate, was regarded as a pariah – his 5 per cent of the vote would have put Jospin comfortably ahead of Chirac and ensured that the two met in the second round.

The electorate had certainly shown a strong streak of irresponsibility – 11 per cent of the French did not want to be ruled by Trotskyites, and, whatever the appeal of Le Pen's pet themes to those who felt abandoned by the major parties, it was hard to believe that nearly a fifth of the French wished to see the blustering, xenophobic snake oil salesman in the Élysée Palace. But the point was not so much the candidates for whom the electorate had cast its ballots, as those against whom it had made its feeling felt. The earthquake of 21 April was a massive rejection of the political establishment, inspired by popular alienation after two decades during which certainties had ebbed away and had not been replaced by anything coherent in which people could believe. The splintering of the vote reflected the state of the nation, which was appalled by what it saw in the mirror, going into a crusade against the National Front that brought out more than a million people in May Day demonstrations. The mobilisation of the left was, in part, an act of remorse for Jospin's elimination. But it was also posited on a fear that Le Pen had a chance of making further inroads. Rather than ignoring him, as it had done in the past, the political class accorded the National Front leader the status of a challenger. Chirac had an obvious interest in doing this to rally the country behind him, but the reaction on the left suggested it took a view of its compatriots which could only further sully the reflection they had glimpsed on 21 April – and the jubilation when Le Pen got only 18 per cent could not hide the fact that the number of votes he received increased.

Chirac's re-election with 82 per cent in the second round was another cause for disorientation after his failure to get more than 20 per cent two weeks earlier – his core constituency was hardly any larger than it had been in his previous two runs at the Élysée. Though it could claim to represent well over a third of the electorate, the whole of the left had been removed from the final choice of the Head of State. By far the biggest majority any president had ever enjoyed was mainly a vote against somebody else. It was certainly not a ringing endorsement of a man whose long career meant that he epitomised the political class the country had so decisively rejected only two weeks earlier.

The process continued with parliamentary elections in June for which the President's men put together a broad tent party to deliver the majority in the National Assembly that Chirac had lacked for the previous five years. His followers took 369 of the 577 seats in the new parliament, to which they could add the backing of another 30 deputies from other sympathetic parties. The left fell from 314 seats to 178 with several leading figures losing their seats, including the ex-deputy premier, Martine Aubry, and Chevènement. The National Front vote dropped to 13 per cent at the first round of voting, and the electoral system, with a first-past-the-post result at the second round, ensured it won no seats. The smaller extremist parties got no seats, either, and the Greens took just three.

Chirac now enjoyed a range of control at presidential, parliamentary and regional level not seen since Mitterrand's early heyday. The contrast between 1981 and 2002 was instructive. Though it was all to go horribly wrong, the left's programme when it finally won power was clear and ambitious. In contrast, the winning presidential platform of 2002 boiled down to a pledge to fight rising crime and to cut income tax. For the Assembly election, the cry was simply to end cohabitation.

Was that all there was for the strongest majority France had seen for twenty years? Where were the deeper issues facing the nation – social divisions and economic inequalities, reforms and deregulation, Europe, France's place in the world, the integration of immigrants and the force of xenophobia and concern for national identity demonstrated by the support for Le Pen? Chirac chose as his new prime minister a provincial politician, Jean-Pierre Raffarin, who was presented as not belonging to the Parisian elite, and who said he would reach out to the French 'down below'. He might be reassuring and in the roly-poly mould that is taken to denote common sense, but Raffarin had begun his adult life as a marketing man, had served in previous right-wing governments and was certainly no stranger to the power structure. When it came to his boss, it was ironic, at least, that the man who had emerged triumphant from the revolt of 21 April should be a politician whose career stretched back to 1967, who had done little for five years of cohabitation, and who epitomised the clannish elites against which the country had voted so emphatically. Before the elections, Chirac had told aides he was sure of winning because the French found him *sympa* – likeable. That was certainly true, but it hardly meant he was fitted to carry out the rebuilding job the nation needed.

The 'blue wave' could not hide the rise in the abstention rate to almost 40 per cent in June – 11 points higher than in the previous Assembly election. Apart from those simply bored with politics, the voters who did not vote were reckoned to include a substantial number who stayed away from the polls as an active protest against the choice before them, and the failure of the system to come up with new politicians and new ideas. Given the abstention rate and the way the National Front got no deputies despite taking 10 per cent of the vote, at the second round, the new Assembly represented only half the people of France. The combined left had 43 per cent of the vote but got only 30 per cent of the seats in parliament. Locked out of political power for five years, its temptation was to use extra-parliamentary methods to press the new government on wages, defence of the public sector and labour regulations. The unions had already shown their muscle in anti-Le Pen demonstrations on May Day; now some of their leaders talked of continuing the fight in the streets. But the Socialists were, themselves, deeply divided between modernisers and those who preached a return to working class roots, while the Communists found themselves out on a very weak limb. The threat of extremism was dramatically illustrated by an assassination attempt on Chirac during the 2002 Bastille Day parade. The neo-Nazi gunman, who hid his rifle in a guitar case, fired only one shot which went far wide, before being overpowered, but the episode evoked memories of the more serious attempts to kill De Gaulle four decades earlier. The earthquake of 2002, and the fall-out, showed how complex the true state of France was. The problems that had been accumulating at the château and in the stables of the song while the elite strutted the stage like the absent Marquise had taken France to a brink of uncertainty about itself.

Move from the political to the practical, and there too, the shining example its leaders claim for their nation turns out to have less luminous qualities. The size of the rail network and the cost of high-speed trains make the SNCF railway service a major loss-maker. State finances are deeply in the red. The health service is wonderful, but is in financial crisis, with the French setting world records for the length of their prescriptions and their consumption of tranquilisers. Despite all the care provisions, a summer heat wave in 2003 killed 15,000 old people. The welfare system has accumulated a deficit of 31 billion euros. Crime has become an obsession, and outbreaks of violence regularly shake the suburbs, such as the burning of 90 cars in one Paris district on Bastille Day in 2002.

The most popular paid-for tourist attraction is the not very French Disneyland outside Paris, denounced as a 'cultural Chernobyl' when it opened. Lift the velvet curtain at those châteaux, manor houses and dovecotes and one finds many are crumbling away. It was a Japanese television network which paid to provide the *Mona Lisa* with a room of her own in the Louvre in 1998. The newspaper *Le Figaro* estimates that state spending on the 40,000 classified sites falls more than 25 per cent below what is required, and that some 100 million euros needs to be spent on the far more numerous, if smaller, unclassified sites. The director of the national heritage foundation says that it would take about the same amount each year for the next quarter of a century to restore 1,500 major monuments. At a time of tight budgets, that can only sound like whistling in the wind.

The divisions of inheritance under the legal system bequeathed by the Napoleonic Code has split up country estates. But it is not only families who sell off their country jewels to divide the proceeds between brothers and sisters. The Defence Ministry put up for sale the eighteenth-century fort at Verdun, the army's headquarters in the First World War battle in which 340,000 French and German soldiers died. The cottage where Joan of Arc was born has been covered with yellow paint which leaves it, in the words of one newspaper, looking like a slice of bread and butter. The French, it has been said, treat their national heritage as they might an ageing mistress: 'Occasionally with indulgence, more often with neglect.'

Or, too often, with concrete. Much of the Riviera has been blotched with ugly but highly lucrative developments. In Paris, one bank of the Seine was ruined by the express road system where the Princess of Wales crashed to her death. The presence of an environmentalist in the Cabinet did not stop the 80,000-seat stadium built on the edge of the capital for the 1998 World Cup being made mostly of PVC.

François Mitterrand's new opera house at the Bastille was the apple of the President's eye in his last years, but it has been battered by the dismissals of a string of directors, money troubles, politics, bad acoustics, a set collapse which killed one person and injured forty – and a tribe of striking musicians, *viz*, 'What is the difference between the Bastille Opera and the *Titanic*? The orchestra on the *Titanic* actually played.' Between them, the 'People's Opera' and the stately theatre at the Palais Garnier in the centre of the city take subsidies that work out at around 700 francs per seat. On top of which, Mitterrand's pride and joy had to be wrapped in netting to protect passers-by from bits of falling masonry.

Paris still likes to think of itself as the world's cultural centre, though most non-French observers would look elsewhere – across the Atlantic or even, perish the thought, over the Channel. This is not to say that artistic endeavour is not alive and well on both banks of the Seine, just that much of the status which France and its capital assume to be theirs is based more on the past than the present. 'In France, they want to always keep things the same,' as Angelin Preljocaj, a controversial choreographer who grew up in an immigrant ghetto outside Paris, puts it. To repeat Gertrude Stein's remark, Paris may be where the twentieth century 'was', but the accent is now on her tense – and the century is over, anyway. Here, as in many areas we will visit in this book, France is torn between the realities of the new millennium and the traditions and achievements of its past. Its enormous cultural heritage buttresses the nation's place among the great civilising influences of world history, but it also raises some awkward questions for the present in both popular and high art, and in the more general field of learning.

True, the government in Paris spends a lot of money on the Culture Ministry and has insisted on the 'cultural exception' to protect national arts by exempting culture from free trade agreements which would open the door to unbridled mass entertainments from across the Atlantic that is such bogey to the French establishment. But the aura of French culture is waning. There are important theatrical and dance troupes, the Odéon and Bouffes du Nord playhouses in Paris, the Lyon Ballet and the Avignon Festival. But where are the new internationally-respected authors and artists? Who is replacing Édith Piaf or Yves Montand or the clutch of singer-poets led by the classic southern troubadour, Georges Brassens, all of whom spoke to the country as a whole rather to segmented groups?

A new breed of philosophers may seek to dazzle by posing for *Paris-Match* or asserting that 'the Gulf War never happened' or with comparisons between the mathematical symbol for the root of minus one and an erect penis. They may, in the words of the writer Pascal Bruckner, 'take, endlessly, the beautiful risk of thinking'. But an analysis of current French philosophy by American and Belgian academics shows some of its leading practitioners haven't much of a clue of what they are writing about, hiding vacuity behind a thicket of meaningless prose.

France still cuts a distinct dash with its well-subsidised and protected national film industry which has built up a record of popular successes from *Cyrano de Bergerac*, to the Montmartre fairy tale, *Amélie*, whose nostalgic power was such that some sniffy left-wing critics accused it of fostering far-right nostalgia. French studios have also turned out a steady flow of more serious films examining the state of society, and have kept esteemed veteran directors active. Putting screen vibrancy to one side, however, this is not a country which leads the cultural world any more. The most celebrated novelist to have emerged in recent years, Michel Houellebecq, is more famous for the political and sexual provocation of his books than for his superb prose, and a runaway best-seller of 2001 was an explicit catalogue of the sexual experiences of a Left Bank intellectual written with all the grace of a telephone directory. A French author last won the Nobel Prize for Literature in 1985 – the previous winner from France dated back to the 1960s. Britain publishes three times as many books as France. Forty per cent of books borrowed from French libraries are comic strips.

In sport, the failure of the national team to get through the initial round of the World Cup in 2002 came as a major jolt to a country which had been used to seeing *les bleus* triumph, not only on the field but as a symbol of racial harmony. The side, itself, was so shell-shocked that, when it flew back to Paris after failing to score a single goal in the Far East, its members brushed past the waiting fans without a word or fled through the underground parking lot at the airport. Hardly the behaviour of the champions they had been.

When it comes to education, the record is far less impressive than might appear from the national pride in the lycée system.

A poll in 2002 showed that 60 per cent of those questioned thought schools were not longer able to do their job properly. The curriculum is often out of touch with the educational level of pupils. Teachers, who make up one of the biggest blocs of Socialist voters, are resistant to change; when the Education Minister tried to loosen up the system in the late 1990s, he ended up by losing his job. As we will see, violence in schools is a matter of growing concern.

France did not make it into the world top twenty when nations were ranked by the numeracy of their nine-year-olds. One survey reported teenagers making two and a half times as many spelling mistakes as in the 1920s, and doing far less well in solving maths problems. A quarter of children entering secondary school do not know how to count; 15 per cent cannot read. A drive begun in the mid-1980s has raised the proportion of young people getting their *baccalauréat* to almost 80 per cent. But in a comparison of examination results in forty-one countries, France finished thirteenth in maths and dropped to twenty-eighth place when it came to science. Only 44 per cent of university students stay the course to get a full degree.

This is particularly serious because language is a particularly serious matter for France. For the post-1789 revolutionaries, it was a means of asserting national unity, a single tongue to replace regional dailects. In the 1970s, President Georges Pompidou declared it was the French language which made his nation more than just another country in the world. In pursuit of purity, the 'immortal' members of the venerable Académie Française spend years dancing on pinheads, reflecting in all their pomp the strength of a conservatism which goes far deeper than politics, and which we will encounter throughout this book. They epitomise the deadly combination of an over-riding faith in codification and a distrust of change which permeates too much of French life. The members of the Académie know, of course, that they are – in the words of one of their members, Jean d'Ormesson – only immortal while they are alive. But this realisation makes the mission of laying down the rules for the future all the more imperative. This is not a scholastic ivory-tower affair. Language has long been a matter for official meddling – it took legislation at the turn of the century to authorise the abandonment of the imperfect subjunctive. More recently, the Académie clashed with Socialist women ministers who wished to be called 'Madame la Ministre' not the traditional 'Madame le Ministre'. The Academicians insisted that, since French does not have a neutral gender, masculine is used instead – in the next government, France's first female Defence Minister got into line by saying she was happy to be called *le*, and was congratulated by the Académie's top official. The real target, however, is English as part of a battle that, in a fluid world, looks like a sign of a lack of linguistic self-confidence.

Whatever the attempts to limit the use of English, its adoption has an unstoppable head of steam, just as the English have taken on so many French expressions when they filled a gap. In London, nobody would be surprised to learn that a louche entrepreneur who enchants his coterie with his joie de vivre was deposited at his pied-à-terre in Beauchamp Place by his blasé chauffeur who manoeuvres his flamboyant limousine into its garage at the end of a cul-de-sac while his wife has a rendezvous for a tête-à-tête with a chaperone. How many French words there? It is only natural that the current should run the other way. So un dealer d'Ecstasy drives le break from le parking to pick up une top-model for un week-end avec le jet-set while his gay brother decides that he and his boyfriend should do un outing. Anglophilia can be unnecessary as when the press writes of a plane having crashé instead of using the perfectly good verb écraser or when managers undergo le training rather than a spot of formation. In the 2002 World Cup, the French coach spoke of his players having failed to scoré rather than not having marqué. But bridge players in London still finesse a trick; Parisian tennis buffs drop un lob. Eat a baguette at Pret A Manger in London, or munch un sandwich on the Champs-Élysées. And what is worse: finding yourself hors de combat and suffering déjà vu in Britain or being blackboulé by l'establishment in France?

It is not only a matter of shuffling existing words; the French are adept at inventing terms out of English – from La Walterscottomanie of the 1820s to les rugbymen of today. Le footing is less in fashion than it once was – what's wrong with a promenade, after all? But, if you are seeking le Standing, you might be tickled to receive a card known as un Bristol telling you to wear un Smoking at a black-tie dinner party. A magazine writes about a manager being scotché to his desk; a food guide describes a restaurant as being cosy; a redesign is known as un relookage; and an airline is surbooké.

But, for the powers that are in France, language is too precious to be left to the ordinary people. So the government limits the number of foreign songs that can be played on the radio, and issues a 74-page list of 'foreign terms or improper terms to avoid or replace'. Not content with its domestic crusade to keep English at bay, France spends a lot of money promoting its own language abroad, through an organisation known as La Francophonie. Since its foundation in 1986, the association's membership and character have followed unexpected paths. Some of the countries which lined up to join, such as Bulgaria and Moldova, were not exactly known as buzzing French-speaking centres. On the other hand, Israel, where there are reckoned to be almost 1 million French speakers, was kept out after Lebanon waved its veto.

The organisation needs members wherever it can find them. Despite the extravagant claims from Paris, only 2 per cent of the world's population speak French, putting it in ninth place in the language stakes. Just 6 per cent of pupils and students around the globe learn French as a foreign language. Five hundred million people live in countries which belong to La Francophonie, but only a fifth of them are reckoned to speak French fluently. The gap between illusion and reality was shown vividly when forty-nine member nations of La Francophonie gathered for a summit in Hanoi at the end of 1997. Paris put up 75 million francs to help stage the meeting. For a few days, the old colonial capital of Vietnam took on the patina of a Francophone city; thousands of waiters, hostesses, porters and drivers underwent crash courses in French, and signs in French suddenly appeared in the streets. The illusion was spread, but the truth is that fewer than 1 per cent of Vietnamese speak French. When I visited Hanoi in 1995, I came across only two men who could converse in the language, both in their seventies. At the main French-owned hotel, English reigns, and the taxi meters are set in US dollars.

That did not deter the proponents of La Francophonie. Having failed to save him his job at the United Nations, France enrolled the ousted Francophone Secretary-General, Boutros Boutros-Ghali, to head the organisation. Mr Boutros-Ghali told the Hanoi meeting that he saw the future of the association in 'cultural diversity and multi-lingualism, which constitute the true quality of the human heritage'. What that boiled down to was an attempt to set up a counterweight to the power and influence of the United States. Nothing new in that as far as France is concerned. The snag, however, was that the enterprise was sailing under false colours, and involved some pretty nasty associates. How heavily Mr Boutros-Ghali's rhetoric weighed in the hearts and minds of the warlords of Cambodia or the despots from Africa who mingled with President Jacques Chirac in the Vietnamese capital was questionable. The hosts showed their devotion to diversity by pulling the plug on French broadcasters who mentioned a damning report about human rights in Vietnam – and cynics noted the French businessmen hovering on the sidelines of the discussions about culture and multi-lingualism who were busy snapping up contracts for telephone lines, a water supply system and a cement works.

Closer to home, there was bad news on the European front for the champions of French: a two-year survey which leaked out early in 1998 revealed that, for the first time, more European Union documents were translated into other EU languages from English than from French. Only two of the eleven countries applying to join the Union in 1998 put their bid in French. Even Romania, a member of La Francophonie, preferred English. One linguistic chauvinist has a simple answer to this. A bow-tied anti-American French aristocrat, with the appropriate name of Hervé Lavenir de Buffon, has set up a Centre for European Study and Action which wants the European Union to adopt French as its single official language and the United Nations headquarters to be moved to 'the centre of the world' – i.e., Paris. There are plenty of precedents for such a view. Victor Hugo once told two English ladies who sympathised with his ignorance of English: 'When England wishes to converse with me, it will learn to speak French.'

If the French language is punted on the kind of rancorous base proclaimed by the likes of M. de Buffon, the result can only demean the land of Rabelais, Flaubert and Jacques Prévert, of the invention of Raymond Queneau and *Zazie dans le Métro* and a language which distinguishes between its varieties of prostitutes with a dozen different terms depending on the way they ply their trade. One might have thought that a tongue with the cultural baggage of French could look after itself. But the protection of

French linguistic virginity is a well-established intellectual industry which foreigners query at their peril. Still, it was striking that, for all the rhetoric in Hanoi, the new Prime Minister of 1997 forgot to assign the ministerial portfolio for La Francophonie to anybody when he took office.

In a further departure from inward-looking orthodoxy, the most vibrant linguistic growth is taking place among people who couldn't give two hoots for the scriptures of the Académie. Young city-dwellers have developed a whole new patois known as *verlan*, from *l'envers* (opposite), in which syllables are wrenched around to produce new words – thus a woman, *une femme*, becomes *une meuf*, while a policeman, *un flic*, turns into *un keuf*. France's linguistic ayatollahs had better seek solace on the line to Madame la Marquise. This is, after all, a world in which the number of French people who emigrate in search of work is rising steadily, and for many of those who jet off in search of a job, the English language is as important as a passport.

If the French still see their language as a badge of international pride, and like to talk about the radiant influence of their culture on the world, it is, in part, because theirs is a country still coming to terms with its post-imperial place in the world. The twentieth century began with France possessing the second most important empire on Earth, spread across large tracts of North and West Africa, through the rubber and opium fields of Indochina to a collection of scattered outposts from the South Seas to the North Atlantic. For the powers that were in Paris, it was a cultural as well as an economic and political exercise: France wanted to spread its ideas, its language, to turn Africans or Indochinese into French-minded people worshipping at the altar of the Republic. An extremely thin upper-crust did, indeed, feel as comfortable on the boulevards of Paris as they did at home, but the motivation for a Vietnamese rice farmer or a Senegalese teacher to become French in mind and spirit was tenuous, to say the least. Now only the outposts remain, reclassified for more correct times into overseas departments and territories, known as Dom-Toms (Départements d'Outre-Mer/Territoires d'Outre-Mer) – the Caribbean islands of Guadeloupe and Martinique; French Guyana, on the shoulder of South America; the islands of Réunion and Mayotte in the Indian Ocean and Saint-Pierre-et-Miquelon off the east coast of Canada; French Polynesia, New Caledonia and Wallis-et-Futuna in the South Pacific; plus French-held frozen wastes in the Antarctic.

Ministers speak of these places as part of a worldwide destiny, and extol the nation's responsibility to people who, even if they live on an atoll on the other side of the world, are officially regarded as being as French as if they were eating tripe and onions in the bistros of Lyon. The overseas departments and territories have twenty-two seats in the National Assembly between them, some with tiny electorates − a presidential supporter elected in 2002 from Saint-Pierre-et-Miquelon won his seat with only 9 per cent of the winning score for colleagues in constituencies in northern France. The truth is that the Dom-Toms are not a comfortable appendage for a modern nation. Few could survive without handouts from Paris. Most have high unemployment. Guyana, once considered only good to house the Devil's Island prison colony, now draws half its tax revenue from the space launch base at Kourou, spends sixteen times as much on imports as it earns from exports, and has seen 1,000 companies go bust in two years. Guadeloupe is mainly notable for having spent 121 million francs on a cycling stadium which is used once a year. On the other side of the globe, French Polynesia has relied on funds poured in for nuclear testing on the atoll of Mururoa: in a corruption case involving a million-franc bribe to a local official from a private clinic, the court said the episode had led to the belief that, in Polynesia, anything could be bought. These territories are stuffed with civil servants who are paid large bonuses to compensate for the high cost of living − that is to say, the cost of buying French goods tens of thousands of miles from the Hexagon. Why, one might ask, should the taxpayer of Clermont-Ferrand or Rennes stump up to keep a middle-rank pen-pusher in a soft life under the palm trees? But that question never seems to be put, and when the government tried to do something about it on Réunion, a couple of protests from the functionaries involved was enough to produce an unseemly retreat.

Not that all the inhabitants of these territories seem grateful for being gazetted as part of France. Presidents in Paris talk emotionally about France's brother citizens spread around the planet, but some recipients of fraternity presume to agitate for independence. Bloody incidents in New Caledonia, including one in which four gendarmes were killed and twenty-seven taken hostage in an attack on a police station in 1988, have paved the way for the gradual introduction of self-government, though Paris will keep control of justice, law and order and the currency. With an unemployment rate put officially at 40 per cent, Réunion is constantly referred to as an island volcano waiting to erupt. At the second round of the 2002 presidential election, the Caribbean electorate showed its lack of interest by recording abstention rates of over 50 per cent – in Guadeloupe only 39 per cent bothered to vote.

More significant than the Dom-Toms has been France's involvement in Africa. For decades, this enabled Paris to see itself as playing an important role in an area from which other big powers were absent. The French began to grant independence to their colonies in the 1950s, but, in many cases, the old links stayed. The interests flowed both ways. Big companies and political parties used friendly former colonial states as handy screens for below-board activities: smaller entrepreneurs set up all manner of businesses – from garbage collection to personal security. A special ministry was established under De Gaulle to handle Africa; when the Foreign Ministry tried to take it over in 1995, African heads of state protested and the President publicly reaffirmed its independence. For decades, France backed its favoured dictators with 8,000 troops stationed across the continent and an equal number on standby at home. In all, they have intervened on more than two dozen occasions since the 1960s to put down rebellions and mutinies, to prop up France's friends, and to perpetuate what the *Wall Street Journal* dubbed a 'virtual empire'.

Three decades after France gave its African conquests their independence, the neo-colonial web which offered protection to dictators in exchange for influence and raw materials looked distinctly tattered, but it took Paris a long time to re-evaluate its role. At the height of the Rwandan tragedy, France helped to supply weapons to the massacring Hutus, who came to be known by the French term of *les génocidaires*, and sent in troops to provide safe havens for the killers. There were persistent reports – denied by Paris – that the missile which ignited the tragedy by bringing down the plane carrying the Presidents of Rwanda and Burundi came from a French armoury, and that French troops turned a blind eye to the massacres. But then Paris had never been squeamish about the clients it picked – no less a person than the third President of the Fifth Republic had accepted the big-game-hunting hospitality and gifts of the mad self-appointed Emperor Jean Bedel Bokassa, whose refrigerator was reported to have contained the bodies of his enemies stuffed with rice.

Bokassa, a former sergeant in the French colonial army, had been authorised to seize power in the Central African Republic by one of the most enigmatic figures of the Fifth Republic, Jacques Foccart. In the early days of decolonisation, the rotund, multi-chinned Foccart acted as paternalistic patron and guide to a succession of African rulers who were encouraged to see themselves as the children of the wise father-figure in the Élysée Palace. He allowed, or encouraged, a coup here and the suppression of a revolt there. All the while, the former colonies were tied closely to Paris through the presence of French troops and a franc-based monetary system, which enabled the ruling elite to export its money to safe havens abroad at highly favourable rates of exchange. In post-De Gaulle days, a string of visitors from former colonies continued to take the lift to Foccart's ornate apartment in central Paris, where a grey parrot kept this man of the shadows company. There, they received advice on how to run their countries and, above all, on the need to repel any attempt by Washington to influence the continent. It was said that some of them entrusted Foccart with standing orders allowing French troops to intervene – only the dates were left blank. When he died in 1997, the great manipulator who listed his occupation as 'exporter' was seen off with military honours in the courtyard of Les Invalides, close to Bonaparte's last resting-place. Eight heads of state and government from Africa joined the President of the Republic at the funeral.

From Morocco to Zaïre, Foccart and Paris had definitely not been on the side of the angels. In early post-colonial days, that may have reflected sheer realism at a time when nobody cared much about what despots got up to south of the Sahara. Africa provided a happy hunting-ground for French business, and its votes were useful in showdowns with Washington at the United Nations. Arms sales to apartheid-era South Africa – sometimes via client African states – helped the trade balance. But, in time, an inevitable conflict developed with the ideals France made much of promoting elsewhere. How to reconcile support for Václav Havel or *glasnost* in Moscow with back-ing rulers who shot demonstrators and looted their national treasuries? Naturally, François Mitterrand blamed others. 'It's an inheritance nobody has ever talked to me about,' the President complained at a meeting of ministers in 1990 when the matter of Africa's aspirations for democracy were mentioned. 'For the past two years, no minister has presented me with a report asking that things change! There has been a misunderstanding between us. I am surprised and pained to hear what I hear.' As if Mitterrand had had no idea of the nature of his host when his helicopter deposited him on the deck of a dictator's yacht with its forty-place dinner setting in rose crystal, or when he enjoyed the sun with his friend the King of Morocco, who kept his opponents in some of the worst jails in the world. The one Socialist minister who had wanted to stand up to the dictators had been quickly ditched, leaving the framing of African policy at the Élysée Palace in the hands of Mitterrand's son, Jean-Christophe, who became known by the nickname of '*Papa m'a dit*' – 'Dad's told me'. Some years later, *Le Figaro* quoted Mitterrand as having said that, in countries like Rwanda, genocide wasn't such a big thing.

But in the end, even Mitterrand abandoned his hypocrisy and threw his lot in with the good guys, urged on by one of his aides, Éric Arnoult, who became better known as a prize-winning author under the pseudonym of Erik Orsenna. 'France cannot remain silent much longer. An announcement of a plan to back the concrete installation of democracy would be welcome,' Arnoult wrote in a note in 1990. 'We cannot continue much longer to struggle openly against the opposition to the ruling regimes, and to expel opposition figures from France as soon as they open their mouths.' At a French–African summit in a coastal resort, the Mitterand finally pronounced the word 'democracy'. His guests were not impressed. As *Le Monde* put it, only the sound of the wind on the sea broke through the silence with which they received his plea for the 'universal principle' of democracy. One head of state made it clear that he was more concerned with why French troops had not put down a mutiny by his own soldiers. Others were ready to hold elections – on condition that the outcome could be written down in advance. And, for all his protestations, the President went on aiding and protecting the *génocidaires* in Rwanda and later in Zaïre.

Mitterrand's successor, a man who liked to put himself forward as somebody who understood non-European values and considered that democracy was not incompatible with a one-party system, was even more likely to be to the dictators' taste. But by the time Jacques Chirac became President, other factors were coming into play. France had already tugged at the monetary carpet by devaluing the Central African Franc by 50 per cent, which forced the countries involved to face up to international competition. Some of the old tyrants were losing their grip. Above all, it was becoming increasingly embarrassing for France to be seen as a principal backer of horror figures like the President, Marshal, Guide and Helmsman of Zaïre, Mobutu Sese Seko, one of the world's leading kleptocrats, described by one French minister as 'a walking bank balance with a leopard-skin cap'.

Zaïre had been a colony of Belgium, not France, but it was also for many years the biggest French-speaking nation outside the Hexagon, and Mobutu's loyalty to Paris was never in much doubt so long as France made sure it was in his interest. He bathed in French perfume, and spent a slice of his pillaged fortune on a sumptuous Riviera property. Whenever he was in Europe, Mobutu was visited by French officials who hurried to his hospital ward when he was treated for cancer and paid court on him on the Côte d'Azur. Even in his campaign for national 'authenticity' he stayed linguistically faithful; when the wearing of suits was banned, the replacement native garment was called an 'abacost' – from the French words 'à bas le costume'.

France stuck by Mobutu to the last. There were reports of French help in despatching Serbian mercenaries to try to prop up his regime. But, in the end, all the efforts of Foccart's successors could not keep the Guide-Helmsman on his throne, though even after he was deposed, some old stagers could not give up the ghost: the deputy to France's ambassador in Kinshasa doggedly kept up contacts with members of the old regime who were trying to stage a comeback – and was expelled for his pains. France's obtuse and murderous policy in Zaïre followed by Mobutu's fall in the summer of 1997 marked a death-knell for the traditional French presence in Africa. Paris had few friends there any more. As a French academic close to African policy put it: 'We had this notion that dictators were good for us and

Africans didn't deserve any better. We have been behaving like slobs, and finally we have to pay the bill.'

What made things even worse was the way the Americans weighed in after decades during which Paris had aimed, above all, at keeping Washington's nose out of Francophone Africa. The great anti-American seer, Jacques Foccart, was gone. Africa was no longer France's backyard. The US Ambassador to Zaïre told journalists that France was incapable of imposing its will in Africa, that the Cold War was over and that 'it is no longer a matter of supporting dictators just because they are pro-Western'. As if that was not enough, President Clinton's first Secretary of State made the Washington view perfectly plain, declaring that 'the time has passed when outside powers could consider whole groups of countries as their own private domains'. Soon afterwards, Jacques Chirac told a French–African summit it was no longer the role of any non-African country to interfere in the continent's affairs. That took a little time to materialise: French troops went into the Central African Republic three times in eighteen months to put down anti-government mutinies. A President of the Congo-Brazzaville Republic who had favoured American oil interests over a French company was overthrown – but the main role was played by other African countries rather than by Paris. Whatever Gaullist nostalgists might feel, the die was cast: the Socialist government elected in 1997 decided to cut its forces in Africa from 8,000 to 5,200, and to shut down its base in the Central African Republic. Ministers insisted that the new force would still enable France to make its presence felt when needed. The government reformed aid policy, in part to fight corruption, and the Prime Minister spoke of a new partnership with Africa, which would demand respect for human rights and growing democratisation. The cost of maintaining a post-colonial empire across Africa had simply become too expensive and, when France sent troops to the Ivory Coast in 2003 it was under a United Nations mandate.

Nobody made the shift plainer than France's most important dictatorial friend of the past quarter-century. Jacques Foccart had picked the name of Omar Bongo from a list of potential Presidents of Gabon in 1967. His country is France's single biggest source of oil. As we will see, Bongo's regime has vital and dubious links with the Elf Aquitaine oil company, French intelligence and French politicians. One of his remarks had for years been taken as a motto for the relationship between Paris and its former colonies: 'France without Africa is like a car without petrol. But Africa without France is like a car without a driver.' Thirty years after Foccart put him in power, Bongo struck a rather different note. 'It is high time for Gabon to erase this image of being France's private hunting-ground [and] to turn towards a partner like the United States, which is more open and more understanding towards it,' he wrote. Washington might not be too thrilled at such an endorsement from a despot for whom a bad election is one in which he gets only 90 per cent support. Still, France's post-colonial edifice was nearing the end of its life. The dictators might find it harder than they expected to live without the unquestioning support of the Foccart machine, but France could no longer presume to be puppet-master of vast tracts of Africa. Its horizons had contracted: it was, in another of Bongo's phrases, just a medium-sized power to which, by implication, its former colonies would no longer entrust their fate.

France's post-colonial experience provides one glaring contradiction of its national motto of *Liberté, Égalité, Fraternité*. But there are also some striking exceptions closer to home, for instance involving the treatment of just over half the population.

The richest non-royal woman in the world may be French (the L'Oréal cosmetics heiress Liliane Bettencourt). The symbol of the Republic may be female; French women writers may stand out as feminist icons; more women may be more highly educated than men; and a masculinist movement claiming 30,000 members may protest at the 'feminisation' of French society. But French women feel hard done by, and with reason when it comes to being in a position to affect the way the country is run. The National Assembly ranks low in the proportion of women among parliaments of the European Union, ranking seventy-second in the world. The only woman to have become Prime Minister, Édith Cresson, calls French politics a 'closed men's club'. Élisabeth Guigou, a former European Minister who later became Minister of Justice, has complained of the 'below-the-waist jokes' directed at her in parliament: she once stared down a macho male minister when he suggested that she could increase her popularity by wearing crimson lingerie. A former Environment Minister recalls the time when a deputy responded to a female colleague with the name of a rap group which means, literally, 'fuck your mother'. Hunters demonstrating against one of her successors in Paris in 1998 waved placards reading: 'Dominique, get back to your housework and leave us alone.' On another occasion, a male member of parliament interrupted a female speaker during a debate on rape to assure her that she wasn't at risk.

Disrespect for women can be traced, like so much else in France, back to the supposed new dawn after the fall of the Bastille. British writers deplored the political influence of women in eighteenth-century France and the first political movement run by women for women, Les Citoyennes Républicaines Révolutionnaires, was established in Paris in 1793. But the Revolution gave rights to just about everybody except women and slaves. Emancipation of the latter only came after the restoration of the monarchy; French women had to wait rather longer. Napoléon declared them to be 'the property of man as a fruit tree belongs to the gardener', and his legal code gave men power over their wives that lasted for more than a century. Up to 1938, French wives needed the permission of their husbands to get a passport, and it was only in 1965 that they gained the right to join a profession without his authorisation. The Revolution proclaimed equality for all, but women did not get the vote until 1944: twenty-five years later, Charles de Gaulle was said to have ridiculed a suggestion that he should establish a ministry for women, by wondering if he should also set up a ministry for his wife's favourite occupation of knitting. Asked when France would have a woman president, Édith Cresson, who went from being prime minister to the European Commission, replied: 'Not in a hundred years.'

Cresson also recalls that when she went to business school, there was a section for '*jeunes filles*'. 'We were told that we would become confidantes to our bosses: "Everybody will be jealous. You'll have to be impeccable." I was about to explode. The boys were going to be the bosses. And they still are.' Women on average earn significantly less than men. For those who succeed professionally, a stereotype was drawn up of the strong, upwardly mobile female who lives a barren personal life, sacrificing the traditional values of husband and children, the warm family hearth and tasty traditional dishes on the altar of ambition, with its consequent stress, empty relationships, snatched holidays and heartache in the early hours of the morning. French men like their women to look good, but they also like them to know their place. 'Swimming teachers concentrate on the times of boys and the style of girls,' according to Élisabeth Guigou. 'Faced with competition from women, men feel obliged to act like fighting cocks,' says France's champion woman cyclist, Jeannie Longo. 'The most unjust thing is that even mediocre performances by a man get applauded, while a woman has to pull off a real exploit to get noticed.' She knows what she is talking about: Olympic gold medallist and a leading world cyclist for fifteen years, Longo is less well known than any flash-in-the-pan Tour de France competitor.

There have, it is true, been strong and popular women ministers on both the right and left. A female Defence Minister was appointed in 2002, and a woman took over the leadership of the Communist Party. But, until very recently, they have been notable by their rarity, and by the way in which they were kept to certain domains – welfare, social affairs, the environment. In 1995, the right-wing premier Alain Juppé appointed twelve women ministers, who immediately became known as '*les Jupettes*' (the miniskirts). Christine Chavet, one of the twelve, recalls that he called her in, asked her which languages she spoke, and told her not to leave Paris. Soon afterwards, she learned from the radio news that she had been appointed Junior Minister for Trade. Some months later, she and the other Jupettes were summoned to the Prime Minister's office in the middle of the afternoon. 'It was like a dentist's waiting room – people were waiting everywhere. Given the crush in the ante-chamber, I guessed why we were there. It was like a Feydeau farce with the doors opening and closing. Some came out in tears. One woman read *Le Monde* out loud to calm herself. Juppé just told me: "I'm sorry. I bring bad news." Not very elegant, that's the least one can say. Afterwards, we arranged meetings among ourselves because we hadn't even had time to say goodbye. We had been shipped out.'

Eighteen months later, Juppé was calling for positive discrimination for women and declaring France to be a lopsided democracy which 'only advances on one leg'. A radio commentator of the time quipped that the role of women in French public life was only slightly better than under the Talebans. And then there was a frisson when a collection of letters appeared in which the feminist icon, Simone de Beauvoir, called herself a little loving frog and promised her American lover, Nelson Algren: 'I will do the washing-up. I will sweep the floor. I will buy the eggs and rum cakes myself. I will not touch your hair, your cheeks, your shoulders without permission.'

Still, change was in the air: the number of women sitting in the National Assembly nearly doubled in 1997 to sixty-three; forty-two of them Socialists. That still only accounted for 11 per cent of deputies, whereas women made up 53 per cent of the electorate, but Lionel Jospin promoted the Labour Minister, Martine Aubry, who had finally outgrown her status of being 'the daughter of Jacques Delors', to be the government's deputy leader and another, Élisabeth Guigou, to head the Justice Ministry – when Aubry stepped down to become Mayor of Lille in 2001, Guigou took her place and another woman became Justice Minister. The Green leader, Dominique Voynet, was Environment Minister, and the Mayor of Strasbourg, Catherine Trautman, the government spokesperson. The Prime Minister's second wife, a philosopher, was seen as emblematic of the advance of high-profile women, though she tried to avoid being pulled into the political spotlight for as long as possible.

The first round of the 2002 presidential election saw three women among the sixteen candidates – they got 10 per cent of the vote, most of it for the perennial Trotskyite and retired bank clerk, Arlette Laguiller. Two years earlier, the Jospin government had introduced legislation requiring parity between the number of male and female candidates in local and legislative elections – Jospin's wife was said to be particularly keen on the measure. Parties that failed to achieve parity would be fined. The outcome in the 2002 parliamentary poll was hardly what had been hoped for. The parties closest to parity were the Trotskyites, Greens, Communists and the National Front which reached 48.8 per cent. Only 20 per cent of candidates backing Jacques Chirac were women while the Socialists managed just 36 per cent – many of them standing in unwinnable constituencies. The number of female deputies rose slightly to 68, including 36 members of the presidential majority, and 23 Socialists. Chirac appointed the secretary-general of his old party as France's first female defence minister, and put a woman associated with the left in charge of European affairs. On the other side of the political fence, a woman Communist leader emerged as the party's main spokesperson as it tried to come to terms with its decline. Among the Socialists, several leading female figures won easy election to the new National Assembly, and Martine Aubry showed she was not deterred by her shock defeat as she made her voice heard forcefully in arguing against veering onto a Blairite path.

Still, there was plainly a long way to go before women played a role in public life in any way comparable with their numbers in the population – they still held only 12 per cent of Assembly seats. Despite Liliane Bettencourt, there are no women among the chief executives of major French companies. Two women who did have considerable impact on the political and business world were examining magistrates who pursued a string of prominent figures alleged to have been involved in major scandals, primarily at the Elf company. But, as if to reinforce old stereotypes, as we will see, the Elf affair also brought to prominence an archetypal mistress figure who branded herself 'The Whore of the Republic' in a book on her liaison with a top politician.

Nowhere have the realities confronting France been more dramatic than in the economy. If the country has a tendency towards manic-depression, or the sleep-revolt dichotomy identified by Philippe Solers, it applies as much to the economy as to politics. Conventional wisdom would link the two – voters unhappy with their material lot are natural supporters of the opposition. But it is not that simple, as Lionel Jospin and his colleagues found to their cost in 2002.

After the pricking of the Mitterrandist dream in the mid-1980s, the Socialists had managed to establish their credentials as economic managers by adopting a monetarist approach that won the plaudits of international financial institutions and fund managers. It was not easy, either for those who had believed in the experiment of 1981 or for the rest of the French. A Mitterrand loyalist, Pierre Bérégovoy, who rose to become first Finance Minister and then Prime Minister, adopted a policy of 'competitive disinflation' preached by the Governor of the Bank of France to hold down prices, keep up interest rates, strengthen the franc and put muscles on the economy, even if this meant double digit unemployment and national depression. At one point, the number of people in financial difficulties was put at 7 million, with 18.5 per cent of householders aged under thirty in poverty. The contrast with the high-living Parisian left – the *gauche caviar* – and the rising tide of scandals surrounding the rich and powerful could only alienate those in trouble. Despite the recession, Mitterrand's skill as a political manipulator minimised the scale of defeat at the parliamentary election of 1986, in part through a change in the voting system to help the National Front eat into the mainstream right. Nonetheless, the ageing Head of State was forced to go through two years of cohabitation with Jacques Chirac as Prime Minister, but he so outwitted the younger man that he easily gained re-election to the Élysée in 1988, and used his prestige to win a parliamentary majority for his supporters. But the economic pain continued for millions of French people, the alienation deepened, and cynicism broadened on both sides. By 1993, as the financier, George Soros, predicted that the franc might become stronger than the German mark, the left crashed to a horrendous defeat.

Despite the ire of the voters, there was little change in policy after the Gaullist Edouard Balladur moved into the Prime Minister's residence at the Hôtel Matignon. So much so that, finding himself facing both Balladur and Jospin in the presidential election of 1995, Jacques Chirac decided that the best way of differentiating himself from them was to denounce the economic approach France had followed for a decade. He thundered against the monopoly of the *pensée unique* adopted by the Socialists and the Balladurians, projecting himself as the friend of those who had suffered from monetarist orthodoxy, and pledging to heal the social fracture. That, plus Chirac's whirlwind electioneering style, was enough to win, but the national mood was also reflected in the 15 per cent of voters who backed the National Front. Once elected, Chirac swiftly switched tack, appointing a Prime Minister, Alain Juppé, who perpetuated the very policies he had denounced, and upped the ante by launching a much-needed, but ill-handled, attempt to reform the public sector. The electorate could only conclude that it had been taken for a ride. 'If it is the Bank of France and the financial world which set the law, what value does the vote of the French people have?' asked a union leader. When Chirac made the mistake of calling a parliamentary election in 1997, the country showed what it thought by giving the left a parliamentary majority. In the flush of victory, Lionel Jospin and Martine Aubry moved to the left by introducing the 35-hour working week, raising corporate taxation and extending welfare cover;

but the effects were far more limited than either their government's supporters or its vocal opponents at the head of the employers' federation supposed.

French-style capitalism thrived; companies expanded abroad at a fast pace. For ideological reasons, Jospin preferred not to speak of privatisation, but the 'opening' of state firms to outside capital, as it was termed, went ahead even faster than under the right. Though the Prime Minister made it more expensive for companies to shed workers, his finance ministers spoke a modernising language and budgeted for tax cuts. At the same time, the social fracture running through France proved much deeper and harder to eradicate than the didactic Socialists could conceive of. Internationally-stimulated growth and make-work schemes brought unemployment down by a million in four years, but it then remained stuck at over 9 per cent. In the last year of the Jospin government, joblessness among men aged under 25 rose by 21 per cent. Long-term unemployment became a mark of depressed parts of the country, and of housing estates in major cities where more than a third of the second generation immigrant population might never have had a job. Even those in employment could feel less and less secure as companies offered only limited-time contracts, and the head of the country's young employers' association talked of a growing 'sub-proletariat'. Social unease was aggravated by rising crime, which became heavily featured in the media. The areas which suffered the highest unemployment and most 'insecurity' were overwhelmingly those where the National Front made it biggest advances.

Despite the effects of the international slowdown in 2001, France still looked good by European standards, with growth well above that of Germany. But issues like crime proved more persuasive than the general economic progress enjoyed under the left. Even the 35-hour week attracted unpopularity from the less well-off who would have preferred to be able to earn more money – the main beneficiaries were companies that used the law to introduce more flexible working patterns and white collar workers who could afford to play golf on an extra day off or take long weekends abroad. Instead of Jospin, it was the man who had been shut out of domestic and economic policy during the five years of cohabitation who got back into the Élysée. Whatever the stripe of those in power, the French have come to realise that far less changes than the politicians pretend. The better-off get better off, and those left behind fall further behind. In that sense, one surprise of the earthquake of 2002 was that it had not erupted earlier.

The aftershocks promised more trouble. The new government promptly ordered an audit of state finances to show what it had inherited. This had an obvious political purpose. Still, the audit and other figures on state finances were sobering. Spending had got out of control, particularly on welfare. The cost of the health service had shot ahead of budget, and the unemployment fund was two billions euros in the red while government revenue had dipped as the slowing economy cut tax receipts. Far from running at 1.8 per cent of the gross national product, as the left had said, the budget deficit for the year was forecast to reach 2.3-2.6 per cent. But the re-elected President demanded tax cuts and spending increases that could only augment the strain on state finances.

All this showed the high-wire act Chirac was going to have to perform to reconcile his domestic electoral pledges with the need to slim down the state and respect France's obligations to its European partners. Having been disappointed so often, and having shown their anger on 21 April, the French people and their rulers were entering a last chance saloon, at which the fate of the Fifth Republic was at stake. The size of the right's victory heightened its responsibilities, not only in its immediate policies, but in restoring faith in the system and the Republic. Just as the country had expected Mitterrand to conjure miracles from his hat in return for having finally given the left a mandate in 1981, so it felt every right to demand the same thing from Chirac and his new Prime Minister, Jean-Pierre Raffarin in 2002. Failure would precipitate a crisis not seen since Charles de Gaulle saved the country from disintegration in 1958. 'We have an obligation not to disappoint,' said Raffarin. Or, as one senior figure in Chirac's movement put it: the end of one road had been reached – the question was where the new path led.

The President walked tall. He cut a dominating figure at a European summit in June 2002, and France got its euro-zone partners to let it off a commitment to eliminate its budget deficit by 2004 so that Chirac could cut taxes and raise spending on law and order and defence. Official forecasts of economic growth for the year were only half what had been hoped for when the election programmes were written, though ministers predicted that the required levels would be reached in 2003-4 – just as the Socialists had done for 2001-2. As Prime Minister, the comfortingly roly-poly Raffarin sounded the right note, talking of decentralising power from Paris and insisting that he would be a listening leader while his Interior Minister, Nicolas Sarkozy, played the tough cop role. A 9 billion euro progamme was launched to strengthen the police and the justice system. Special security squads were set up in high-crime areas; 11,000 new prison places were to be built; and police were equipped with pistols fitted with *flashballs* – rubber pellets that can incapacitate at short range.

The relief the country felt at having blocked Le Pen had induced a Republican euphoria. The wicked witch had been banished – for the time being, at least – even if the winner's use of smoke and mirrors might well equate him with the Wizard of Oz. The fact remained that Le Pen had increased his vote between the two rounds to 18 per cent.

There was a growing awareness that things were not as they should be. A doom-laden book called *La France Qui Tombe* (*The France that Falls*) shot up the bestseller list. The state debt was one of the highest in Europe. Taxes and social security payments took an inordinate slice of national wealth. State spending was 52 per cent of gross domestic product, higher than in any other euro-zone country except Austria. Trade unions were in militant mood, while major companies which had set off on ambitious international expansion trails were reporting huge losses and laying off battalions of staff. In a competitive ranking drawn up by the World Economic Forum, France slipped to fifteenth place. The steadily ageing population contained a financial time-bomb for the pension system in which payments are met from contributions from those still in active employment. The ratio of retirees to workers at the start of the century was 4:10, it will be 7:10 by 2040.

Instead of mainstream politics, protest voting, the street and direct action beckoned. The militant anti-globalisation farmer, José Bové, who had became a national folk hero for trashing a McDonald's, made his way to jail in the summer of 2002 on a tractor at the head of a cortège of followers. Even before the Socialists crashed out of power, a major public sector union leader talked of strikes if the new government dared to cut staff. Between the two rounds of the parliamentary election, stoppages by doctors led Raffarin to reach a hasty agreement to raise consultation fees. During its first 18 months, street protests and fear of losing votes led the government to water down vitally needed changes to the pension system and to put off university reforms. Action by tobacconists made it reduce a rise in cigarette taxes. Railway workers defended their privileges with strikes, and 2,000 researchers resigned en masse to complain about lack of funding.

The Chirac administration had all the formal powers required for the reforms the country needed, and promised the Commission in Brussels that it would get to grips with public sector spending. The question was how far it would dare to go, with the President mindful of what had happened when his first government had tried to change too much too fast in 1995-7. Beyond the overwhelming centre-right electoral victories of May and June lay the old shadow of clientelism, of pressure groups pursuing their individual agendas regardless of the general good – and of a nation deeply cynical about its rulers. The demoralised left could all too easily be tempted to play to essentially conservative themes to try to regain its working class support. The smaller parties that had made such an impact at the first round of presidential voting subsided in the parliamentary contest six weeks later, but their showing in April demonstrated the fragility of the political system, and how easily discontent could well up against the establishment.

Anticipating Philippe Solers by two centuries, the British political philosopher, Edmund Burke, noted in considering their first revolution how the French prefer to seek a new dawn rather than going through a national process of reform. Their politicians repeatedly pander to this, and then do not deliver, provoking the bad temper of a people being woken from its dream and finding that the night is colder than had been promised. In the words of the former president, Valéry Giscard d'Estaing, they tend to be 'centred on the individual, on the defence of personal interests, and on the conviction of always being right on every subject'. That makes for a lively country, but all too easily ends up in the absence of the broader basis needed for lasting reform. Giscard's description of the French applies to far too many of their leaders. Law and order and tax cuts apart, the Chiraquian broad tent has little ideological coherence or purpose. The Socialists have still not made a full-scale conversion to social democracy. Extremists feed on disappointed individuals. Whether the individualistic Chirac, a man who has lived all his adult life as a full paid-up member of the clannish, inbred elite, could put right the weaknesses that had grown up over two decades was the major question that came out of the earthquake of 2002. What was plain was that neither he nor his country could afford to see him fail.

Into the questioning of where France is heading there comes, crucially, the matter of Europe. Properly, the French see themselves as pillars of the community. The bargain struck in the 1950s between their agriculture and German industry provided the core of a continental system which made a repetition of their three wars in 75 years impossible. It has brought great economic advantage to France, which sends 60 per cent of its exports to the European Union, and receives the highest farm subsidies of any of the EU states. But Europe has changed radically in the four decades since Charles de Gaulle and Konrad Adenauer celebrated the friendship treaty between the two nations in the cathedral at Reims.

The Franco-German duo remains the core of the European Union, as is evident when Britain tries to make it a threesome. Unity between Paris and Berlin against the war in Iraq has served as a cornerstone of French foreign policy. France then drew comfort from the victory of the anti-war Socialists in Spain in 2004 which destroyed the London-Madrid partnership that had challenged Paris in backing the invasion. But Chirac and Gerhard Schröder do not enjoy the rapport of their predecessors – the President backed the Chancellor's opponent in the 2002 German election. German federalist impulses run counter to France's defence of national sovereignty. Enlargement of the EU to the east will increase Berlin's influence, and place it, rather than Paris, at the geographical centre of the new Europe. Germany's drive to acquire greater EU voting rights to reflect its bigger population is a direct threat to the political leadership of Paris.

On the institutional front, a community of up to two dozen members could not be run in the centralised system the French had grafted on to it in the 1950s. The Chirac–Jospin cohabitation seriously weakened the impact of Paris, as France's partners did not know who spoke for it, and there was a growing clash with the increasingly federalist Commission, particularly after Chirac backed the idea of appointing a powerful president for the European Union who would overshadow Brussels.

France is at the centre of any European project. In Jacques Delors, it provided one of the strongest president of the Commission, and then made sure that Giscard d'Estaing chaired the convention mapping out the future of the Union's institutions. But there has always been a reservoir of ambivalence towards the loss of sovereignty. The Maastricht Treaty on monetary union was only approved by a slim margin at a 1992 referendum. In 1997, the left's victorious platform was tinged with euro-scepticism on the financial front. 'Everywhere, people are asking themselves what interest there is in building a Europe on the ruins of the welfare state,' wrote the editor of the left-wing review, *Le Monde Diplomatique*. Forty per cent of the votes in the first presidential round of 2002 were for Eurosceptic candidates.

Concern about Europe melds with the political alienation and economic concerns of the lowly-paid and the unemployed. Public-sector workers worry about their jobs as frontiers are opened to competition. Farmers fear for their subsidies, and fishermen face big cuts decided in Brussels. Successive governments have reflected these concerns by putting off the application of European directives which would menace specific interest groups, from insurers and the state electricity company to market stalls – and maintained the ban on British beef well after the Commission decided that the mad cow danger had passed. Europe's opening of frontiers, deregulation and anti-cartel policies are an evident threat to a country that believes it is an economic exception, and has grown used to Europe serving its national interests. For Jacques Chirac, the natural course will be to put France first. With his re-election, the Gaullist vision of a *Europe des patries* associating sovereign states rather than pursuing federalism was set to make a big come-back. If that meant shading the European beam, so be it – though the rhetoric will always be one of denial as Paris seeks to have its cake and eat it.

Society is changing around the world. The transformation is never easy, but a rough-and-ready distinction can be drawn between those who look forward with hope and those who peer apprehensively over their shoulders at what they may be about to lose; between those who believe they can turn the new century to their advantage and those who would like to stop the clock – or, preferably, ratchet it back a couple of decades. In France, the great shift in social conditions that occurred from the 1950s is ancient history. It is hard to remember the days when less than a third of homes had a bath or shower and under half had a lavatory of their own. Below the coverlet of *la France éternelle*, national life has altered out of recognition, and will go on doing so, despite the rearguard action of traditionalists. The extremist parties of 2002 may have appealed in part to those nostalgic for an older France and to those left on one side by material progress, but many of the young people who voted for Le Pen or the Trotskyites live thoroughly modern lives, if on the less advanced side of the tracks.

Private morality in France has evolved as fast as in any other Western country. While the population has risen by 3.4 per cent since 1990, family sizes have shrunk since the 1960s when government paid people to have more children. As life expectancy grows, France is becoming an ageing country, particularly in its southern half. The number of marriages has fallen by a third per cent since 1970. There are five times as many couples living outside marriage as there were 40 years ago. Births out of wedlock increased sixfold since the mid-1960s, and there is no shortage of prominent examples; actresses Catherine Deneuve, Isabelle Adjani, Emmanuelle Béart and Sophie Marceau have not seen the need to marry the fathers of their children, nor have two of France's leading television news presenters. The First Secretary of the Socialist Party and a prominent minister in the Jospin government had four children without visiting the register office. Homosexual couples have been given the tax and legal benefits of heterosexuals, and qualify for the same fare reductions on the state railway. A successful film comedy was based on the plot line of a downtrodden worker suddenly gaining sympathy and avoiding the sack when he pretended to be gay. The country, according to its President, is entering an era when 'test-tube babies will be surfing the information superhighway'.

Such trends contribute further to the breaking down of the old structure. The new French society has little place for that which used to be taken for granted. Satirical television programmes have spread a 'culture of derision' for the men and women meant to be leading the nation – a trend which undoubtedly contributed to the low votes for Chirac and Jospin in April 2002. Two-thirds of the French say they expect their politicians to lie to them. In a study of twelve European states, they ranked only ninth in expressing faith in their nation's democracy. Asked if they were being told the truth about the way public money was being spent, three-quarters of those questioned said no. A survey by the Sofres polling organisation among young white collar workers at the end of 2001 reported that only 9 per cent expressed confidence in political parties. While Raffarin won immediate popularity, the fall-out from the elections of 2002 could hardly inspire greater trust. Despite all the assurances from both sides that the lessons of popular alienation had been understood, and that politicians would change their ways henceforth, old patterns of behaviour emerged even before the voting was over. The self-absorption of what was known as the political *microcosme* seemed able to withstand any earthquake from outside.

Attempts to reform education and the pensions system ran into popular opposition, and the bid by Jean-Pierre Raffarin to introduce changes gently left him looking weak and ineffective. As the economy stagnated and the government was held responsible for the deaths of 15,000 old people in the summer heat wave of 2003, the Prime Minister's popularity dropped steadily, as did that of Chirac. The one man who won widespread support was the hyper-active Nicolas Sarkozy who was Interior Minister for two years before moving to the Finance Ministry in 2004 – but he was deeply distrusted by the President for having betrayed him in an intra-party power struggle a decade earlier. Discord ran through the big tent party set up to back Chirac, the Union for the Presidential Majority (UMP). Its leader, Alain Juppé, the former Prime Minister whom Chirac hoped would succeed him, was found guilty in a political corruption case, and sentenced to be barred from politics. In March, 2004, the UMP suffered a major reverse in regional elections, which became a referendum on the Raffarin government and Jacques Chirac, himself. Less than two years after its sweeping presidential and parliamentary victories, the centre-right was back on the ropes, winning only 37 per cent of the second round vote to the left's 50 per cent and holding on to control of just two of France's 22 metropolitan regions.

Though the Socialists could rejoice at this, the vote was more of a fresh manifestation of the power of protest voting than an endorsement of the left, with the 15 per cent score for the National Front taking support from the orthodox right and emphasising the appeal of the far right to those who felt abandoned by orthodox politicians. Feuding among Socialist chieftains, which had broken out as soon as Jospin had been eliminated in 2002, rippled on, centring round the presidential ambitions of Laurent Fabius, a former Prime Minister from the 1980s, who divided the party into fervent supporters and die-hard opponents. To the right of Fabius, another former Finance Minister, Dominique Strauss-Kahn, stood for the modernising wing of the party. To the left, the number two figure in the Jospin government, Martine Aubry, nurtured national ambitions from her power base in the northern city of Lille while the ambitions of the party's First Secretary, François Hollande, seemed to rise as he grew into the job. As Socialist leaders succeeded one another on television programmes on the night of the regional election, the impression was of a multiplicity of voices coming from politicians who could not quite believe their luck.

For Chirac, the outcome was a nasty repetition of his humiliation in 1997 and he decided to resist, keeping Raffarin as Prime Minister despite the heavy vote against him and his policies. But there was a deeper significance to the result. Though less dramatic than the first round of the 2002 presidential election, the regional results in 2004 showed a country that continued to vote into office leaders whom it then promptly turned against. For its part, the political class remained remarkably impervious to change, with the same cast playing the same games of revolving door administrations unshaken by defeat. The deeper problem was that neither right nor left offered a coherent road map for the nation. The requirement for reform was evident; the link between the rulers and the ruled had to be restored. But achieving that involved the fundamental questions which reach to the heart of the nature of France, and are the subject of this book. Most difficult to resolve was the conflict between the need to make the system more flexible, more attuned to the different parts of the nation, more modern – and the way in which the French look to the state as their protector from the challenges of the modern world. In the past, the second had predominated, however poor a defence it had proved to be during the hard years of the 1990s.

There was no more fervent defender of the importance of *l'État* than Chirac. For many who had voted for him to block Le Pen, the votes of 2002 had been, above all, a re-affirmation of the Republican state as the highest value in the land. For all their individualism, the French feel a need to be able to believe that the Hexagon is something special. The political and economic history of the years between 1981 and 2002 had severely shaken that faith. Year by year, the stakes had grown as the old self-confidence came under growing strain, and no alternative emerged to restore the exceptional nature of the nation. After the latest earthquake, France found itself on the edge. How it reacted would be vital for its own future, with important repercussions for its neighbours, and for the world it so dearly wants to illuminate.

2

Behind the Mask

Diminishing faith in leaders is a general phenomenon in the West, but has a particular impact in France because of the quasi-monarchical status of the man in the Élysée Palace. With a term that was cut from seven years to a more sensible five only in 2002, the President of the Republic is Head of State and is meant to personify the nation. He is boss of a major political party which usually, but by no means always, forms the biggest group in the legislature. He names the Prime Minister, and approves the composition of the government. He has the last word in foreign policy and any other domains which attract his attention – one former minister told me that he was blessed because the President of the time had no interest whatsoever in his field of responsibility. Commander-in-chief of the armed forces, he controls France's nuclear strike force. Vast acres of patronage are at his disposal, together with a state apparatus that is both extraordinarily pervasive and excessively powerful. He can call a referendum when he wishes as a means of rallying the country behind him. And his influence is not just a matter of politics: speaking of one of his grand cultural projects in Paris, François Mitterrand put it in a nutshell: 'I choose, I decide, I build.' In what may not be an apocryphal story, another President was told on a foreign trip that his country no longer had a leading world novelist. 'When I get home, I'll call a ministerial meeting to deal with the matter,' he replied. It is not surprising that, for much of the Fifth Republic, commentators have spoken of 'our president-monarchs' down to the way in which many of the trappings of power and personal behaviour that surrounded the kings at Versailles find echoes at the Élysée, including the illegitimate daughter born to the mistress of the longest-reigning President and the roving eye of his successor.

It may be all too much for a single human being, calling for discrimination in the exercise of power hardly to be expected of those who spend their lives fighting their way up the political ladder. The experience since the mid-1970s certainly argues in that direction, as the men France chose fell short of the heights expected of them while the interplay of party and electoral systems repeatedly excluded others apparently well fitted for the job. The concentration of power might be acceptable if exercised to the broader benefit of the people, but national politics has become the domain of self-interested clans which put their own struggle for power above everything else. Periods of cohabitation between presidents and prime ministers from different camps after the Heads of State lost legislative elections in 1986, 1993 and 1997 became rehearsals for future battles for the Elysée, with each man jockeying for the contest ahead. From 1997 to 2002, in particular, this produced damaging fragmentation at the summit, to the disadvantage of France and the bewilderment of its partners.

Faced with the huge task of reviving the nation from the ruins of the Fourth Republic, liquidating the cancer of Algeria, quenching military revolt and avoiding a repetition of his post-war defeat by the political establishment, it was not surprising that Charles de Gaulle opted for an imperial presidency when he returned to power in 1958. He had to hold the divided, dispirited country together and provide the leadership needed to take it into a new dimension. His success marks him as the greatest French leader of the twentieth century. But, a decade after riding roughshod to power, the General was an old man clearly incapable of driving the great presidential engine he had constructed. So, adopting the logic underlying the Gaullist system, the people turfed him out in a referendum in 1969. After a five-year interlude of pragmatic conservatism under the presidency of Georges Pomidou, France embarked on another adventure, with the brilliant, conceited and ultimately fragile Valéry Giscard d'Estaing, who ended his term dragged down by rising unemployment, vicious in-fighting on the right and allegations that he had accepted jewellery from the unsavoury Emperor Bokassa. The man who vanquished him in 1981 enjoyed a De Gaulle-like monopoly of the levers of power – the Élysée Palace, a faithful Prime Minister, an obedient Cabinet, an adoring party, and control of the National Assembly. He could, personally and politically, speak about it being a time for dreams. To nobody's surprise, the fervently anti-Gaullist François Mitterrand, who had once denounced the permanent *coup d'état* of the Fifth Republic, found that, once in power, the presidential raiment suited him very nicely indeed.

But Mitterrand misplayed his hand in a domain he took pride in knowing nothing about – the economy. As a result, his presidential leadership was rapidly undermined by a rolling crisis which led to one of the greatest policy U-turns seen in modern Europe. Although most of it was hidden at the time, the regime was also being sucked down into a mire of scandal, which reached from the everyday business of raising political funds to the destruction of the anti-nuclear ship, *Rainbow Warrior*, by French agents in New Zealand. Mitterrand held on to the Élysée in 1988 thanks to clever tactics and the widespread distrust of his main opponent. But, almost as soon as his second term began, the *après*-Mitterrandist jockeying started, and the President devoted himself to playing favourites with his courtiers and ordering up grandiose building projects worthy of the Sun King. Once again, France had found that the man of its choice could not live up to its hopes. Seven years after his first victory, the first President of the Fifth Republic to claim to come from the left confided that he had 'learned to distrust dreams'.

Some of Mitterrand's achievements will last – the commitment to Europe, the abolition of the death penalty, the encouragement of culture, the renovation of the Louvre Museum, and the great buildings he commissioned. Above all he showed that France did not have to be ruled eternally from the right, and that an alternance of power was possible. But he also led France to the edge of disaster and, when he went, the country deserved a new start. What it got was Jacques Chirac.

The new President was hardly a fresh face: he had been a junior minister at the time of the 1968 general strikes and student riots, when he was said to have attended a secret meeting with union leaders in a prostitutes' hotel in northern Paris with a revolver in his pocket – presumably none of the labour bosses made the Mae West joke about him being glad to see them. His career has gone in twos – two spells as Prime Minister and two in the Élysée after his re-election in 2002. For eighteen years, he played the twin roles of Mayor of Paris and Gaullist party boss. Each of his premierships lasted for two years, so did the period he ruled with a parliamentary majority after getting to the Élysée in 1995. Multiply by ten and you get Chirac's basic political support, which has fluctuated around 20 per cent for two decades. After seven years as President, he scored 19.8 per cent in the first round of his re-election bid in 2002.

The paradoxes of Chirac's character are enough to give a psychiatrist a lifetime's work. His energy and charm co-exist with periods of detachment and depression. He combines a grasshopper attention span and nerve-end impetuousness with grinding long-term ambition. He revels in grand occasions, and lived a gilded existence as Mayor of Paris before becoming President, but harbours contempt for what he once called the 'salon hamsters' of high society. He operates through a mix of loyalty and ruthlessness. A fervent Gaullist, he was among those who prepared the way for the General's downfall by helping in the emergence of a credible successor. His attachment to republican legality is not in doubt, but he can also play the Bonapartist card and cultivates semi-clandestine networks which have always been a hallmark of Gaullism. A man of the right, he organised his party on Leninist lines. In the 1995 presidential election, he portrayed himself as an outsider ready to put right the wrongs of French society, but he has lived for so long in the palaces of the regime that the editor of *Le Monde* punningly baptised him 'le Résident de la République'.

For all this, when he finally won the presidency at his third attempt in 1995, nobody knew what made up the real Jacques Chirac. He seemed to live on nervous energy – the first time his wife met him, his legs jiggled so much that she concluded he must drink too much coffee. After beating him in the 1988 presidential election, Mitterrand told an aide: 'Basically, this man is mad, and does whatever comes into his head. He may get elected after me, but he'll soon be the laughing-stock of the whole world.' Chirac's image marked him out as somebody whose tastes stop at hearty food, Western films, military music – and a passion for sumo wrestling. In fact, he has greater depths. Passionate about primitive civilisations and their art, he refused to have anything to do with the 500th anniversary celebrations of

Columbus' voyage because of the havoc wreaked on the people of South America. Adoptive father of a Vietnamese child, he is a man who would hide a volume of poetry in a copy of *Playboy*, remarks the journalist Françoise Giroud, who served in one of his governments. But show him a crowd and he rises to the surface at the first handshake. On his emotional bottom-line, he seems to fear failure above all else, and he knows plenty about it. In the 1988 presidential election, he was humiliated by Mitterrand. The French, his wife is reported to have told him at the time, just didn't like him. That was something he simply couldn't bring himself to accept. Following him at election meetings and on the streets seven years later was to witness a man who was, literally, reaching out for support each time a hand came into view, a man who longed to be loved and had to prove that he could surmount the final hurdle – he should have appropriated the Paul Anka/Claude François anthem of doing it his way before Frank Sinatra got hold of it.

So, to fill its imperial presidency, a post requiring massive vision and deliberation, France found itself with a man who picks up ideas like lint and who cannot resist going after the gallery. As a former premier put it: 'For him, thinking is, first of all, thinking about what others think.' Back in the 1980s, when Chirac was out of national power but still an important figure as Mayor of Paris and leader of the neo-Gaullist party Rassemblement Pour la République (RPR), I had breakfast with him at his office in the Hôtel de Ville. He was going to Bonn later in the day, so we spoke about Franco-German relations and I wondered if, in the spirit of greater co-operation, there might be some scope for Paris to offer the Germans a finger on the French nuclear trigger. It was a silly idea – there was nothing Germany wanted less than to be involved in nuclear weapons. But that evening, the television news reported that, on his visit to the Konrad Adenauer Foundation, Chirac had suggested that the Germans might like to share in turning the key that would set off France's contribution to an earth-shattering war.

Given the vim and vigour of the man who moved into the Élysée in 1995, it was entirely natural that the new presidency began on a high, sweeping away the cobwebs of the Mitterrand era as Jacques Chirac zoomed to unprecedented heights in the polls and upstaged the much younger Bill Clinton and John Major when they gathered for their first summit with him. France is back, alive and kicking, was the message. *Vas-y, fonce*: crack on, and damn the consequences. So it was also entirely predictable that one of Chirac's first major acts was to arouse and ignore world opprobrium by resuming nuclear testing in French Polynesia. And, as night follows day, the new President's popularity slumped after the initial honeymoon. Plans for welfare cuts and proposals to reduce the huge losses of the railway system, where staff were entitled to retire on a full pension at the age of fifty, brought hundreds of thousands of protesters out in the streets. Pessimism reached the levels of the darkest days of Mitterrand. Scandals began to swirl around the new administration. Unemployment rose to a record level and his Prime Minister's popularity slumped.

Achieving the goal of his political life at the third attempt might have induced a certain serenity in another man. When things began to turn sour, another politician might have sat down and drawn up a long-term plan to make the maximum use of his seven-year term. In philosophical mode, Chirac once reflected that political life was 'a succession of reflections on life and on oneself'. But the ups-and-downs of his own career had produced a deep insecurity that sat uneasily with the office he had won at long last. After his defeat by Mitterrand in 1988, he was, aides recalled, physically present at meetings but his mind was absent. His victory in 1995, confounding opinion polls which had cast him initially as an also-ran, restored his manic side. So the decision to meet the rising tide of discontent head-on by calling a premature parliamentary election in 1997 was in character, but also doubly dangerous.

Not only did he risk defeat, he also created a formal blurring of lines between two great institutions of state, the presidency and the legislature. Presidents had always thrown their prestige into parliamentary elections to aid their own party, but this time Chirac was, in effect, putting the presidency on the line for his Prime Minister. It was sheer folly to expect a grouchy electorate to supply the shot in the arm he was seeking. France was fed up with its rulers, annoyed that yet again they had failed to come up with a miracle remedy as promised by witch-doctor Chirac two years earlier. Voters were deeply worried about unemployment and the social cost of Europe, and felt that the men in power did not understand – or even care – about the fears that kept them awake at night. So it was not surprising that Chirac's gamble went horribly wrong, that the right lost its majority in the National Assembly, that the President had to appoint the Socialist Lionel Jospin to head a new government, and that the National Front became the electoral arbiter in more than sixty constituencies.

In many ways, the episode provided a sharp snapshot of the trouble with France – an out-of-touch elitist leadership, an electorate grasping for straws from politicians it had rejected only a few years earlier, a rise of extremism, and widespread disenchantment reflected in a 31 per cent abstention rate. As Jospin ruled with a broad left coalition including Communists and Greens, Chirac was marginalised. Mitterrand had known how to manage cohabitation, but Chirac was pushed to the sidelines as a tide of political scandal allegations from his time as Mayor of Paris rose. The decline in the status of the presidency raised questions about whether the nature of the Fifth Republic was changing to make the Head of State less of an executive and more of a figurehead. As Chirac and Jospin girded up for the 2002 presidential election, opinion polls showed them running neck-and-neck – a sign of the times since an incumbent prime minister had never made it to the Élysée. Then, in an extraordinary reversal of fortune, the splintering of the left led to the elimination of Jospin, the presence of the National Front in the run-off ballot, and an 82 per cent vote for Chirac in a second round vote that became a referendum against Jean-Marie Le Pen. This saved France's honour, and gave the President the opportunity of re-establishing the Gaullien pre-eminence of his office. The issue was whether, aged 69 and after 35 years in the corridors of power, he would prove to be the right man to lead a fractured France through the challenges of the new century.

When Jacques Chirac entered government in 1967, as a junior minister for employment, the French were shielded from economic and social reality by inflation, corporatism, self-defensive politicians, a provident public sector and the belief that the state and its servants would always look after them. In the three decades after the Second World War known as *Les Trente Glorieuses* (The Glorious Thirty), prosperity brought telephones and washing machines to almost every home; rat-infested city buildings were replaced by tower blocks; and, under De Gaulle, France walked tall on the world stage.

As the Glorious Thirty slipped seamlessly into what were later dubbed the Lazy Ten, other countries were marching to a different drum. Margaret Thatcher was doing her utmost to change Britain. Ronald Reagan was altering America. Germany was pushing its productivity to new heights, and Japan was leading Asia's economic charge. But the French refused to change, and when the crunch came at the end of the 1970s, they blamed their President for the threat to their comfortable way of life posed by the oil price crises, the shifting shape of the world economy and growing cost of the welfare state. And when Giscard d'Estaing rightly noted that the country was caught up in a world crisis, he was ridiculed for seeking to evade the blame, as if any French Head of State worth his salt should be able to buck international trends.

The narrowness of Giscard's defeat in 1981 showed that France was not all that convinced of the merits of swinging to the left, but the temptation to reject his stern medicine proved irresistible. So France flew out of the window of reality on a rip-roaring expansion jag which all too soon slammed with sickening inevitability into the tough monetarist wall of the Ten Fearful Years of deflation.

After more than a decade of fear and belt-tightening, George Soros was far from alone in admiring the way successive Finance Ministers of right and left kept to the straight and narrow anti-inflationary path. France's trade balance with the rest of the world rose to record levels of surplus as the 1990s progressed. In a country which had never been entirely at home with modern business (and often preferred to leave finance to Protestants or Jews), market capitalism became the flavour of the decade. The head of a pharmaceuticals company told me that the crisis 'makes one more intelligent'. It also enabled managers to award themselves large pay rises and plentiful share options. French workers, on the other hand, have been classed as the most insecure in Europe, with the lowest identification with their companies and the least positive relationship with their employer. The fact that unemployment soared under a government of the left elected to usher in economic expansion was an irony which many found hard to stomach.

The combination of deflation and high unemployment, lack of convincing leadership, mounting social tensions and gnawing uncertainties at home and abroad encouraged the process of fear and contraction to feed on itself. The relief that came after the Socialist victory of 1997, thanks to the world economic upturn and the increased efficiencies introduced during the harsh years of the 1990s which boosted productivity, provided a time of enormous relief – at least for those who benefitted. But a degree of complacency crept in as France saw itself set to outstrip Germany, and become the centre of an European alternative to the America of George W. Bush. The rush of confidence fed an assurance that is always latent in the regard France feels for itself. Then came the slowing of the economic expansion, and the political earthquake of 2002, with an immediate analogy from the other side of the planet. France's football team had been world beaters, adding the European championship to the World Cup which, it was assumed, they would capture again in the Far East in 2002. But then the side of Zidane and company crashed out of the top international competition at the first round without scoring a single goal while French companies, whose fortunes we will follow in a later chapter, came a huge cropper. What did they have in common with the Socialists who plunged to defeat at the same time? Arrogance, to start with – *les bleus* thought they were assured of reaching the second round, as did the equally unhappy Jospin. Beyond that, a failure to recognise opponents – be it Senegal or Le Pen. And, finally, the ultimate winner was the very one they had beaten the last time round – Brazil and Chirac. And, as Jospin retreated into silence, the football team emerged from Roissy airport on its return without a word for the waiting supporters.

By that time, economic growth had more than halved. The European statistics agency put France twelfth among European Union countries in terms of gross national product per inhabitant, ahead of only Spain, Portugal and Greece. The national planning commission said the wealth disparity among communes was the highest in western Europe. In the countryside, the gulf between rich and poor farmers widened. France had become a country of two nations, searching for a moral foundation, with a ruling clan of both right and left that had become accustomed to living in a world of its own and behaving in such a way as to deprive itself of the claim to leadership on which the Republic rests.

*

Public morality certainly ain't what it used to be. The ranks of role models are shrinking. Even the country's long-time saint in waiting, a Benedictine priest called L'Abbé Pierre, who had regularly been voted the most admired man in France as he spent his life helping the poor and homeless, ran into trouble when he talked of the 'international Zionist lobby' and accused Jews of having committed a genocide in Palestine eleven or twelve centuries before Christ. A cancer research charity which had enjoyed about the same high repute as the abbot was revealed to have spent only a third of its donations on medical work, and to have funded political parties by the back door. Its seventy-year-old president, who used to appeal for donations on television surrounded by pale children, was reported to have diverted tens of millions of francs from the charity, known by its initials as the ARC. As the net closed around him, Jacques Crozemarie had a heart attack; he was charged with fraud in his hospital bed. The charity, which had attracted around 600 million francs a year in donations, was found to have paid out a billion francs to contractors without requiring tenders: in return, kickbacks running into tens of millions of francs flowed to the men running the organisation. If this scummy scandal seemed to show that nothing was sacred, it was promptly followed by the disclosure that nurseries of Paris were buying milk from corrupt suppliers in exchange for bribes.

Champions of cancer charities and suppliers of children's milk should be above reproach, but, as realists, the French do not expect their politicians or businessmen to be as pure as the Alpine snow. There has always been politico-business sleaze. The Third Republic saw a great scandal over the financing of the Panama Canal in which bribes were handed out to some 100 National Assembly deputies, and a series of high-rolling swindlers who bought political protection and helped to undermine respect for the regime in the 1930s. The first two decades of the Fifth Republic saw the kidnapping of a Moroccan opposition leader on the Boulevard Saint-Germain in Paris with French connivance – and his subsequent assassination in a suburban villa; the murder of one minister and the mysterious death of another; plus murky rumours involving Yugoslav gangsters, a film star couple and the wife of Georges Pompidou, probably inspired by his opponents as he prepared to run for the presidency. There was a long-running controversy over whether the immovable head of the Communist Party had gone voluntarily to work in Germany during the war; awkward revelations about how little tax one Prime Minister had paid; the treacly matter of state-subsidised repairs done to a château bought by Jacques Chirac while he was still an up-and-coming politician; and the affair of diamonds given to Giscard d'Estaing by Emperor Bokassa of Central Africa.

The funding of French politics has always been opaque, but a series of judicial inquiries in the 1980s and 1990s lifted the veil in a manner that deepened public cynicism about those who presumed to lead them. Some Mediterranean regions have a long tradition of graft. The state audit court found 'serious irregularities' in the management of the public finances of the Bouches-du-Rhône and Gard departments in the south while, in the neighbouring Var, the former president of the departmental council was sentenced to two years in prison and a million-franc fine over the payment of bribes for a public construction project. A National Assembly deputy from the Var, Yann Piat, who had declared war on the local mafia, was gunned down by a man on a motorcycle as she drove along a rural road in 1994. She left a letter mentioning a local senator and a gang boss. Soon after she died, two of her associates were found dead in a car in their garage. A tube ran from the exhaust pipe into the car. The verdict was suicide. Eastwards along the Mediterranean, the Mayor of Cannes, once known as 'the Kennedy of the Croisette' after the resort's sea-front boulevard, was handed a suspended prison sentence and a large fine for corruption. Another Riviera boss who liked to call himself 'the Godfather' and was arrested for taking kickbacks amounting to 1.8 million francs, put up the ultimate defence. 'I did not demand money,' he said. 'I was offered it.'

In this Provençal gallery, nobody could rival Jacques Médecin, the swaggering, high-living Mayor of Nice, a one-time Minister of Tourism, an all-too-typical scion of a local political dynasty, author of an excellent cookbook and escort of starlets in see-through blouses. Médecin was put under the spotlight in the 1980s by one of the Riviera's most eminent English residents: Graham Greene accused him of running a mafia system in his city. Once, telephoning me after lunch on a Sunday, Greene rambled on about former torturers from French Algeria working for the mayor's camp. When I later tracked down a man whom Greene fingered as a secret underworld boss, he turned out to be a petty criminal who appeared to have crossed one of the author's local friends. Still, Médecin's way of running France's fifth biggest city was deeply rotted by kickbacks, corruption and flirtation with the far right. Naturally, Médecin blamed the attacks on the Socialists and Communists. They were, he once told me, after him because he was 'the most offensive' politician in France (despite being married to an American, his English was not as good as he thought it to be). Eventually, the burly, moustachioed mayor was jailed for siphoning off millions of francs from municipal funds. On his release, he went to Uruguay where he sold hand-painted T-shirts and died at the end of 1998, lamented by Jean-Marie Le Pen as a man who 'was no more guilty than others'. What the National Front leader had in mind was the growing tribe of politicians who lived far from what the commentator, Alain Minc, identified as 'a Latin predisposition to deals and fiddles'.

When the Gaullists sought new faces in the 1980s, no two politicians better represented the coming spirit of the party than Michel Noir, mayor of France's second biggest metropolis of Lyon, and Alain Carignon, who ran the Alpine city of Grenoble. They were each thoroughly modern men, good communicators and managers who could hope to rise to the very top of government. Tall and handsome, Noir became Minister for Foreign Trade, but, in 1995, he was given an eighteen-month suspended jail sentence for a political funding affair centering round his flashy son-in-law, whose pharmaceutical franchising business he helped to promote – the affair was given added appeal by the involvement of the presenter of France's main nightly television news programme who, unlike Noir, kept his job.

Alain Carignon was even more of a star, running Grenoble which had become a showplace for French modernity. His election as mayor in 1983 seemed to mark a neat fit between the man and the place. The dapper Gaullist became France's Environment Minister at the age of thirty-seven, and was spoken of as a potential Prime Minister. Behind the scenes, some more old-fashioned games were being played. A local official recalled meetings at which the mayor fixed the distribution of the spoils of sleaze – the Gaullists got as much as the Socialists and Communists combined. (This official, himself, received a monthly salary from four construction firms which worked for the city.) As Carignon's self-confidence grew, he doubled his party's take, and accepted a rent-free flat in Paris, plane tickets, holidays and finance for his campaign newspaper from a lobbying company representing a big public-works group. He billed the city government for trips of doubtful value to Grenoble, and kept the councillors of the surrounding Isère department sweet by doubling their stipends.

In 1995, Carignon was arrested and held for 200 days in the jail cell in Lyon once occupied by the Nazi war criminal, Klaus Barbie. While there, he went on receiving a special monthly allowance of 20,000 francs for his promotional activities for Grenoble. When he was put on trial, his supporters declared their love for him from the public gallery. A group of stars, including actor Gérard Depardieu and philosopher Bernard-Henri Lévy, issued a statement in his defence. It did no good. Carignon was convicted of having accepted 21 million francs in return for awarding a water supply contract to one of France's biggest companies. He had also interfered with witnesses, the court ruled. The once dashing hope of Gaullism got five years in jail.

'Other countries have political crises, we have scandals,' a former high official reflected. Sleaze oozed out of the very summit of power. The Socialist Party which came to office in 1981 promising new ethical standards was found to have been taking widespread pay-offs for public-works contracts – there were even suggestions that it was François Mitterrand himself who had dreamed up the scam. The President of the National Assembly Finance Committee was sentenced to a suspended eighteen-month prison term, fined 30,000 francs and deprived of his civic rights for two years after being found guilty of being involved in the scheme to raise money for the party through false bills issued to firms which got contracts in Socialist-run towns. A former member of parliament revealed a series of large kickbacks from supermarket groups to give the Socialists illicit funding. A minister and his chief of staff plundered 20 million francs from a fund set up to help pay for a Franco-African summit. A huge scandal erupted at the state oil company, Elf, with a cast ranging from international fixers to the novelist Françoise Sagan, which we will hear more of in a subsequent chapter. On top of which, some leading Socialist figures appeared to bear political responsibility for delays in testing HIV-contaminated blood in the national blood bank which infected 1,250 haemophiliacs. Nor were the Communists immune –

some of their officials were found guilty of raising illegal funding on municipal contracts.

The first President of the left liked to denounce the immorality of money and of all who sought it, but it turned out that one of Mitterrand's oldest friend had used his position to wring commissions out of French state contracts, to sell his near-worthless company to the state for a hefty price and to use privileged information for insider dealing. In a move which even some of his loyalist followers found hard to stomach, Mitterrand invited a rogue in recurrent trouble with the courts and the tax authorities into the Cabinet. Two of the President's closest associates killed themselves. Illicit telephone tapping from the 'black box' unit at the Élysée targeted around 1,500 people, including journalists, lawyers, magistrates, a nightclub, a cleaning company, an actress, a prominent Socialist politician, the Aga Khan and the President's mistress – at least Mitterrand spared his wife. The sleaze continued to seep out after Mitterrand's death in 1996 – three years later, for instance, a former secret agent said $2.5 billion had disappeared from a secret Saudi loan to France at the start of his presidency. His son and one of his aides were alleged to have been caught up with a wheeler-dealer who sold arms illicitly to Angola. (Beside all this, news that the Socialist Defence Minister had supplied information to the KGB in the 1950s and 1960s in return for payments that more than doubled his earnings and paid for his election expenses seemed almost conventionally reassuring.)

On the other side of the political fence, a wave of allegations broke about the way Paris was run during Jacques Chirac's two decades as mayor, and about the funding of his neo-Gaullist party, the RPR. As examining magistrates dug into his past, they came up with accusations of everything from using fake municipal jobs to pay party workers to plundering state funds to finance family trips abroad, sending a driver with envelopes of large-denomination bills to buy the tickets at a suburban travel agency. Stories about the President surfaced weekly, including one that, as mayor, he kept piles of five hundred franc notes in a safe in the toilet beside his office – when he went inside, his visitors did not know if it was to urinate or to fetch a bundle of cash. A videotape by a property developer, who had been a big fund raiser, spoke of a pervasive system of kickbacks. Other businessmen who had worked with the municipality and the Gaullist-run region round Paris told of stumping up cash contributions to get contracts to build schools and public housing. A charitable foundation to which the City of Paris contributed purchased land round the President's country château, thus protecting it from development that would have impinged on his privacy. Grocery bills from the city hall showed extraordinarily high spending, with the same bills being reimbursed time and again. After losing his job, Chirac's chauffeur published a book recounting his former employer's active extra-marital sex life, including encounters with an unnamed Italian actress – women at Gaullist party headquarters were said to refer to the President as a 'three minute man, shower included . . .'

By the 2002 election, Jacques Chirac's denials of anything untoward had earned him the nickname of 'SuperLiar' bestowed on him by a satirical television programme – if politicians found themselves in trouble all they had to do was to summon SuperLiar who would show them how to brazen their way out. But a ruling by the highest constitutional court confirmed his immunity so long as he remained in the Élysée – not only from prosecution but also from questioning. There was a certain amusement and world weariness in the popular reaction: what else could one expect of a politician? 'Better a crook than a Fascist' became a rallying cry for left-wingers voting for Chirac to block Le Pen. It was hardly a slogan calculated to inspire respect for the system and the man holding its highest office. The President's refusal to have a televised debate with the National Front leader was attributed, in part at least, to his reluctance to face a no-holds-barred rhetorical onslaught on the scandal front – his opponent said he would have come to the studio with a large pair of handcuffs to be clamped on the wrists of the Head of State.

Charles Pasqua, the former Interior Minister who had been close to Chirac before falling out with him, was alleged to be involved in various sleazy undertakings ranging from arms dealing in Africa to kickbacks in a Paris suburb where he ran the local administration. One of Pasqua's officials there fled to the Caribbean after a murky incident involving an apparent attempt to smear a magistrate, and then returned with tales of malfeasance in awarding public housing contracts. Alain Juppé, Chirac's right-hand man in the Paris city government who served as his first Prime Minister, was found to have lived in an apartment owned by the city in a smart Left Bank street at an extremely low rent. More seriously, in 2004, he got an 18-month prison sentence and was barred from elective office for ten years for having used municipal funds to pay workers for Chirac's party – though appeal proceedings meant he was able to hang on to the party leadership for the time being. The President's successor as mayor, Jean Tiberi, also faced a string of allegations that contributed to his defeat at municipal elections.

While the President reacted with a mixture of denial and disdain, safe behind his immunity, Lionel Jospin adopted a stricter morality, though, given the Socialists' own past record, he was careful not to launch a frontal attack on the party funding front. However, the climate was such that even the squeaky-clean Prime Minister came under the spotlight with suggestions, which proved unfounded, of sharp practice in connection with his holiday home. He had also suffered embarrassment when his long-standing denials of a secret Trotskyite past were shown to have been, at best, economical with the truth, raising not so much the issue of whether he had kept up friendships on the far left after joining Mitterrand's party as why he had bothered to hide what was hardly a badge of shame. The Socialists also faced judicial pressure when their Finance Minister, Dominique Strauss-Kahn, was obliged to resign over an inquiry into legal work for a student organisation that funded the party – he was cleared in time to re-appear in the 2002 election campaign.

The stream of cases was the result of investigations by a new breed of examining magistrates who made it their business to take on prominent figures in a way that would have been inconceivable in more deferential times. As well as the politicians, a line of leading business figures has, as we will see, been put under investigation for alleged tax evasion, money laundering, false accounting and buying favours. In the face of a self-protective establishment with plenty to hide, the magistrates emerged as men and women ready to buck the system and act in the public good. But, by the time of Chirac's re-election, their crusade appeared to be running out of steam. There was a reaction against the sledge hammer tactics some of them used, wielding draconian powers to lock up suspects for long periods without bringing charges. The magistrates, themselves, complained of political pressures, and lack of resources. Several took early retirement. Some big cases collapsed. One judicial bloodhound, who had conducted an eight-year probe into Chirac and kickbacks in Paris, was taken off the job at the end of 2001, and resigned early the following year, complaining that he had been blocked at every turn.

A broader question is whether, as well as protecting the ruling class, the nature of the hermetically sealed elite that runs so much of France actually encourages corruption as small groups of men and women work together for decades at the junction of politics, business and officialdom, believing, at least until recently, that they are beyond the reach of the law. The widespread practice of politicians holding several elected offices at the same time, which successive governments have sought to end but with only partial success, extends their ambit and limits the number of players. The way in which bureaucrats move between politics and business creates another layer of mutual understanding. Their common background, often as students at the country's top colleges, creates another bond. As a Socialist minister put it: 'In the relatively narrow world of the administrative universe, everybody knows one another.'

The parade of politicians and businessmen wending its way through the courts, or fighting to keep out of them, underlines the extent to which France, though priding itself on being a meritocratic society dedicated to equality, has a highly impermeable ruling class, rigorously removed from the common run of mortals and lifted to a pedestal which encourages a distorted view of life and engenders social division. That might not be a surprise coming from the right, but the Socialist Party has also developed its own ruling caste, drawn from the elitist background and increasingly cut off from the working class, as shown by the vote of 2002. 'We make fine speeches about equality of opportunity,' a former minister reflected. 'But France is the European country where the selection of elites is the fiercest, and the division between good and bad pupils perpetuates the cleavage between social classes.' When the 'good pupils' are seen to fall short and to be concerned primarily with their own interests, the rest of the class inevitably begins to wonder why they are up there in charge of things and whether they deserve the respect which any governing group needs to be effective. At the least, that breeds an unhealthy degree of corrosive cynicism; at worst, it could lead to a desire to tear down the temple of the elite which rules the nation.

★

Britain has Oxbridge, America the East Coast college mafia, France the Grandes Écoles. Once again, France is different. You may get an intellectual sheen and start to build up networks at Oxford or Harvard, but you are not specifically educated to take charge of a nation. Margaret Thatcher read chemistry; Bill Clinton law. Neither of them was set on a course of administrative and political power, as such. But that was precisely what was laid out for Presidents Jacques Chirac and Valéry Giscard d'Estaing, and for Prime Ministers Édouard Balladur, Michel Rocard, Alain Juppé, Laurent Fabius and Lionel Jospin when they emerged from the final oral examination for the hundred bright young people who graduate each year from the leading finishing school for the elite, the École Nationale d'Administration, known by its initials from one end of the country to the other simply as *l'ÉNA*.

In all, 184 establishments come under the umbrella of France's network of state-funded administrative finishing schools, the Grandes Écoles. Their 75,000 students sit at the peak of an educational selection process and come mainly from the middle and upper classes in what one writer has called 'pure and simple social reproduction'. Each student costs the taxpayer an average of 12,000 euros a year, but, at one top establishment, *Polytechnique*, 65 per cent of graduates go into the private sector rather than working for the state, and another 10 per cent go on to do research. Those who stay with the service of the Republic enter one of eleven *corps d'état*, drawing appropriate prestige in the process – a luncheon guest told the *Finacial Times* a big takeover of a state conglomerate had gone in favour of a company because it had been able to boast a member of a leading *corps,* an *Ingénieur des Mines*, among its top brass: it was a joke, but only just. The careers of the man from the École des Mines who has run the Peugeot car company since 1997 and of his predecessor provided good illustrations of the way such men move. Jean-Martin Folz had gone through the Industry Ministry, the Rhône-Poulenc chemicals group, Péchiney and the Eridania Béghin-Say food firm before being hired by the Peugeot family to head their enterprise. His predecessor, Jacques Calvet, had moved from ÉNA into the civil service in 1957, ending up as chief of staff to the Finance Minister and then moving on to the Banque Nationale de Paris, where he became chairman before spending fifteen years in charge of Peugeot.

The aim of ÉNA is to teach its students how to order and present their ideas, how to produce a seamless presentation on any subject under the sun in which style vies with substance. From any set of data, a true graduate of ÉNA, or Énarque, should be able to extract a convincing case for either side in an argument. The system is hermetic – and not by accident. Set up after the Liberation by De Gaulle's fervent follower, Michel Debré, the aim was to produce an irreproachable mandarin sect whose only duty would be to serve the nation above and beyond partisan politics or personal advancement. The rankings of students on leaving the college would provide an objective, scientific gauge to who was capable of running the administration of France, in contrast to the way in which pre-war civil servants and Vichy collaborators-to-be got their jobs through social and family connections at interviews which they attended in morning coats and white gloves. As Debré's master, the General, told the students of 1959: 'You are called by your vocation to exercise the most important and most noble function which exists in the temporal sphere – I mean, the service of the state.'

'We are defined by our jobs,' one ÉNA graduate who rose through the civil service to the summit of the French business world reflected. Some break free – one Énarque became *Le Monde*'s presidential correspondent, and another, a businessman called Marc de Lacharrière, came out of a ruined provincial aristocratic family to put together a major conglomerate with a turnover of 8 billion francs. Not that either lacked the contacts which an ÉNA background helps to nurture. The journalist's dinner parties were truffled with top civil servants with whom he had studied, and he was France's principal presidential scoop merchant for many years. As for M. de Lacharrière, he has known Jacques Chirac since the 1970s, was a good friend of the head of the Gaullist party, funded a social body set up by the second-ranking minister of Lionel Jospin's government, employs former leading aides of ministers of left and right, and backs the classic politico-literary monthly, the *Revue des Deux Mondes*.

Around 4,000 Énarques – 20 per cent of them women – are at work in France: three-quarters in the civil service, 600 in senior positions in public-sector companies, and 200 in private firms. They run state banks and arms companies, private-sector firms and planning bodies. They guide the country's political destiny from ministries and parliament, conduct its diplomacy, and offer counsel in weighty tomes of futurology. At the very top of the tree sit 300 *Inspecteurs des Finances*, a band of super-auditors drawn from the top 10 per cent of ENA graduates. A former minister, Albin Chalandon, describes them as 'a monolithic, conformist, self-assured group'. Many go on to run big public and private sector enterprises, leading the journalist, Ghislaine Ottenheimer, to write in her book on the *Inspecteurs* in 2004 of a 'hold-up by this aristocracy of the State on whole swatches of the economy'.

As De Gaulle instructed them to be, these technocrats are ecumenical servants of the state. The importance of *l'État* in France is something we will come to in more detail later: for the moment, it is enough to say that the legitimacy of this elite class is based on the Republic which they are meant to serve through thick and thin. They could not exist without the republican state; nor it without them. The result is a sealed circle which leaves little room for self-examination but which risks imploding or exploding if it does not live up to its own proclaimed expectations of itself.

François Mitterrand, who finished his education before ÉNA came into being, and who wouldn't have got in anyway, had four Énarque Prime Ministers – two each from the left and the right. When one graduate, Michel Rocard, challenged his leadership of the Socialist Party in the late 1970s, another old boy, Jean-Pierre Chevènement, rode to the rescue at the head of a Marxist faction – and then went on to show the seamless adaptability of the true power-player as a fiercely left-wing Industry Minister, a patriotic Education Minister and an anti-Gulf War Defence Minister before becoming Interior Minister in Lionel Jospin's government. (He is also said to have invented the term 'Énarque'.) When the right lost its parliamentary majority in 1997, one Énarque succeeded another at the prime ministerial office at the Hôtel Matignon, not far from the college's Paris headquarters. Lionel Jospin's new government contained the highest proportion of Énarques for a decade, and his own 35-strong staff included twenty-five graduates of the finishing schools for France's rulers. The most senior of them was reported to have justified his refusal to offer a suitably elevated job to the head of the national planning office by observing, 'That's normal, he's not even an Énarque.' When the Socialist Prime Minister confronted the leader of France's employers over cutting the working week, the two men could look back to the time they spent together at ÉNA in the early 1960s.

Even at the most egalitarian stage of Socialist rule in the early 1980s, nobody had the President's ear more than another Énarque, Jacques Attali. Attali's brilliance was constantly on display: everybody knew that he could talk about everything, but, equally, nobody knew if he was actually capable of doing anything. That wasn't the kind of petty matter to worry an Énarque, however. Didn't François Mitterrand say Attali had so many ideas that, if one turned out to be good from time to time, he would have earned his keep? Subsequently, the directors of the European Investment Bank proved less indulgent after Attali cost them a fortune turning their institution into 'the Glistening Bank' with its marble halls and expansive expense accounts. Showing the true confidence of his breed, Attali once invited me and two other journalists to breakfast at the Élysée during a currency crisis, and planted a false story about France being ready to sell its gold reserve to defend the franc without having bothered to consult the Finance Ministry. On another occasion, he defended himself against accusations of literary plagiarism by saying that, since he got up at four in the morning to write his books, he must be excused if he copied out some of his notes from other works verbatim. When the first edition of this book appeared, he wrote me an indignant letter asking why I had mentioned these episodes, and not his academic honours and the number of languages into which his works had been translated. After the Socialists returned to government, he was given the mission of finding a way to bridge the gap between the Grandes Écoles and less elevated universities. Naturally, it was a job for an Énarque.

Politicians can be voted out of office; not these fellows. One day a ministerial adviser; the next, in charge of a big company. As one graduate told me, ignorance about a new job was a positive blessing, since it meant one was not saddled with preconceptions. 'ÉNA creates a self-reproducing caste which has completely conquered the key political positions and confiscated the apparatus of the state, making politics very technical with the same approach by left and right,' according to the author of a recent study carried out for another elite college, the École Normale Supérieure. Or, as a member of the 1986–88 government puts it: 'The big failing of top civil servants is their superiority complex towards ministers. Their class, made up of technocrats and technicians of governments and administration, only really respects the President of the Republic.' They are the experts – why search any further? 'When one looks for people who can understand industry, public finance or the reform of the social security system,' observes a former chief of staff at the Prime Minister's office, 'one quickly turns to the pool which provides the administration – for ever.'

Despite the array of graduates who have become Presidents and Premiers, relatively few Énarques actually go into party politics at anything below the top level; they hardly need to. Their role is more likely to be exercised behind the scenes, and there have been notable examples of their survival capacity in serving different political camps with equal aplomb. One ran a major state firm through eight governments of different political complexion; another served as the spokesman for a President of the right and then headed the state broadcasting authority for six years under a Socialist Head of State. In the public mind, they can almost make politics and its practitioners irrelevant, which may be one reason why the people take directly to the streets rather than trusting their elected representatives in parliament to make their concerns felt. When the Prime Minister of a neighbouring country expressed concern about the zigzags of Jacques Chirac's European policy in the 1995 presidential election, a French elder statesman reassured him that, whatever the politicians might say in public, the officials had laid down the unalterable tracks for the future behind the scenes – and so it proved.

At any one time, half the chairmen (they are all men) of France's top 200 companies are likely to be from ÉNA. A few have failed in an embarrassingly public fashion: it was an *Inspecteur des Finances*, no less, who presided over the biggest losses in French banking history. The growing ranks of critics of this elite relish the occasion to shrug their shoulders and exclaim, '*Ah, encore un Énarque*' as though that explains everything. François Mitterrand complained mildly that they used too many adverbs. More trenchantly, the business magazine *Le Nouvel Économiste* asked in a cover story, 'Should we kill off the nation's elite?' A populist former Interior Minister, Charles Pasqua, suggested a novel way of doing down France's economic rivals: 'We should export half our ÉNA graduates. And send them to our main competitors.' Or, as the arch free-marketeer of the right, Alain Madelin, told an election rally: 'Britain has the IRA, Spain has the ETA, Italy has the Mafia – and we have the ÉNA.'

A group of less elite civil servants has set up an association called Against the ÉNA System, whose rallying cry is, 'Yesterday the Bastille, today the ÉNA.' The sociologist and historian, Emmanuel Todd, compares attitudes of the elites to the flowering of the authoritarian, Catholic tradition in the wartime Vichy collaborationist years – for them, he adds, 'The infallibility of the central banks has replaced the infallibility of the Pope.' The far right delights in alternately denouncing and ridiculing the tyranny of the ivory-tower technocrats. In his man–of–the–people mode, Jacques Chirac dismissed a Socialist who came to challenge him in an election in his rural stronghold as 'an Énarque no better known than Mitterrand's Labrador dog' – ignoring the fact that he, himself, went to ÉNA and was surrounded by an army of its best and brightest at the Élysée Palace. One of Chirac's deputies tabled a bill for the college to be abolished, on the grounds that its graduates have become a self-interested caste and 'we can no longer accept Martians making laws for earthlings . . . We need a ritual sacrifice.' Drawing a comparison with the Japanese civil service, that fan of the strong franc, George Soros, worries about 'the French elites who listen to themselves talk and pay no attention to the real world, not even to the state of mind of their fellow citizens. They think they know better than the people what is good for them. There is too much statism in France. Too much value is placed on the management by brilliant pupils, reared in elite institutions.'

Or take one of the recurrent crop of Énarque jokes.

A young man stops his car beside a field. He goes over to a farmer he sees walking on the pastureland with his dog and a flock of sheep.

'If I can tell you how many sheep you have here without counting them, will you give me one?' he asks.

'Okay,' says the farmer.

'Eighty-one,' says the smart young man.

'That's amazing. How did you know?' asks the farmer.

The young man does not reply. Instead, he picks up an animal and walks back to his car.

'Now, let *me* try something,' says the farmer. 'If I can tell you where you were educated, will you give me my animal back?'

'Of course,' says the young man disdainfully.

'You're from the ÉNA,' says the farmer.

'How did you know?'

'Because that's my dog you have under your arm.'

ÉNA is, as it happens, beginning to reform itself. In a symbolic piece of decentralisation, it is moving to the Euro-city of Strasbourg, and there is a proposal that its graduates should no longer be guaranteed civil service posts. Prominent graduates like former Prime Minister Laurent Fabius have come out of the closet to acknowledge the unhealthy nature of a system which picks up bright young people in their early twenties and anoints them as rulers for life, and some of the top students of recent years have recognised its failings.

But, still, when a people feels unhappy, it seeks a target to blame for its frustrations. Inevitably, the bureaucracy figures high on the grouse list. At an everyday level, the French rail against the weight of administrative controls, the fiscal burdens that constrain small businesses from growing, the uneven application of valued added tax, and, behind all the daily irritations, at the technocrats who run the nation through an ocean of directives and controls. The topsy-like growth of official paperwork seems unstoppable – the main social security form now has twenty-nine separate boxes to be filled up. Sitting on top of the bureaucratic pyramid, the Énarques risk becoming like eggheads in 1950s America or social workers in Thatcherite Britain: figures to be viewed with suspicion and ridicule, held up as the worst examples of the one-track mindset, *la pensée unique*, which bedevils France. There was great amusement, for instance, when it became known that the move of part of the college's activities from Paris to Strasbourg had been so mismanaged that it took more than twice as long as planned and ran 70 million francs over budget. It was a perfect example of the imperial caste which could not run itself with the standards it demanded of others.

But if the college is an irresistible populist target, the criticism it is attracting may be yet another evasion of responsibility. Abolishing ÉNA would be only a ritual sacrifice, like killing off social workers or eggheads. It would, in itself, not change the way the French elite thinks and operates. If it disappeared tomorrow, the upper civil service might become even more restricted in its social background and ways of thought. ÉNA has become a convenient symbol as the French, emotionally rather than rationally, sense that their seamless, self-preserving master-class is coping poorly with the challenges of the turn-of-century world. When things were more comfortable, the elite could take the credit; now, it cannot escape the blame, and its responsibility cannot be narrowed down to a single college which has become a facile demon figure for those who seek easy targets and avoid a deeper reality.

What is clear is that the technocrats have not re-thought their role and outlook. On a higher plane, the growing concern about Europe jeopardises the elite's reputation for infallibility if only because it was so closely identified with the restrictive, strong-franc policies of the 1990s. An Énarque at the head of the Bank of France can produce analytical demonstrations of interest rates till the cows come home, but, as one magazine noted, a word which seems to have no place in the discussion is 'unemployment'. Economic and social engineering does not take account of either the deep changes the world is going through, or the alienation and anger being felt on a deeply personal level which exploded in April 2002. In the mind of the Énarque, everything can be resolved by the exercise of logic and reason – as in the seeming inevitability of a Chirac–Jospin second-round duel. That is not exactly the way a man who has never had a job, or a single mother limping by on welfare, sees things. Nor are the international fund managers who invest in France too happy when they watch their cash going down the plughole of a bank run like a branch of a Grande École. As one of Chirac's close friends, the author Denis Tillinac, points out, the mindset of ÉNA graduates would be fine for a country with a 6 per cent growth rate, but it was inappropriate for a nation in a monetarist vice. Or, as the President of the Republic himself noted: 'Our technocrats are neither amoral nor incompetent: they are the heirs and guardians of a thirty-year-old system. They knew how to manage a stable society, whose sustained growth ensured social progress. But this society no longer exists. Society is shifting and divided. To govern it, old reflexes have to be wiped out. The intellectual effort needed for renewal will be great: it will not come from technicians.'

None of which seems to faze those concerned. A poll of Énarques published by *Le Monde* showed a remarkable degree of self-satisfaction. Only 8 per cent felt that they might have too much power in carrying out decisions for the state – and 28 per cent thought they did not have enough.

France's mandarins see little need to prepare public opinion for the tablets of wisdom they hand down from the administrative heights. Did Confucius worry about public relations? The people are told what is good for them, and should gratefully accept. But now the superior style grates and proves counter-productive, setting off a call-and-response pattern in which the orders from the summit are met with popular revolt. Everything then either runs into the sand or ends with one side backing down. Though they would shudder at the very thought, the Énarques and their peers are, in their way, part of a disjunction at the centre of French life. Seen in historical terms, they are playing out a game which repeats the themes of the Revolution of 1789, and in which they represent the rulers against whom the people rise up. They are also natural heirs to the philosophers and revolutionaries of the eighteenth century who believed that intellectuals can reshape society: in his black frock-coat and powdered wig, Robespierre would have made a tip-top *Inspecteur des Finances*.

Within six months of Chirac's election in 1995, his Prime Minister and fellow ÉNA man, Alain Juppé, known as 'the computer' for his lack of human touch, had come to personify all that the French disliked about the self-assurance of the elite. When Juppé sprang on the country his programme to slash welfare spending, shrink the heavily-indebted railway network and reduce social benefits in the public sector, the people knew their part, too. The sacrificial lambs were trotted out, from train-drivers to priests who were to be made to pay the same social security charges as salaried workers. The streets were filled with protesting crowds; the provinces attacked the metropolitan elite in Paris, and the Prime Minister became a national hate figure, not helped by the way he looked like a calculating egg head.

A third of the Socialist government that ruled from 1997–2002 were fellow graduates from the college, and Jospin surrounded him with technocratic staff members from the Grandes Écoles. His professorial manner smacked of his educational background as he made it all too plain that he would rule by the exercise of his superior powers of reason. By 2002, however, Jospin's electorate lay mainly among those who would be impressed by an Énarque – the professional classes, teachers, and the left-wing elite. When confronted during his campaign by workers who were about to lose their jobs, the Prime Minister was lost for words. His voters were those who were on the safe side of the social fracture, not those the left had once set out to help – and, in any case, France was no longer in a mood to be lectured by a caste which had lost touch with so much of the nation it presumed to govern. The wife of one ÉNA graduate who had made it to the top still delivered some home truths in the summer of 2002. 'Some technocrats have no idea of what everyday life is,' said Bernadette Chirac. 'Some of them have never taken the *métro*.' As if it was a badge of merit, she noted that the interim government formed after her husband's re-election contained fewer Énarques than the Jospin or Juppé administrations.

The irony is that, more than ever in its history, France is looking for guidance. But, given the gulf between the people and the elite, and the inability of the latter to find new ways of helping the former, the natural tendency is to fall back on the past, on old comforts of national life that predate such convulsions. More than most nations, France lives with traditions – but they are no longer a suitable guide for the twenty-first century. As the economist Alain Minc has put it: 'Our political culture, our history predetermine us. But they will not prove eternally right against the whole world.' Particularly since the bedrock on which France has lived for so long is ebbing away. The result is a national identity crisis with which France lives, usually unconsciously, each day. The French may want to seek refuge from the present in the past, but, once they get into the cork-lined room, they find that the little cakes of history which they seek are crumbling away.

3

Vanishing Madeleines

—◦◦◦◦—

Modernists and technocrats may scream, but a set of images traditionally defines France – the beret and the café, dark pungent cigarettes, baguette breadstick and red wine, accordions, garlic and the Seine. Air France put a beret on top of a globe for instant recognition in its international advertising. A compilation of French songs by a British record firm is subtitled 'the garlic and Gauloises world of French accordionists and singers'. At the reconstructed citadel at Verdun, where hundreds of thousands of French soldiers died repulsing the Germans in 1916, the table is laden with baguettes and red wine. Nothing stirs more nostalgia for the older French than the evocation of the *bal musette*, the popular dances at which lovers sway to squeeze-box strains. No film is complete without a café scene – the biggest recent box office success, the sentimental comedy, *Amélie*, was set in one, complete with retro music and roles. Any travel documentary on Paris has to have a long, lingering shot of the Seine and its bridges.

So now move from the general to the particular, and consider the symbols of everyday life reflecting France's character – in its own eyes, as well as those of the rest of the world. Their current condition tells much about the shifting sands of national life.

Start at the top. Medieval stone carvings show French beret-wearers. More recently, Sartre sat in Left Bank cafés philosophising with one on his head. Picasso, a Spaniard turned French resident, painted in one. France produces a million of them each year, and the beret-making city of Pau in the Pyrenees plans to introduce beret motifs on its lamp-posts and bus stops. The stereotype seems firmly in place.

But, though berets may be more common in France than bowler hats are in Britain, you could drive from Calais to Cannes without seeing one. (The only beret-wearer I know lives in Berkshire.) A third of the berets produced each year are for the French army. France now has only three beret-making factories, one-tenth of the number before the Second World War. All three turn out what are known as *bérets basques* – though, confusingly, they are located around Pau in the Béarn region, rather than in the neighbouring Basque country. Employing a grand total of 180 people, these companies have only survived by diversifying into wool caps and 'event headgear' emblazoned with logos and decorations – a 'Just Married' (in English) model for newly-weds or an Eiffel Tower version for tourists.

Then take the baguette. Again, things seem well-settled. Three-quarters of the bread produced in France comes from outlets that call themselves bakers – compared to one-third in Britain. While the amount of 'industrial bread' rises each year, it only accounts for 16 per cent of the 3.6 million tonnes sold each year.

But dig below the crust. A celebrity chef who appears on a popular knock-about radio show has made a speciality of denouncing frozen, pre-constituted dough from which even baguettes are made these days. He has a point. The baker who stays up all night kneading dough and supervising its passage through the oven has been overtaken by more convenient and financially rewarding methods, even among self-proclaimed *boulangeries*. The process of making dough from flour, water, salt and yeast can take up to three hours by the traditional method. After that, the dough is divided into sticks and fermented to increase its volume before going into the oven. The longer the dough is left, the better it is; but that takes time, and time is money. So the baker uses frozen dough containing two or three times the normal dose of yeast. Intensive kneading, as it is known, increases the end volume by up to 30 per cent, but produces inferior dough. At the next two stages of production, the mechanical shaping of the dough sticks toughens the inside of the baguette, while modern hot-air ovens do not give a thick crunchy crust.

Traditional bakers remain, mainly in the country and in up-market city enterprises. On the southern slopes of the Massif Central, an Auvergnat bakes his bread once a week in the oven in his farmhouse, and sells it all from his van around neighbouring villages. But the industry as a whole faces long-term decline. As people grow richer and more urbanised, they eat less bread. A century ago, the average French person consumed 219 kilograms a year. By 1967, that was down to 82 kilos; in the 1990s it fell below 60 kilos. Parisians now average only 36 kilos a year, and the national record for bread-eating is in the deeply rural south-western department of Gers. Not surprisingly, the number of small bakers has fallen steadily from 54,000 in 1960 to a little over 30,000 today.

This is more than the decline of a cottage industry. Bread has a resonant place in French life. Members of the Annales school of social historians would say that its price was more important than which nobleman happened to be Foreign Minister under King Louis the Whatever. A top Paris baker, Lionel Poilâne, calls bread 'the key to social peace and stability for every French government'. The theft of a loaf by Jean Valjean set off the saga of *Les Misérables*. Traditionally, the French find it hard to start a meal without a chunk of baguette by the plate. Bread plays the same role as rice for Asians: it is more than a simple means of calming the pangs of hunger or mopping up sauce. Not quite the staff of life any more, perhaps, but still a food with deep social roots.

In 1995, the future Prime Minister, Jean-Pierre Raffarin, who was then Minister for Small and medium Companies, established an annual Bread Day on 16 May — the day of the profession's patron, Saint Honoré. Two years later, he took action on behalf of non-industrial bakers by decreeing that only those using the five-step traditional method could call themselves bakers. Industrial manufacturers got that overturned, but Raffarin had a similar law passed by parliament three months later — remembering the debt to him, the President of the Bakers' Federation welcomed Raffarin's appointment as premier in 2002 as 'a recognition for the whole profession'. A scheme was launched to give the best bread a special stamp. Bread served to children with school meals was improved to catch them young. A television commercial warned, 'If you don't eat bread any more, one day there won't be any!'

All this showed how close bread is to France's idea of its own identity. And in national symbolism, bread means, above all, the baguette, preferably with its crust still warm from the oven. Sandwich shops around the world sell themselves on the idea of its appeal (even if they are run by English or Asian entrepreneurs). As part of the overseas aid effort, an expert from eastern France teaches bakers in developing countries how to make French bread. In the Élysée Palace, Jacques Chirac eats one and a half baguettes a day, and a hundred bakers compete each year for the Grand Prix de la Baguette and the honour of supplying the President with his daily bread. Crunching his crust, Jacques Chirac stigmatises industrial bread as 'not even a Christian food'. An author of a book called *Vive la Baguette* says the breadstick should sound like a drum, and 'flatter the palate with its slightly-caramelised hazelnut flavour'. But how many French people these mornings have the time or inclination to walk down to the *boulangerie* to buy a freshly-made baguette to flatter their palate while the coffee is percolating? One survey shows that the French idea of really good bread is round *pain de campagne* loaves or bread studded with nuts, not the crunchy stick of national imagery. Another cliché bites the dough.

Now drop in at the greatest French social landmark of all, the café. For Balzac, it was 'the parliament of the people'. A century later, the novelist Nathalie Sarraute sat writing at the same table every morning for forty years. The café was hailed by the poet, Léon-Paul Fargue, as the soundest of French institutions: no revolution, he wrote, had been able to rock its foundations. That was in 1946. Seven years later, Robert Doisneau took one of the great photographs of everyday French life at the Bouillon Tiquetonne café in the Paris market district of Les Halles. A man in a thick jacket and cap stands in front; an accordionist is on the right by the wall-sized mirror; a stout gesticulating woman fills the middle ground; empty glasses and wine bottles sit on every table. The reality of today is a long way from that post-war world. Surveys report that half the French hardly ever set foot in a café and most have modernised with plastic, pop music and neon.

In 1910, France had 510,000 cafés and bars for 38 million inhabitants: nowadays, there are one-tenth of that number for 50 per cent more people. Between 1960 and 1995, the ratio of cafés to people fell by a factor of five. Three thousand close each year, up to half of them in Paris. Knocking back a quick calvados on the way to work or propping up a zinc bar while downing a *pastis* or three on the way home is no longer in fashion. Ingeniously, the president of a café-owners' association blames the decline in spirit-drinking on the better quality of coffee now being served. 'It used to be so undrinkable that it encouraged customers to lace it with a small glass of calvados, kirsch or rum,' he says. 'Nowadays, the coffee you get served is of such high quality that anyone adding a dash of spirits to it would raise an eyebrow or two.' As for another icon in the Doisneau photograph, despite the invention of 'rock-musette' combining accordions with heavy bass-lines, and strolling players in the Paris underground and a few retro-restaurants, you have to go a long way to hear an accordionist in the flesh these days. France's principal factory, in the town of Tulle, produces 800 instruments a year compared to 6,000 before the Second World War. One of the last heroes of 'the piano of the poor', Jo Privat, ended up as a born-again star in Japan after work dried up in France.

With average daily viewing rising by one hour to 5 hours 45 minutes between 1993 and 2001, television keeps people at home. Villages which once had three cafés are lucky to have one. An inhabitant of a caféless village in the south-west was reduced to petitioning the visiting British Prime Minister in a bid to get one opened there. For speedy eating, people flock to more modern outlets. The opening of a fast-food establishment is estimated to cut trade in nearby cafés by up to a third. Even the tax system is against them – café food bears value added tax more than three times higher than at take-aways.

Half France's fast-food outlets are *hamburgeries*. One estimate reckoned that the French spend three times as much on hamburgers as on eating at restaurants with rosettes in the Michelin guide. In 2002, Kentucky Fried Chicken announced plans to open between 100 and 150 outlets in France by 2006. It is still politically correct to turn one's nose up at McDonald's as a threat to the national way of life – the protesting farmer, José Bové, made himself a national figure by trashing an outlet being built in the Aveyron department, and parents in the south-eastern town of Romans protested when the local McDonald's laid on a free bus service for schoolchildren. However, ordinary French consumers seem indifferent as they line up for *un Big* and *un Cheese* or for more locally-targetted offerings like croque-monsieur and pastries. With more than a thousand outlets, France is the most profitable McDonald's operation in Europe, and accounts for ten per cent of new branches worldwide. When the chain launched healthier meals in Europe, its French manager headed the initiative – and nobody could gainsay the 42,000 jobs which McDonald's supports. If things go on at the present rate, the model Frenchman of the twenty-first century will not be emerging from a café in a *pastis* haze but leaving a fast-food joint with his take-away burger in one hand and a packet of sliced bread in the other.

The pungent smoke of another cliché has wafted through national life for most of this century. Tobacco entered the French conscious-ness after the ambassador to Portugal treated his injured cook with a patch made from a herb imported from the New World in 1559. News of its therapeutic qualities got back to France and the ambas-sador was soon supplying the court with tobacco grains. The Queen used them against headaches, and such was their popularity that Louis XIV restricted worshippers at mass to only one sniff of the stuff from the spiritual staff. By the beginning of the eighteenth century there were 1,200 snuff and tobacco establishments in Paris; the smartest still exists in the Place du Palais Royal. In 1818 the special property of tobacco was given a name, inspired by the original ambassador to Portugal, Jean Nicot. Three centuries after his discovery, the manu-facture of cigarettes began after French soldiers came across them while fighting in Spain.

At the turn of the century, tobacco was estimated to cause 45,000 premature deaths a year in France, one of the highest rates in the industrialised world. Among men, lung cancer is the leading cause of early mortality, well ahead of alcoholism. It is a particular killer among the working class, but a killer which has long been close to the Finance Ministry's heart. Tobacco taxes came in under Cardinal de Richelieu in the seventeenth century, and a state monopoly followed. As well as the tax takings, the state cigarette company, Seita, provided large revenues to the public purse in three decades of nationalisation: today, privatised Seita ranks as one of the country's dozen biggest agro-food businesses. In a country which looks after its agriculture, tobacco is an important crop and is given appropriate government protection.

It was not until recently that French politicians had any reservations about being photographed dragging on a cigarette in a way that would have been unacceptable in, say, the United States. A classic photograph of the Tour de France from the 1960s shows a cyclist giving a team-mate a light from his stub as they freewheel at the head of the pack. At a time when the rest of the developed world was cutting down, the number of cigarettes smoked in France rose from 85.7 billion to 97.1 billion during the 1980s. Twenty per cent of men smoked more than fifteen a day. Then, in 1991, the government got tough.

There had always been isolated pockets of anti-tobaccoism. If a client at the restaurant run by the godfather of modern cuisine, Fernand Point, was seen lighting up during a meal in the 1950s, coffee and the bill were immediately brought to the table, even if the cray-fish or *poularde en vessie* had not yet been served. Some anti-smoking measures were introduced in public buildings in the mid-1970s. When these were extended to provide for no-smoking areas in restaurants and cafés, they were much honoured in the breach. One café in the Paris suburbs put up a notice proclaiming that its owner would rather go to prison than infringe his customers' right to smoke; another des-ignated a single table in the middle of the premises as the no-smoking area. When my wife asked for the tobacco-free zone in a Left Bank restaurant, she was told simply: 'Outside' (the owner insisting that the odour of perfume was far more detrimental to the enjoyment of food than tobacco fumes).

A serious-minded Socialist Health Minister banned smoking in canteens, public areas in hotels, lifts and offices containing more than two people. Offending individuals or employers were threatened with fines or imprisonment – the state railway was found guilty of failing to put up big enough anti-smoking posters at a station in Lyon. Cigarette advertising was outlawed. An opinion poll said 84 per cent of people supported the measures. The consumption of cigarettes fell steadily through the 1990s, and the Jospin government announced plans to increase taxes on cigarettes and tobacco – not, of course, to raise rev-enue but as a way of discouraging young people from smoking. But, if the French are smoking less, where the cliché really comes apart is in what they actually puff.

For decades, there was something exotic about French cigarettes; even the brand-names were peculiarly resonant. As cigarettes swept the nation at the turn of the century, smokers could chose from 242 different products. There was a name for everybody to identify with – Odalisques and Jockeys, Boyards and Havanaises. The Hongrois brand changed its name to Gauloises in 1910 and became the market leader ten years later. Gitanes–Vizier put a woman on its packet in 1927, the year it dropped the Turkish second half of its name. The Belle Époque brand, *élégantes de luxe*, turned butch after the First World War by altering its name to Amazones. For chauvinists there were Celtiques, Royale and, most simply, Les Françaises; those with more distant horizons could buy packs of Congo, Maryland or Égyptiennes.

Despite the range of choice, French cigarettes were epitomised for decades by Gitanes and Gauloises, in conventional white paper cylinders or more exotic maize paper. Gitanes had a characteristic flat box that opened like a drawer; Gauloises were tapped out of a soft packet with a card-shuffling motion. No French film was complete without a cloud of smoke round Jean Gabin or Jean-Paul Belmondo; no existentialist nightclub or corner café was authentic without the tobacco haze; no Paris taxi ride was real without a throat-twitching, stomach-churning stink wafting back from the driver. In the early 1970s, when the Head of State appeared on the cover of a biography with a thick dark French cigarette clenched between his lips, *les brunes* accounted for 86 per cent of sales. The songwriter Serge Gainsbourg, who lived in a perpetual cloud of smoke, appeared quite content when Catherine Deneuve told him in a duet that, while God puffed Havanas, 'you are only a smoker of Gitanes'.

Now, as with the café and the baguette, things are different. Law suits have been launched against cigarette companies for allegedly giving insufficient warnings of the health dangers of smoking. An illustration on a stamp of the writer and former Culture Minister, André Malraux, was doctored to eliminate the cigarette between his lips. 'Given the law, we had no choice,' explained a spokeswoman for the postal service. The traditional French brand which Malraux was smoking in the photograph was still the individual national favourite with 20 per cent of sales, but, overall, dark tobacco cigarettes are now outsold two to one by light tobacco ones. *Blondes* put out under the Gitanes mark sell almost as many as its *brunes*. When Marlboro went on sale in France in 1924, it was as a niche product aimed at women, complete with a red tip to go with their lipstick. Seven decades later, the brand takes 17 per cent of the market, and even the President of the Republic smokes Virginia-style cigarettes. Foreign brands account for almost half total sales; filter-tips rule. Perhaps that is why French films seem to show less smoking these days. Gérard Depardieu drawing on a Stuyvesant wouldn't be quite the same as the gangs of the great *films noirs* plotting heists in a pall of smoke you can smell off the screen. And even the packet for Gitanes Blondes has taken on a new look from the other side of the globe. Its new fliptop box with a little yellow figure dancing against the traditional black gypsy silhouette on a stonewashed jean background is the work of a Japanese designer. But then, a baker born in Portugal won the Grand Prix de la Baguette in 1998, a sommelier from Japan has carried off the top prize at the Bordeaux wine fair.

If brown tobacco, bread and cafés are three essential elements in the traditional image of France, another is red wine. But here, too, late-twentieth-century reality chips in. The French still drink a very large amount of wine overall, and there are restaurants where you are automatically brought it with your set menu. But just as it is rare these days to see a zinc bar topped with a row of glasses, so the number of people who drink wine every day has almost halved since 1980. Even Jacques Chirac makes no secret of his preference for beer (although, after being elected, he had the patriotic decency to switch from his preferred Mexican brew to Kronenbourg). Less than a third of the population takes wine with their meals each day. Soft drinks sales are rising steadily, and the proportion of young people drinking wine on a regular weekly basis is reckoned at under 20 per cent.

The world's largest wine-producing region is behind the Mediterranean coast in south-west France, where a few good growths are swamped by a multitude of *vins de table*. The makers of ordinary wine face a crisis, with prices dropping by up to 20 per cent in 2001. Falling demand means they have built up huge stocks. The number of people employed in the industry has halved since 1970. Though some growers have sought survival by trading up into better quality, changing tastes mean there is no prospect of the low end of the industry experiencing a revival – tomorrow's consumers are not going to want a litre of *gros rouge* to wash down their evening meal. There is also a serious survival issue: despite France still holding records for alcoholism, premature deaths due to drink are waning. A couple of glasses of wine may help ward off heart attacks and reduce the chances of cancer or senile dementia, but even the French have been shocked to learn that 40 per cent of their fatal road accidents involve drunken driving.

Worst of all, some of France's own experts have rounded on the quality of some of the home-produced drink. Most French wine is excellent, and no country has a greater range of regional vineyards, each with its own distinctive taste. However, the head of the institute which monitors standards acknowledged at the end of 1995 that even wines bearing labels attesting to their status as coming from an Appellation d'Origine Contrôlée (AOC), which is supposed to guarantee quality, were sometimes undrinkable. On occasion, they were even 'scandalously bad'. There should have been nothing too surprising about this. Anybody who has drunk any quantity of reasonably priced wine in France or anywhere else will have come across poor bottles. Whatever their labels may say, some wines will always turn out to be below standard in some vintages. Real or apocryphal stories have been around for years about tanker lorries filled with cheap southern (or even North African) plonk turning up in Beaujolais and Burgundy to add strength to the produce of up-market vineyards in thin years. The pursuit of higher yields, sometimes by late watering which makes the grapes swell, has jeopardised quality in some areas. So has the addition of sugar to the fermenting grape juice to raise the alcohol level. More seriously, questions have been raised about pesticides getting into the wine from the wooden barrels at one leading Bordeaux château, and about the practices of some top Burgundy growers. But the local committees of growers rarely deny the AOC label to their neighbours; one estimate puts the failure rate at only 2 per cent.

What was striking was the strength of the reaction to an article in the consumer magazine, *Que Choisir?*, which detailed these shortcomings. It was as if nobody had ever even considered the possibility that there might be something wrong with some French wine. The industry association tried to get the article withdrawn because of 'the harm caused to an entire group of honest producers and products'. Silence was golden when it came to such an integral part of France's existence. The official who acknowledged the scandalous quality of some growths resigned. The French drink less and less of it, but the renown of their national drink has to be defended come what may.

This raises a real problem. The French believe that their wines are the best in the world, and they are right. Though they sell a smaller proportion of their output abroad than Spain, Italy or Germany, France's vineyards still account for almost half the world's exports, measured by value, and a French company is busy taking the message to the other side of the world by planting 3,000 hectares of quality grapes in China to nurture the nascent wine industry there. Led by the great growths of Bordeaux and Burgundy, and by legally ring-fenced Champagne, wine sales rank second only to aerospace as an earner of foreign currency, with annual exports of wines and spirits the equivalent of the sale of 135 Airbus planes or 560 high-speed trains. Prices of the finest French growths spiralled beyond reason in the later 1990s as Americans increased their purchases by one-third and Asian buyers circled Bordeaux. The Saint-Emilion vineyard, Château Cheval Blanc, was sold for 860 million francs by French and Belgian businessmen at the end of 1998. A case of 1945 Château Pétrus which had been bought for the equivalent of $42,000 fifteen months earlier went for $75,000. Prices at the annual auction in the Burgundy wine capital of Beaune and for top clarets staged another burst at the start of the twenty-first century.

Such inflated prices will not be achieved by New World wines and the greatest French growths have acquired a speculative value as a way of making money for people who may not be able to tell a Corton from a Corbières. But more everyday French wines face a major international challenge. Exports have tailed off from their peak in 1997, falling by 10 per cent in 2003. Branded Australian and Latin American wines offer a predictable drink for people who are baffled by the multiplicity of different regional products and vintages from France. There is also growing quality competition. In 1998, the highly respected wine critic of the *New York Times* declared the best reds of California and Oregon to be worthy rivals of the great Burgundies. Australian wine exports have risen tenfold in a decade. Cloudy Bays from New Zealand and the best of the Napa Valley can even be found in timid corners of the wine lists in some French restaurants: one sniffily entitles the section '*Vins d'ailleurs*'. Simply saying that French is best is no answer. Some producers in the Hexagon have actually learned from methods used in California and Australia to raise the quality of the output. Domestic consumption may remain resolutely national, but, as the advance of New World wines in Britain has shown, there is a big battle to be fought abroad for reliable everyday wines which ordinary drinkers can afford to take home in the evening.

All right, so things are changing, but one fact about the French is surely unshakable – they stink of garlic. Indeed, they may be so imbued with the vegetable that they don't notice its aroma: a gourmand academic from London, Keith Walker, once ate a whole chicken stuffed with forty cloves and rode the train back to Paris from Orléans without anybody pursing their nose. The truth is, however, that France does not even rank in the world's top half-dozen producers or consumers of the vegetable. There is, indeed, an association devoted to its folklore and promotion in the middle of France, whose members parade at jolly ceremonies wearing hats shaped like the clove. But the leading academic expert on garlic is American, and the South Koreans use far more of it than the French. The self-proclaimed garlic capital of the world is to be found in Gilroy, California. At an 'officially regulated tasting' of a dozen varieties held there, Spain took the top prize.

One by one, landmarks crumble, or are not quite as they used to be. The franc has been subsumed into the common currency of the euro. Changing tastes and European rules have forced the biggest maker of camembert to produce a new version with pasteurised milk. Mad cow disease led to the outlawing of calf sweetbreads and the cattle intestines that previously made the best casing for sausages – one artificial substitute has been compared to greaseproof paper. The madeleine on display at the house in the country town of Illiers-Combray which has been turned into a museum to the memory of Marcel Proust's most famous novel turns out, on inspection, to be made of plastic. France's most popular soft drink, Orangina, has been sold to Coca-Cola. Fewer than 10 per cent of bathrooms built in France have a bidet. The famously rotund Michelin Man, Bibendum, was slimmed down for his hundredth birthday in 1998 to demonstrate, as the company put it, that 'we can adapt to changing circumstances'. France may still be the world centre of the game of pétanque, but Tunisia has dented Gallic pride by taking the world championship. Crooks are not what they were, either: a top cop, Robert Broussard, says old hoods have been replaced by a more discreet, more intellectual, more financially astute class of criminals who send their children to private schools. Less discreetly, a new breed of heavily armed robbers hit security vans delivering cash, and then turned their attention to jewellers in the capital, escaping in high-speed stolen cars. Police said they came from housing estates round the capital where some still lived with their parents and where they sold the proceeds to other criminals, sometimes for a twentieth of their value. As for the prostitutes with gold-plated hearts who were long part of the popular imagination, they are now often from Eastern Europe, and advertise electronically. Modern society and fear of Aids have undermined the image of the headstrong French lover – in an opinion poll men expressed their preference for a partner who would bring a condom along with her in case he forgot his, rather than for an impromptu unprotected coupling. There has even been an offensive from the north on a worldwide French icon, claiming that French fries are actually a Belgian invention. The home team appears to have a good defence – Thomas Jefferson spoke of 'Potatoes, Fried in the French Manner' thirty years before Belgium came into existence as a country.

Once-sacred traditions like the business lunch and long summer holidays have been affected by social shifts. Business meals eaten in restaurants are reckoned to have fallen to less than half their level of 1980; in part that was due to changing lifestyles (mineral water and a salad instead of Cahors and *cassoulet*) but also because of cost controls and the spread of breakfast meetings, instead. For their part, chefs can no longer care only for the freshness of their vegetables, the quality of their fish and the unctuousness of their sauces. 'Before I make money, I have to pay overheads,' as a three-rosette cook put it as he joined a scheme to offer half-price meals to diners who took tables on a standby basis. 'Maybe I won't make a profit tonight – but at least I won't lose money.'

As for holidays, the month-long vacation in August is becoming less sacrosanct, with people ready to go for shorter periods, particularly after the 35-hour working week gave them more flexibility and long weekends. The Club Méditerranée has added one-day breaks in France to the traditional offering of long stretches in far-away places. Money-conscious holidaymakers have been avoiding the Riviera and frequenting cheaper areas of the country. Those who still go south often rent simple *gîtes* away from the coast. Feeling has swung against the conspicuous consumption of the Côte d'Azur in favour of the more bracing and less polluted west coast, against the gilded palaces, intensive suntans and over-priced lounging chairs on the beaches at Nice and Cannes in favour of woolly jumpers, sailing and family walks through the wind-swept Celtic heather. When Lionel Jospin bought a holiday home, it was not in his south-western constituency but on an island off the Atlantic coast, and even Princess Caroline of Monaco was sighted in the same area. The change of scene was not just a matter of the amount of cash spent – Brittany can be as expensive as the Mediterranean – but more a matter of mood. 'I see in this fashion the generation of those in their forties who have done it all,' says the publisher of magazines for the smart set of the south and the west coasts. 'They want a return to the family, which is even more sacred to them because they are often starting out for the second time after a divorce. They remember the quiet family holidays in Brittany during the 1950s. For years, they made fun of them, but now they realise they weren't so bad after all.'

In a final cliché challenge, the river along whose banks lovers traditionally stroll on the screen, in romantic imagination and in real life, may even be misnamed. The Seine rises in Burgundy, hundreds of kilometres from the capital. On its way to Paris, it joins another Burgundian river, the Yonne, at the town of Montereau. Their waters are, from then on, known as the Seine. But the custom is that when two rivers meet, the one which has the largest volume of water gives its name to the combined flow. And the flow rate of the Yonne at the junction is 105 cubic metres per second while that of the Seine is only 75 cubic metres. The Mayor of Montereau has no doubts: 'The rivers are of different colours. It is easy to see that the Yonne beats the Seine.'

In this moving set of stereotypes, however, one thing seems certain: the name of France's best-known river will not be altered. But plenty else is changing in the countryside where the Yonne, the Seine and all France's other great rivers flow, for the most basic of all madeleines is undergoing a metamorphosis which is more crucial to the nation than all the Virginia cigarettes, Euro banknotes or McDonald's in the world.

4

COUNTRY LIVING

If there is one thing which the French have long held particularly dear, it is the rural land that covers some 90 per cent of the surface of their country. Agriculture is a major element in the wealth of the nation, but the status of the countryside is not to be reduced to mere economics. The pull goes far deeper than that. The rural world is a pole around which national sentiment has revolved ever since the Romantics saw fields and lakes as more than a way of scraping a life from earth and fresh water. But now it, too, is changing more than the French would wish to admit. Ninety per cent of rural households do not contain anybody working in agriculture. Farms are being deserted, villages are emptying. Pig factories flourish while the streams are empty of crayfish. *Foie gras* is as likely to originate from Eastern Europe as from a farm in the Périgord. The seeds for Dijon mustard come from Canada. Traditional evenings around the village fountain exist only in books and on the screen. Hypermarkets are killing off rural shops. All of which is so disorientating because what is vanishing is crucial to the nation's idea of its own basic character.

Country life has deep roots in the French imagination. The tale of a harassed town-dweller escaping to peace and contentment in a rural idyll is a constant theme of popular books and films. France has a set of diverse and thriving regional cultures. Many of its greatest writers have drawn on their direct link with a country region – Balzac with the Loire Valley, Flaubert with Normandy, Mauriac with the Bordelais, Mistral, Giono and Pagnol with Provence. As Jacques Chirac has pointed out, the regional appeal in fiction lies in 'the rediscovery of a source of popular memory which the French are afraid of losing for ever'. Up-market pop singers record hymns to their native corner of the land, and regional cultural centres keep traditions alive, if sometimes rather artificially. A remarkable encyclopaedist, Marcel Lachiver, has collected 45,000 rural terms in a book running to 1,816 pages. In the heart of France, the annual literary fair of Corrèze draws 100,000 people to the departmental capital of Brive. For some who have risen to the summit of power and glory, the essential link with the countryside is one which harks back to an innocent childhood. Through his long political career in Paris, François Mitterrand never shook off the sentimental appeal of his native region of the Charente, which his fellow south-westerner, François Mauriac, described as 'an unchanging landscape where I can still believe I am an adolescent'.

French townspeople have more country homes than any other Europeans. Nearly 70 per cent of France's 12.5 million gardens have a vegetable plot. A million and a half people count themselves as hunters – 150,000 of them marched through Paris in February 1998 to proclaim their right to shoot migrating birds and their presidential candidate got 1.2 million votes in 2002. Scratch an urban French man or woman and they will speak nostalgically of the village or small town where they grew up or where their parents hailed from. Their taxes pay for services which would be hard to find in many other advanced economies – for the electricity network which takes no account of distance or inaccessibility, airports that handle a hundred or so travellers a day, the country train network with its neat little stations, and the highly efficient postal system which supports rural offices with annual turnovers of just 50,000 francs. In person or through television, many more join the great annual celebration of the French countryside that is the Tour de France, as riders sweep across plains, climb mountains, swoop down on coasts and rocket through a hundred villages in *la Grande Boucle* which brings the nation together.

In a country which has always appreciated feminine virtues of an old-fashioned kind, the land is essentially a woman. There is plenty of stereotypically rugged masculine mountain terrain on the edges and in the middle of France. Still, the traditional image of the rural lands echoes the remark by the historian, Emmanuel Le Roy Ladurie, about France being, first and foremost, a beautiful woman. This is '*la douce France*' immortalised in Charles Trenet's songs. Today's writers shrink from genderised descriptions, but the inventor of the modern French novel had no inhibitions. For Balzac, his native Touraine was 'a woman going to meet her lover'; nature resembled 'a woman rising from her bed' and the Loire estuary became an older woman 'swollen with all the disappointments and tribulations of life'.

In the French tradition, stock characters pop out from the hedgerows: the ruby-cheeked priest preaching to a tiny congregation of old women, and the earnest left-wing teacher trying to instil republican values in a class of bored children; the dried-up widow in black peering at passers-by from behind her curtains and the amply-breasted, loosely-dressed village flirt who leads the farm boys off into the long grass; banquets without end on market days and the old-fashioned farmer eating his soup as his wife stands humbly behind him; the poacher lying in the bushes watching for rabbits on the edge of the local hunting estate and the gamekeeper who waits till the owner has driven back to town before inviting his friends round for a feast behind the château. It is not all a matter of imagination. In one village we visit regularly, an old woman sat for many years watching the passers-by from behind her curtains, and the priest drinks cheap wine from tumblers as his housekeeper serves his meagre supper. Bernadette Chirac recalls that, when her husband began campaigning in the Corrèze in the 1960s, local dignitaries held dinners at which their wives remained standing behind them after serving the dishes – now, in her role as a local councillor in the department, she, herself, soldiers through the eight-hour annual banquet of the local firemen. Some years ago, I spent a long Sunday at an open-air banquet in the grounds of a hunting estate amid the forests and lakes of the Sologne region, where the increasingly drunk gamekeeper denounced his employers, opened their finest wines and terrines of *foie gras* – and ended the day by lurching off into the woods with his wife.

France is a patchwork of local *pays*; *paysans* are not peasants but the people of their stretch of the land. Frenchmen living ten thousand miles from the Hexagon define themselves as Berrichon or Provençal as much as French. As La Rochefoucauld put it: 'The accent of the country where one is born remains in the spirit and the heart as it does in the language.' Roots count, up to the very summit. Though born in Paris, Jacques Chirac talks of his adopted homeland in the

Corrèze as though it were more important to him than the Élysée Palace.

The untranslatable expression '*la France profonde*' refers not just to areas like the great central region stretching from the Limousin through the volcanic peaks of the Massif Central to the Cévennes. It is not just a matter of geography, of what a Parisian friend used to refer to as 'the French desert'. Rural France is a state of mind. Towns breed politics and division; farmers get on with life in a down-to-earth manner, and stand together in adversity. 'With bare arms and pure hands, we will go to clean up Paris,' proclaimed a pre-war quasi-Fascist rural movement, the Green Shirts. Sixty years later, the President of the Republic speaks feelingly of 'a land peopled by humble, brave, honest and hard-working folk'. Though the Île-de-France region around Paris was, as its name suggests, the kernel of the nation from the Middle Ages, there is a lingering and unshakable feeling that the real France lies in the countryside, not in the capital.

Farmers, proclaims Jacques Chirac, 'are the gardeners of our country and the guardians of our memory'. Provincial, rural knowledge is a natural gift as opposed to an acquired skill – folklore rather than culture, a natural wisdom absorbed from the ebb and flow of the seasons instead of being learned from books. The country is a place where people have proper old French names rather than being called after American film stars, where the tombs in a graveyard by the Aveyron river deep in the Rouergue region commemorate Albertine and Armand, Baptiste and Blaise, Calixte and Célestin, Firmin, Germaine and Marise, and where the living old folk get a twice-yearly free banquet of soup, asparagus quiche, stuffed veal, duck, cheese, dessert and cakes at the Michelin-rosetted restaurant opposite the church. Like Bouvard and Pécuchet, Gustave Flaubert's classic couple of city-dwellers who think they have found paradise in a crumbling farmhouse in Normandy where the vegetables wither, the cabbage is inedible and the neighbours mocking, the French stand ready to be swamped by a rural idyll.

On this hymn-sheet, city people are bad-tempered, materialistic seekers after money and slaves of empty fashion who jostle one another on the pavement, have heart attacks in traffic jams and only escape from their concrete jungle by roaring out on multi-lane motorways at murderous speeds. In contrast, country folk are easy-going and friendly, ambling up leafy lanes behind their herds of cattle, or driving their old cars gently along empty roads bordered by poplar trees. This view is not confined to the French. 'Parisians,' declared a letter-writer to the *Independent*, 'are rude, ignorant and in a hurry. Provincial people are pleasant, attentive and relaxed.' The contrast is seductive, as the creative directors of advertising agencies know when they conjure up rural images to sell processed food. In 1981, Mitterrand's presidential bid was greatly boosted by a poster showing him against a soft-focus village complete with church tower. Thirteen years earlier, it had been fitting that the great urban student revolt and general strike of 1968 should have been brought to a peaceful and mutually profitable conclusion by a head of government who hailed originally from the iconic-sounding Auvergnat village of Montboudif.

Much of this is rubbish. 'The land is tough,' as a local landowner remarked to Bouvard and Pécuchet while their haystacks burned down. Less so today than when Flaubert wrote, but there are few lotus-eaters on the land, and the idea that proximity to the earth brings with it a sunny disposition is strictly for the birds. Many more people die on country roads than on motorways. Farmers are notoriously aggressive demonstrators, and there has never been any shortage of village money-grubbers. Rural folk are as likely as anybody to name their children after pop stars and film idols. The highest rates of suicide are in largely agricultural areas of the north-west. The countryside's good sense often equates to reactionary conservatism.

Still, the ideal provides a mattress and a vital prop for the nation. The politicians in their ministries in the far-away capital certainly recognise the need to keep the non-urban world happy. Almost 20 per cent of voters are reckoned to depend for their livelihood on farming and the countryside in some way. Nearly one-third of French mayors are farmers. Few government posts are more sensitive than that of the Agriculture Ministry. An attempt by the left to alter the power structure of the farm organisations in the early 1980s ended in farce when the minister was marooned in a muddy field by demonstrators who prevented her helicopter from rescuing her. (The appointment of a woman to deal with such a chauvinistic group of men as the farmers was seen as either a provocation or a massive miscalculation, or perhaps both.) Later, when he wanted to do down a rival, Mitterrand put him into the Agriculture Ministry and dared him to do something about subsidies. On the other hand, Jacques Chirac's stint in the job in the early 1970s made him the farmers' friend for life – his vehemence in defending their interests led his German counterpart to advise him to see a psychiatrist. A quarter of a century on, the farm vote kept Chirac in the presidential race in 1995, ahead of the distinctly unrural Prime Minister, Édouard Balladur, whose inability to hold a lamb in such a way that it would not urinate over him caused much mirth among the farmers when he visited the Agriculture Minister's south-western town of Rignac. Once installed at the Élysée, Chirac the born-again Correzian repaid the compliment by devoting five hours to visiting the Paris agriculture show; in all, 200 politicians went to the exhibition that year to pay their respects to the farming world.

The countryside counts not only in politics and the national psychology, but also where it really matters – in the stomach. Food in France is linked to the land in a way that is not the case in many other nations. This, after all, is a country where an academic writes a 152-page treatise on one sort of Auvergne cheese and where, for many years, food pirates found it worth their while to buy cheap brown lentils from the Cantal department, die them green and pass them off as the prized pulses from the neighbouring Haute-Loire. Paris has excellent chefs, but it is the regions, the *pays*, which make French cuisine what it is. A 440-page compendium of national menus by the Maîtres Cuisiniers de France contains only half as many pages on the Île-de-France region around the capital as on Brittany, Guyenne or Languedoc. Pollution may have driven the famous *sandre* from the Loire river, and the *boeuf bourguignon* served up for dinner may have been produced on an industrial estate, but food remains rooted in the countryside, and most of the top restaurants are still located in the provinces. Each product has its specific local link. The best butter comes from the meadows of the Charente, the sweetest melon from Cavaillon in the south, and your favourite wines from any one of a hundred individual vineyards, each with its own taste. Those green lentils from Le Puy have an Appellation d'Origine Contrôlée to honour and protect their excellence, as do poultry from the wetlands of the Bresse east of Lyon, nuts from Grenoble, potatoes from the Île de Ré in the Atlantic, and the olive oil from Les Baux-de-Provence and from Nyons in the foothills of the Alps. These are national treasures, as much a part of France's glory as Notre Dame or the nuclear strike force. The AOC accolade has even been extended to a foodstuff not consumed by humans, the 100,000 tonnes of hay harvested each year on the plain of Crau at the mouth of the Rhône which is exported as far away as Hong Kong for the delectation of thoroughbred racehorses.

To illustrate how the countryside and village life imbue French gastronomy with its real strength, let us take a short tour around three sides of the great Massif Central mountain range to visit three cooks who have made their birthplaces objects of gastronomic pilgrimage. On the heights rising above the northern Rhône Valley below Lyon lies the village of Saint-Bonnet-le-Froid, a lost place in the Haute-Loire department at the meeting of the Vivarais and Velay regions. Son of the local café-owner, Régis Marcon wanted to be an artist but turned to the kitchen instead. After travelling to London and learning his trade under the Roux brothers there, he returned to his native village and transformed the family café into a restaurant and simple hotel – at the same time running the village petrol pump. He used the extraordinary natural local ingredients, and made a few mistakes along the way – his cèpe mushrooms in vinegar were inedible back in 1986. But by the mid-1990s, Marcon was a deserved gastronomic star. Though he has a fine hand with fish, which is not common in these parts, his food remains rooted in the countryside around him, many dishes using wild mushrooms from the surrounding hills brought in by locals. By the new century, he had two Michelin rosettes and a mark of 19 out of 20 in the GaultMillau guide. His success brought new life to the austere village, and, if Marcon's place was full, you could always stoke up on the seven-course menu at the café across the road.

To the south-west, across the volcanic Puy-de-Dôme and the high Aubrac plateau, is the market town of Laguiole, long famous for its knives but now also known as the home of another son of the local bistrot owner, Michel Bras. The first time I ate at his first restaurant-hotel, the most expensive menu was 60 francs, and a room for my wife and myself and our two small children was half that. Now, Bras, an intense man who runs the New York marathon and picks wild herbs on his runs round Laguiole, has built a futuristic establishment on a hill above the town where he brings back to life forgotten regional specialities such as the *Gargouillou* vegetable broth made of three dozen ingredients prepared in twenty-seven different ways. In country fashion, you get one knife for the whole meal, being expected to wipe it clean on bread between courses. Bras' return to the sources of the local cooking can lead him to the edge of pseudery – on one visit, the pre-starter *amuse-bouche* was a boiled egg with a cheese-encrusted bread soldier and a poem on his childhood. But there is nothing pretentious about his chestnut soup, pork with *foie gras*, pigeon in olive and orange sauce, spit-roast Aubrac beef with parsnip butter, and *sorbet à la verveine-citronnelle*. With a kitchen that looks like a laboratory, and quotations from Saint Augustine about the importance of passions, Bras ended the century by winning his third Michelin rosette, and 19 out of 20 in the GaultMillau.

Take the main road down to Rodez, capital of the Aveyron department, and head west until you see a sign to Belcastel, rightly billed as one of the most beautiful villages in France. There, by the river that gives the department its name, the Fagegaltier sisters have carried out a similar transformation as Bras and Marcon. Their establishment was once a café run by their rock-like father. Born on the plateau overlooking the valley, he started out building roads and other public works, and rose to become a foreman. Then he and his wife took on the café by the bridge in the middle of the village, specialising in frying little fish plucked from the river outside. One day, a retired miner came to stay, and began fishing. He became a fixture, spending the last fifteen years of his life in the village, where he was remembered years later as 'the king of whitebait'. One day, father Fagegaltier recalled, a party of a dozen people turned up unexpectedly – 'and within a quarter of an hour, we'd caught enough fish to feed them all'.

The excellence of Nicole Fagegaltier, the sister who does the cooking with her shy husband while her sister, Michèle, runs the front of house and buys the wine, would be unthinkable away from the family roots. The restaurant has been named the best value in the whole country by the GaultMillau, which gives it 16 out of 20 though the Michelin, shamefully, grants only one rosette. Nicole received a supreme local accolade when she was rewarded with her weight in prunes for winning a cookery competition. Again, it is the rural dishes which make their mark – cèpe mushroom tart, salt cod, superb stuffed rabbit, veal and lamb with herbs and berries in the sauce, stuffed cabbage, cream of bacon, and local cheeses, all washed down by Marcillac wine from over the hill. For the big menu, you need a solid appetite – on one occasion, this might mean artichokes and asparagus with truffles and powdered ham, red mullet with sweet onions flavoured with anchovies, duck liver with young turnips and a sauce made from a local liqueur, sweetbreads, local cheeses and four desserts; on another, crispy potato cake with shrimps and cèpe mushrooms, sea bass and leeks with cèpe oil, grilled duck's liver with green beans and a sauce using a Marcillac liqueur, pigeon breast in breadcrumbs with garlic and rosemary oil, local cheeses and four desserts. At one recent Sunday lunch, every table except ours was taken by local family parties, and several of them were eating the big menu.

In times of trouble, the country is a source of valuable supplies: one of the staple Second World War tales is of food being smuggled into Paris, preferably involving a squealing pig which has to be kept quiet while the police patrol passes by. At such moments in history, the contrast between town and city becomes all the sharper. While food was hard to come by in the occupied capital, a marriage banquet in an isolated village in the centre of the country consisted of a *macédoine* of vegetables, ham and butter, home-made *foie gras*, rolls of ham with cream, guinea fowl in sauce, chicken with truffles, vegetables, turkey with watercress, cheese platter, apple pie, almond cakes and fruit, with red and white wine, champagne and liqueurs.

For some, at moments of great danger, the countryside provides an even more important succour as a haven to escape into the vastness that is rural France. The isolated town of Le Chambon-sur-Lignon, with its reserved Protestant inhabitants, won fame for sheltering thousands of Jews from 1940 onwards. When the German army swept by on its regular patrols, the refugees were hidden in the rough countryside of the windswept plateau that surrounds the town. After the war, Chambon was offered a Garden of Thanksgiving in Israel but, in its modest manner, refused the honour.

Two hundred kilometres to the east, it was the snow on the foothills of the Alps that dazzled a five-year-old girl who didn't know what she was escaping from. 'We arrived in the village in wintertime,' she recalled half a century later. 'Snow covered the countryside. I was five and tired from the long journey. My father carried me on his shoulders up the path that led to our new home, the farm of the Vieux Colombier which we had rented in the Free Zone to escape from the persecution in Paris. Years later, the family would repeat my first words when we got there: "Oh, look at the white snow, it's like pre-war snow." I had heard everybody saying, when they saw anything good, that it was like before the war – so I guess I thought that was the best thing I could say about the snow.'

Her father had been taken prisoner by the Germans in 1940, and had escaped from his camp. His wife and two children avoided deportation from Paris to Auschwitz by a mixture of hiding and good luck; some of their aunts and cousins died there. In 1942, they decided to flee the city. The little girl was entrusted to her nine-year-old brother. The two children were taken to a group of *passeurs*, people living by the demarcation line between the occupied zone of France and the Vichy-run 'Free Zone' where the Germans had not yet arrived. Some *passeurs* took Jewish children to safety in the south; others sold them to the Nazis. This brother and sister were lucky. Their mother travelled separately to join them in the Free Zone, hiding in a crate of coal on a goods train from Paris. Before it left the capital, police with dogs searched the train for people like her fleeing death, but they did not find her. When she emerged from the crate and met relatives in Grenoble, they could not help remarking on her face. At such a tragic time, how did Fanny have the vanity to put on mascara? It was coal dust.

In the Alps, life was different. The father came from rural stock in Poland: he told rousing stories about repelling bandits and riding through the family forests with a rifle in his hand. In Saint-André-de-Rosans, the war was far away. 'Our farm was one kilometre from the village,' the daughter recalls.

We lived in the back of the building. A family from Marseille and then a group of resistance fighters were in front. We had a garden and a courtyard where the poultry ran. One evening my brother and I gave the chickens the wine left over in the glasses from supper. They tottered about, completely pissed. On one side of the building was a mysterious room; later I was told it was occupied by a member of the collaborationist militia.

My brother, five years older than me, went to the village school, and learned to talk the local patois with his mates. Once, I remember, the whole village was gripped by fear: word spread that a German was marching across the square. But it was only a teenager who thought it was a good joke to dress up in a Wehrmacht uniform – where he got it from we never knew.

The family pretended to be Turks and called themselves Vartil rather than Wartski. Not that the demons stalking France at the time would have been fazed by a name. Appearance counted for more, and there they were fortunate in their father.

One day, the schoolteacher came up to our farm. He'd slung a satchel over his shoulder so that it would look as though he was out hunting, or picking berries. 'They're here,' he warned. My mother, my brother and I ran up the hill to hide in another farm. My father stayed behind, working in the garden. The Germans, who were retreating from Italy, stopped and said they had been told that Jews were being sheltered in the area. At a time like that, all they could think of was rounding up some more of us. With his green eyes and white hair, my father looked like a Kirk Douglas Jew. He shook his head and said no, he didn't know of any Jews in the area. So they drove on, and nobody in the village betrayed us.

But even far away in the countryside danger remained ever present. The Wartski–Vartil parents kept an empty tube of toothpaste in their barn with rolled-up banknotes tucked inside. They told their young son: 'If anything happens to us, take the money and look after your sister – and God help you.' North-east of Saint-André, an anonymous tip-off in March 1944 led the Germans to a farmhouse near the mountain village of La Martellière, in which eighteen Jews were staying with a resistance group led by a rabbi. All were sent to a transit camp on their way to their deaths. One escaped. The others were deported to Auschwitz, where all but one died. Fifty-three years later, a plaque with the names of the dead was unveiled in the village – and still nobody knew who had tipped off the Germans.

★

In view of all the emotional investment in the idea of the land and those who live on it, nobody should be surprised if France's stout defence of the European subsidies paid to its farmers is more than a matter of money and votes. One of the key tasks of the central government is to protect the rural fibre which underpins the nation: ministers may deplore violence against prefecture buildings and the blocking of roads by tractor barrages, but they cannot afford to be seen to be hostile to the *paysans*. When farmers spread manure in the streets or pelt officials with rotten fruit, they find an echo which would be unthinkable across the Channel. Town and city dwellers see their compatriots in the countryside as victims of modernisation who deserve support, not as subsidy-absorbing leeches on the tax structure. They view them as giving something to national life that goes well beyond their economic contribution – though, since France is the world's second biggest food exporter and accounts for nearly a quarter of agricultural output in the European Union, their weight as wealth-producers is very considerable indeed. 'Tillage and pasturage are the two breasts of France,' a royal official declared in the seventeenth century. The economic statistics may indicate that this is still the case, but, behind the billions of francs earned by France's farms each year, the mother's milk is turning somewhat sour.

Take, as an example, a series of snapshots over thirty-five years. In the 1950s, the woman who had sheltered in Saint-André went back to live in her wartime haven 600 metres up in the southern foothills of the Alps. 'In the summers then, Saint-André-de-Rosans was always busy,' she recalls.

The women gathered around the fountain to gossip and exchange secrets as they did their laundry in the public wash-house. Farm-hands sipped *pastis* while they waited their turn to play pétanque in front of the three cafés round the main square. On summer evenings, the young people danced to the music on the portable gramophone – *le pickup* – set up outside Madame Roland's café down the main street: the priest warned us we were courting damnation. In the winter, after supper, we wandered from house to house, chatting and listening to the old folk recounting their memories in the local Provençal dialect. Our favourite stopping-off point was the post office, where Madame Estienne had a wireless for us to listen to the hit shows from Paris. The schoolteacher taught all his pupils in a single class. Those who graduated to secondary school moved to the town down on the plain to study.

At weekends, we sometimes went to visit relations in nearby villages for lunches that stretched on till the evening. Each commune and village had its own fête, held in August when the harvest was in. The day-labourers who moved around from village to village would join in before going on to their next place of work. We danced late into the night under lanterns in the trees. The music was by little country bands in which the accordion-player was always the star.

Once a month, the travelling cinema came by. A white sheet was hung on the wall of the mayor's office and the whole village trouped in, everybody bringing their own chair. The sound and picture sometimes got out of sync. The noise of the projector drowned out the actors' voices. There were gaps while the projectionist changed the reels. None of that mattered. It was always an evening to remember.

The food sprang from the earth, and I can still taste the flavours to this day. The salad of big shallots with walnut oil from Léon Jean's farm. The gratin of wild herbs which Granny Augustine collected on the slopes above the village in the skirt of her apron held out in front of her as far as her arms could reach. The thrushes and rabbits which the Estienne boys brought back from their poaching expeditions . . .

Now fast-forward to the 1970s. Like the rest of France, Saint-André has been modernised. The houses have running water. The jolly Madame Estienne is delighted that she no longer has to press the nuts and olives from her garden: she can buy her oil ready-made in a plastic bottle. Washing machines have destroyed the convivial gossiping round the communal wash-house, but have made life easier for the women of the village. There is only one café in the square now: it serves meals for tourists as well as *pastis* for the locals. Most of the elderly people have died or moved to old folks' homes. Madame Roland is as alert as ever in her café. Every year, she goes on a package tour for pensioners, once all the way to Ibiza. The young people have left to work in the town on the plain, or further afield. Several are in Marseille; others in Lyon or Paris. Some come back in the summer with their families to spend their holidays with their parents. The village fête is still held in August. One year, we meet two of the Estienne sons there. At night, one of them leads half a dozen of us out on the ridge beyond the furthest-flung farm, from where there is a superb view of the Milky Way. The other son is the life and soul of the party, organising beds for visitors and roasting a whole lamb on a spit in the garden of a mill he is rebuilding nearby. Following in the footsteps of his father, Venance, he has become a postman. Venance delivered the letters on foot across the hillside, winter and summer in snow and sunshine. The son drives the mail in a van in the Paris suburbs.

In the early 1980s, the ruin of a chapel opposite Madame Roland's café was declared a historic monument and added to the official route of the Romanesque churches of southern France. By then, the village had so few inhabitants that many of the fields were left untended. But the remaining villagers nurtured the dream that the tourists visiting the ruins might stay, seduced by the beauty of the place. They could walk in the fields, climb the neighbouring rocky outcrop of Mont Risou and write postcards to their friends in Paris congratulating themselves on having found an undiscovered corner of paradise in the Hautes-Alpes. A potential new source of revenue seemed to be there for the taking: Madame Roland installed showers in the rooms below her café. But tourists these days want swimming pools and tennis courts, good food and service – not stuffy rooms in the basement of a village café run by an eighty-year-old.

So the visitors stopped, looked and drove on. Before they left, some wandered through the narrow, winding streets between the crumbling stone houses with their collapsed beams and heaps of fallen masonry on the floor. We were told that we could have a fine old ruin if we simply paid the legal fees. But there was nobody around to rebuild the houses, install bathrooms and kitchens and make sure the walls weren't going to fall in. And who wants to live in a place where the only distraction is a village fête once a year and where the remaining inhabitants are dying all around you?

'It's so sad,' lamented the woman who had first gone to Saint-André as a little girl in the war and took me back there after we married. 'Saint-André is one of the most beautiful villages on Earth. When we were feeling energetic, we used to climb Mont Risou and light bonfires on the top for the festival of St John. You could see the glow from far away.'

On the paths around the village, the scent of lavender still hung heavy in the air – ancient, straight-backed Mélanie gathered it to sell to the perfume-makers of Grasse down south. Up the hill, in the farm to which my wife and her mother and brother had fled when the Germans came through, Monsieur Richard dispensed his home-made *pastis* and advises against a third glass – can it be the long-banned absinthe that drove Verlaine crazy? On the slopes below, the goats munched the wild herbs that give their special flavour to the cheese made by the bachelor brother and spinster sister, Marcel and Marcelline. At the bottom of the ravines, the river water was as fresh and pure as ever.

Some years later, we revisited Saint-André one day in August. That used to be the busiest time of year. But now all was silence. The square was deserted. The big old building which had housed the Estiennes' post office, the school where my wife learned to read and write, and the mayor's office was boarded up. The walls were peeling, ugly amid so much natural beauty. The clock on the top floor from which the children had learned to tell the time had stopped long ago. The café had closed when the owner's wife left him and he went to a teaching job in the town down the hill. The school bus no longer came up the hill; there were no children to collect any more.

As we stood in the shade of the trees in the square where *le pickup* once played and the men tossed boules outside the café, Marcel and Marcelline walked by, bent with age. Madame Roland still kept her café, but there was nobody to sit at her two tables. The earth mother, Madame Estienne, was in an old people's home in the Rhône Valley, said to be in poor health.

'The others?' my wife said. 'Dead – like my old village.'

Rural depopulation is not a new trend. The appeal of urban jobs, a falling birth-rate and the loss of life in the First World War reduced the population of some country regions significantly from early in the century. But the outflow has generally speeded up since 1960. The quintessentially rural Creuse department, for instance, has lost half its population since 1901. Forty per cent of those have gone since 1960, and the numbers are still falling year by year. It is now the least populated department in the country. In 1929, France had almost

4 million farms; by the 1950s, that halved; in 2000 the number of farmers was under a million. The mad cow disease delivered a major blow, and reform of the Common Agriculture Policy after enlargement of the European Union loomed as a fresh threat.

Farmers constitute only 5 per cent of the active population. Their numbers have fallen by a third in a decade. In the same period, more than 50,000 shops and small rural businesses have closed. Itinerant farm labourers who were once a feature of life at harvest time have virtually disappeared. So have rural artisans who roamed the country offering their services – masons from the Limousin, tree-cutters from the central Forez region, chimney-sweeps from Savoy. Those who stay in farming are progressively older, living in villages without shops. In the Creuse, one-third of the people are over sixty; in the Auvergne, nearly half the farmers are over fifty-five. Despite buoyant prices in some areas, helped by foreigners buying holiday homes, the average value of agricultural land fell continually after 1980.

The French have a word for the emptying of the countryside, *la désertification* – not that these wide open spaces bear any resemblance to the Sahara. The official definition is a population level of thirty people or less per square kilometre. That makes half the land area of France into a green desert. But, while the emptying of the countryside has been a long-term phenomenon, it has been balanced in recent years by a shift in the way the rural population earns its living. One study shows that only 20 per cent of those in the countryside work in agriculture. Some rural areas have become the home for small-scale industry and services. A growing number of people commute from the country to work in towns, resulting in an overall growth in the rural population of 247,000 between and 1992 and 2001. In 2002, 'rurality' came into fashion. *Le Monde*'s agricultural correspondent was moved to write of its renaissance, and the leader of the Hunting, Fishing, Nature and Tradition party won a respectable 4.23 per cent of the vote in the first round of the presidential election, one point more than the Communist. After becoming Prime Minister two weeks later, Jean-Pierre Raffarin called himself 'the messenger of rurality'.

But it was a message that has to deal with a much changed rural world. The image of France as a nation of small farmers has been overtaken by intensive, large-scale agriculture – just as rural backwardness has been punctured by consumer goods, one of the best rural road systems in Europe and the Minitel data terminal network, which brings train timetables and sex on-line to the most isolated of farms. In the north and the east, huge grain and beet fields are farmed as efficiently as anything in Britain or Germany. Agriculture is a compartmentalised business. Once regions aimed to be self-sufficient: now they are part of a global market, and concentrate on what they do best. The west contains half of France's dairy farms. Brittany houses 60 per cent of the country's pig plants and grows most of the nation's cauliflowers. Paris is at the centre of a great grain belt. In the east, fortunes are made from sugar beet, not to mention champagne. One-third of south-western farms concentrate on maize and oilseeds (and the poor uplands of the centre have made a speciality of living on European subsidies). Wine-making has become a science as well as an art. The old regional languages of the land have been submerged in a common glossary of terms for agricultural machinery and scientific aids to greater productivity: a whole list of traditional names for farm implements no longer appear in the dictionaries of today. And, in a tiny village in the middle of the country, the grave-diggers drive to the churchyard in a Toyota four-wheel-drive land-cruiser with a large Coca-Cola logo on the bonnet.

Off the coast, farming at sea has run into rough weather. The fishing fleet has been halved since 1988, to around 6,000 boats. Even oyster producers have been hit by disease and lack of breeding space. It is not that demand is lacking – French fishermen provide only half the 600,000 tonnes of fresh fish France eats each year. The trouble is that domestic trawlers cannot compete on price with East European fleets. On top of which, the mark-ups along the wholesale and retail chain make fish a relatively expensive dish without benefiting the fishermen too much. A French magazine which priced a kilo of cod at the various stages between Brittany and a Paris fishmonger found that the fisherman got only 10 per cent of the final selling price. Trawlermen from north to south express their anger in the habitual way by blocking the entry to ports for foreign boats, pouring oil on imported mackerel and attacking lorries carrying rival catches. The government reacts by giving in. It doles out money and imposes health tests that ensure foreign fish goes rotten by the time it gets to market. None of this does any good. On sea as on land, the small harvesters of food face a future of decline.

Still, it is the old agricultural ways which loom large in the national mind, and the countryside still calls to the city-dweller. Some follow the rural siren. An Air France executive gave up his career at the age of thirty-five, spent seven years moving from farm to farm to learn the ways of the land, and then set up in Normandy to raise goats and ducks, and make cheese, *foie gras*, sausages and pâté. A fertiliser salesman from a big multinational bought a vineyard in the Rhône Valley and now sells 110,000 bottles year. Such experiences warm the French heart. When there is good news from the deep heart of France, everyone cheers. So visit the small village of Calvinet, perched 600 metres up in the very south of the Cantal department, between the blustery heights of the Massif Central and the sunny uplands to the south.

On the face of it, Calvinet should have had no more reason to survive than Saint-André-de-Rosans. It lies in a region known as 'chestnut country', because the nuts used to be its main resource – they were the staple ingredient in the local flour. Today it remains much as described by a local carpenter, Joseph Lavigne, in a 26-page memoir he wrote in a notebook discovered after his death in 1994 at the age of eighty-two:

> My parental home was by the pastures. The silence was broken only by the crow of the cockerel or the snorting of the cows. My commune stood on the rise of a hill and it got the first light of day. To the south were the big fields where the wheat rippled like a rough sea. To the east and west, there were chestnut trees under whose shade the cows passed by. To the north were the poor people, scratching a living from the soil. There, too, were sheep grazing amid swarms of bees sucking the honey from flower to flower. In the village, the houses were mostly white, low-standing and with slate roofs. They looked charming from a distance; a group of homes with a bell tower in the middle, a schoolhouse and the big lime tree on the square, known as the tree of liberty.

Calvinet has gone through many changes since then. It was rent by a long and searing battle between reactionary Catholics and a pioneer of lay education: a *Romeo and Juliet* saga was played out between two young people from either side. In the 1930s, peddlers hawked their wares in *patois* at the market: '*Boutous de braguas, de comijias, de couls, de giletas, de broguetas.'* (Sixty years later, there were still vestiges of the local dialect. The nearby fifteenth-century village of Marcolès put up signs for visitors in both French and *patois*. Walking through a farm-yard on the hills one spring day, my wife and I were surrounded by a pack of dogs. We implored them in French to leave us alone. They took no notice. Then the farmer came out of a barn and shouted at them in *patois*. The dogs turned tail and ran off into the woods.) During the last war, a local inventor built a bicycle made of wood, but his plans to commercialise it came to nothing. The population declined, and the village became increasingly dependent on subsidies from Brussels. Around 1980, several of the younger men decided to take its destiny into their hands. While they had no intention of demanding any less in the way of European funding, they believed that Calvinet should avoid becoming another rural basket-case.

'It would have been easy to have sat back and done nothing, and watched the young people leaving for the town, and their parents being reduced to watching the television because that was all there was to do,' said one of the younger generation. He, himself, works in the departmental capital of Aurillac, forty kilometres away – but the road has been widened and improved and the journey takes half the time it used to. Calvinet is part of the wider world: there was even talk of building a branch of the Auvergne motorway in the hills down towards the Lot river.

The son of the local *charcutier* went off to learn to be a cook in Toulouse. He returned with a host of new ideas and ambitions, but was sage enough to draw on his mother's old recipes and his father's ham and sausages. Soon he was in the national guidebooks. He mar-ried the daughter of the local chemist, and they undertook the renovation of the hotel above the restaurant. Foreigners started coming for their holidays, and one day a fleet of bright red Ferraris called by for lunch on a sponsored rally through the region.

The village now has five places to eat or drink. The main square has new curly lamp-posts and a wooden notice-board with a large guide to the surrounding area. The main restaurant has won a Michelin rosette. There are two tennis courts in the woods by the camping site, a convenience store and a swimming-pool of sorts in the reservoir. The baker still serves up good old-fashioned bread. Naturally, Calvinet is not free from complaints, or concerns. The farmers worry not simply about the age-old uncertainties of the weather, but also about how well they are being defended in Brussels, and what trickery the Americans are up to in world trade talks. A local producer of *foie gras* once told me that, if this delicacy were banned in the USA, it would not be because the Americans really thought force-feeding was cruel – who could imagine any such thing? – but as a non-tariff barrier aimed at France, which should ban McDonald's in retaliation. As for the matter of mad cows, a farmer outside Calvinet was convinced that it was all a plot dreamed up by Washington to boost exports of American beef to Europe – ships full of transatlantic cattle were, he assured me, heading for Spain at that very moment, ready to be driven over the Pyrenees and supplant the Salers cattle in the fields below him. Another shook his head when the name of Jacques Chirac was mentioned. 'He thinks he can count on us, but he doesn't do anything,' he said, adding ominously: 'There are others who will look after our interests better.'

Cheap imports from Spain and Italy are a constant source of concern. Oh, and don't forget the Arabs: they used to import a lot of local lamb but they aren't buying any more. When I mention the way in which farm incomes have been rising, I get a dismissive shrug and expulsion of breath: as a city-dweller, not to mention a foreigner, how could I possibly understand that, whatever the statistics may say, France's farmers are always on the edge of disaster? That, Monsieur, is a fact with which nobody had better argue.

If its rural roots permeate France, the worry and self-absorption that periodically sweep the nation may be simply a translation of countryside concerns into the national bloodstream. In Calvinet, familiar national obsessions punctuate the conversation about falling beef prices and the grand wedding being held next Sunday on the street known as the Avenue de la Grande Armée because a couple of retired military officers live there. The restaurateur expostulates against the tax system which, he insists, makes it impossible for him to expand, and may encourage him to go back to his father's trade as a *charcutier* since VAT on cold meats is a quarter of the rate on cooked meals. Still, I say, he must be happy with his Michelin rosette. Yes, but his reply is complex. He reckons that he got the award for his traditional local dishes, like his mother's recipe for duck in a secret thick sauce (which I think contains both blood and bitter chocolate). Those are what the customers want when they drive up with the red guide in their cars. But what he'd like to be famous for is more adventurous recipes. Still, I say, things are going well in Calvinet. In return, I get a grudging *oui, mais* . . . the undefined 'but' which could mean that the weather may turn bad tomorrow, the crops may fail, the cattle may fall ill, the volcanoes may erupt, the world may come to an end.

On a ridge outside the village, a sharp-faced weather-beaten farmer sits at a huge wooden table and keeps watch on the herd in his cow-shed via closed-circuit television. He went to Paris once, but found the city so dirty and airless that he had to get home fast. His farm-house has walls a metre thick. In the courtyard outside, there is a hundred-year-old drinking trough hewn from a solid block of vol-canic rock. In the big, stone-floored main room, a stuffed fox stands on a ledge, copper cooking utensils hang on the wall, a grandfather clock reaches to the ceiling, three hunting rifles are racked over the huge fireplace and a big old television set sits on a dresser. By the door, a pair of horns has been mounted on the wall. The farmer's strongly-built, smiling wife explains that they belonged to a cow which was a treasure at the farm, never caused any trouble, but which went berserk when taken to the slaughterhouse. The farmer and his wife shake their heads at the memory, as though the cow was an inexplicably wayward child.

We had telephoned that morning for a couple of rabbits for dinner. The farmer's wife couldn't supply them immediately because her husband was out harvesting, and she had nobody to hold the animals while she killed them. By afternoon, she had found help, and she brought the cut-up meat in on a plate from the pantry. Over our protests, she added a large chunk of stuffed cabbage – layers of vegetable and minced meat with herbs – and half a dozen eggs. Then her husband led us out into the kitchen garden, looking out on to a horseshoe-shaped wood and an endless vista of countryside all the way down to Rodez. He gave us a handful of cucumbers and a couple of big courgettes, and told us that what he really needed was a good downpour. On the way back to the house, we passed the rabbit hutches, two of them empty and with their doors open.

Down the road, the local nobleman shows me round the wood-panelled rooms of his château one evening, and then sits and sips whisky and talks about his daughter's wedding, and about a young man from the village who went to Paris after the Revolution and made a fortune out of floating brothels on the Seine. A century ago, the nobleman's family held aloft the clerical standard in Calvinet, boycotting the village council when their lay opponents replaced the cross in the main square with a statue representing the Republic. After peace broke out, the baron became Mayor of the village, and used his contacts to ensure it got a bite at any financial cake on offer. After he gave up the post, his presence was still felt up to his death in 2000, standing in the queue at the local self-service store or sitting at a window table in the restaurant across the road for Sunday lunch, a bottle of Bordeaux on the table. 'Oh, Calvinet will always be here,' he says at the end of our conversation. 'We just have to make sure it is in as good shape as possible.' He accompanies me to the door of the château, and as I motor up the long driveway to the road, I see the baron in my rear-view mirror, urinating against the wall of his ancestral home. An image from a book of clichés about rural France, but a cliché that seems alive and well.

There may be a hundred re-awakened Calvinets across France; even Saint-André-de-Rosans tried a revival, hoping its position on the old pilgrim route to Santiago de Compostela would draw tourists, opening a hotel-restaurant and having T-shirts made to sell to visitors – but not many came, and the hoped-for revival boiled down a few sons and daughters of the village who had moved elsewhere buying holiday homes in the village. The waning of country customs cannot be denied. The annual killing of the pig and the use of every morsel down to the ears and tail for food has been supplanted by preserved cold cuts in cellophane from the local supermarket. A professor remembers how, in her childhood in the Vendée region, a rope was traditionally hung between two houses after church weddings with a jar of sweets attached to it; the mother of the bride then took a long pole and broke the jar with heavy symbolism for her virginal daughter as the children ran forward to scoop up the bonbons. Today, in the same area, church confessionals are sold as big bird cages.

Much as he puts himself forward as the farmer's friend, the Head of State can do little to slow down the change in rural life, even if he wants to. After Chirac's re-election, it was notable that France decided to stop diverting part of its European farm subsidies to rural development in poor areas. This carries political dangers – in a mirror image of its advance in old industrial areas, the National Front has increased its votes in rural areas of the centre and south-west which feel left behind. But it is possible to wonder if the countryside really deserves special treatment and over-representation in parliament when some industrial areas feel as much pain, but farmers benefit from favourable tax treatment and France heads the beneficiaries of Europe's Common Agricultural Policy.

The EU treasure trove has gone increasingly to big farms which become even larger as the small ones die out: grain producers in the Oise department north of Paris get subsidies nearly three times the national average. Departments with above-average farm income are mainly in the north-east while the lowest incomes are in the areas of *la France profonde* whose problems are held up as justifying all those subsidies – and where Le Pen raised his score in 2002. In the south-west, wine producers joined the ranks of the discontented as their incomes fell by 18 per cent in 2001 and their stocks rose by 62 per cent in three years amid talk of a re-run of the vineyard revolts that shook the region in the early 20th century.

Agriculture has produced its boutique farmers, grafting wild and cultivated strawberries to create a new fruit called the *mara des bois*, pressing exotic vegetable oils or breeding silkworms in the Cévennes. Thousands of 'bio' farmers raise vegetables and cattle without chemicals. Down south, in the Hérault department, the 430-inhabitant village of Avenge-les-Bains sells 2 million sprays made from its local waters in Japan each year. In Le Puy in the Auvergne, the number of lentil-growers exploiting the unique combination of volcanic soil, altitude and climate has doubled in a decade, and, by the Lot river, a market gardener does a nice line in Asian vegetables.

Still, the clear trend is for the big boys to grow bigger and the small folk to go to the old people's homes, or to be bought off active farming by a handout from Brussels. In one quintessentially rural village, a plump farmer's wife with tree-trunk arms who used to drive the fly-infested cattle to and from the fields lived placidly for years with her hard-drinking husband until he died, at which point, by coincidence, the European Union decided that it had too many cows, and would pay her and others like her to get rid of her beasts. This she duly did, using the money to refashion her house, buy a smart little car, have her hair done, and generally appear happier than she had ever been, free at last from the tyranny of the land.

As the average size of French agricultural holdings has doubled in the past thirty years, banks have taken to arranging seminars for their urban customers on the attractions of putting spare cash into the soil. Financial institutions buy up agricultural land as a good investment for themselves or their clients. Some farmers who rent their land have never seen the owner. The nature of farming changes year by year to meet the requirements of the bottom line, and maximise the return on capital for owners who would not know wheat from barley. For all the small farmers who dump their produce on the roads and drive their tractors in noisy demonstrations, the agricultural union is controlled by the big operators in the north who make sure that they reap a double benefit from high prices and rising productivity. Intensive pork and poultry farmers of the west saw their revenues go up by 50 per cent over only two years; at the same time, earnings of cauliflower-growers fell below the levels of the 1980s – and they were soon out blocking the roads of Brittany in protest. Ducks now provide far more livers for *foie gras* than geese because they are easier to force-feed with machines. Proclaiming that scientific advances did not always bear 'the mark of the devil', the government lifted a ban on growing genetically modified maize, boosting France's position as the European Union's biggest producer of the plant. Increasingly, farm houses are sold separately from the land to city-dwellers or foreigners, and then the fields are amalgamated into larger holdings.

All of which exacerbates the conflict between the way agriculture is going and the image the nation cherishes of its land. It is difficult to wax sentimental over a grain baron from the Beauce, south-west of Paris, who runs his fields with a computer, buys genetic crop strains from a Swiss drugs firm and flies off to an exotic holiday twice a year. And equally difficult to expect a twenty-year-old son of a hill farmer to remain on the land. 'I can't wait to move to the town,' a youth in Calvinet said at the football pitch one afternoon. 'Except that I won't find a job there, will I?'

Some resist. Deep in a forest off a main north–south route, but light-years from the world of motorways and high-speed trains, a farmer in his thirties lives in a muddy, fly-infested hovel at the end of a track. He ekes out a living with his wife and three children, tilling a small plot of earth and tending a herd of goats which produce fine cheese. It looks a miserable existence but, he says, 'I am from the earth. I live with my beasts. This is my life.'

As the rural world meets the twenty-first century, that life becomes rarer. The identification between the countryside, agriculture, tradition and the nation is breaking down into an economic bargain. One demographer has worked out that active farmers make up only one-fifth of the 15 million people who live outside towns and cities. Farmers, one of their leaders remarked, have believed for too long that the countryside belonged to them alone. Now, if they want to survive and prosper, they have to jump on the latest bandwagon, drawing the maximum in European subsidies and convincing the banks that they are a step ahead of the market. The new race of rural entrepreneurs approaches the countryside with the logic of modern business. One year they grow grain; the next, maize. One year they raise battery poultry; the next, they go for calves. Behind them, they leave breeze-blocks and corrugated iron, drained fields and an abandoned work-force. 'Farmers are their own worst enemy,' remarked a landowner whose locality had been devastated in this manner. Tradition fades, and another divorce develops between a vital element of national life and the way the French actually live now. And as the icon of the small farmer at the heart of France dissolves, we should turn to look at the condition of the other pea in the national pod.

5

MODERN TIMES

The country which invented the modern popular revolution naturally gave its working class and its urban life a historic place in society. Now, as with the traditional rural world, the rush of present-day realities cuts deeply into the fabric of town and city life while the industrial transformations of the past decades have eaten into the cherished old ways.

The Great Revolution may have been directed by the bourgeoisie and petty nobles, but the storming of the Bastille has gone down in history as a defining moment of popular passion, and the legitimacy of France's Republics through five manifestations over the last two centuries is based on the people. A rolling saga of revolt carried on from the Revolution to its more timid successor in 1830 and a rising by Lyon silk workers seeking a minimum wage, which left hundreds dead the following year. In 1848, another revolution brought in the Second Republic and inspired Karl Marx. The violence of the Paris Commune of 1871 terrified the middle classes and helped to ensure that, despite its greater tenors of the left, the Third Republic was their regime for nearly all of its seventy years. In this century, the nation's greatest sacrifice of lives was by millions of working-class men from both urban and rural France in the trenches of the First World War.

In the 1920s and 1930s, mass culture celebrated the workers; the icons of the age were not just popular but populist – the actor Jean Gabin in his vest; the actress Arletty making the most of her Parisian street accent; the songs of husky-voiced women bewailing the loss of their men; Marcel Pagnol's moving trilogy of plays and films about Marseille port life; Jean Renoir's cinematic celebrations of everyday existence; and the imperishable photographs of cafés with accordion-players, of a family picnicking on a river bank, of a narrow suburban street under a railway viaduct. Amid the tumult of the 1930s, the granting of the right to holidays with pay to workers – *congés payés* – has a historic resonance which may seem strange beyond French borders. The arrival of crowds of city workers and their families on hitherto middle-class beaches symbolised a social revolution. If the trains from Paris to the coast of Normandy were not quite a new storming of the Bastille, they came close in their way. As the eminent British historian of France, Douglas Johnson, has put it: 'It was dramatic. There were those who saw the sea for the first time. There were children who at last met their grandparents. Men whose families had come to Paris to find work visited the countryside their forefathers had cultivated. And there are other memories. Bourgeois families who had enjoyed the privilege of using certain beaches . . . were invaded by "louts wearing caps" and their followers.'

The Popular Front governments of 1936–38 which introduced paid holidays were a political and social watershed, bringing together Socialists and Communists, cutting the working week, nationalising the Bank of France and trying to show that France did not always have to be ruled from the right or the bourgeois centre. They certainly scared a lot of proper-thinking people. Charles de Gaulle's deeply reactionary mother described the Socialist leader Léon Blum as an agent of Satan, and a right-wing refrain of the time proclaimed 'Better Hitler than Blum'. In many ways, the left lacked a true cutting-edge. It let down the Republican peers in Spain, and quailed before the rampant slanders of the right. But it bequeathed an imperishable mark on society which France would not forget. When Blum was released from imprisonment at the Liberation, he took a suit to the cleaner. When he collected it, he found a handwritten note in one pocket: 'Thank you for the *congés payés*.'

The military importance of the French Resistance to the Nazi Occupation is open to debate: Hitler's architect, Albert Speer, once responded to a question on the subject with a scornful: 'What Resistance?' But the fact that some did stand up to the Nazis was essential to the salving of national pride after the Liberation. The

Army of the Shadows was the essential counterpoint to the civil ser-vice collaborators who did not even have an ideological excuse for what they did. While there were resisters from the right, the domes-tic fight against the Occupation was primarily a movement of the left, particularly after Hitler invaded Russia and thus freed the Communists to participate; the murdered Resistance chief, Jean Moulin, was even suspected by some Gaullists of being a secret agent of Moscow.

The left's role in fighting the occupiers gave the working class a special badge of respectability after 1944, and led some alarmists to fear a Marxist coup. In some cities, Communist Resistance leaders seemed poised to take power. But General de Gaulle used his position as the Great Liberator at the head of a Government of National Unanimity to carry out a ruthless amalgamation of the Resistance with the reg-ular army and to exert control. He also showed a distinct lurch to the left in preaching the virtues of the public interest, of using national wealth for the benefit of all, and of the right of everybody to live, work and bring up their children in security and dignity. To show that this was not a matter of empty rhetoric, his government nationalised coal, gas and electricity, banks, insurance businesses and some major industrial companies. Family allowances were introduced, together with unemployment and sickness pay, and women finally got the vote. Soon afterwards, long-term state planning was instituted at the behest of the future Father of Europe, Jean Monnet. Implicit in the Resistance and the victory of 1944 was a rejection of the static con-servatism that had contributed so much to the shame of 1940. The Fourth Republic, which came into being with the Liberation, would degenerate into a regime far more splintered and impotent than its predecessor, but the bright dawn of 1944 gave it a socialist–statist base which became entrenched in national life. Much as foreigners might scoff at France's political instability, and De Gaulle might rail at his successors after he lost power in 1946, the inflationary, state-cushioned economy that ushered in the Glorious Thirty Years represented a tri-umph for a system which catered to the desires of France's workers under the guidance of powerful trade unions.

When the General returned to office and changed the political system in 1958, the economy and the position of the working class altered little. Ministers might be Gaullists rather than members of the myriad small parties of the previous Republic, but managers and workers went on cutting easy deals in both private and public sectors. De Gaulle's Premier, Georges Pompidou, ended the nationwide strikes of 1968 with the simple expedient of a budget-busting pay agreement. Labour leaders were great national figures, and a former union official called Jacques Delors became a top-level governmental adviser with new-fangled ideas about industrial relations and worker participation in companies. De Gaulle sprang from the old-fashioned right, but he drew support from voters on the left – even the Communists liked his independent attitude towards Washington. In its early years, the Fifth Republic bound French society together and, though more in appearance than in reality, offered the working class a stake in society.

The politics of the 1980s changed all that. Not that anybody would have guessed it while the crowds danced in the streets to celebrate the Socialist victory of May 1981, and the newly-elected President proclaimed it to be 'a time for dreams'. As frightened businessmen smuggled money across the border to Switzerland, the Social Security Minister announced that her job was to spend money without bothering about the accounts. The government decided on the most expensive and inefficient way of nationalising a dozen key companies, followed by a deeply misguided attempt to build up stand-alone French production chains overseen by that Énarque of the left, Jean-Pierre Chevènement. It was all done in the name of the workers, even if there were more teachers than labourers among the Socialist Party faithful.

When three rapid devaluations of the franc, a bounding trade deficit and out-of-control inflation woke the President from his reverie, it was those workers who suffered. After the Socialists were forced into their economic volte-face in 1983, redundancies ripped through coal-mining, textiles and ship-building. François Mitterrand returned from a visit to the United States and said how impressed he had been by the automated steel plants he had seen there: in the ensuing years, job cuts in the great mills of Lorraine ran at 8 per cent or more a year, and those thrown out of work could only look for employment across the German border to the east. Robotisation of factories hit France with a vengeance. Unemployment shot up in the industrial bastions of the north and centre and along the Mediterranean, where the presence of large numbers of immigrants and of former settlers from Algeria exacerbated social tensions and gave the far right its deepest wells of support. Parisians grew accustomed to seeing teenage beggars huddled in doorways. The solidarity proclaimed by the Socialists in 1981 gave way to selfishness: it was increasingly difficult to be a good Samaritan if your job might no longer be there when you got back from helping one of your less fortunate fellow men on the other side of the road.

As the crisis bit ever deeper, and poverty became a way of life among the one-time workers of the old industrial areas, a reporter for *Le Monde*, Corine Lesnes, travelled to the northern mining basin and brought back a telling piece of reportage from a typical town of brick houses and paved streets. In Fresnes-sur-Escaut, 800 were out of work and 200 families lived on welfare. To save money, dozens had moved out of their homes and into old, abandoned caravans. One woman cooked for a community of fifteen living in a Second World War blockhouse.

'A woman of thirty-four died after her lungs were contaminated by toxic fumes: she burned rubbish and electric wires to recover the copper inside and sell it,' Lesnes wrote. 'The four children of last year's Father Christmas at the parish church are in care; Santa Claus spent five days in prison for a tax debt of 1,800 francs. Women get pregnant younger and younger – the children's allowances are like a wage for them.

'The most common way of making money is to collect scrap metal and sell it to the foundry for 3 francs a kilo. Anything goes – skeletons of cars, railway tracks, drain covers and even, last year, the railings of the bridge in the neighbouring town. Misery has a particularly black tone here.'

One woman, Nadine, divorced from a drunken husband, had seven children aged from one to seventeen, one of them a chronically ill truant of a teenager. The children did their homework by candlelight because it would take two years to pay off the debts to the electricity company. An older woman, Marcelle, lived on 15 francs a day, dropping in at neighbouring houses at mealtimes and watching for the days when rotten apples were thrown on the local dump. 'All one can do is to share their worries as winter comes and applaud the government's ritual anti-poverty plan,' Lesnes wrote. 'Or re-read Zola and Dickens. And flee.'

Under succeeding governments led by Socialists and Gaullists, things only got worse for the working class. With the number of jobs falling in three-quarters of France's regions, 9 million people were unemployed or in part-time posts or 'precarious' jobs. Star industries stumbled. Household names took the shears to labour costs: the loss-making appliance firm which gave the world the vegetable mixer (under the slogan 'Moulinex frees women') shed a quarter of its full-time jobs. Even the smile of the pneumatic Michelin man couldn't save 15 per cent of the tyre firm's workers from getting the chop. The French term for downsizing – *dégraissage* – moved out of the kitchen and on to the factory floor. Four former homeless men marketed social problems with a board-game in which players had to dodge dole queues, debt, alcoholism and the police to reach the ultimate prize of a job – it was packaged in the brown cardboard from which street sleepers make their shelters.

Moving to the upper end of the working class, the number of office staff and white-collar employees signing on for benefit doubled over five years. The slowdown in hiring meant there were fewer and fewer jobs for young people, and those who did get work found it mainly in small firms and on short-term contracts.

The process which started with a series of political decisions by an administration which had come to power supposedly to promote the interests of the working class rapidly took on a life on its own, arching beyond politicians. Because they could not control events, ministers could not explain what was happening to their voters – or, more painfully for the Socialists, to their own party members. The language of the early 1980s became archaic as the habits of past generations were blown away. The working class was abruptly removed from its sentimental pinnacle and made to feel useless. The old notion of long-term relationships between workers, managers and owners evaporated in the face of the pursuit of survival, as the old anchors were pulled up and the ship of everyday existence was cast to the winds. Take three examples from urban life – shops, cars and the party which claimed to stand for the workers of France.

In the panoply of French working life, small shopkeepers, trades-people and artisans have long been a key element in the nation's daily

existence. They give many city streets an essential part of their character. In the countryside, they served a far-flung community out in
the fields and villages. Before the Germans destroyed it in 1944, the
small town of Ouradour in the middle of France counted around fifty
family or one-man enterprises – hairdressers and butchers, shoe- and
dress-makers, bakers and iron merchants, carpenters and dealers in
agricultural produce, a dentist, a tailor who also sold insurance, and a
bunch of weavers – plus six cafés. In the capital, even the smartest districts have traditionally been alive with a variety of small shops that
made them self-sufficient: a 200-metre stretch of a street on the Left
Bank of Paris where I lived in the 1980s contained three butchers, a
stationer, a greengrocer, a dry-cleaner, a cheese shop and an outlet
from the Félix Potin chain of grocers.

Launched in 1844, the Potin chain made its reputation by promising honestly weighed goods, quality products bought by the founder
in person and a low profit margin. The firm established the first
French food-processing factories owned by a retailer, and pioneered
home delivery. Its clients included the Élysée Palace. The main Potin
factory in the north of Paris stretched over four hectares. The shops
were a unique kind of enterprise. Though small in size, they used
bulk-buying and a standard range of goods to undercut stand-alone
rivals. They were mini-supermarkets and, as such, overcame smaller
competitors. Yet, being neighbourhood establishments, they carried
with them none of the looming size and power of the hypermarkets
which were to follow. They kept a local feel, and a family atmosphere.
They were often run by a couple whom customers knew by name; in
the early days, employees had to obtain the firm's permission before
getting married. Many of the managers lived in company flats above
their shops. And there was a fine nostalgic resonance of their founder's
first name: very few French baby boys are called Félix these days.

In 1956, self-service was introduced to the 1,200 Potin outlets.
Soon after that, two revolutions shook up French retailing for ever.
The first saw a boom in the mail-order business. The second involved
the huge growth of giant out-of-town shopping centres. France has
more hypermarkets per head of population than any other European
country. Municipal authorities made the most of the planning powers
devolved to them under decentralisation measures to attract shopping
centres. Consumers are estimated to buy 90 per cent of their groceries

from such places which saw their sales rising by up to 10 per cent a year at the start of the new century. In services as well as retailing, big chains took more and more of the market. From McDonald's to exhaust-pipe fitters, franchises spread across the nation. Eighty thousand small shopkeepers gave up the struggle in the 1990s, with the closure of 40 per cent of grocers and 35 per cent of furniture and clothes retailers. The survivors complain vociferously about high taxes and rents, and the effect of the 35-hour week, plus fear of crime. They say they cannot find staff ready to work hard. In big cities, immigrants from North Africa have taken over neighbourhood groceries, *l'Arabe du coin* replacing the traditional shopkeeper couple. But it is the hyper-markets which have wrought the major change. Take the town of Avallon in Burgundy as an example. After the appropriately named Mammouth chain opened a complex on the outskirts, the number of butchers in the town dropped from twelve to two. As well as offering cut-price goods, the commercial centre became a focus of social activity, in a reversal of the old image of the locals hailing one another as they move from one small shop to another. 'Mammouth has become the town centre,' said a fishmonger. 'People go there to meet their friends as well as to do their shopping.'

Social intercourse apart, shops like the Félix Potin chain simply could not compete on price; and saving money became steadily more important for consumers in the harsher climate that set in during the early 1990s. A new Anglicism emerged, *les hard discounters*. It was not just poorer customers who flocked to them; plenty of middle-class mothers sorted through the cheap clothes, cut-price food and do-it-yourself gear on offer. A sociologist, Denis Stocklet, dubbed bargain-hunting a national sport. In 2003, 15 million households used the cheapest stores. France, said one pollster, had adopted 'a discount attitude'.

There had always been stores which piled the goods up high and sold them cheap. The Tati chain, set up by a Tunisian immigrant in a former brothel in the down-at-heel Barbès area of Paris, had the atmosphere of an Arab market as customers, many themselves immigrants, sorted through goods heaped on counters before taking them away in the chain's distinctive pink gingham-pattern shopping bags. 'Keep the thieves out of my shops, and you'll take away part of my clientele,' the founder once remarked. He knew how humiliating it could be for poor people to ask superior shop assistants for the price of goods which they might not be able to afford, so he did away with the assistants and let his customers check the prices themselves before taking them to the cash tills. At its height, the chain attracted some 25 million customers a year in nine cities. Then other retailers noticed how keen the French had become to save money on clothes. By 1996, one-third of garments were being bought at discount houses or in sales. Smarter stores which had once let Tati have their unsold stock at knock-down prices began to sell it cheap themselves. Turnover slumped in Tati's souks. To restore its fortunes the chain looked overseas, and cashed in on its kitsch image with disposable cameras in shades of its trademark pink, a Fifth Avenue store in New York, and a jewellery outlet on the smart Rue de la Paix. Everybody was in the cut-price game now, and, as the lines of hypermarkets grew for kilometre after kilometre on the edge of provincial cities, Denis Stocklet reflected that, without realising it, the French had gone back to nineteenth-century Catholic ways of parsimony and economy. That made a few people very rich indeed: three of the country's half-dozen largest fortunes belong to big retailers.

Governments have tried to check the mega-stores, but with scant success. The bottom line rules, and the bigger the store, the greater the profit. French hypermarkets have spread their message round the globe – Carrefour is now the world's second largest retailer after WalMart. At home, they have become the hallmark of the outskirts of provincial towns and cities. When predatory pricing was banned to try to protect small shops, one supermarket boss reacted with glee to the news that he would not have to offer bread at below cost price to lure customers. Jacques Chirac thundered about the 'extraordinarily negative' effect of supermarkets in drawing people to 'unfriendly' suburban centres; a move to make planning permission more difficult for new hypermarkets only set off takeover battles as the bigger chains sought to grow ever larger by acquiring their weaker brethren. For all the rhetoric of regret for the cosy past and the place of small shops in the social blanket, the die was cast. Even if they shudder at its social cost, one thing successive governments have pursued with success is low inflation, and the discounters help to achieve that – the harder the better.

Some of the cut-price retailers see themselves as playing a positively crusading role in forging a better way of life for their compatriots. One cut-price pioneer, Édouard Leclerc, has been deeply hurt by official criticism. 'We're attacked like the Jews once were,' he says. 'They used to be held responsible for everything that went wrong. Now it's us.' Leclerc is a phenomenon of post-war France. Born into a poor family of thirteen children, he opened his first shop after the war in the west of Brittany, selling chocolates, biscuits and sweets at half the artificially high wartime rates still charged by other stores. The secret of his success was simple: 'I sold retail at wholesale prices.' As Centres Leclerc sprouted throughout the country, small shopkeepers demonstrated against him and his methods. Local farmers refused to sell him milk or vegetables. Leclerc, a man who loves to upset established ways, relished the battle. Sometimes things turned violent. Lorries were stopped by force; a leader of protesting shopkeepers was hit in the face by a rock and lost two teeth. Then Leclerc had the idea of selling discount petrol to attract car-owners to his stores. Once there in their Renaults and Peugeots, what could be more convenient than to load up with goods from the adjoining store? A believer in astrology, Lerclerc adopts a quasi-religious approach to retailing. 'He taught us that the only thing that counts is our intellectual capital,' one of his sons says. His local managers are known as disciples or adherents.

Though the founder has never taken much money out of the business, his followers do very nicely. Lerclerc often gives his managers an ownership stake in their enterprises, and insists that they share the takings with the staff. They are invited to conferences to listen to his vision of the future. 'As the years have gone by, one has seen them turning up in thicker and thicker furs, with bigger and bigger rings and in more and more powerful cars,' one observer of the Leclerc phenomenon told *L'Express*. 'Édouard is their god. It isn't a limited company he set up, but a movement. A man who lets you build up such a business for yourself without asking for anything in return except that you follow certain moral rules (don't rob the customer, sell as cheaply as possible and distribute a quarter of the profits to the staff) is unique.'

So, in an age when families drive scores of kilometres to shopping centres for a Saturday expedition, eat lunch on the spot, fill the car with goods and go home feeling they have passed a day well spent, shops like Félix Potin found their backs to the wall. The founding family sold out, and the new owners realised that inner-city property prices meant the real-estate value of their assets might well outweigh the revenue to be earned from retailing. Little by little, the stores were hived off for development. At the end of 1995, the remaining 400 Potin shops received a terse note from the central management: 'You can stay open until December 31 at 20.30.' Given that New Year is a more important occasion for celebration than Christmas in France, it was a Christmas carol from a Gallic scrooge, a death-knell for an institution.

The French love affair with the motor-car has been charted by writers, lyricists, photographers and academics. The greatest modern French novelist, Albert Camus, died in a road crash; a far poorer writer, Roger Limier, won fame as 'the French James Dean' for dicing with death – which finally caught up with him – in fast cars. The revolt of shopkeepers and small businessmen led by Pierre Poujade in the 1950s would not have been possible had its leader not been able to drive about the country from one village meeting to another. The reputation of the novelist Françoise Sagan as a symbol of modernity was inflated by the way she ignored speed limits. Despite the efficiency of French public transport, 82 per cent of local trips are still made by car. France has more motor dealers than any other European nation. In 1973, a French sociologist was moved to write an article entitled 'Automobile Accidents and the Class Struggle'. The philosopher Roland Barthes devoted an essay to the semiology of the Citroën DS. An American academic, Kristin Ross, entitled a study of post-war French society 'Fast Cars, Clean Bodies', noting that, after the 1950s, a revolution in attitudes towards mobility and displacement had permeated every aspect of life with 'the dismantling of all earlier spatial arrangements, the virtual end of the historic city, in a physical and social restructuring'. So it is not surprising that France's main car manufacturer should have played a key role in national life, going beyond the mere construction of vehicles, and that its history should tell a story about the evolution of French industry and those who worked in it.

For six decades, the Renault plant on the Île Séguin on the Seine in a suburb of Paris was France's greatest industrial citadel. Built in 1929 by Louis Renault, 'Fortress Billancourt' sprawled over sixty-five hectares. It brought major assembly-line production to France, and was immortalised as an industrial monument and shrine of the French working class in photographs, books and even poetry. In the 1930s, the town of Boulogne-Billancourt became a treasure-house of modernist buildings by the urban pioneer, Le Corbusier, and a dozen other leading French architects. During the German Occupation, the plant was turned over to the Nazis, who used it to produce military vehicles – Allied air-raids killed more than 1,000 workers. After the Liberation, Louis Renault was arrested for collaboration, the company was nationalised and the Communists turned the factory into a union stronghold. Before she discovered silk stockings, Cyd Charisse's Ninotchka put a visit to Billancourt high on the list of things she had to do on her first visit to Paris. Édith Piaf moved into a villa across the river. Renault set the norms for pay and conditions – for a fourth week of paid holiday and for the wage rises that ended the 1968 strikes. When Jean-Paul Sartre launched a revolutionary newspaper, he sold it at the factory gates. A line from one of his plays – 'We mustn't make Billancourt lose hope' – became a catch-phrase for the need to cater to the workers of France. When the left finally won power in 1981, a former chairman of the motor firm became the Minister for Industry. The company symbolised a society in which more than a quarter of the workforce looked to the state for employment. It was as solid as the nation itself.

With car ownership booming in the 1960s, Renault and other motor companies expanded production beyond their urban citadels, setting up new plants on green-field sites in Normandy and importing cheap labour from Africa. Many of the immigrants moved to dormitory tower-block estates on the outskirts of neighbouring towns. One such place was Dreux, a market town west of Paris which had once been a key frontier post between the Kingdom of France and the Duchy of Normandy. In the town itself, there are brick buildings with stucco façades, a Renaissance bell-tower, a bridge over a slow-flowing river and an arrow-straight avenue which points up the hill to the railway station and the ride to the Gare Saint-Lazare. Drive ten minutes out of the middle of Dreux and you land in a very different environment, where the local give-away newspaper carries advertisements for witch-doctors and the lifts in the tower-block are covered with Arabic graffiti. The flats are occupied by immigrants who came to work at the car plants and other factories in the area in the boom years. In the 1980s, robotisation and downsizing threw many of them out of jobs, but they had no wish to go back to Africa. The town's left-wing mayor devoted much money and effort to catering for the new arrivals. The French natives of Dreux resented this, and grew fearful of unemployed Arabs from the car plants and their teenage children. They wanted nothing to do with multi-cultural experiments. And so Dreux became the unexpected testing-ground for France's National Front extremists whose anti-immigrant, law-and-order programme made such an impact that, in 1983, the orthodox conservatives in the town forged a pact with the devil. In return for his support, they appointed the local Front leader to the town council. After his death in a car accident, his wife went on to win the parliamentary seat for Dreux with 61.3 per cent of the vote.

Just as the National Front was exploiting the explosive seeds of unemployment, industrial mutation and racism unwittingly sown by the motor industry in Normandy, Renault was reflecting other changes in France as well. Amid an upsurge in extreme left-wing terrorism, the chairman was murdered in the street as an evil paragon of capitalism. A quarter of Renault's capital was opened to investors in France's privatisation programme. Volvo took a stake in an ill-fated attempt at European co-operation. The management even summoned up the nerve to defy a 22-day strike at one of its factories. And *dégraissage* hit Billancourt with a vengeance. When its workers had led the charge for more pay in 1968, the plant employed 24,000. By 1991, it had 1,230. At 2:30 P.M. on 27 March 1992, France's most famous assembly-line came to a halt. Four days later, the Billancourt plant closed for good. The men went home, and the management looked for buyers for the land. It used to be said that 'when Billancourt sneezes, France catches a cold'. By 1992, France was already ill.

Three and a half months after its Paris plant closed, Renault got a new chairman, a former senior government official called Louis Schweitzer. His first year in office saw another 7,000 jobs cut. Renault had lost 37 per cent of its labour force in the dozen years since the left won power in 1981. Back then, Schweitzer had been the principal aide to the Socialist Budget Minister, and reacted with cold irritation if one dared suggest that the government's plans for reflation and nationalisation might be just a little unrealistic. As for France itself, the experience of the 1980s had been a steep learning curve for him. An Énarque who was distantly related to Jean-Paul Sartre, he had dealt with ministerial problems over HIV-contaminated blood supplies, telephone tapping and the blowing-up of the anti-nuclear Greenpeace ship *Rainbow Warrior* by French secret service agents. In the early 1980s, Schweitzer wore shoes with unusually thick soles; by the time he took over as chairman and chief executive of Renault in 1992, his footwear was a good deal more elegant.

The early 1990s were a bad time for the company. French car sales were soggy as the economy struggled on the edge of recession. Renault lacked attractive new models, its prices were high, its productivity low, and its workers older and less flexible than at some rivals. One new model had to be modified after critical safety reports in motoring magazines, and 160,000 cars were recalled after static electricity triggered off their airbags. Investors who had bought into the firm's first share offering in 1994 watched the value of their stock decline by nearly a third in eighteen months. By 1996, the company plunged to a loss of 5 billion francs. The Industry Minister suggested that the very survival of the company might be at stake. 'Renault is developing a device to stop drivers falling asleep at the wheel,' remarked the *Financial Times*. 'Shareholders could be forgiven for hoping the company's top brass have it installed in their offices.'

As French car registration slumped by 20 per cent to their lowest level for twenty-two years, Schweitzer's wake-up call began with changes in working patterns in France, and the closure of a factory at Villevorde near Brussels. The loss of 3,000 jobs brought a protest from the Belgian monarchy, and the newly-elected Jacques Chirac wondered if the company was doing the right thing. Still, the share price rose – as the Communist-led CGT union federation remarked, 'Renault has chosen the stock market over jobs.' But, like a number of his colleagues from the Socialist glory days who had moved to run big firms, Schweitzer had to face the fact that sacking staff was not enough; Renault also had to re-make itself for the new world in which it found itself. So it embarked on a transformation into a far more international undertaking, opening plants in low-cost countries of Latin America, Eastern Europe and Asia, and buying into local firms in trouble in the developing world. The one-time bellwether of French heavy manufacturing did not exactly turn its back on its homeland and the tight European market, where it sold 160,000 cars a year, but it decided survival as a significant player meant taking a world view, turning out cars modelled for different geographical markets from regionally-situated factories that could use coordination to achieve worldwide economies of scale.

While the other big French vehicle maker, Peugeot Citroën, stayed closer to home and turned losses into profits through reduced costs, increased productivity and popular new models, Renault moved its strategy into top gear in 1999 by taking a one-third stake in the debt-crippled Japanese company, Nissan. Its top operational manager, Carlos Ghosn, flew east on a mission that would once have seemed unthinkable – to teach the Japanese how to produce cars more efficiently. Known as 'le cost killer', the Franco-Brazilian Ghosn was so successful that Nissan headed back into profit from what its new boss called 'a near death experience'. As Japanese women voted Ghosn one of the four men with whom they would most like to have a child and the *Financial Times* described him as the hottest property in the car industry, he was earmarked to succeed Schweitzer as chief executive of Renault in 2005.

Though the question remained as to whether France could continue to maintain two separate car-makers, the change in Renault symbolises the distance the nation's industry has travelled in the decade since the last days of Billancourt. In April 2002, the government in Paris added another ingredient to the new Renault by selling a quarter of its stake, and announcing that it would cut its shareholding in stages to 25 per cent. Still, as the company drove into the globalised world chosen by Schweitzer and Ghosn, new risks appeared. The sagging world economy cut demand and mid-range models that had powered Renault's revival started to look old-fashioned. In 2001, operating profits dropped by 75 per cent. Though sales rose, the margin fell by three-quarters. Economic crises in Latin America and Turkey threatened the company's regional expansion there which had been at the heart of Schweitzer's strategy. Becoming a world company involves meeting competition everywhere while, at home, Peugeot Citroën had a fresher fleet. This meant Renault had to be more nimble, planning twenty product launches between 2002 and 2004 and cutting the time taken to develop new models in half.

The radically changed character of the former national industrial icon was underlined when its first half results for 2002 included a contribution of 425 million euros from Nissan where Ghosn's medicine had made the market value of Renault's stake worth more than its own total capitalisation. The French raised their holding in the Japanese firm to 44.4 per cent while Nissan took 15 per cent of Renault. The two firms developed common production platforms and common engine types, and melded their accounting systems. They each wrote their management documents in English to ease mutual understanding round the globe. A joint holding company to plan strategy and co-operation was set up, registered in the neutral territory of the Netherlands, with three directors from each partner. Renault described the evolution as having moved from 'international mutual assistance to strategic coordination'. It was all a long way from the Île Séguin. Another working-class totem had been submerged by new realities.

No political movement has caught the chill that emanated from Billancourt more than the Parti Communiste Français. Since its split with the Socialists in 1920, the PCF had seen itself as the true champion of the working class. Once it had terrified the bourgeoisie and frightened the CIA as it brought hundreds of thousands of supporters out on to the streets. Under the charismatic leadership of Maurice Thorez, it had played a leading role in promoting the Popular Front, and, after initial hesitations during the Hitler–Stalin pact, had been as important as the Gaullists in the internal Resistance. During the Fourth Republic, the party routinely outpolled the Socialists. In the strikes of 1968, it made the rest of the left look like dilettantes; the world might watch images of students occupying the Sorbonne, but what really mattered was how the PCF played its hand. If De Gaulle was to be overthrown, that task could not be accomplished without its solid battalions. But the Communists did not want the General to go – and, above all, they did not want their troops infected by the springtime elixir of young people who declared themselves 'Marxists – Groucho wing'. At the presidential election of 1969, less than twelve months after the crushing of the Prague spring, the Moscow-loyal Communist candidate took four times as many votes as the Socialist.

If Georges Pompidou was the major winner of the battles of the late 1960s, the PCF counted itself a close second. But it was in grave danger of losing the war.

Two decades later, the electoral relationship between the two main parties of the left was more than reversed, as the still highly orthodox Communists got just under a fifth of François Mitterrand's score in the 1988 election. In return for its support in the run-off ballot, Mitterrand gave the PCF four places in his first government. They were very much on the second rung of power; their most important post was the Transport Ministry. Still, the chance of participating in the left's first administration of the Fifth Republic could not be resisted. Before long, it proved a poisoned chalice.

The party had lost its way. This was not simply a matter of the diminishing appeal of Communism. On the one hand, there was Mitterrand's superbly orchestrated long-term campaign to build up the Socialists as the major party of the left, taking the Communists into a one-way alliance which sapped their strength. Reformers might talk of forging a new brand of Marxism: a senior Communist civil servant spoke to me at length over a slab of pink calf's liver in a smart Left Bank restaurant of how the Communists could use the Socialists to broaden their appeal. But the party had been so dragooned into Moscow-directed orthodoxy over the decades that it could not get the worm out of its bud, and establish itself as a real working-class party for modern times which would think for itself and stand apart from both the temporising Socialists and the rampant forces of the far right. More than any other political group in this retrospective nation, the PCF is a prisoner of its past, to a degree which the vast majority of its members are unaware. For proof, meet one of the more shadowy figures of French political history, Eugen Fried.

It was not until 1997 that two tireless chroniclers of French communism, Annie Kriegel and Stéphane Courtois, uncovered the extent of Fried's role in ensuring that the supposed white knight of France's workers had been the slave of Moscow. As a young man, he had proved his worth to the Kremlin by organising a campaign against Social Democrats in Czechoslovakia in the 1920s. Fluent in Slovak, Hungarian, Yiddish, Czech, German, English and French, Fried was sent clandestinely by Moscow to France in around 1930. Once installed, he promoted Maurice Thorez and other trusted figures in

the trade unions and politics – and blocked the rise of a popular tribune, Jacques Doriot, who switched to the far right and ended up
being executed as a Nazi collaborator. Fried made each senior party
official fill up a 74-part questionnaire covering everything from his
education to his private life; the forms were immediately dispatched
to Moscow. Fried himself regularly travelled to the USSR to report to
the Kremlin, returning with Stalin's latest commands.

In 1934, Fried came back to France from one of these trips with an
order that the PCF should set aside the rancours of the 1920 split and
work with the Socialists again. The left was on a major upswing at the
time, buttressed by the economic slump, fear of what was happening
across the Rhine in Nazi Germany and the activities of fascist groups
in France. But when the Popular Front won power two years later,
there was another order from Moscow – the Communists were not to
join the new government.

Instead, they must put bourgeois politics on one side and concentrate on building up industrial muscle through their labour federation,
the Confédération Générale du Travail (CGT). The instruction was
loyally followed by Thorez and the party's labour boss, Benoît
Franchon, and a future presidential candidate, Jacques Duclos. The
loyalty to Moscow was not confined to politicians and unionists; a fair
number of French intellectuals also made fools of themselves. 'Death
to the saboteurs of the Five-year Plan,' ran a line by the much-
honoured poet, Louis Aragon, who also confided later that his pain at
Stalin's death was only equalled by the sense of sorrow and personal
loss he had felt when his mother passed away.

Rewriting history is a futile exercise, but all the same: what if the
PCF had been more independent of its puppet-master answering to
Moscow, what if Thorez had grabbed the destiny which seemed to
have been his to take at national level in 1936, what if the anti-fascist
parties had formed a united bloc in government in the late 1930s?
Would France have acted differently at Munich? Would Paris and
London have been able to check Hitler sooner? And, if so, would
Charles de Gaulle have retired to his country home as an obscure
prophet of tank warfare? So much for speculation; the reality was that,
after the Nazi invasion of 1940, Fried told the French Communists to
collaborate with the occupying power. He himself moved to Belgium,
but kept in touch over a clandestine radio linked with Moscow and

with Jacques Duclos in Paris. He instructed Thorez to desert from his regiment, and Duclos to open political negotiations with the Germans. Hitler's invasion of Russia finally freed the Communists to join the Resistance, but Fried did not live to resume on-the-spot control after the Liberation: in 1943, the Gestapo killed him during a raid in Brussels. They had no idea who he was. Nor did any but a handful of the French.

After the Liberation, the control from Moscow continued, reinforced by the emotional strength which at least some of the resisters had drawn from news from the Eastern Front as they fought their lonely battle in the west. The first post-war elections gave it a quarter of the vote, but it remained aloof from the twisted manoeuvres of Fourth Republic Cabinet-making, and so could claim a certain purity. It reacted with a famous court case when a former Resistance fighter revealed the nature of the Soviet Gulags in 1950 and, though it lost, could still count on the allegiance of Jean-Paul Sartre and the intellectual left. But the true nature of communism in the East gradually seeped home, and the PCF's devotedly Stalinist leadership became increasingly isolated though it, again, won credit for its opposition to the colonial war in Algeria. The advent of the Fifth Republic did the party no harm, since the Socialists were humbled and De Gaulle's independent foreign policy created a certain warmth with Moscow. But the sands began to shift more decisively in the 1970s, when the Communists became epitomised by a man who hit a political nadir on their behalf.

Georges Marchais, Secretary-General of the PCF from 1972 to 1993, was a scary remnant from the caverns of Stalinism whose outbursts provided regular occasions for national mirth. Under his long rule, the survival of the least fittest became the be-all and end-all of leadership. A bushy-eyebrowed, potato-headed thug whose lack of style could make him almost endearing on occasion, Marchais supported the crackdown on Solidarity in Poland and the Soviet invasions of Czechoslovakia and Afghanistan (the latter in a television interview direct from Moscow). Earning his nickname of 'Jojo' for his admiration for Stalin, he developed ties with Leonid Brezhnev and Nicolae Ceauşescu, and viewed Mikhail Gorbachev's reforms with trepidation. 'What's a Gulag? he once asked. 'What we call a prison, they call a Gulag.' When deportations and executions in the Soviet Union under

Communist rule were mentioned, he retorted: 'I tell you, they didn't arrest enough! They didn't imprison enough! If they had been tougher and more vigilant, they wouldn't have got into this situation they're in now.' After pulling back from a tilt at Euro-Communist liberalism in the 1970s, he proclaimed the glories of 'democratic centralism' and muzzled anything approaching *glasnost* in his party. Famously dogmatic, he once told a television interviewer who had cornered him that the man was asking the wrong questions. Such braggadocio behaviour earned him high ratings on the box – higher, it was said, than football matches – but party membership fell by around 70 per cent under his leadership.

Following the lines originally laid down by Eugen Fried, the PCF had always been an outsider. Marchais's leadership ensured that, more than ever, it would not evolve into being seen as a natural party of government, in the way that the Socialists were from 1981 onwards. But then, contradictorily, Marchais allowed himself to be drawn into Mitterrand's web, ensuring that the PCF got the worst of all worlds. As unemployment rose in the 1980s, it failed to make itself the party of those hit by economic change in old industrial regions, and thus lost votes to the far right which emerged as a powerful rival for protest votes among laid-off workers.

Revelations about financing from the KGB and the siphoning off of cash by Communist-run local councils further tarnished the image. Marchais himself could never explain away the fact that he had signed on as a wartime worker at a Messerschmidt plant before the Nazis introduced compulsory labour for young Frenchmen. But all this paled into insignificance beside the huge political failure of the would-be party of the masses to capitalise on the growing discontent with successive governments among its natural supporters. The 1980s should have been the moment the PCF had been waiting for, with soaring unemployment showing up the harsh side of capitalism as administrations of left and right took ever more unpopular measures, and voters searched for new panaceas. Instead, the PCF's woes mounted, as did those of the nation. In the first round of the 1981 presidential election, Georges Marchais, for all his faults, had won 15 per cent of the vote to Mitterrand's 26 per cent. Seven years later, Mitterrand got about the same level of support but the Communist candidate managed to muster only 5.4 per cent.

In 1993, the party eventually got a new leader, Robert Hue, a bearded, friendly-looking former nurse with an unusual wit who resembled a large garden gnome. At the National Assembly elections of that year, the Communists did so badly that the minimum requirement for a parliamentary group had to be changed to enable their deputies to sit together. In the 1995 presidential poll, Hue took 8.6 per cent of the first-round vote. Georges Marchais, who was to die at the end of 1997, said nothing in public, but sniped at his successor. Undeterred, Hue set out to bring the party into the modern world. Internal discipline remained tight, but reformers were no longer banished. Jacques Chirac's gamble in calling legislative elections in 1997 gave fresh reason for hope. United by pledges to slash unemployment and by scepticism about the demands of the Maastricht Treaty, the Communists and Socialists reached a broad policy agreement that, despite some decidedly grey areas, enabled them to campaign in the name of a united left.

Hue set a target of 10 per cent of the first-round vote; in the event, the PCF got 9.9 per cent, and boosted its representation in the National Assembly from twenty-four to thirty-eight seats. The election result meant the Socialists needed Communist support to achieve a parliamentary majority. Hue overcame opposition from some old hard-liners, including Marchais, and agreed to join the new government; the central committee celebrated with a 1992 *grand cru* claret, cheese and strawberries. A member of the party's national secretariat followed the 1981 example to become Minister of Transport. He lost no time in getting 20 billion francs written off the debts of the state railway system and freezing a job-reduction plan. Flying down to the south-west for the weekend, he told his fellow passengers he was confident that France was facing a new start, with the PCF up there in the driving cab. Not that his new responsibilities had gone to his head: standing behind him at the counter in Rodez airport, I noticed that his hire-car was in the cheapest category, like mine.

The party might be back in government, but it was very much a junior partner alongside ecologists and left-wing Socialists. There was no doubting the decline of the once-mighty Communist machine. The mutations through which France had gone had profoundly altered the nature of its one-time supporters. The collapse of communism in Eastern Europe dealt it a heavy blow. Its past associations could not be easily shaken off – an 846-page account of the crimes of communism went to the top of the French best-seller list in 1997. In that year's parliamentary election, the PCF won substantially fewer votes than the National Front, and polled less than one-third of the non-Communist left. On election night, Hue asked a reporter if he looked like a frightening person; but that was not the point.

When the PCF had been frightening, it was because of its disciplined mass following. Now, the marchers in the street were a far more disparate lot, following different drums; it was the extreme right, not the benign Hue, who inspired fear. The CGT labour federation could still lay down the law in bastions like the state railway system, but trade union power was not what it was. Membership dropped by more than a third in a decade. The more pragmatic CFDT took over as France's biggest labour grouping by recruiting in the private sector and the service industries and, at the beginning of the new century, 20 per cent of CGT members were pensioners. Once the Communists had been sure history was on their side; now it did not know where to stand as events passed it by. Symbolically, a guide taking visitors round the PCF's new headquarters remarked on how the building contained no angles, only curves. The party newspaper, *L'Humanité*, dropped the hammer and sickle from its masthead, relaunching a glossy Sunday edition with advertisements from privatised companies. And, all the while, the Communists twisted themselves into knots as the price of being in government – denouncing the sale of state assets and the common European currency while sitting in a Cabinet which sold state assets and oversaw the introduction of the euro. Doctrinal certainty had been replaced by the basic need to keep the oxygen supply Jospin offered.

The Prime Minister was certainly keen to give the Communists face, modifying legislation on key areas of concern such as employment law to keep them happy. Jospin's electoral calculation was transparent – counting on Hue to tell his voters to back the Socialists in the second round of the presidential election of 2002, Jospin thought he had every interest in the Communists scoring decently in the first round as he, himself, went on to the showdown with Chirac. The cerebral Premier was horribly mistaken. Hue scored just 3.39%, a fifth of Le Pen's showing and less than two of the three Trotskyites. It was under half his score seven years earlier, only a third of the

PCF's performance at the legislative elections of 1997. The strongest Communist showing was in its traditional stronghold of the Limousin where Hue came fifth with just 6 per cent, behind the Trotskyite, Arlette Laguiller. In the ensuing legislative elections, it attracted 3.06 per cent of the votes, and lost 14 of its 35 seats in the National Assembly, barely getting enough deputies to form a parliamentary group. Hue lost his seat in the Paris suburbs, blaming the defeat on National Front voters backing his opponent. As supporters wept at his headquarters, the Communist leader spoke of the need to 'rebuild what is necessary for this country and to propose to its inhabitants something other than the rule of money'.

But, for all except the inner core of true believers, there was simply no point in voting Communist. The party had nothing to offer. Protest voters, who would have backed the party in the past, went straight to the extreme left or right, or abstained. The PCF had chosen the worst of both worlds, and its survival as a serious force came into question. Its weakness had placed it in a humiliating position vis-à-vis the Socialists while long-running enmities dating back to the tribal warfare of Stalinists and Trotskyites stood in the way of a link with the far left. The plight of the party that had once stood as the beacon of the working class spoke volumes about the changed state of a nation where the unemployed outnumber trade union members, and where business rules the roost – even if not always with all the success its captains would wish for.

6

BUSINESS MATTERS

As the twenty-first century dawned, French business seemed to be on a roll. Company chieftains became stars. Stolid old companies were shaken up. Privatisation continued under the left as it had under the right. The Paris Bourse boomed. L'Oréal was the biggest cosmetic company on earth, making its septuagenarian principal shareholder the richest non-royal woman in the world with a fortune put at more than 100 billion francs. After a buying spree that took it to Hollywood, Vivendi Universal became the world's second largest media and entertainment outfit, and its subsidiary, Canal+, was the main pay-television service in Europe. The Elf oil group formed part of the world's fourteenth biggest company after merging with the Franco-Belgian, TotalFina. Electricité de France (EdF) acquired energy concerns across Europe. AXA was a major international force in financial services. LMVH led the market in luxury goods, with its boss, Bernard Arnault, reckoned to be sitting on 90 billion francs. Pinault-Printemps-Redoute, headed by the country's third richest person, François Pinault, became an international retailer, buying the Gucci fashion house along the way.

The French ran water systems in America, waste collection in Asia and trains in England. Alcatel reorganised itself at the cutting edge of communications. France-Télécom snapped up third generation wireless licences, and bought mobile telephone businesses in Britain and Germany. Air France turned long-running losses into a profit of more than 400 million euros. Airbus Industrie, the European group based in

Toulouse in which France plays a major role, soared as Boeing floundered. Alstom sold power and transport equipment in seventy countries. Banque Nationale de Paris (BNP) took over Paribas to become the biggest bank by market capitalisation in mainland Europe. Michelin made a fifth of the world's tyres; Renault saved Nissan. Internet companies sprouted, and Riviera high-tech parks aimed to become second Silicon Valleys. As growth shot up towards 4 per cent, the feeling spread that France was on its way to overtake Germany as the motor of Europe's economy.

A couple of years on, things looked quite different though French executives were well enough regarded to win a *Business Week* poll to pick Europe's best managers, with Gérard Mestrallet of the Suez group in first place. But there was no mistaking the downturn which went well beyond the bursting of the Internet bubble, thought that had its effect. Growth fell steadily to only 0.2 per cent in 2003. The trade surplus shrank. Unemployment rose to 9.8 per cent. State debts reached 63 per cent of GDP. France broke the euro-zone currency rules on budget deficits. The main Bourse index crashed. France-Télécom racked up steep losses and huge debt as a result of prices it paid in the telecoms boom. Alcatel laid off 40,000 staff, and AXA's shares hit a five-year low. Canal+ was deep in red ink. Alstom recorded its first loss since it was floated in 1998. Michelin axed 7,500 jobs. Though it forged a merger with KLM to make it one of the world's biggest lines, Air France saw profits slump. The Channel Tunnel company, Eurotunnel, ran into financial trouble as did EuroDisney. Despite making the Queen Mary 2 and high speed trains, the giant Alsthom group needed an eight billion euros state bail-out to stay in business. Smaller firms shed staff and shut factories, sapping public morale as unemployment stayed stubbornly close to 10 per cent. A third of the French said they felt close to the aims of the anti-globalisation movement which gathered 100,000 people for a rally on a stony plateau in the centre of the country.

Against that background, French big businessmen take a more cautious view of the world than in their glory days. Even as they saw signs that things might be getting better in 2002, they were careful to speak of 'a soft recovery' and 'a mediocre outlook'. Investment was flat, with falling orders for everything from trucks and machine tools to telecommunications equipment. Banks toughened credit terms; clients took longer and longer to pay. A downturn in Germany raised the question of whether France could grow while its principal partner stagnated.

Still, there was no doubt of the changes which the turn-of-century experience had brought. Companies which had once been content to exist as national monoliths were imbued with American management techniques, and saw their futures in global terms. Forty per cent of the shares in French companies were in foreign hands. As one American observer put it: enterprises like Vivendi, Renault or AXA are 'global companies with headquarters in France'. But the ups and downs they went through in the space of a few years raise questions that go to the root of French identity. Having become international players did not mean the shooting stars of 2000 stopped being French, or that they fully relinquished their Gallic frame of mind.

As they launched themselves into the world, the country's business leaders performed like seventeenth century musketeers racing to outstrip the competition. Overnight, they came to see themselves as world-beaters, dazzling others – and themselves – with their superior intelligence and bravado. But stock markets get suspicious all too easily, and figures are implacable. The more global a company is, the more open to scrutiny it is from international investors, and the more share prices fall the less deferential the domestic audience becomes. Punching above your weight is harder to do in business than in politics or diplomacy.

Few French firms figure among world leaders in absolute size, or revenue. Many successful enterprises tend to be niche players, even if their niches can be sizeable. German companies may not have the pizzazz of their counterparts west of the Rhine, but they are often bigger and look more solid. The *Fortune* magazine list of world companies for 2001 put six German outfits in the top 30, compared to two from France – TotalFinaElf and AXA. The oil firm was the only French entry in the *Business Week* index of the 50 leading companies for 2002. In a ranking of most respected companies by the *Financial Times* and the consultants, PWC, L'Oréal was the top French entry in thirty-first place – three French firms figured in the top 50, plus Airbus, compared to seven from Germany and five from Britain. When it came to individual business leaders in that listing, Vivendi's boss, Jean-Marie Messier was placed twenty-first, one rung below Carlos Ghosn of Nissan. Three months later, Messier unveiled the biggest corporate loss France had ever seen. The story was one which, in high-profile mode, could stand as symbolic of what can happen when French business set out to conquer the world.

Nobody has ever accused Jean-Marie Messier of lacking ambition, or chutzpah. The chubby-cheeked son of a Grenoble accountant, he says he was so insulted when a school teacher told him his maths was not good enough to get him into a top college that he worked so diligently that he got into two – the École Polytechnique and ENA. After working on the early French privatisation programme and then at the Lazard Frères investment bank in Paris, he was appointed to run a shambolic conglomerate called Compagnie Générale des Eaux (CGE) which had 2,700 subsidiaries in everything from casinos to laundry services. Messier, then 30, hacked away at the corporate undergrowth, and emerged with two core operations under the new name of Vivendi. One, Vivendi Environment, was in traditional public works and services – it supplies water to 110 million people, collects the rubbish of 70 million; provides energy for 40,000 clients, mainly local communes, and runs 4,000 local transport systems round the world, including the Connex train service in southern England. Solid as those revenues were, the glamour was in the other branch, which became Vivendi Universal, and amassed an ever-expanding media and entertainment empire stretching through films, television, music, the Internet, books and the press on both sides of the Atlantic.

Messier was known as J2M for his initials. As he made Vivendi a soaraway company, a satirical television show dubbed him J6M for *Jean-Marie Messier, moi-même maître du monde* (Jean-Marie Messier, myself, master of the world). The show was on Canal+ which Vivendi owned. The way the chairman took J6M as the title for a book showed he had a sense of humour, but it may also have been a nickname he relished as befitting his ambitions. After buying Universal Studio and its big music business for $34 billion in 2000 in a final negotiating session that lasted till 3am, Vivendi Universal jumped ahead of Rupert Murdoch's News Corporation and stood behind only AOL Time Warner in its sector. In short order, it then purchased a leading Internet music services provider, mp3.com, and the big American educational publisher, Houghton Mifflin. At the end of 2001, Vivendi bought the film and television divisions of the sizeable USA Networks cable operation for $10.3 billion, installing its heavyweight boss, Barry Diller, at the head of the merged film and television operation.

His vision was to bring together content and delivery systems in a seamless high-tec whole. Vivendi moved another step forward by taking a $1.5 billion stake in a US satellite system, EchoStar satellite system, with six million subscribers. Universal's film, *A Beautiful Mind*, won the Oscar for the best picture of 2002. In Europe, Messier conducted running battles with Murdoch, who was said to have hung up on him during an argument about Vivendi's 25 per cent stake in his Sky satellite television station, which the French company subsequently sold. Canal+, France's biggest film producer, expanded in digital services across the continent. The group acquired fresh assets at home, including the venerable Olympia music hall in Paris. Its subsidiary, Cegetel, became the country's largest private mobile telephone operator. Its Internet services included a big directory service, Scoop, and the Vizzavi joint venture with Britain's Vodafone. In a knife-edge battle with the French government, Messier got the price Vivendi would pay for a third generation mobile telephone licence cut to an eighth of the level it had bid at an auction at the height of the telecoms bubble.

As Vivendi Environment provided a strong flow of cash, the seemingly unstoppable Messier proclaimed Paris to be a mere suburb of New York. He moved into a $17.5 million duplex apartment high above Park Avenue, and proposed a 2 billion euro stock option plan for himself and senior executives. But, by the beginning of 2002, investors, particularly in the US, started to grow concerned not only at the breakneck speed with which Vivendi was moving but also at the lack of information they were getting. Even the Chairman admitted that 'the pace of change in our company has made us difficult to follow'. In the first two months of the year, the share price dived by a quarter. A stock sale fell flat, with the underwriters having to step in to absorb a third of the offer. Despite some big films from Universal, its music division – the largest in the world – was hit by declining demand. Canal+ failed to expand its subscriber base for the first time in 2002; a venture into pay-TV in Italy had to be abandoned, and the company sold to Rupert Murdoch; Vizzavi fell well short of expectations; and Scoop required a provision of 280 million euros.

In March 2002, Vivendi declared the biggest loss in French corporate history – 13.6 billion euros – as it was obliged to write off large amounts of goodwill booked during its acquisitions. Messier hardly endeared himself to investors by saying that, since he had done his acquisitions mainly with Vivendi shares, there had been no real destruction of value, as if paper losses somehow did not count. To add to the company's woes, Messier's tactics were far from clear, as he first denied any intention to sell part of Vivendi Environment to raise cash – and then moved towards doing exactly that.

He also set off a storm by declaring that 'Franco-French cultural exception is dead'. With Canal+ and its other media properties in France, Vivendi was particularly important to those who see their country as a standard bearer against the spread of American-English popular entertainment. The new culture minister warned in May 2002 that foreign acquisition of the company would 'threaten the cultural diversity to which we are so attached'. Messier said all he meant by his remark was to express his belief in multi-cultural globalism. But the television station's position of Canal+ as France's biggest cinema producer made domestic film-makers very nervous about any synergies it might exploit with Universal and Barry Diller. France would also have been unsettled if Messier backed American attempts to break down national cinema quotas such as those imposed by Paris. In the spring of 2002, the Canal+ boss, Pierre Lescure, was sacked. Given the scale of the station's losses, this gave investors some cheer, but it raised an outcry in the French cultural world where Lescure had many friends and protégés. Lionel Jospin expressed concern, and some Socialists wanted to make it an issue in the electoral campaign. Staff took over the station for a while, and a demonstration forced Messier to use the back door when the broadcasting regulator called him in for questioning.

The heat soon rose further when the application of American accounting rules pushed Vivendi Universal's loss even higher. As the firm's debts rose, the ratings agency, Standard & Poor said it was close to a 'credit cliff'. With the share price 40 per cent down on the year, the former owners of companies Vivendi had acquired started to cash in their shares at preferential rates or to grow restive. For the first time, Messier faced a hostile annual general meeting which rejected the executive stock option plan – the company said electronic voting machines had been tampered with, but the Chairman still got a 5 billion euro salary and bonus payment. Talk of a take-over bid, possibly by foreign companies, did the rounds, leading the new government to say it would seek to block any attempt by non-French predators to force the dismemberment of the Vivendi empire – apart from Canal+, it did not want the group's municipal services round France to be run by outsiders.

'With meticulous care, I set myself to try never to be found wanting in whatever I do, in small matters as in big ones,' Vivendi's Chairman had written in his book, *J6M*. His critics thought the trouble was that he had been dazzled by the big picture, seeing himself as the equivalent of one of the Oscar winners his company employs. The influential former head of AXA, Claude Bébéar, spoke openly of a problem of decision-making at Vivendi, and the need for change. It was hard to see synergies between the different parts of the empire, and the attractions of a break-up were evident, with the sale of a big slice in Vivendi Environment a first step. A board meeting in New York at the end of May 2002 set up a watchdog committee of directors to supervise Messier. In his email to staff only three months earlier, the Chairman had sought to reassure them by reflecting: 'We also have to understand that all speculation eventually comes to an end, and that end is much closer when absurdly low levels (of share prices) are reached. The only solution is to hang in there.' By the summer, American shareholders, headed by the Bronfman family, which had sold Universal to Vivendi for shares, were insistent that the would-be mogul from Paris must go. Amid a row about his severance package, J6M resigned and the deflation of the company began. He said he was leaving in order to save the company. True enough, but his self-confidence and refusal to accept that he could not be master of the world smacked all too much of the arrogance of the elite ranks from which he came – but which, in the end, proved no match for the power of the market he had presumed to lead by his brilliance.

Despite the problems which Vivendi and its peers ran into, their engagement with the world promised a distinct break with the traditional French way of doing business which had not, in the main, welcomed innovation and competition, particularly from abroad. In the 1980s and 1990s, France's competitiveness had lagged behind in world rankings, and its economy remained less open and deregulated than many others. The authorities in Paris might pay lip-service to free trade, but protectionism and state regulation lie deep in the French soul. It was Louis XIV's mighty minister, Jean-Baptiste Colbert, who gave his name to the doctrine of the state ring-fencing the economy from foreign depredations – and his spirit lived on into the late twentieth century. Companies speak the correct management school language and benefit from a surge in overseas investment in the Bourse – at least until the market turned down in 2001. But old ways die hard. The picture is more nuanced than prophets of a brave new business world suggest, which may be a relief to a country whose political leaders reject the 'Anglo-Saxon' market economy, and which makes a national hero of a man who trashes a McDonald's.

In keeping with this national mode, business in France has been conducted inside a charmed circle. The question now is whether this can last, or whether the price of French companies launching themselves on the world will be to force them to act under 'Anglo-Saxon' external constraints which can only make life a lot harder for their managements. In some ways, the internationalisation is evident – from the globetrotting chairmen and chief executives to the introduction of *le business plan* and *le benchmarking* into companies. As one executive remarked, it is no longer enough to invite American analysts to a three-star dinner; nowadays, it's more likely to be a dawn breakfast meeting with a video conference link to New York. But, until France develops pension funds as big investment vehicles or more people invest in the Bourse – currently only some 12 per cent do so – its companies are going to need all the foreign capital they can attract. In 2002, more than half the shares in major enterprises such as TotalFinaElf, Vivendi Universal, AXA, the pharmaceutical company, Aventis, and the water, waste and energy group, Suez, were held by non-French investors.

The implications of this are obvious, but were not recognised for some time by the media or the public at large. There was, for instance, a sense of national shock when it was realised that an attempt by the BNP to take over two other banks would be decided by how investment managers sitting in New York or London voted on the basis of the shares their funds and banks held in all three. The foreigners will apply the judgements they would make about domestic stocks in their home countries. They want representation and responsive management in return for their money. They will not sit by quietly and let the business establishment go its own way, as American fund managers showed with their assault on Messier. Large domestic shareholders have also been showing themselves more ruthless with non-performing senior executives, a dozen of whom lost their jobs in the last three months of 2001, leading *Le Monde* to conclude that French bosses were now sitting on 'an ejector seat'

At the same time, another pressure for change appeared from French small shareholders attracted to the Bourse during the boom of the late 1990s who turned increasingly vociferous when the market slumped. Investors in the Eurotunnel project set the pattern by showing up at a company meeting in Paris to tear apart copies of the annual report. In 2004, led by a financial tip-sheet journalist, they voted out the board. Another group, the Association for the Defence of Minority Shareholders (Adam), has had some success in influencing a couple of big companies, and was a vocal critic of Messier. 'The powers of chairmen and chief executives are enormous because their companies are becoming multinationals with huge capitalisations,' says its leader. 'It is indispensable that these growing powers are counter-balanced by the strengthening of controls. But these counter-balancing powers do not work; neither at board level nor from shareholders.'

For, against the pressures for change, French companies still have considerable defences in depth, starting with the near-universal practice of the same person acting as both chairman and chief executive – *le Président-Directeur-Général* (PDG). Though they have grabbed headlines, small shareholder revolts are still rare. The number of annual general meetings at which management has come under attack doubled between 1995 and 2001, but only to 1.42 per cent. As Colette Neuville, chairwoman of Adam, reflected, the revolt of small shareholders is a sideshow since 'most PDGs arrive with the majority of the votes in their pockets'. Shareholder lists are a closely-guarded company secret, making it hard for critics to rally support.

Almost 60 per cent of leading firms quoted on the Paris Bourse use double voting rights for a favoured few as a means of bolstering control. Large groups hold stakes in one another, and the same men sit on one another's boards to offer mutual understanding. Non-executive directors more often see their role as being the support management rather than control it on behalf of shareholders – and the corporate accounting scandals across the Atlantic in 2002 provided plenty of ammunition for those who resisted change. In keeping with the Catholic taboo about money, family firms which have prospered in recent years in everything from retailing and battery farming to medicine and starch guard their positions and privacy jealously – 'it is not done to show off one's wealth', as the sociologist, Michel Pinçon, observes. Hostile takeovers are not part of the French model, particularly if they come from abroad. Globalisation is best if it serves as a one-way street, enabling firms from the Hexagon to move into America, Britain or Asia, but with a red light in the other direction to protect the domestic bastion.

So, despite their differences, Jacques Chirac and Lionel Jospin stood shoulder-to-shoulder in slowing down the opening up of France's electricity market to foreign suppliers whatever the European Union treaty said. In 2002, France played a leading part in resisting the lifting of tax breaks for road hauliers as ordained by the Commission in Brussels. European law on insurance companies which went into effect in 1994 had still not been applied in France eight years later in order to help the country's 3,000 mutual societies. Paris worked hard to delay liberalisation of European postal services till 2009, and ensured this would affect only 10 per cent of the turnover of *La Poste*, one of only two European services not to have been privatised. In May 2002, the internal market Commissioner named France as the worst country at implementing laws on the single market. Compensation paid by the state to Air France for losses because of the 11 September attack continued long after American air space was re-opened, and was almost as much as received by British Airways which ran three times as many flights across the Atlantic. France pays out more state aid per person in work than any other major European Union country and almost as much industrial aid as a percentage of gdp as Germany, with all its problems in the backward former Communist east.

Within the protected flexagon, the public sector naturally looms large, employing a quarter of the country's workforce, many of them assured jobs for life. Public spending in France rose from 49.5 per cent of gdp in 1990 to between 51 and 53 per cent at the beginning of the new century, while falling elsewhere in Europe. Despite privatisations, the state still has majority control of 1,500 companies, employing 5 per cent of France's workers but producing a profit margin of only 3 per cent. Nationalised companies account for 15 per cent of the gross national product – four times as much as in Britain. At the huge state electricity firm, EdF, one expert forecast that applying the rigours of privatisation might deprive 30 per cent of the workers of their jobs. An economist, Jacques Marseille, calculates that, if France ran its public sector along the lines of other European countries, it would spend almost 15 per cent, or 107 billion euros, less. He reckons that France could get rid of a million civil servants and still operate as efficiently as Germany. 'Which private sector firm has not been able to cut its expenditure by 10 to 15 per cent in recent years?' asks the magazine, *L'Express*. Cushioning the introduction of the 35-hour week cost an estimated 26 billion euros in 2000-1, or a third of the income tax collected in those two years. Each year, the top audit committee comes up with a long list of wastage of public funds, from unnecessary jobs to botched construction projects. But, as we will see, the state holds a very special place in France, and those whom it employs benefit accordingly.

Public service workers enjoy a privileged position denied to the increasingly tough world of the private sector. Under the Jospin government, hostile reactions from teachers and Finance Ministry staff to reform proposals led to the sacking of the two ministers concerned – one of them an old and close friend of the Prime Minister. France is the only European Union country not to deduct income tax at source in large part because staff at the tax offices say it would mean too much work although they are 40 per cent more numerous than in Britain, Holland or Spain. In the run-up to the 2002 election, one public sector union chief threatened a general strike if whatever government emerged tried to reform the welfare system, or affect his own movement's power within it. At the same time, the growing imbalance between old and young is putting a major strain on the pensions system, while the main social security funds plunged into the red just as Chirac was winning re-election.

The big state has to be paid for. Tax takes 45 per cent of gdp. Though the government's income is reduced by evasion and low levels in the bottom bands, the top rate at the time of the election in 2002 was 52.5 per cent – 12.5 per cent higher than in Britain. That pushes governments to raise funds by deficit financing, high levels of indirect taxes, a wealth levy, and big welfare contributions. State companies are allowed to run up debts that make Vivendi look prudent. In one of its first acts, the Jospin government increased company tax from 36.6 to 41.6 per cent The excellent welfare system requires high social security charges – at one point, AXA reckoned it was paying more in this way than in wages to its workers in France. Taxes and social security contributions from employers are among the highest in Europe. Businesses say this inhibits growth and stops them hiring more workers. Start-up firms grouse about the time and paperwork needed to get into business; the number of new firms that come into being each year remains static at around 175,000 – the official who runs the agency that encourages company creation reckons the rate should be 100,000 a year higher. A survey by the Economist Intelligence Unit puts France behind the Netherlands, Britain and Germany among European countries as the best place to do business.

To escape the burden, a growing number of small businesses began to move their operations across the Channel during the 1990s, attracted by lower levels of tax social security contributions and employment flexibility at the other end of the Eurostar line. 'Explain to me why it is better to be unemployed in France than a worker in England,' asked one businessman, who reckoned that his profit potential quadrupled by moving his electronics firm from Paris to Kent. Such was the influx that the *Daily Mail* reported concern among Conservative MPs at the number of young French job-seekers crossing the Channel. A hairdresser from Valence in the Rhône Valley used her European rights to register her business in Wales while keeping its operation in France; she saved more than 100,000 francs a year in the process. Such people earned a furious rebuke from the Labour Minister who insisted, 'If you want to cut French hair, then you have to be in the French tax regime.'

According to a calculation by the OECD, it takes the earnings of the average French worker from 1 January to 12 June to cover all annual payments to the state: in the USA, the end date is 11 April, in Britain 9 May. Since 1965, the period needed to cover all taxes has gone up by thirty-six working days in France, twelve days in the United States and seventeen in Britain. The bias towards indirect taxes is socially regressive, particularly for the unemployed and those on the minimum wage. On his re-election in 2002, Jacques Chirac pledged a 5 per cent cut in income tax during the year at the start of a rolling five-year programme of reductions. The snag with this was that, at a summit in Barcelona earlier in the year, the President had committed France to the European Union target of eliminating budget deficits by 2004. With slower growth reducing government tax revenue in any case, and a programme of spending on police and prisons to meet his law-and-order pledges, Chirac faced a major conundrum of how to cut tax and keep to his EU promise. Though ministers spoke of spending cuts, these would take time to implement and the experience of the Juppé years from 1995 to 1997 had shown the dangers of taking a scalpel to public sector expenditure, particularly when the unions were in a feisty mood and the cost of introducing the 35-hour week into the civil service had to be met. So Chirac broke the euro-rules and in 2004, the state debt rose to over a billion euros – 63 per cent of 90p. The President could only see a way out in playing for time, hoping for a strong revival of growth, selling off some more of the state's silver to pad the receipts and handing the poisoned chalice of the Fincance Ministry to his main rival, the ambitious Nicolas Sarkozy, who proclaimed his devotion to creating growth and jobs but was constrained by the President's reluctance to embrace politically sensitive structural reforms.

In the parliamentary election campaign of 1997, the Socialists proclaimed their opposition to the privatisations which had begun during Chirac's first premiership, and had resumed during the prime ministership of Edouard Balladur from 1993 to 1995. Once in office, Jospin's broad left government found itself waving through even bigger sales of state assets than in the past. To assuage the Communists and old Socialists, the P word was avoided – the sales of shares were described not as privatisations but as 'opening up' the capital of nationalised companies to outside investors. The Prime Minister became known for a *Ni Ni* policy – neither nationalisation, as if they were on the cards, not privatisation, as if that was not happening. By temperament and conviction, Jospin was a natural exponent of a command economy, but the pull of the market was too strong. So France Télécom became the biggest stock-market flotation on his watch, launched on Wall Street to the accompaniment of cancan dancers, accordion-players and croissants. The big steel group, Usinor, followed. Then came financial institutions, and the state's holding in a maker of semi-conductors. In its last budget, the government ended its five years in office by selling off motorways in the south and part of a nationalised consumer electronics group.

As in other domains, the French establishment has kept a careful hand on the process. There has always been the search for a hard core of reliable investors to ensure privatisations maintain control of the companies. At the top, chairmen often come from the small circle that binds the public and the private sector, men who are properly mindful of the continuing role of the state as the source of big contracts and a safety net of succour in times of difficulty. The general approach has been to privatise in instalments, starting with the state selling a quarter or so of shares and disposing of others by stages, thus retaining a decisive voice until late in the game. This means that, while private investors buy into the companies, they lack the final power of decision for a long time. So the Jospin government was able to get rid of the successful head of Air France when he clashed with it, ironically over the pace of privatisation. Some international investors saw this as another case of the administration seeking to have its cake and eat it. When it sold 20 per cent of France Télécom, the government laid down that the new shareholders were to have a say in the appointment of only three of the twenty-one directors. And when the CIC bank, the country's fifth largest, was floated, the majority stake went to a mutual trust, not to a commercial buyer. No wonder one analyst called such partial privatisations an opportunity to buy 'a share in the French civil service'. Still, the process was unstoppable. It even applied to the nationalised bank which, in the 1990s, had epitomised much of what was wrong with the cosy world of finance where the political and business establishment overlapped.

From its stately white building covering a city block beside the Paris Opéra, the Crédit Lyonnais set out to build the equivalent of Germany's all-powerful Deutsche Bank with what the European Commission later called a 'bulimia of investments and acquisitions'. Enthusiastically backed by the Mitterrand regime, it plunged into the property market, and opened its coffers to lending at home and abroad. Its largesse was extended to Robert Maxwell to keep his empire afloat. It advanced $1.3 billion to an Italian waiter turned financial buccaneer, Giancarlo Parretti, to buy the MGM studio in Hollywood – a subsequent investigation by *Fortune* magazine produced an allegation that the loan had been tied to a French bid to sell high-speed trains to Italy, with a senior Italian minister acting as broker. Control was sadly lacking as the bank threw good money after bad. Starting with a single investment outside Paris, one subsidiary ended up owning thirty-six loss-making golf courses, and plunged 1.5 billion francs into a retailing business which racked up a loss of 700 million francs. There were juicy commissions for go-betweens, a 600,000-franc payment through a Swiss subsidiary to an adviser to a Socialist minister in Paris, and a 2-million-franc deposit in a Swiss bank to an editor on the main French state television channel for his help in keeping the press sweet.

French banking was in a crisis at the time. The country was, by international standards, 'overbanked', with too many competitors vying for business. Controls were lax and bad judgements multiplied. Big banks poured 200 billion francs into the increasingly sick property market and other poor investments, often failing to get proper collateral and overestimating rental incomes. In this increasingly difficult environment, the Crédit Lyonnais gave its figures an upward tweak by revaluing assets. That made the gap between the figures on paper and the reality outside all the greater when the final reckoning came. In 1994, the government had no alternative but to step in with an injection of 4.9 billion francs. At that point, losses were estimated at 14 billion francs. A year later, they were put at ten times that figure. By the end of 1997, dozens of judicial inquiries were being conducted into the bank.

The Economist dubbed the affair 'banking's biggest disaster'. The head of another major French bank publicly blamed it on the 'megalomania' of Jean-Yves Haberer, the Crédit Lyonnais boss in its go-go days who was taken into custody in 1998 for questioning over the bank's role in the bankruptcy of a food transport firm. One issue which was rarely raised was how the board, including some leading names, had allowed the bank to race out of control. But then, Haberer was a member of the elite *Inspection des Finances*, and had headed the French Treasury. And which body was charged with supervising France's banks? Why, the Treasury. So he must have known what he was doing.

Even the rescue effort aroused controversy, and not just for its cost to the taxpayers. The European Commission wondered why a state bank in France should be propped up to such a huge degree when its competitors in the private sector were subject to the rigours of the market. The Socialist Finance Minister accused his predecessors of political interference in the sale of assets stripped out of the bad bank to be put into a new company and sold off. The fact that a time limit was set on these sales gave buyers a clear edge. One troubled subsidiary was cleaned up, injected with new capital – and then sold back to the bank without others being able to put in a bid. Another transaction involved a stake Crédit Lyonnais had bought in a holding company controlled by a close friend of Jacques Chirac, the retail king, François Pinault. After Pinault made it plain that he refused to work with a minority shareholder, the Finance Ministry in the Juppé government ordered the outstanding stake to be sold to him for 1.5 billion francs. Since Pinault's holding company is not public, the value of the stake is not known, but estimates put it between 4.5 and 6 billion francs. On top of which, the President's friend got bonds with a face value of 1.5 billion as part of the deal.

With the taxpayers paying off its debts, Crédit Lyonnais returned to profit. But fate seemed to have it in for the bank. It found itself with a $12 billion exposure in Asia as the region crashed in late 1997. Fire, apparently deliberately started in two separate places, ravaged its headquarters in Paris, causing major damage. The sixty cases which arose out of the scandal took an extremely long time to come to court. The Governor of the Bank of France went on trial for his responsibility – he was acquitted. After a tug of war with the US judiciary, the bank paid a $600 million settlement in a case arising from its acquisition of a Californian insurance firm, in which François Pinault's name surfaced again.

Its subsequent privatisation in 1999 showed the care with which the government controls such undertakings. Forty per cent of the shares went to the public while the big Crédit Agricole bank took 10 per cent; the state kept the same amount; French financial institutions took around 20 per cent. To give the ownership a European element, the remaining 10 per cent was handed to the German insurance giant, Allianz. After the slimmed-down bank announced a 75 per cent rise in profits, the government began to negotiate the sale of its stake to Crédit Agricole and Allianz in 2002. A former finance minister who had drawn up the privatisation plan for the bank joined its board. Another non-executive director became Finance Minister in the interim government set up in May, 2002. The overall cost of the rescue of the Crédit Lyonnais was put at 15 billion euros. But now, the French state could leave banking behind, having ensured that no other company in the sector had been able to gain control, with all the threats of consolidation and job losses that would have brought.

The Crédit Lyonnais scandal of the 1990s was only the biggest of a wave of *affaires* that brought prominent business figures to book as investigating magistrates went after corporate chieftains as well as politicians – and, sometimes, both at the same time. By the end of the decade, some fifty chairmen and chief executives of big firms had been fined, gone to prison or were under investigation for illegal behaviour of one kind or another. Among them:

The managing director of one of France's biggest construction firms was charged with the misuse of company funds, and the head of a large retail group was had up for fraud and corruption over alleged bribes to get planning permission for stores from Socialist local government officials.

A major developer was charged with insider dealing, and thirty-six companies were fined for rigging public-works contracts.

The chairman of a leading industrial group was thrown into jail in Belgium for alleged breach of confidence, and then became the target of an international warrant. The boss of one of France's main aircraft manufacturers was the object of another international warrant from Belgium, issued to try to get him to answer questions about alleged bribery. As a result, neither man could travel outside France without risking being arrested.

The head of a large investment bank was charged with falsifying accounts.

A property developer made a video recording telling of buying contracts from the Paris city government – the tape only became public after he died.

The boss of Alcatel–Alsthom, once described as the most powerful private-sector businessman in the country, was given a three-year suspended jail sentence and fined 2 million francs for having had security work at his six-storey home in the Paris suburb of Neuilly paid for from company funds. He was also ordered to pay the money back. Several other big bosses were being investigated for allegedly having used company funds for work on their private homes.

Even such totems of modern French life as television and the national lottery are not sacred: a prominent executive was held in connection with an affair involving rights to screen the weekly lottery draw. Then there are the cases in which the state or its representatives appear to have been remarkably indulgent. The national audit court put at 1.5 billion francs the value of a contract between a state television station and production companies linked to its star presenters which had 'contributed to enriching the companies concerned' but had produced doubtful benefit to the channel. Another report from court, which warned of heavy cost overruns at the main stadium for the 1998 World Cup, noted that the building contract had been signed by the Prime Minister between the two rounds of the 1995 presidential election with a consortium that included a company which also owned the country's main television channel. As it happened, the Premier had just been eliminated from the presidential election, and would soon lose his job, meaning that he would no longer be in a position to sign anything. And, as it also happened, the television channel was widely viewed as having been most supportive of him in his bid for the Élysée.

'Money flowed freely, everybody seemed buyable,' *Le Monde* wrote in a retrospective article after legislation was passed to regulate public works contracts. The activism of the investigating magistrates had a distinct dissuasive effect while tighter government budgets meant there was less money to be syphoned off. Instead of the old-fashioned suitcases of cash, companies operated in more sophisticated ways through offshore fronts in tax havens where no question could be asked. In 2001, a ranking by the monitoring organisation, Transparency International, still put France in only eleventh place for virtue among the fifteen EU members, ahead of Belgium, Portugal, Italy and Greece. The investigators, meanwhile, kept turning over new stones.

At the start of 2002, ninety people were questioned over allegations of tax evasion and money laundering by ready-to-wear clothing firms in Paris. As part of the probe, dozens of banking executives were hauled in – the chairman of the Société Générale had his pockets searched before being interrogated, and the chief executive of another big bank was kept all night in a brightly lit cell, having to hold up his trousers after his belt was taken away. The head of AXA and his predecessor were questioned, and then freed on bail, over an alleged tax evasion scheme. Members of the family that owns the big regional newspaper in Toulouse were given fines and suspended prison sentences after being found guilty of misuse of corporate funds. Magistrates probed contracts for building schools in the Île-de-France and the conditions under which casino licences were granted. In California, allegations surfaced that the Crédit Lyonnais had infringed banking laws in buying a failed American insurance company, and then tried to carry out a cover-up. This long trail of scandal even affected the public transport system so close to French hearts.

On 18 May 1993, President Mitterrand and his former Prime Minister, Pierre Mauroy, ceremonially rode on France's latest high-speed train link, between Paris and the northern city of Lille, which had been Mauroy's political barony as mayor and boss of the Socialist Party for decades. Since the old industrial belt around Lille was suffering economically, Mauroy had been an ardent proponent of building the line as a means of bringing new vigour to the north-east and providing plenty of construction jobs in the process. It would also provide the French section of the Channel Tunnel connection with London. One of Mauroy's successors as Prime Minister, Michel Rocard, had given the go-ahead to build the line in 1988 on the basis of a dossier from the board of the Société Nationale des Chemins de fer Français (SNCF). Rocard said later that he thought the dossier might have been 30–40 per cent accurate in its forecast that rail traffic between Paris and Lille would double once the TGV was in service. In fact, it rose by 2 per cent.

A senior civil servant wrote in a confidential note that some fifty or sixty kilometres of track was not needed, ending a missive on the subject to a colleague with the salutation '*Bon courage*'. A station built in the middle of the countryside had one stopping train a day – except for weekends and public holidays, when it had none. The SNCF noted with satisfaction in 1997 that this station's passenger traffic rose by more than 25 per cent in twelve months – to 480 people.

It took years for the truth to come out. When it did, the Audit

Court concluded that the SNCF had shown the TGV line's prof-
itability at up to twice what could reasonably be expected on the basis
of revenue projections overstated by up to 13 billion francs. If the
politicians and the SNCF were pleased at the building of the line, the
public-works companies were ecstatic. There is no more juicy
prospect for construction firms than a massive state contract, and here
was a 40-billion-franc monster, a major new railway line to be built to
the most modern and demanding specifications. And that was not
all: a subsidiary link was to be laid between the northern TGV and
networks serving the south and west of France. Why spoil things by
competing for contracts? Much simpler to sort things out in private.
An internal note found at one firm put it quite plainly: what was
needed was 'an overall strategy with the other major public-works
companies instead of classic competition'. When an Italian company
refused to join in the price-fixing, it was offered a 'non-participation
fee' of 5 million francs to withdraw. The Italians persisted, only to find
that a tender from a French rival had been mysteriously changed in
handwriting to undercut its offer – after they had both been submitted.

In many cases, it was evident that there was only one serious
tender, and that others had been thrown together without proper
research. Apart from the actual construction of the track, there was
plenty of ancillary jam to be shared around. For some stations, the
Audit Court found that the SNCF had over-estimated costs by 75 per
cent. At the Lille terminus, it contracted for a dozen escalators to be
built; only two saw the light of day, but the railway still paid for all
twelve, only discovering the mistake four years later. Officials scrawled
out acknowledgement of the tenders on pads that looked like casual
café bills. Supposedly secret documents were kept in a cupboard
whose key hung on a nail nearby. That was the degree of care which
a hugely loss-making state enterprise showed over how it spent 20
billion francs of taxpayers' money. The Competition Council spoke of
SNCF officials participating in 'various practices, including understandings', while the Audit Court uncovered internal memos which
showed that the tender-rigging had been known to senior railway
management. Even worse was to come.

After being hauled in by the police and an examining magistrate for
a routine check on his tax affairs, a sub-contractor from Lorraine

who had acted as a bagman blew the gaff. Quizzed about some unusual items in his accounts, he admitted that he had passed SNCF executives such inducements as Porsche, Ferrari and Mercedes cars, jewels worth a million francs, and up to twice as much in cash. One man, alone, had received five cars to keep him sweet. Others had had their rents paid, or received salaries for fictitious jobs invented for their wives. In all, the sub-contractor drew up a list of around sixty SNCF managers who had taken bribes. Since the amount he had paid out exceeded his company's turnover, the assumption was that he had acted as a conduit for other firms anxious to buy work from the railway.

Four years after Mitterrand and Mauroy walked down the flag-decked platform of the Gare du Nord to board the first TGV-Nord train, the Competition Council fined thirty of the country's major public-works firms for having rigged tenders for the construction contracts. The penalties totalled 388 million francs. It was an embarrassment, but the size of the fines was only half what L'Express estimated the corruption had directly cost the SNCF. Lawyers for the railway board reckoned that forty-six separate contracts were involved. Notes seized by police showed that public-works firms were already carving up tenders on the next TGV route, in eastern France.

Once again, the scandal raised questions which went to the heart of the French way of running things. First, there were the politicians. Nobody accused them of doing anything wrong, but the enthusiasm of senior figures in government for the Paris-Lille line gave it a following wind that made it virtually unstoppable. Then there was the way senior figures who were meant to control the project were interlinked. The impression was of the SNCF as a fortress in which the managers held sway with the complaisance of powerful friends in positions of authority. Nothing seemed to affect those inside. After briefly breaking even, the SNCF went on to rack up the second biggest loss of any company in the world in the mid-1990s, with debts accumulated over the years reaching 203 billion francs. When Alain Juppé's government set about trying to introduce serious staff changes and boost productivity in 1995-7, strikes crippled the network. Railway workers were able to draw on a long-held folk image of heroic train-drivers à la Jean Gabin getting the express through on time against all obstacles. That applied to staff who had never stepped on a footplate – in a dinner conversation one night, a middle-class couple insisted that booking clerks had just as much right to early retirement as the drivers. They were all part of the great family of railway workers, *les cheminots*. So the management backed off, and public transport workers won another battle. By 2001, the system's losses had risen to 135 million francs, boosted by the botched introduction of a computerised traffic management system. It also suffered 150,000 days of strikes, double the figure for the previous year – SNCF staff make up 1 per cent of the working population, but accounted for almost a quarter of the number of days lost through stoppages.

In the Socialist governments of 1981 and 1997, Cabinet responsibility for the railways was given to a Communist as if in deference to the train staff's folkloric roots. In 1995, coming from the other side of the political spectrum, Jacques Chirac had tried a rather similar tactic by appointing a former Socialist senior civil servant and state industry boss called Loïk Le Floch-Pringent as chairman of the SNCF. It was a bold move, which some of the new President's advisers opposed. Chirac overruled them. He believed that 'Pink Le Floch', as he had been known in the 1980s, had the right mixture of business acumen and links with the unions to pull the railways back from the brink. The bearded Breton had headed major companies nationalised by the Socialists in 1981 and had later been appointed to run the big state oil concern, Elf. Asked what it was like to be a left-wing boss, Le Floch replied that he knew how to keep his business activities and his personal feelings apart. To set Le Floch off on the right tracks, the government announced a plan to take over 125 billion francs of the railway's debt. The new boss opened negotiations with the unions to cut the 180,000 workforce. Then the reasons why the President's advisers had counselled against appointing him became evident as a huge new scandal broke that would still be running through the courts when Chirac was elected for his second term.

Two months before the election season opened in the spring of 2002, forty-two French business and political figures received hand-delivered packet of documents they could have done without. Inside the envelopes delivered were papers setting out the conclusions of a long-running probe into *l'affaire Elf*, the oil company Le Floch-Pringent had headed from 1989 to 1993. The basic allegation was that, in the first half of the 1990s, 3 billion francs was looted from the state-owned oil company, at the time France's largest firm. That would have made it a big enough case. But the character of Elf, its political links and its top-level contacts gave the scandal a special dimension, making it an affair of state in a country where the state is sacrosanct.

Among those who received the envelopes warning that the recipients were about to be charged were Le Floch-Pringent, and the company's 'Mr Africa', André Tarallo. A lawyer for the Gaullist former Interior Minister, Charles Pasqua, made plain his client was involved even before the papers were sent out in February. Then there was the former Elf number two, Alfred Sirven, a short, squat 75-year-old who had been brought back to France under arrest the previous year after fleeing to the Philippines where he was tracked down by journalists from Paris rather than by the French police. He was thought to know where the Elf bodies were buried, but he remained largely silent, even taking the precaution of swallowing the chip from his mobile telephone as he was nabbed. More shadowy elements were provided by former intelligence agents and the clan of Corsicans who have long played a prominent role in the police, the underworld and France's former colonies. Then there was an international go-between, André Guelfi, known as Dédé la Sardine from the fishing boats he once owned in Africa. Now in his mid-eighties, Guelfi had laid on Elf private planes for Pasqua. He had also persuaded the novelist, Françoise Sagan, to use her influence with François Mitterrand to try to get him to lobby the visiting president of Uzbekistan to give Elf an exploration concession – Sagan had been paid 4 million francs in return, and was subsequently prosecuted by the tax authorities for failing to declare it.

From its foundation in 1965, Elf had been an arm of government, its boss as powerful as a member of the Cabinet. The first chairman was a former Gaullist intelligence chief. As France's colonies became nominally independent, what better channel than Elf to retain the old imperial links? The company had fields in the North Sea and the Middle East and the Americas, but its core was in Francophone Africa, from where it drew 60 per cent of its oil. As Le Floch wrote in a private note, oil and Elf had been France's twin ambassadors there.

Alongside its conventional energy activities, Elf has always maintained very special top-level connections. Le Floch's note named Chirac and Pasqua as the bridgeheads between politics and the company. The firm's operations in France's former colonies provide a convenient cover for spies and political agents. Through a banking subsidiary in Switzerland, it was in the habit of paying 'royalties' of up to 150 million francs a year each to various African leaders. The dangers of falling out of favour were shown vividly in the Republic of the Congo, where Elf produced 70 per cent of the oil output, and paid royalties that amounted to 40 per cent of the country's budget. When a friendly President lost power in 1993, his successor brought in an American firm which paid a higher royalty. Four years later, an invasion by the former leader turned the clock back. Two months after returning to power, the restored ruler conferred with the chairman of Elf in Paris before seeing Jacques Chirac. To the south, Elf had also invested time and money in Angola, sending a member of the National Assembly to talk to rebels and then celebrating the discovery of a huge offshore oil field with the government. But it is in Gabon, to the north of the Congo, that Elf really came into its own as a state within a state, blending business, *raison d'état* and politics.

Its relationship has been particularly close with Gabon's long-time dictator, Omar Bongo, the unpleasant figure picked as his country's ruler in 1967 by De Gaulle's African adviser, Jacques Foccart. During Bongo's decades in power, his country's oil riches have not saved it from piling up a mountain of debt, while the President himself has become a byword for repression. He also hit the headlines briefly for his use of 'models' flown out from the metropole who reported that he did not use a condom, setting off a flurry of speculation that he might have Aids which provoked a diplomatic incident in 1995. Bongo belongs very firmly to the ranks of dictators for whom France acted as a protective godfather over the decades, using his country, in return, as a base for military and intelligence operations. He makes no bones about his debt to the Hexagon: his remark about Africa without France being like a car without a driver was much quoted by defenders of neo-colonialism. France accounts for three-quarters of foreign investment in Gabon, and its political parties, especially the Gaullists, have long found its capital of Libreville a handy transit point for illicit funding, the 'black chests' of the oil company acting as useful conduits. In some years Gabon provided more than three-quarters of Elf's profit. 'Here in Paris, we don't need to know too much of what goes on in Gabon,' a top executive at the firm once told me. 'But what we do know is that it is very good for us as a company.'

Despite its strong Gaullist connections, the oil company ingratiated itself with the 'caviar left' court round Mitterrand, among other friendly gestures, buying the country house of the president's golfing partner, and letting him remain in residence. It also employed a dashing, dark-haired lady called Christine Deviers-Joncour, whom it set up in a 17-million-franc Left Bank apartment where she held lavish parties, and enjoyed a 200,000-franc monthly allowance. Deviers-Joncour was the mistress of Roland Dumas, a long-time Mitterrand aide a quarter of a century older than her who was Foreign Minister from 1984 to 1986 before going on to become chairman of the Constitutional Court. As Le Floch said, the way Elf operated was the result of 'interweaving' its activities with the French state and, as a man who moved seamlessly through top jobs in nationalised industries after the Socialists took power in 1981, this is a subject on which he may be considered an expert. 'I spoke to ministers as equals,' he recalled. Politicians made such frequent use of the company's private jets that it became known in their circles as Air Elf.

Among Le Floch's social acquaintances was a Paris nightclub queen, Régine, who introduced him to his Algerian-German wife. He also met Régine's brother, a textile magnate called Maurice Bidermann, known as 'the King of the Sentier' after the Paris rag-trade district. The two men became friends: the future Elf boss, who was then a civil servant, acted as arbitrator in a financial dispute in which he ruled for the businessman. Bidermann had ambitious plans to expand in America – one lunchtime, I was among a group of journalists invited to a smart Paris restaurant to eat *langoustines au beurre blanc* and be told how his company had a new international vocation. When his expansion failed to live up to expectations, Bidermann found succour both from the Crédit Lyonnais, and from Elf, where his friend, Le Floch, was in charge. The oil company sank money into the textile firm, and Bidermann showed his gratitude by inviting Le Floch and his wife on holidays in the United States, including a stay in the Hamptons.

The connection would, however, set the fuse ticking under Le Floch and Elf. A stock market investigation into the textile empire was sparked off by a complaint from an American investor which led to a judicial investigation. It was headed by a formidable magistrate called Eva Joly, who had come to Paris as an au pair girl from Norway before marrying and taking up the law. Joly was one of the new breed of investigators who believed in throwing aside the old taboos and pursuing wrong-doers however highly placed they might be. In the process she and her colleagues made themselves utterly unpopular with the establishment in France. The chairman of one big company told me that the magistrates were all the children of the 1968 student revolt out to destroy French society. Another businessman noted that Eva Joly, who was investigating the Crédit Lyonnais as well as Elf, was not of French origin, and that her colleague, Laurence Vichnievsky, and one of the earliest judicial diggers, Renaud van Ruymbeke, did not sound very French. The chairman of the giant Alcatel group blamed his problems with the law on a 'cultural gap' between him and the examining magistrate. But the legal lions showed no signs of relaxing the pressure. When one of them, Thierry Pierre-Jean, left the judiciary to join the European Parliament, he warned: 'The magistrates are determined, and nothing will stop them.'

Joly and Vichnievsky needed all their determination on the trail that led to the delivery of the forty-two envelopes in 2002. Along the way, they had to be given bodyguards because of death threats. They worked in cramped offices without proper back-up. From time to time, political tensions within the magistrature threatened to explode as politically-appointed judicial administrators wavered. But the probe gathered steam after two Elf executives told Joly the investment in the Bidermann group had been made at Le Floch's insistence. A right-wing victory in the 1993 legislative election had cost Le Floch his job at Elf, and the new Chairman, Philippe Jaffré, decided to clean out the stables, launching legal proceedings against the previous senior management.

By then, Floch had walked out on his wife, who received a settlement of 19 million francs, apparently courtesy of Elf. According to the former Madame Le Floch, her husband ditched her on Mitterrand's instructions because she knew too many of Elf's secrets as the result of accompanying him on his international trips and attending top-level dinners at which business was done. Before the marriage broke up, the President invited her to a dinner at his private home – though she sat opposite Mitterrand, she says nobody spoke to her. After keeping quiet for ten years, she published a book to deny that the 19 million francs had been blackmail money – and to hit back at her former husband's remark that she had been the worst mistake of his life.

As the new head of the SNCF moved in to the job Chirac had given him in 1995, Joly was going to work on his friend, Maurice Bidermann, raiding his office and home and calling the portly businessman in for questioning. At the first session, the one-time King of the Sentier complimented Joly on her dress sense. Second time around, he gave her a book inscribed 'to my magistrate'. Such gestures did him no good. At their third encounter, Joly locked Bidermann up, accusing him of having taken out a backdated insurance policy on a factory which had burnt down. The policy, written by an offshore Caribbean company, allegedly had Elf's backing.

While Bidermann was held in jail, the judiciary and the police delved into Elf's international connections and, in particular, its African subsidiaries. Ten executives were hauled in – a couple of others either skipped the country or refused to come across the border from Switzerland to be interrogated. The head of Elf Gabon was questioned. Omar Bongo and the President of Congo sent emissaries to Paris to find out what was going on. Then the magistrate called in Le Floch himself – just after he had announced his restructuring plan for the railways.

At the end of twelve hours of questioning, he was taken to one of the single-occupancy cells in the Santé prison in Paris kept for special inmates and the mentally ill. There, he was allowed to retain his own clothes, but was forbidden scarves, ties, belts, paper handkerchiefs or a bath towel larger than 1.2 metres square. The Appeal Court refused to free him. Joly said she feared he might try to intimidate witnesses or arrange for the disposal of embarrassing documents. Le Floch was accused of having abused his position as chairman and chief executive to seek 'enrichment of himself, his family and friends' through Elf's Swiss and African subsidiaries. He had to resign from the SNCF, and occupied his time teaching bridge to a fellow inmate of La Santé.

While Le Floch languished behind the twenty-foot prison walls for six months before being let out on bail, other intriguing aspects of the case peeped out from the shadowlands surrounding the company. Allegations of corruption and corner-cutting surfaced in connection with deals in Spain and Venezuela. A secret company payroll discovered in Geneva included French politicians and journalists. There was also a scheme by which Elf was said to have been a channel for bribes connected to the sale of French frigates to Taiwan in which Deviers-Joncour was used to try to persuade her ministerial lover to get France to lift its arms embargo on the island. Even more exotically, a confidence trickster from the Ivory Coast by the name of Anna Rose 'Lise' Thiam, surfaced, boasting of knowing Le Floch well. After she was arrested on fraud charges, *Le Monde* reported the finding of a note in her car signed 'Loïk' suggesting that he had given her money. A former refinery manager said he had been threatened with death over a disagreement about an investment in the North Sea. There was talk of Masonic links, and a computer containing details of payments made by a company foundation was stolen – rumours said it might contain evidence of half a million francs paid to a prominent politician.

Raids on company headquarters turned up sheaves of incriminating documents – Elf felt confident enough not to have engaged in Enron-style shredding but some sensitive papers later disappeared from a police station. Through it all, the Africa connection kept surfacing. A company came to light run by the chairman of Elf Gabon, André Tarallo, which seemed to serve no purpose except to pass large sums of money through obscure financial channels. Tarallo, an Énarque who had known Jacques Chirac for decades, was investigated for misusing corporate funds, and had to put up 10 million francs in bail. Among other things, he was reported to have bought a luxury villa in Corsica for 90 million francs and to have spent 45 million on improving three of his homes: there was immediate speculation that he was acting as a front for Elf-friendly African potentates. Then there was the matter of an unexplained $2.5 million payment into a Swiss bank account called 'Collette' – the name of Tarallo's wife. According to the fixer, Dédé the Sardine, who talked after five weeks in preventive detention, the payment was part of the proceeds of a $20 million commission paid by Elf for a deal in Venezuela.

As the revelations dripped out, the spotlight edged towards the President of Gabon. Acting on a request from Eva Joly, a Geneva magistrate blocked an account in the British Virgin Islands where Bongo had deposited funds. The Elf Gabon chairman broke his silence to say that the Collette account had been to buy a plane for a private airline in Gabon. In a long telephone conversation to Jacques Chirac, Bongo threatened economic sanctions in retaliation to what he saw as attacks on his country's sovereignty. Taking up his pen, under his habitual pseudonym of 'Makaya', he wrote an article in Gabon's main newspaper, saying the French were 'desperately trying to pick the nits in the President's head', and describing Eva Joly as their 'Norwegian bird [who] smells of salt cod'.

Philippe Jaffré, who later left Elf after it was taken over by TotalFina, was scathing about Le Floch when questioned by the investigating magistrates. 'All imaginable methods were used to remove funds from Elf in the time of my predecessor,' he said. While denying the political payments mentioned by Le Floch and Tarallo, Jaffré did acknowledge the use of go-betweens to secure contracts, and payments which followed 'procedures aimed at ensuring the discretion wished for by the countries concerned'. For his part, Le Floch brushed aside allegations that the oil firm helped to pay for his château in Normandy as well as for everything from hundreds of compact discs to his garden furniture. He said that, if others used company funds on his behalf, it was not at his behest. He blamed colleagues for shuffling money through Swiss and American bank accounts without his knowledge. His successors at Elf would have to answer for their actions one day, he warned darkly.

In 2001 – French justice moves very slowly in high-profile cases – Le Floch came to trial together with Roland Dumas and his mistress. Le Floch, now 58, got three and a half years in prison and a fine of 2.5 million francs for misuse of company funds. On the same charge, Deviers-Joncour, 54, who had written a book about her experiences entitled *The Whore of the Republic*, was sent down for three years, half of the term suspended, and fined 1.5 million while Dumas, the 79-year-old former Foreign Minister and head of the country's highest court, was initially sentenced to jail and a big fine. The verdict was reversed on appeal, but the glimpse France had been given into the scandal could not be erased.

Further trials followed which earned Le Floch, Tarallo and Sirven additional prison sentences of up to five years. Running through the whole affair was a suggestion of a game within the game as insiders not only profited directly, but also syphoned off part of the enormous sums Elf was secretly circulating for bribes and commissions. Alfred

Sirven was reported to have admitted under questioning that he had pocketed part of the money he handled. *L'Express* said he had put aside 200 million francs in Liechtenstein before escaping to the Philippines. According to the magazine, the money was then taken to Switzerland in cash in an armoured truck, and half of it moved to Manila by a French former policeman, who acknowledged knowing Sirven but said they met by accident in the Philippine capital.

Even more intriguing was the matter of an alleged payment to the German Christian Democrats, perhaps suggested by Mitterrand, to help 'my friend' Helmut Kohl. Le Floch told the German magazine, *Die Zeit,* of 'high-level political talks' with German leaders about the purchase by Elf of a refinery at Leuna in former East Germany. That deal was said to have been accompanied by large payments that found their way into the treasury of the Chancellor's party. At the end of 2001, a parliamentary inquiry in Berlin found no evidence to back up the allegations. But the equivalent of £25 million was moved out of Elf's coffers, supposedly in connection with the Leuna contract through a series of bank accounts in Switzerland and Liechtenstein. If the money did not end up in Germany, the question was where it was, and who was sitting on the cash. A French former secret service agents suspected of involvement was sought, and a German intermediary arrested.

When the 42 envelopes were delivered in February 2002, it was evident that the case had years to run. Acting as a recurrent reminder of the corruption that had been conducted at the apex of the state and business, it could only deepen the cynicism of the French towards the business–political nexus around their rulers. There was also a final indignity for the oil company. In the summer of 2002, the TotalFinaElf group announced that the 2,500 Elf petrol stations in France would be reduced to 300 selling cut-price fuel to compete with supermarket outlets. Elf garages on motorways would be put under the Total name. Even its logo would be redesigned.

The cast in the Elf affair was pretty unappealing, but the gallery of dubious characters who have popped out of France's business undergrowth in the last decade does contain one figure whose exploits won him a place, however morally equivocal, in the national heart. For a while, Bernard Tapie was even taken to epitomise a new breed of entrepreneur, before the born-again turn-of-the-century managers came to the fore. A one-time car salesman turned asset-stripper and wannabe pop singer, he rose to sit in the Cabinet as an anointed favourite of a Socialist President, a legend in his own lifetime for a year or two at least, who came to represent one aspect of what was wrong with France.

As a wheeler-dealer in the early 1980s, the swaggering, dark-haired Tapie had swept through a swathe of ailing companies, buying them for knockdown prices, selling off the pieces he didn't need and posing as a crusader for modern, efficient industry. The sheer momentum and bombast of the man kept his house of cards standing; though two of his early enterprises went bust, the Crédit Lyonnais inevitably fell under his spell and loaned him francs by the billion. Tapie moved up a notch by acquiring companies that were not in great trouble, but that had funds with which he could juggle. His firms made batteries and scales, jeans and perfume. He bought the sports goods firm, Adidas, and backed a Tour de France team led by the best French and American cyclists. In 1986, he took over a leading football club, Olympique de Marseille (OM), and bathed in reflected glory as it triumphed at home and in Europe. In Paris, Tapie treated himself to a pre-Revolutionary mansion behind high walls in Saint-Germain-des-Prés. A huge yacht with a fourteen-metre-long drawing-room, a dining table for twenty and ten bedrooms awaited him in the Mediterranean. In 1987, he floated a holding company on the Paris stock exchange. With all this going on, he still found time to record sub-Julio Iglesias records, put his name to a book of advice for aspiring tycoons, give magazine interviews and appear in television and radio shows where he dispensed his wit and wisdom to the nation.

When the Mitterrand regime staggered into a swamp of unpopularity, the old man in the Élysée fastened on to Tapie as a rejuvenating force. 'That man's a winner,' the President remarked. 'We've got to have him with us.' Self-assured as ever, the chancer had no hesitation about plunging into politics at the head of a small party allied with the Socialists. With the President behind him, which state-owned bank would query his loans and which official would blow the whistle on his fragile empire? His astuteness was shown when the Budget Ministry decided to do nothing about a tax report proposing a thorough check on his businesses, and his personal situation, with officials carefully covering their backs in the process. Tapie was a bruiser, flash and nerve all the way through. That only impressed the salon Socialists even more. He was their rough trade to set against the growing appeal of Jean-Marie Le Pen with whom he fought a televised debate in which he showed an ability to take on the old bruiser of the extreme right. Then, the tycoon turned politician went south, to the National Front's heartland, to reclaim the heritage of the non-Communist left in Marseille, and to lead a small left-wing group that did well in European elections.

The port's long-time mayor died in 1986, leaving a great vacuum in the politics of the city. Tapie's ownership of the football team eased his entry. After an initial defeat, he won a parliamentary seat, and bested the far right in regional elections. He renamed his luxury yacht the *Phocéa*, after the port's Latin name, and moored it opposite the city hall as if threatening to storm ashore and take the ornate Ancien Régime palace. But, important as Marseille might be, there were greater prizes up north where Mitterrand had him appointed to the Cabinet as the Minister for Towns.

Within two months, Tapie was forced to resign when an examining magistrate threatened to charge him with misuse of company policy and receiving stolen goods. He got out of that after a former business partner suddenly changed his mind about testifying against him. Though he was restored to his government position, news of his return was sneaked out on Christmas Eve in the knowledge that no newspapers would be published the following day. Even Mitterrand loyalists were unhappy: one of the President's friends publicly called Tapie 'a lout'. Another judged the appointment an act of contempt to the nation. Moves quickly began to strip Tapie of his parliamentary immunity from prosecution – and his real problems began.

Given the range of his activities, his positions in Marseille and Paris, the luxury of his yacht and the fine furnishings of his Paris establishment, there was something pathetic about the fact that Bernard Tapie's greatest disgrace came from a hole in a garden in the drab northern town of Valenciennes. The garden belonged to a member of the local football team which had played Tapie's side in a key match in the OM glory season of 1993. The northern team had been bribed to throw the match, with Tapie participating in the conspiracy. A Marseille player admitted to having handed over the money, which a Valenciennes team member hid in the ground in his back garden. The newly-reinstated minister denied everything, and demonstrated his political appeal by taking over a small part of the centre-left and leading it to a good result in the European Parliament election, which gave him a place in the parliament in Strasbourg. But, in March 1995, he finally came to trial on the football bribery charges.

It was not a pretty case. A woman employee of another Socialist minister was hounded out of town when she revealed that her boss had lied to give Tapie an alibi. There were sexist jokes about women's figures. Tapie snapped his fingers as though he were in charge of the courtroom, and gestured to witnesses to shut up, obliging the judge to ask him: 'Who is running this trial, you or me?' At one hearing, the accused was asked if he had tried to interfere with witnesses. Yes, he replied – but he said he was acting from the best of motives, just trying to get his pals off, like 'what people did to help the Jews during the Occupation'.

Tapie was sentenced to two years in prison. He was dropped by the French *Who's Who*, and the bank which had loved him, the Crédit Lyonnais, tried to seize the belongings from his Paris palace – only to find that most had already been moved out; what remained was worth less than the mortgage valuation. There then followed a marathon run of cases involving personal bankruptcy, handling stolen goods, misuse of corporate property, the millions spent on the annual upkeep of his yacht, tax fraud – and another over funds from the OM club treasury. His wife spoke movingly of the strain of seeing the man she loved in tears, and told a story of how their eight-year-old daughter had thrown her arms around her father as a policeman walked towards them at an airport, crying, 'Don't take my daddy to prison.' In true Tapie style, the tale ended with the self-regarding twist that the policeman had only been after an autograph from her dad.

The courts were not impressed. Tapie got three more sentences, and was banned from business activities for years to come. At the end of 1996, the one-time minister who had been privy to Cabinet secrets was stripped of both his national and European parliamentary mandates. A magistrate who investigated his ownership of the Marseille club found that 100 million francs had been spent on seeking to reduce 'the hazards which inevitably exist in a football match' by rigging games and under-the-counter payments to players to join OM.

As the cases moved slowly through the courts and he bought time with a series of appeals, Tapie found a fresh vocation – acting. 'I have paid too dearly for the mix of roles,' he said as he announced he was quitting politics, though he still found the bombast to express his desire to 'resume my responsibilities in the great movement of European integration'. His first film role was as a high-priced lawyer in a film by the director Claude Lelouch, entitled *Men, Women and How to Use Them*. He made the most of his notoriety to negotiate a contract which a magazine reckoned could earn him up to 8 million francs. He turned his hand to television commentating for the 1996 Olympic Games where, it was said, he enjoyed covering the women's gymnastics. Reflecting on his new career in an interview with *Paris-Match*, he hit all the cliché buttons about the world being a stage in which one had to know how to act to survive. 'The scenarios of life are often more cynical and cruel than those of films,' he reflected. As for the prosecutors, 'they're not interested in justice, they're just interested in getting me'.

On 3 February 1997, Bernard Tapie telephoned Loïk Le Floch-Pringent to ask what life was like in prison. Next, he made inquiries about whether mobile telephones were allowed in jail (the answer was no), and how often convicts could take a shower. Then, described by his lawyer as being 'ready to meet his fate, resigned and courageous', the one-time political and business whiz-kid was driven to the Santé prison. There, he became convict number 265 449G.

The Santé was getting used to housing one-time business celebrities who had fallen from grace. Apart from Le Floch, another inmate was Pierre Botton, the son-in-law of Michel Noir, the disgraced former Mayor of Lyon. Tapie and Botton had clashed over a business deal some years earlier, and their enmity quickly flared up behind prison walls, with each man striking an appropriately macho pose. Tapie warned that he might give Botton a punch on the nose if their paths crossed: Botton banged on the walls of his cell, accused Tapie of running scared of him, and complained to the warders that they were giving the former minister favourable treatment, including solo use of the gymnasium. Mitterrand's one-time protégé whined that he was feeling lonely and wanted to mix with other prisoners. His self-esteem was hit when a sale of paintings from his collection attracted only one buyer – 'his name is no longer a draw', the auctioneer explained. Before long, Tapie was moved from Paris to Marseille, where he faced questioning on an alleged 10-million-franc bribe to the former head of the national lottery. To take his mind off his troubles, he was allowed out of jail one day a week to work for a naval construction firm which had once renovated his yacht.

In the spring of 2001, out of jail, he popped up again at the football club whose supporters associated him with its glory days despite the scandal he had brought upon it. Olympique de Marseille had fallen on hard times though local loyalties meant it still attracted crowds of 50,000 to its shiny new stadium built for the 1998 World Cup. Tapie bought a 15 per cent stake in the club, paying, he said, only a symbolic franc. He had an option on another 20 per cent. As he walked out onto the immaculate turf, with the rocky Provençal hills rising in the background, he said he was happy, but shaking at the knees. The club was in need of a saviour. It had slumped down the First Division, and racked up debts beyond the level allowed by the football regulations. If they were not reduced, the punishment would be relegation – a prospect that horrified loyal supporters and the whole city of Marseille. OM's chairman, Robert Louis-Dreyfus, who had bought the Adidas sports goods firm once owned by Tapie, came up with the financial undertakings to prevent that. The ex-minister was barred from any financial role by his prison sentence; so he became sporting director, quickly firing the manager and plunging into the transfer market.

Tapie insisted that Louis-Dreyfus was the boss but, as *Le Monde* commented, it was hard to see him allowing himself to be told what to do. He was the local hero come home. Inevitably, speculation grew that he might try to relaunch a political career in Marseille. The mayor, Jean-Claude Gaudin said everything would be all right if he restricted himself to OM, but another local right winger and former minister was more outspoken. 'Given what Bernard Tapie represents, his return to OM is shameful for professional football,' he said. 'Where has the most elementary requirement of ethics and transparency gone?' Local Socialists said they would never allow him to stage a comeback with them, but there was no doubt of the man's abiding popularity. Visiting Marseille on the day the city awaited confirmation from Louis-Dreyfus that he would come up with the necessary financial guarantees, I found the sense of excitement at the return of Tapie evident. When the news came through on the radio, my taxi driver

lifted both hands from the wheel and clasped them in a victory gesture. Despite everything, he represented hope for the city which had
suffered heavily from economic downturn, unemployment and racial
tension. Tapie so evidently believes in himself that he has the ability to
make others believe in him. As he ordered the players to go on a diet
and to stop eating pizza, a local radio journalist remarked 'a lot of
people pardon him because they think Tapie was the victim of a
plot', and the head of the supporters club declared, 'We never forgot
him, we will never forget him.'

A year later, the club had spent 50 million euros and gone through
five trainers. Fifty-eight players had come or gone. While Zinedine
Zidane, the boy from a Marseille housing estate whom Tapie had
chosen not to sign during his first spell at the club, was the pre-World
Cup national hero, OM could only manage to squeak into the top
half of the First Division table for the 2001-2 season in ninth place.
Though he swore that he had given up politics for ever, he found
himself invited to a lunch given by the new Minister for Towns in
June 2002. By a coincidence, the minister was Mayor of Valenciennes.

Tapie was a born survivor, and he earned some public admiration
for that. But he had, in the end, simply made a fool of the establishment, sporting, political and banking. OM had taken him back. One
of France's most venerable banks had lost more than a billion francs
backing a shyster whom nobody in their right mind would have
trusted with their first centime. A supposedly wise President had
chosen a charlatan to join his Cabinet. If Bernard Tapie was the best
the ruling class could find, that said more about them than it did about
him. The government job Mitterrand entrusted to his protégé was
highly symbolic. Picking a man like Tapie to take charge of improving life in France's towns and cities underlined just how great the gulf
had grown between the governing elite and the realities of urban life.
The appointment of a con-man to handle France's urban condition
can stand as a metaphor for the more general failure of successive
administrations to get to grips with parts of the country which most
visitors don't ever reach.

7

ANOTHER FRANCE

The French city has played a key role in the development of the modern metropolis. The *bourg* gave its name to the middle class; a score of conurbations from Lille to Montpellier, Rennes to Nice are regional powerhouses in business, politics, culture and social life. Many of the greatest works of French literature, art, cinema and song – not to mention the evocations of photography – have been set in the city streets and apartments, particularly those of the greatest metropolis of all.

Each big city has its story – Paris as the capital, the City of Light and the seedbed of successive revolutions; Marseille as the colourful capital of Provence and gateway to the old Empire; Toulouse in the south-west, once a great bastion of regional power now reborn as an aerospace centre; Lille in the north and Nancy and Metz in the east, struggling to free themselves from the decline of their nineteenth-century industrial base; Lyon projecting itself beyond its reputation as the capital of gastronomy to become a home for new technologies and pharmaceuticals; Bordeaux trying to move away from a legacy of elegant complacency.

Smaller cities and large provincial towns have lives of their own, too, a tradition of links with the surrounding countryside, a specific character which sets a town in Brittany apart from one in the Pyrenees, which distinguishes Toulon from Brest, Arles from Dijon. It is not just a matter of geography and climate; though the effect of television and mass food distribution is breaking down old regional

particularisms, the distinctions of attitudes, accents and ways of life
remain sharp, as we will see in a later chapter. But, between these
towns and cities which jump off the map as symbols of the multi-
faceted nature of France, there has also grown up an entirely different
urban culture. Half-submerged, a source of concern and outright
fear, this world is growing in ways that the orthodox society neither
understands nor is able to cope with. As such, it presents one of the
biggest challenges to confront the nation today. Britain or the United
States have inner cities; France has the *banlieue*, and the people who
live there.

Though it has become the accepted term, the word is, in fact, a mis-
nomer for what we are going to be talking about here. *Banlieue*
means, literally, the suburb. When a couple at a dinner party in Paris
say they live '*en banlieue*', they probably mean that they are the proud
owners of a trim house surrounded by a garden in a place with a genteel name like Fontenay-aux-Roses or Saint-Germain-en-Laye, the
neat town which gave its name to the main Paris football team but is
now well separated from the roar of the crowd in the Parc des Princes
stadium. However, when newspapers run headlines about the problems of '*les banlieues*', they do not mean the suburbs to which many
inner-city inhabitants have moved in recent decades. What they are
talking about are places like the Tartarets estate on a hill in the
Essonne department south of Paris.

Down below lies the nineteenth-century heart of the town of
Corbeil-Essonne, dominated by a huge red-brick flour mill. For
decades, this town of 40,000 people was run by the Communists, but
then the voters swung to the right and elected Serge Dassault, a
Gaullist from the aircraft-manufacturing family which has long been
close to Jacques Chirac. His town hall stands on a tidy, tree-lined
square. Faded lettering above a row of shops opposite proclaims '*Hôtel
de la Mairie – Déjeuners, Dîners*'. Another old sign offers '*Graines en tous
genres*'. There are trompe-l'oeil paintings on some of the walls. Up the
road by the railway station, past a shop offering '*Produits Cosmétiques
Afro-Américains*', the atmosphere becomes less relaxed. The main café
sports a notice informing clients that they are under permanent video
surveillance. The barman shouts at an African who has asked for a

sandwich as though he is an idiot. I ask a swarthy man with chains on his chest for directions to Les Tartarets. He grunts and lies: 'Don't know it.' Another man, wearing a black Guns N' Roses T-shirt comes out of the café after me and points to a bus stop. 'Be careful,' he calls out as he ambles off. 'It's another world up there.' In a nearby telephone box, an Arab yells into the receiver while two teenagers play with an Alsatian in the road.

The estate of Les Tartarets consists of twenty-eight buildings, most of them reaching up fifteen floors. The streets have the names of French artists like Cézanne and Gauguin. The bus stops on the way up from Corbeil station are called Gustave Courbet, Charles de Gaulle, Auguste Renoir, Léon Blum and Henri Matisse. The concierge's room at the foot of each block has a sign offering '*Accueil*'. There is an adventure playground and a large open green space in the middle of the estate where a few elderly men sit talking at wooden picnic tables. The municipality has also erected a number of 'free expression' boards for people to inscribe their thoughts.

Though nobody seems quite sure of the exact figures, unemployment here is reckoned to be well over 20 per cent, and for all the street signs, this is a foreign place for the French. Groups of young black men sit on the pavement chatting the day away. A Mercedes car suddenly appears, its black driver stopping to talk for a couple of minutes before roaring away, giving a clenched fist salute as he goes. Arab music blares from the open window of a ground-floor flat, and the names on the letter boxes are from the other side of the Mediterranean or the Sahara. While the free-expression board is blank, the walls and bus shelters are covered with graffiti – 'Fuck la police', 'La Zone Rouge', 'Tartarets fuck la Police'. One local road is known as 'la Rue de la Mort' (the Road of Death) – more graffiti proclaims 'Fuck la Rue de la Mort'. Alarms sprout from doors, garages, cars. Under a bridge, somebody has inscribed a familiar *banlieue* mantra: 'A man falls from the fiftieth floor. As he passes each storey on his way down, he says, "It's not falling that matters, but how you land."'

On the side of one tower-block, somebody has written countergraffiti with a felt pen. The wording is not entirely coherent, but the message is plain: 'I have friends of all races and colours but not the scum of the Tartarets who screw in front of the television to produce children to get social security and put them outside even late at night – this scum breaks and steals, burns cars, drops its trousers – I owe 1,400 francs in rent and I can't afford to buy an aerosol to tag this wall, I haven't got enough to live on to the end of the month.'

Fabien, a 17-year-old whose parents came from the Ivory Coast, put the other side of the story to a reporter after his gang had seen off incursions from enemies from a nearby estate. 'You have to understand where we live, it's a state of war,' he said. 'We are fighting for our territory, we have to protect ourselves from the police and from other gangs and we have to have respect. That's the most important thing. It's very clever. They put us all in these desolate places and we fight each other, when we are not fighting the police. This is misery and hell. Nine out of ten young people here are unemployed. The police are racists who are out to get us.'

The Mayor says he'd like to provide young people like Fabien with a place to meet and socialise and have a non-alcoholic drink. Dassault comes from the establishment which runs France. His photograph appears in the national press chatting to the President of the Republic. His father, a concentration-camp survivor, built the famous Mirage military jets. Inevitably, his life and his language are a million miles from the young Arabs and Africans of Les Tartarets. Graffiti on a big back door to one block on the estate brands him a 'whore's son'. When a government minister paid a visit with the mayor, the youths at the local community centre told him: 'We're not asking for the moon, just get us out of the shit. As for the moon, we'll see about that.'

There are a hundred Tartarets in France, many of them in worse shape than the estate in Corbeil. Though the streets of Paris, Marseille or Lyon are not always the safest of places at night, France's key urban problem is the outer rather than the inner city. These estates are part of a bad dream constructed from high unemployment, social and racial tension, brutalist architecture and decades of neglect. Once they were proud examples of modernity: 'Here, there was a field of beetroots; now I have planted a flag; thousands of flats will sprout,' as one of the first masters of urban development put it in the 1960s. They replaced the shanty towns – the *bidonvilles* – where immigrants once huddled. Now they have become known as rabbit-hutches, symbols for the plight of French people who have been left behind by the economy, and for dark-skinned foreigners who were imported by the million and then abandoned. One former Socialist minister calls them places of despair; another urges 'an effort of solidarity from the nation equal to the one that set up the social security system after the war'. The former Premier, Michel Rocard, has spoken of their crime-forming architecture, but when his government decided to paint such blocks in bright colours to cheer up the residents, only the outside walls got the treatment and the insides remained as drab as ever.

Rocard's initiative was one of a string of official schemes over the years to breathe fresh life into the *banlieues*. From Bernard Tapie on, governments of left and right have appointed Ministers for Towns, whose prime job has been to deal with the social divide in urban areas. But the problem gets steadily worse, with the Audit Court judging at the beginning of 2002 that it was impossible to decide what progress had been made over the previous quarter of a century. Yet, until recently, this has not been a subject that the French establishment has been ready to face for a number of reasons, notably for what it said about the submerged tenth of the country's population.

At the start of the twenty-first century, France has around 6 million immigrants. In the name of racial equality, it does not separate them into those who come from former colonies in Africa and those who come from Europe or Asia. So the *banlieues* cannot be seen officially as a racial problem, and the problem that their young inhabitants pose on the law-and-order front has to be dismissed as a matter of political correctness. In this, once again, the political elite was sadly out of step with popular beliefs. Though France's overall crime rate lies in the middle of European Union rankings (well below Britain but above Germany), it rose by 7.7 per cent in 2001, with violent crime increasing by 9.8 per cent. Petty delinquency has risen steadily, and the number of young people arrested reached 177,000 in 2001 – 21 per cent of the total number of people detained compared to 14 per cent seven years earlier. With the National Front hammering on about 'decent' French people not being able to walk home at night in safety, right-wing Gaullists joined in, one thundering in the National Assembly about France becoming a land 'of fire and blood'. Chirac made the need to strengthen law and order his main campaign plank and, looking at the polls showing crime far and away the main popular concern, the left joined in.

Despite once expressing his sympathy for those who objected to the noise and smell of intrusive foreigner neighbours, the President has resisted any temptation to beat an anti-immigrant right-wing drum, but there is an inescapable conjunction in the popular mind between crime and young immigrants. Since no statistics are kept which could prove or deny that link, the argument is one that rests on perception, on television reports showing brown-faced youths being taken from court after receiving sentences for violence, or newspaper reports which name the young men involved as Salim, Soufiane, Sami or Mohammed. Since the subject is taboo, no serious attempt can be made to get at the roots of the problem. To speak of a *banlieue* culture that lies behind the alienation of so many of its young inhabitants is to risk being accused of racism. To say that run-down housing estates and deprived inner-city areas are beyond the reach of the Republic is considered inadmissible on two counts – it suggests that the state has lost control, and it points to a long-running failure by the country's rulers to assure the social framework of an integrated nation. The police may have identified 120 no-go areas where ambulance and fire services can only penetrate with heavy guards, but few ask why this state of affairs has been allowed to evolve. Facing facts could, indeed, give Jean-Marie Le Pen ammunition, but avoiding them in the name of anti-racist humanism has only meant the problem has festered, and given more grist to the mill of the National Front.

There has been some realisation of this recently, not by politicians but by a few figures who know from experience what they are talking about. At the end of 2001, Christian Delorme, a priest from the deprived suburbs of Lyon, told *Le Monde:* 'In France, we do not bring ourselves to say certain things, sometimes for praiseworthy reasons. That is the case with the high delinquency of young people from immigrant families, which has long been denied on the pretext of not stigmatising them. To recognise this publicly, we have had to wait for the reality of their districts, of the police stations, of the courts and the prison to impose the evidence on us. And, still, the politicians do not know how to talk about it.' At the same time, the newspaper's ombudsman acknowledged that for years, it had 'given the impression of hiding part of reality in order not to feed racism.' The following spring, the head of an anti-racist organisation, SOS-Racism, Malek Boutih, crossed another hurdle when he remarked in a book that, at a big prison outside Paris, 'you can count the whites'.

The different world of the *banlieues* is, of course, exactly the opposite of what the planners in Paris and the well-meaning left aimed for. But, in skirting round the real problems in places like the Tartarets, and pretending that everybody owed a similar allegiance to the Republic, the establishment ended up by failing in its duty towards the men and women it had brought to work in the factories of France in the 1960s. The same goes for their 1.5 million children who had grown up on the margins of a society that often did not accept them, and have become known as *beurs* in reverse slang for Arabs. The resulting alienation was shown dramatically when young immigrants whistled in derision during the playing of the *Marseillaise* at a France-Algeria football match in 2001 – the Socialist Prime Minister stood rooted to the spot, not knowing how to react. The youth gangs of the suburbs who stage armed robberies on shops inside the city limits live in a world far removed from the received truths on which mainstream politicians like Lionel Jospin base themselves. As a teacher in Vitry-sur-Seine, outside Paris, puts it: 'They leave school without any certificates, with an educational level near zero. From the age of ten, they are in a parallel economy. Armed robbery is a logical conclusion'. Or, in the words of a social worker in the same district, 'To be somebody, you have to have carried out an attack with a gun.'

'These districts need everything except for charity and hand-outs,' Malek Boutih said just before the 2002 elections. 'One is charitable towards people whom one does not think are one's equals. Society should have the same requirements from us as from others. That is what equality means.'

Equality of employment is certainly not something immigrants and their children can expect. Twenty per cent or more are out of work. In the 1990s, their unemployment level increased at almost double the overall rate. The industries that brought them to work in France are those which have suffered the biggest cuts. Just over half are in manual employment compared to a third of those born in France. A third have no qualifications, and the large majority remain at the same job level all their working lives. In the mid-1990s, a survey carried out with the help of the CFDT trade union federation revealed a devastating account of racism at the workplace. A wife coming to meet her African husband for lunch heard his colleagues calling for 'the monkey'. Two firms in a high immigrant area of the south employed six dark-skinned people among their 1,000 staff. Hearing that an Arab employee of the railway system had prayed on the platform of a station, one of his colleagues explodes that: 'If I'd been there, I'd have kicked his arse till he left.' Or the reaction of a watchman at a housing estate: 'We'll go in with machine-guns and bury them.'

In 1998, the Socialist government launched a campaign to fight racism in the labour market, but, three years later, a report from the Economic and Social Council found that discrimination 'remains and has a tendency to grow'. It identified three barriers to getting work – immigrant applicants were less likely to be invited for job interviews; if they did get called, they might be asked for qualifications not required from others; and, if they were offered a post, it would be at a low rate of pay. In every sector, children of immigrants were under-represented. Unemployment among those with professional qualifications was double that among those with French parents. Merely saying one comes from a troubled estate is enough to put employers off. At one job centre in the north, those with Arab or African first names were encouraged to change them to help get to the interview stage.

Those who do make it and escape from the *banlieues* still often find promotion slow and limited. The unemployment rate for under-thirties from Algerian families with the *baccalauréat* is 30 per cent, compared with 17 per cent for the children of Spanish immigrants and 15 per cent for French as a whole. Only a third of *beurs* with professional qualifications get a job straight away, compared to the majority of native French. Among white collar workers, unemployment of immigrants is double the national level.

Though there is an increasing number of success stories and media appearance, immigrants remain on the fringes of mainstream life, most prominent in the bread and circuses of sport and show business, rarely featured in advertising. The French have voted the footballer Zinedine Zidane the man they most admired, but a government report in 2004 decried the 'abject failure' of television to reflect multiculturalism. There was just one immigrant among the pro-Chirac candidates put forward for the National Assembly, and only a tiny number for other parties. As the newspaper, *Libération* noted, the immigrants were 'the forgotten ones of politics' and, not surprisingly, they lost whatever confidence they once had in the ruling classes of left and right. For the Paris suburb of Saint-Denis, with its big immigrant population, rather than running somebody who knew the problems of the *banlieue* the Socialists parachuted in the ultra-establishment Labour Minister, Elisabeth Gigou, who was looking for a seat after being humiliatingly defeated in municipal elections in Avignon. To establish her bond with the *banlieue*, she put on basketball shoes to visit her constituency.

In the northern city of Amiens, capital of Picardy, there are districts within distant sight of the cathedral where nearly half the children aged under six live in families dependent on welfare. In 1996, Jacques Chirac visited a huge, sprawling complex housing 25,000 people on the edge of the city. The President spoke of the need for a 'pragmatic' urban policy; he threw his arms around a group of young Africans; he climbed down to a basement to listen to a band called Bestial Overdrive. When he embraced a six-year-old daughter of immigrants, her brother shouted, 'Chirac, don't touch my sister!' From behind the barriers, another child noted the redness of the President's face as he glimpsed the underside of his country. Unemployment ran at up to 33 per cent from tower-block to tower-block. Among the residents were Arabs who had fought for France in colonial wars: half were out of work. One-third of residents were behind with the rent. The President's visit was punctuated by cries of 'Work! Work!' as police sharpshooters kept watch from the rooftops.

Six years later, the President visited the biggest estate in the country, Val-Fourré, outside Mantes-la-Jolie west of Paris. Twenty-five thousand people live there, and 220 million francs have been spent over the years to give them a better living environment after riots sparked off in 1991 by the shooting of an Arab by a policeman – he was acquitted after legal proceedings that stretched over ten years. But unemployed residents say merely mentioning where they come from is enough to prevent them getting a job. 'When you live in Val-Fourré, it's as if you had a label on your face,' one 27-year-old Arab told *Le Monde.* 'when a pal moves, he finds work. He's no longer got Mantes-la-Jolie written on his identity card.' A would-be entertainer, who works at a local social centre, says he wrote two letters applying for a job with a state television channel. One gave his African name and his real address; the other bore a French name and a different address. The first received a refusal, the second an invitation for an interview. He gave up the game, but wonders if he should have gone to show his true identity and said to them: 'You agreed to see a Frenchman, but not the other one – give me an explanation.'

To stop gangs attacking passengers, a special police unit patrols the railway station at Mantes, and security forces keep watch inside the trains to and from Paris; in 2001, 4,000 infractions were recorded on the line. In the autumn of that year, ten youths at Val-Fourré were arrested and accused of having carried out forty armed robberies in ten months. Four months later, 13 young people were wounded in a gun and knife battle in the estate's shopping centre. Choosing Val-Fourré to make one of his main law-and-order speeches in his re-election campaign, Chirac was greeted by a small crowd of *beurs*, some of whom shouted his nickname of 'SuperLiar'. In the Charlie Chaplin cultural centre, the President insisted on the need to enforce the law and not to allow 'impunity' – the code was understood; he had no need to add the words 'of young delinquents'. As he walked from the hall to his car, surrounded by security men, he was spat at while youths shouted 'Chirac, thief'.

In the centre of France, Saint-Étienne, once a symbol of heavy industry, with big factories and a triumphant football team, is now a high unemployment zone, and the imported workers suffer most. On the Montchovet estate, with its 971 flats, 70 per cent of the inhabitants are immigrants, and half are out of work. Outside Lyon, the town of Vaulx-en-Velin has a special place as the scene of the killing in the street of a young Arab, Khaled Kelkal, whose fingerprints had been found on a device used in an unsuccessful attempt to blow up the TGV high-speed train. His death at the hands of uniformed security forces was filmed by a television crew, and he became a martyr to *banlieues* youths as the town was torn by riots. The Mayor laments how places like Vaulx-en-Velin are watched by the French on the television news as though they were in a different country.

Down on the Mediterranean, crime rates are as high as in the Paris area, unemployment is well above the national average, and racial tension leads to repeated clashes. For many on the crumbling concrete estates outside Marseille, Toulon and Nice, demoralisation has become a way of life. A priest who sought to help people find work on one estate recounted: 'I went with one of them to the job centre,' he recalled. 'We waited two hours, and then we were told to look at the notices on the wall.' But many of those he tries to help cannot read French. A local councillor set up a scheme for young people to earn some money cleaning up the estate. 'After three days, none of them came any more.'

On the estates and in the *quartiers difficiles* of big cities, drugs are, inevitably, a recurrent and growing problem. Lunching with one of his successors as Minister for Towns, Bernard Tapie told him he would never succeed unless drugs were legalised. Small deals are conducted in the street, with boys as young as eight or nine keeping watch from the nearby rooftops. Any patrolling police are spotted long before they arrive on the scene. A young French narcotics runner recalls his trips to estates south of Paris. 'You made sure you only went to places where you were known. Otherwise, as a white kid, you could be in trouble. And when you got there one of you stayed in the car: otherwise it might be stolen within five minutes. The outsides of the blocks of flats had been repainted, but inside it was just the same – dirt, graffiti, human and dog excrement on the landings. And inside the flats, you had this Ali Baba cave of hi-fi equipment, videos, all the latest gear. And any drugs you wanted. The law didn't exist; they didn't give a shit. It was their world, and they were going to make the most of it.'

Nathalie knows that attitude as well as anybody. She joined the police in the mid-1980s after coming to Paris from the Mediterranean. She patrols an estate in the Seine-Saint-Denis department outside Paris, checking cellars and lift-shafts and the concrete alleyways between the tower-blocks. When she joined the force, she thought her blue uniform would win her respect. Instead, 'the young people treat us like shit . . . the insults rain down on us'. Two of her colleagues killed themselves in despair.

Nathalie dreams of being posted back to her home region on the southern coast. Instead, the local hoods sidle up to her and tell her she could make much more money as a prostitute. Others set fire to a car and call the police; when they drive up, a dozen youths run out into the street and bombard their vehicle with stones and metal bolts. Her windscreen has been smashed several times; once it was broken by a flower pot dropped from ten floors up. 'You just have to hope that the doors are well locked and the reverse gear doesn't jam.' Her bus-driver husband finds her growing more bossy at home. 'I've lost all my sensibility as a woman,' she says. 'Seeing only the bad side of society means I trust nobody any more. I feel as if the whole world reproaches me for being a cop. My only friends are in the police. At least they understand me.'

Early on, she was shocked by the language of the streets, the petty crimes, the drug trafficking; then she absorbed the ultimate survival technique of *banlieue* cops – the shrug of the shoulders. Just as her husband no longer reacts when youths get on his bus without paying, kick the doors and horse around. But, still, there are moments which even a dozen years on the beat cannot deaden. One evening, Nathalie was called out on an emergency. A man had fired his rifle by mistake while cleaning it. The bullet went through the floor into the flat below and hit a two-year-old baby in its cot. It died in her arms. When she got home at two in the morning, her uniform was still stained with blood.

Places like these are, to all intents and purposes, ghettos, where, fewer and fewer white French people live any more – and those who stay often have nowhere else to go. As even the National Front has to admit, the prime victims of the degredation lawless instability and isolation are the immigrants, themselves. The *cités*, as the estates are known, are marked, in the words of the sociologist, Azouz Begag, by 'failure at school, unemployment, crime and drugs. People are at a stage where they have nothing more to lose, in a situation of complete blockage.'

A pattern of youth violence has become all too familiar, spreading well beyond the familiar areas of tension round the biggest cities and in the south to Normandy, Brittany and Alsace. An incident between local youths, and then between the gangs and the police, all too easily escalates into assault, burning and looting. 'If you go to a party now, you need your crew,' said a young man in Chanteloupe-les-Vignes, outside Paris, where the raw ghetto film, *La Haine*, was shot. 'They come in a group of ten, somebody disrespects your girl, all of a sudden your ten have to fight their ten.' One night, a chubby teenager called Imed Amri, who appeared in the background in some scenes in the film, went to a rap evening organised by a local Franco-Algerian solidarity organisation to raise funds to pay for a skiing holiday for immigrant children. The youths from his estate and visitors from the nearby *banlieue* of Argenteuil got into an argument. Going outside, they traded punches. Knives came out. The boys from Argenteuil went to get a gun. When they returned, they shot Imed in the head. He died in hospital. Now his mother pleads with her elder son not to take up a job as a monitor on school buses for fear of what he could face.

A priest in the town of Montataire, near Paris, where an irascible Frenchman shot a young immigrant dead, spoke of 'a generation of young people who have no chance, without work, without housing, without money, facing a world of adults who judge, condemn and exclude them without understanding'. At a murder trial after the shooting of a teenager from Les Tartarets by a 21-year-old from another estate, the judge asked each witness what motivated the hatred between estate gangs; only one replied, saying simply 'It's free'. As the trial went on, fighting between rival groups broke out in the courthouse, itself, with one youth suffering a bullet wound.

Casual violence is commonplace. In a Marseille suburb, three youths who had been tormenting a handicapped boy stabbed his elder brother to death for objecting. In Lyon, an 18-year-old died from injuries inflicted by a gang after he refused to hand over his chain necklace. In one month in 2001, a 17-year-old Arab was shot in a café in Montpellier by an adolescent who said he just wanted to frighten people'; a 14-year-old died walking in a road outside Paris as two gangs start shooting; a 17-year-old was stabbed to death in a bus where he sought shelter from street fighting; and a 15-year-old had his throat cut in a cellar in Grenoble after falling foul of two gangs. 'What is astonishing is the low price these young people attach to life,' said a local judicial official in the Alpine city. Charles Rojzman, a specialist on violence in run-down urban areas sees a 'rotting' of the environment in which young immigrants live. They have less and less contact with the outside world and adults. One-parent families are common. Role models are on the street rather than at home. 'They do not believe what their teachers or the judges say,' Rojzman told *Le Monde*. 'Some fall back on themselves and become very solitary, capable of going off the rails at any moment.'

In the Paris suburb of Grigny, a rumour spreads that a local man has killed an Algerian. A dozen youths try to break into the flat of the man's parents, thinking that he is hiding inside. The police are called, and meet a hail of stones. The youths burn a police car and spread out through the neighbouring estate, pillaging shops and trying to attack a petrol station. South of the capital, half a dozen youths walk up to a building on the Cité d'Orgemont estate in Épinay-sur-Seine. They are from a similar estate in another suburb. After a row with some youths from Orgemont, they are out for revenge. One carries a rifle, another a sawn-off shotgun. One has fair hair; one is black; the others are Arabs. They fire an aimless shot at the window of a shoe repairer. Another bullet wounds a five-year-old who came running up to see what was going on. A third round hits a pregnant 25-year-old woman who was visiting her brother. She dies in his arms. Where did they get the guns? 'If you want a weapon, boys of between twelve and thirteen will find you one within a quarter of an hour,' the Mayor of Épinay explains.

In a Lyon suburb, rioters burn cars and a supermarket after a policeman arrested a man, confiscated his shotgun, pointed it at his face and pulled the trigger, not realising it was loaded. On a housing estate outside Paris, the fatal police shooting of a 16-year-old Arab who crashed through a roadblock sets off nights of mayhem. In the late 1990s, a report by a senior police officer pointed to 700 'sensitive' districts, two-thirds of them scenes of gang violence. In eighteen, the report found 'collective rebellion and premeditated attacks against the police, ambushes, throwing of paving stones and metal balls, Molotov cocktails, shots from firearms'.

Before he resigned over the autonomy offered to Corsica, the Socialist Interior Minister, Jean-Pierre Chevènement, spoke of the problem of 'wild children' and put in place a tougher law-and-order regime to control them. But this ran into the opposition of some magistrates and social workers who believed that repression, on its own, would achieve little. In the summer of 2001, some cities imposed a curfew for children under 13 in 'difficult' areas, though the newly-elected Socialist Mayor of Paris rejected this as representing 'a segregationist logic that threatens to worsen the problems [it is] supposed to solve'. With concern growing about violence in schools and colleges — a total of 16,382 aggressive acts in or near education establishments were recorded in two months in late 2001 — some teachers have launched imaginative schemes to deal with unruly pupils; given the scale of their difficulties, they are but well-intentioned pinpricks.

Reflecting on a suggestion that youth crime might be reduced by more civil education in schools, the Mayor of the town where *La Haine* was filmed shrugs and says: 'Imagine a child who has been breaking into cars and stealing radios with impunity for years because he's under thirteen. Do you think he'll stop it because he gets a civil education class once a week at school?' After one outbreak of riots, a cartoon in *Le Monde* showed a schoolmistress teaching her pupils to decline their verbs: on the blackboard was 'I want to burn a car; you want to burn a car; he, or she, wants to burn a car' – and the teacher is warning the class not to forget the circumflex accent on *brûler*. Writing in the magazine, *Le Point*, in the summer of 2002, a 28-year-old teacher explained why he had given up the job after two years at a *lycée* in the Paris suburb of La Corneuve, providing, in the process, a striking example of the gulf between the French establishment, with its set notions exemplified by the school curriculum, and the alien-ated, rebellious world of the youth of the *banlieue*. His lessons included instructing teenagers who had a vocabulary of a few hundred French words the 'presuppositions' to be borne in mind when reading an autobiography. 'I was asked to develop concepts at almost university level when I couldn't talk for more than fifteen seconds without being interrupted by a pupil getting up, or another shouting, or by the ringing of a mobile telephone,' he recalled. 'For these kids, schools represents their only interface with the world outside their estates. That brings out all their rebellious feelings. Rebellion against culti-vated, bourgeois society, rebellion against the language, the country . . . The only time I felt useful was when I helped some of them write a letter to get a job at a local fast food outlet.'

Among non-immigrants, the depressed suburbs and run-down inner city areas are a natural breeding-ground for the political extremes – once it was the Communists; now anti-immigrant voters seek another vehicle for their fears and concerns. The Socialist mayor of one *banlieue* town south of Paris compares the way members of the far right have targeted French residents in tower-blocks to the tactics of the Nazis in the tenements of Weimar Germany. 'Every day,' she writes, 'the precariousness of life gathers ground, public services wither, the Welfare State retreats . . . and when these words take shape in the faces of men and women, the unbearable leaps to your eyes and touches your heart.' For many immigrants caught in the vice of the *banlieue* and rundown city areas, it is not surprising that France's second biggest religion offers an increasingly attractive means of escape from the rejection so many feel in their daily lives.

France is home to between four and five million Muslims. It is probably true to say that the majority are not strongly religious – only between 10 and 15 per cent are reckoned to worship on a regular basis (about the same proportion of Catholics who go to mass each Sunday). For most Arabs and some Africans, Islam is above all a social and community glue in a foreign land, an assertion of their identity rather than any threat to those around them. A poll for *Le Nouvel Observateur* magazine in 1998 reported that only 24 per cent of them felt any affinity with fundamentalism. But, for many of the French, the imams, mosques, veiled women and Halal butchers have become a symbol of the separateness of the immigrants. Muslims and Arabs are seen as being pretty much the same. One poll in the late 1990s showed nearly two-thirds of the French equating the two in thinking the country had 'too many Arabs' and 'too many Muslims'.

There are regular rows over whether Muslim girls should be allowed to wear religious scarves to state schools. The number of mosques has grown to more than a thousand. Muslim religious schools have been set up in back rooms. The Arabic graffiti on city walls shouts for itself. In prisons, warders keep watch on fundamentalist terrorists to prevent them making converts. An imam who was subsequently expelled from France spoke openly of imposing Islam on the country. A police association has warned of the religion's potent appeal to 'young delinquents who are seeking their identity and are ready to wage a struggle against the country's institutions which is presented to them as legitimate'. One of the nation's most politically correct newspapers ran a headline about 'Islamic gangrene'. In a Lyon suburb, *Le Monde* reported, militants of a Koranic teaching association warned immigrant parents in the street: 'If you don't send your son to the class, we know your family in Algeria and we'll deal with them.' Nearby, a nun who has spent her life working with young people in the housing estate told how a young man walked into a neighbourhood fair and spoke a few words in Arabic. 'Immediately, all the *Maghrébins* left; outside, bearded men in djellaba robes were waiting for them.'

For the resentful youth of the *banlieues*, Islam meets a psychological need which all the anti-racist, integrationist movements of the 1980s never touched. 'Better to count yourself as a Muslim than as one of the unemployed,' as a saying goes. To which one of Bernard Tapie's successors as minister responsible for towns and social integration responded: 'They do not want mosques but jobs. They may not have the same roots, but they want the same pay-slips.' The trouble is that the jobs simply aren't there. A growing number of *banlieue* families have two generations without work. Islam, whether actively practised or not, is a counter to what they see as the indifference of French society to their plight. The evident suspicion that officialdom shows towards the religion only increases its appeal to those who already regard mainstream society as hostile to them.

Behind this lies the colonial legacy in North Africa and the support Paris gave to the repressive, anti-fundamentalist regime in Algiers. Well before 11 September, France felt itself to be a prime target for Muslim fundamentalists, bent on attacking the West. In Algeria itself, five people died in an attack on French diplomatic quarters, a French bishop was blown up and seven French Trappist monks had their throats slit after being kidnapped by the main fundamentalist group. A French airliner was hijacked across the Mediterranean. France was hit with a series of bomb attacks, one of which killed seven people in a Paris station – and Khaled Kelkal tried to blow up the TGV train track. The combination of terrorist bombs, the threatening cloud of violence in the suburban housing estates at home and the horrific bloodletting in France's former colony makes it easy for the far right to warn of France being swept by a murderous horde from the Maghreb, poised to cross the Mediterranean and join up with their brothers in Corbeil, Vaulx-en-Velin or Marseille. One of France's most famous names thinks they have already landed. Brigitte Bardot, who married a National Front supporter as her fourth husband, said she might have to emigrate because of the overpopulation of foreigners, especially 'manic throat-cutter' Muslims, with their ritual slaughter of sheep. 'We have to submit against our will to this overflow,' the actress turned animal-rights fanatic declared. 'Year by year, we see mosques flourish across France while our church bells fall silent because of the lack of priests.' Such language earned her a 10,000-franc fine for inciting racial hatred, by which time she had publicly pledged support for the National Front in an election in southern France and, against the background of horrifying massacres in Algeria, was ratcheting the rhetoric up a gear with a vision of how the fundamentalists would 'slit our throats one day – and we'll deserve it'.

The perceived Islamic threat has been given a new edge by an emerging link with organised crime. Police report having broken up a web of Islamic groups involved in hold-ups, explosions, gun-running and forged documents in Paris, Toulouse, in the east and on the Mediterranean coast. The network was said to have ties not only with North Africa but also with Bosnia, Chechnya and Afghanistan. One gang, based west of Paris, raised millions of francs for Algerian fundamentalists by selling forged documents to immigrants. In the capital itself, a front company specialised in shipping stolen cars to the brothers across the Mediterranean. There have also been cases of native Frenchmen who converted to Islam, underwent military training in Afghanistan and returned to France to join the fundamentalist movement at home. And then there was Christophe Caze.

The son of a cleaning woman and a unemployed worker, Caze became a Muslim while a medical student in the northern city of Lille. He changed his first name to Walid, grew a beard and began to attend a fundamentalist mosque. In 1993, he abandoned his studies and went to Bosnia, where he worked in a medical outfit, fought on the Muslim side, and married a seventeen-year-old nurse. Two years later he returned to France and was called up for national service. Within two weeks, he had deserted. Christophe-Walid had brought weapons back with him from Bosnia. He also acquired a police scanner radio. With a band of sympathisers, including another French convert to Islam, he established a headquarters in a brick house in a suburb of the depressed northern town of Roubaix.

Ten days after he deserted, Caze and his gang held up a supermarket, killing a motorist. Six weeks later, they attacked a Brinks security truck with a rocket launcher. The money they stole was dispatched to Muslims in Bosnia. Next, Caze left a car with three bottles of gas in the boot outside the main police station in Lille, where the leaders of major industrial nations were due to meet three days later. Only the detonator went off. The following day, heavily armed police moved in on the brick hide-out house at dawn. If they thought they would catch the gang asleep, they had got their religion wrong. The four people inside 59 rue Henri-Carrette were already at their morning prayers. The police opened fire on the house. According to an eyewitness, one of the attackers went to the back of the house with a rocket launcher, lay down in the street and fired. 'The roof went up like the lid from a saucepan. It fell back in flames and set the whole building alight. It was like a house of cards that had caught fire.' From inside, a man engulfed in flames went on shooting with a Kalashnikov rifle. When four bodies were pulled from the ruins, they were so shrunken by the heat that some locals thought they were children.

Caze was not among the dead. He had been out of the house for the night, and picked up news of the attack on his scanner radio. With another member of the gang, he drove towards the Belgian frontier. Police were waiting for him. Their fusillade killed Caze outright. His companion, wounded, took two women hostage before giving himself up.

Roubaix, a forgotten part of France's industrial decline, suddenly came under the national spotlight. One-third of the town's population are immigrants, and few Arab women do not cover up in the streets. An English journalist, Mary Dejevsky of the *Independent*, reported seeing teenage boys with Arafat-style headgear in the streets a few days after the shooting. There is a raging drugs problem in the largely immigrant southern suburbs. The porous border with Belgium up the road makes it simple for illegal immigrants to slip into France, and for drugs to be brought from the Netherlands. Unemployment stays stubbornly high in the shadow of the old spinning mills and the factories that once provided work for all in the great northern urban sprawl around Lille. Five months after Caze and his companions died, journalist Sara Daniel visited the Alma-Gare district where the gang had established itself:

In summer here, nobody goes on holiday. But round rue Henri-Carrette, the silence of the dead reigns. A silence of mourning. Approaching Number 59, a woman draws the edge of her veil across to cover her face. So as not to see the little charred house with its windows covered with planks. Between the Alma district and Christophe Caze, a kind of love affair has come to life. A strange alchemy. Here the problems of living bring people closer. Everybody knows each other. Here, the young man who had converted to Islam found a new family. Christophe was something of the favourite son of the district. The kids in the street speak of him with respect. 'He tried to persuade us to go to the mosque. He was intelligent, educated, but not haughty. We talked about football, anything and everything. He was tolerant. As for religion, he said it was up to us to make the decision, nobody could force us.'

In the once bustling textile centre of Tourcoing to the west of Roubaix, a different tone is to be heard. Tourcoing has also fallen on hard times. Racism, fear, unemployment and extremist politics meld into a sour brew on a run-down estate. 'My father told me: Arabs are worse than mice,' a 31-year-old mother of five told a visiting reporter from *Le Monde*, pointing at a little Arab boy. 'What we need is a boat to put them in, or a good bomb.' Another woman sounded a softer note. Her neighbour, Fatima, is nice – during Ramadan she hands out her couscous and cakes. That did not stop the second woman referring to the Arabs as 'wogs'. The first woman's husband had never had a job; their evening meal was bread and cheese. 'And to think that my mother and father changed jobs in the cotton mills whenever they wanted to.'

People in places like this tell of young Arabs attacking old French people in the cemetery, of police who either turn a blind eye or suggest that they take the law into their own hands. A municipal basketball court was built just for Arabs, they say: a Frenchman who went there to play was turned away. A 28-year-old woman has had to put up wire fencing around her garden to keep out the Arabs who used to shoot up with drugs and leave the syringes behind on her grass. Racism and unemployment feed off one another. A former trade union official recalls how, in the old days, you could break off from work to have a cigarette; now, there will always be an Arab standing in line to grab work, while an army of illegal immigrants is pouring into the country in search of jobs and the shopfloor manager will remind you that there were two thousand people waiting to take your place. A retired Frenchman with a Socialist Party card who keeps several guns in his flat says he votes for the far right in local elections 'to stop the wogs getting above themselves'. In the 1995 presidential election, the Front began to make inroads in Tourcoing. Seven years later, Le Pen scored 22 per cent there in the first round – to 18 per cent each for Jospin and Chirac. In the second round, his score increased to 23.7 per cent.

What fuels French racism is the changing face and colour of those who come from abroad. Throughout the century, France has attracted a large flow of immigrants, starting with Polish mineworkers and Jews from Eastern Europe. Immigration accounts for 40 per cent of the national population growth since the Second World War, and a quarter of the population has immigrant family links. In the 1960s, 75 per cent of those who came to live in France were from Europe, most of them Catholic Spaniards and Portuguese. Generally, they looked like the natives and fitted into a comfortable pattern; the men worked in factories while their wives were concierges or cleaning women. They kept to the rules, and their children grew up in the French system. A Portuguese concierge in our street on the Left Bank told my wife proudly that her daughter had voted for the National Front in 1995, as if that was proof of belonging.

Today, half the immigrants are from Africa. When the French talk of the foreigners in their midst, they do not think of Portuguese concierges or Spanish waiters but of the brown-and black-skinned people living in run-down sections of major cities or in the suburban housing estates – the substantial Turkish population usually manages to avoid notice, though it has been at the centre of some incidents in northern industrial cities. Whenever possible, the French put immigrants out of their minds, and pay little attention to the conditions in which they exist. In the mid-1990s, a member of the National Assembly investigated how one group of immigrants lived. He found over-crowding, black markets, drugs, prostitution, health problems, the growth of Aids and tuberculosis. One place he visited contained three times as many people as its legal entitlement; another had four people or more sleeping in the same room; a third served 3,000 meals a day with no health controls. Was the deputy, Henri Cuq, writing about a hide-out for illegal immigrants? No, these were some of France's 710 official hostels for foreign workers.

Cuq's report emphasised not only how the nation had given up on its immigrants, but why men from Mali or the Maghreb were so intent on coming to France. If they could find work, the economics are simple. The minimum wage was 4,900 francs. In an immigrant hostel, meals cost 7.50 francs, and the monthly price of a bed was 450 francs. So there was no problem in saving 3,000 francs a month to be sent home to a country where that was a great deal of money. 'This can only encourage a flow of illegal immigrants,' as Cuq concluded. Soon after his report was published, a fifteen-year-old Moroccan travelled 1,200 miles from Tangiers to France hidden in the luggage compartment of a bus, and a group of Chinese was found making shoes in a garage in western France in conditions of virtual slavery. Others died locked up in containers, or were thrown overboard from ships after they had paid to be smuggled to France.

How such people are received once they arrive in France has become a touchstone of the tension between the humanism on which the country has always prided itself and the more visceral reactions encouraged by unemployment, social discord and national uncertainties. After a highly publicised incident in the summer of 1996, in which 220 Africans without residence papers were hauled from sanctuary in a Paris church to be expelled, the editor of Le Monde described immigration as 'that moment of truth in which an age is plainly revealed and generations radically divide'. The immigration laws were rewritten three times in five years in a left–right tussle over how tight controls should be. But legislation only scrapes the surface of a deep social divide. The inevitable gulf between a North African family in a banlieue tower-block and an orthodox French family has become immeasurably deeper because the feeling of non-acceptance is mutual. Increasingly, immigrants are asking what France is going to do for them. The jobs that brought them north are drying up, but they do not want to leave. Religion is the only rallying-point in which they can have confidence but, by its nature, it sets them even further apart. When a right-wing Interior Minister spoke of developing 'a French Islam', an imam from northern Paris countered: 'What is being asked of us is not integration but assimilation, which requires us to leave our identity behind. Individuals can be assimilated, a community cannot . . . the arrival in France of Protestants and Jews required changes in French society; now it is the time of the Muslims.'

Before he embarked on his brief career as a terrorist, the would-be bomber of the TGV train, Khaled Kelkal, spoke of what being a Muslim meant to him. 'I am neither Arab nor French, I am Muslim,' he said. 'When I go into a mosque, I'm at ease. People shake my hand, treat me as a friend. When I see another Muslim in the street, he smiles, we stop, we chat. We recognise one another as brothers.' The contrast between his words, published after his death, and the television image of a policeman turning the young man's body over with his boot summed up the cleavage between the world of the *banlieues* and mainstream French society. Fundamentalist terrorism had become a home-grown threat to society. The terrorists were no longer wild figures from the Middle East or North Africa, but young men who had been brought up in France itself. Some, like Christophe Caze, were even Frenchmen who rejected the ways of their homeland. In their desperate way, they had come to be an archetype of the submerged world of the other France.

That frightens a lot of people. They see the Arabs and Africans as outsiders who can only be a threat to the cohesion of their country and their own lives. Racism against black and brown people thus takes on a wider resonance than simple 'wog-bashing', and draws on the image which France has had of its own social fabric for two centuries. The French do not see themselves as living in a land of separate ethnic communities: Islamists, as a Gaullist Interior Minister said, should be French. The country may receive people from different nations and cultures, but it requires them to conform to the unity of the Republic. The education system and the authority of the state are meant to impose a uniformity which ensures that the melting-pot produces a single national stew. There are exceptions – in the immigrant communities of Marseille or the Jewish traditionalists of the Marais district in Paris – but, as a general rule, multi-culturalism and the right of different ethnic groups to be treated on an equal plane with the native French are new, and often uncomfortable, concepts. 'If immigrants, no matter where they are from, settle in our country, then they must adopt our civilisation and bend to our rules, habits and lifestyles' – the formulation from the Comte de Paris, the Pretender to the late throne, is an unequivocal expression of an attitude widely shared across the nation. Or, as an adviser on immigration to Alain Juppé's government said: 'When somebody emigrates, he changes not only his country, but also his history. Foreigners arriving in France must understand that henceforth their ancestors are the Gauls.'

Such a message takes no account of places like Vaulx-en-Velin, with its thirty-eight different nationalities; or the tower-block suburbs outside Paris in La Courneuve, Aubervilliers and Saint-Denis; or the tower-block estate of Les Bosquets, north of Paris, where the 9,000 people come from scores of ethnic backgrounds and the youth centre is the only public building not to have been attacked during recent troubles. As well as Arabs, many *banlieues* are home to substantial numbers from black Africa who bring their cultures and traditions with them. In the suburb of Montreuil, where 5,000 immigrants from Mali live, the mayor fights an uphill battle against their polygamy. More than a hundred African religious sects have set up in the hinterland of France's cities. Each weekend, a bare, neon-lit hall in La Plaine-Saint-Denis north of Paris resounds to a *Zaïrois*-style band of electric guitarists and singers laying down the path to salvation. At a Sunday service of the Cherubin Christians of Drancy, black immigrant girls parade in immaculate white dresses and bonnets. A woman in African costume slumps to the floor in a trance while a young man is taken through an exorcism ceremony. In another suburb, a pastor from Madagascar preaches to the faithful in an annexe to a fast-food restaurant. The quest is for roots as much as for religion. At the end of one service, the mighty brass of the Kimbanguiste Fanfare band blares out. However drab and cold their suburban world may be, however threatening the shadows of xenophobia, the faithful can almost feel at home for the space of a Sunday morning.

Sarcelles, the suburb in which the pastor from Madagascar exhorts his flock each weekend, counts sixty different nationalities among its 58,000 people. Its bus stops strike a high French cultural note, being named after César Franck, Camille Saint-Saëns, André Gide and Albert Camus. But the walls of the bus station are covered with posters advertising concerts by Le Sénégal en Musique, Le Afro-Jazz and Le Turbo de l'Afrique, or offering the services of Le Plus Grand Coiffeur Afrique-Antillais. In the big square housing blocks by the train tracks, the vast majority of faces are black. In the sprawling street market, each immigrant community is represented in the food stalls – mint and North African spices, sweet potatoes, soja and kosher meat. Nobody can pretend that Sarcelles is French in the way that the Comte de Paris or most traditionalists would define the word. But it has become home to the immigrants, many of them of the second generation, and they refuse to conform to a straitjacket forged by France's past. As an imam in the 19th *arrondissement* of Paris pointed out to the American writer Milton Viorst, his flock was part of the French family, and accepted their responsibilities towards it, but it could not be alone in making accommodations. If such mutual understandings remain as elusive as they are at present, or are actively rejected, the *de facto* distance between communities can only grow. After a lengthy study of the Paris *banlieue*, the publisher and author François Maspero was led to observe that, if a plan for ethnic separation was regarded as viable for the former Yugoslavia, 'one day, we must expect such a plan, in the name of the same logic, to be set out for a just ethnic division of the people of Aubervilliers and La Courneuve'.

France's difficulty in coming to terms with the dysfunction between the old, all-encompassing idea of the nation and the ethnic separations which it cannot ignore is heightened by the high profile of Arabs born in France. The first generation of immigrants were overwhelmingly single men recruited from North Africa to work in factories and mines. According to a recent compiler of an oral history of the immigrants, Yamina Benguigui, their minds were set on returning home one day; at first, they kept their belongings packed, ready to make the journey back. But the longer they stayed in France and the more their families joined them, the further that prospect receded. 'If you go to Algeria, you will see the houses the immigrants had built for them,' Benguigui notes.

'Often there is no more than the first storey: the building stopped at that.' For their children, the process went a step further. The idea of returning to North Africa became a non-starter, but, at the same time, France was not a real home. 'We were neither from here nor from there,' as Benguigui puts it. For teenage *beurs*, the process is complete. No question of crossing the Mediterranean, but little question of adopting traditional French ways either. They see themselves as a community – the second most numerous in France – which has the right to live in its fashion by its own rules. They want to have their cake and eat it;

but their cake can be pretty thin and discriminatory – an official report showed that 40 per cent of twenty- to thirty-year-old children of Algerians who had moved to France were out of work compared to 11 per cent of offsprings of native French parents at the turn of the century.

Amid such dark shadows of *apartheid à la française*, one outcome of *beur* pride is a vibrant alternative street culture, expressed mainly in rap music which has bred a true international star in the singer MC Solaar and claims brotherhood with the Bronx, Watts or Brixton – a self-conscious lexicon of *banlieue* language lists terms like 'gangsta' and 'homeboy' (no *Académie Française* gurus here). But, despite sometimes high record sales to a wider public, this is essentially an outsider culture which loses its edge if it allows itself to be embraced by the mainstream. Its base in the youth of the *banlieue* lives resentfully and with a clannish pride on the edge of society. There may have been cause for national pride when the formidable black athlete Marie-José Pérec notched up an Olympic double in the 200- and 400-metre races at the Atlanta Olympics and a *beur* won a gold medal for judo, but, for many white French people, the young blacks and Arabs are a threatening force. Inevitably, the separateness reaches into that sacred area of French unity, the language.

The *banlieues* have a slang which can be virtually impenetrable and can act as a wall in both directions. 'We are not like them, the words we use are not the same as them because they speak old French, we talk our slang,' as a twelve-year-old from the suburbs said about white children from inside Paris. 'Traditional French language finds itself in a foreign land,' remarked a film-maker after finishing a documentary on the housing estates. In a further twist away from the universal language spread across France by the centralisers of the nineteenth century, this new tongue can vary from estate to estate, from race to race. In Noisy-Le-Grand, outside Paris, Africans call white French people '*babtou*' while Arabs call them '*gaori*' or '*gouère*' and gypsies call them '*roum*'; elsewhere one popular term is '*from*' – from *fromage*. There is nothing inherently menacing in young immigrants calling a condom a '*passeport*' or talking about '*dunk*' to mean hitting somebody. But, to those not in tune with ghetto life, it is a considerable step further when the slang for 'leave me alone' becomes 'fuck your mother'. And when the rap band of that name – Nique Ta Mère – performs a song urging 'kill the cops', the liberal establishment was in a quandary. Condemnation meant lining up with the racists who wax indignant when the band is booked for subsidised music festivals. But to shut one's eyes and ears in the name of racial harmony is, as the journalist Élisabeth Schemla points out, to renounce moral values needed to stand up to the extremism which threatens civil society. If NTM can get away with it, how about a band that sings a ditty entitled 'Kill the Jews'?

The law eventually stepped in: two members of NTM – one from white Portuguese parents, the other a West Indian black, both of them French citizens – were given suspended prison sentences for singing a song which declared: 'I piss on the courts. The police are fascists and murderers. It's those motherfuckers in blue and the courts who break our balls all the year. Our enemies are the men in blue and we piss on them.' Soon afterwards, two other rap singers were fined for another cop-baiting song entitled 'Sacrifice de Poulets' – *poulet*, or chicken, being the slang term for the police. The fear is that it is not all a matter of words. As the sentence was being handed down to NTM, two teenagers were arrested and accused of dropping a block of cement on a policeman from a tower-block on a suburban Paris estate, breaking his skull. And on the Paris Métro, four Arab youths and one black slashed a woman officer's face while shouting: 'Filthy cop! We're going to kill you!' as they repeatedly raped her.

The tension that surrounds the presence of native-born children of immigrants has given rise to recurrent suggestions that French nationality should be defined by blood rather than by simply having been born on French soil. The questioning of a hallowed element in France's tradition as a land that welcomes foreigners has gone as high as a former President of the Republic. At a less elevated but more pertinent level, an immigrant living close to Valéry Giscard d'Estaing's Auvergnat homeland in Clermont-Ferrand issued a striking appeal entitled 'To My Brothers':

In this land of welcome, we meet two attitudes. One regards us as the source of all the country's social ills – that's the extremism of hatred, demagogy, of people closing in on themselves, sometimes the result of ignorance and naïveté. The other imagines us to be angels, simple victims of the economic crisis and its 'natural' corollary, racism. That's angelic racism, smart, romantic and sometimes condescending.

Come what may, the results are the same: we are disliked more and more; we irritate; we are always on display.

Unfortunately, it is not simply a matter of racism. People speak about us for good or ill without really knowing us. They think for us. Really, it's time to realise that we upset them. Nobody can talk about us without passion, and we can't talk about ourselves without emotion.

The presence of foreigners in the West in general, and in France in particular, is the direct result of colonialism and the demands of the flourishing industry of the 1960s and 1970s. You have to take the consequences of history. To justify violence in the suburbs by blaming unemployment and people's feelings of helplessness is easy. But how many French farmers work sixteen hours a day for less than 3,000 francs a month? How many unemployed French people who no longer get benefits live in destitution without drawing attention to themselves?

And where would you be in a similar situation back home? You'd be without work, without benefits, without rights and subject to totally arbitrary regulations. You couldn't even smash up the lifts because, when there are any, most are already broken. You couldn't tag the walls because, back home, there aren't any aerosol canisters. Even less could you hassle the police – you'd be risking your life.

So why do you feel this contempt for the country that welcomes you? For its laws, for its leaders. All they ask of you is not to impose your culture on those who don't want it. I listen to African singers and to French singers. I read French and North African writers with the same admiration. I watch a European or an African football match with the same passion. I watch *Cyrano de Bergerac* and *Omar Gatlato* with the same emotion. All that without my neighbours knowing it. That's what integration is all about.

Such voices are rare in France today on either side of the racial divide. A lot of French people find street gangs of Arab or African teenagers genuinely threatening, while many immigrant youths, and at least some of their parents, see themselves in a separate world, marginalised by the way society operates. The nation's growing sense of insecurity leaves little room for strangers from another culture. Government schemes to spend money on improving living conditions on the estates of the *banlieues* are not as popular as they might be with the population at large: law and order counts for more than what are seen as hand-outs to unemployed Arabs who don't deserve charity. With its finger on the pulse as ever, the National Front hammers on about the 'exclusion' of native French people from housing and benefits which should, by rights, be theirs – to the advantage of invasive immigrants sucking up welfare, homes and jobs and getting away scot-free with breaking the law. The gang rape of a Dutch tourist on an Atlantic beach and the fatal stabbing of a young man during a gang fight outside a discotheque by the Mediterranean became *causes célèbres* when it emerged that, in each case, the attackers were youths on subsidised holidays from the ghettos. Each *banlieue* riot involving young immigrants sends more votes to the far right.

The exact degree of racism in France is impossible to define, but there is clearly a lot of it about. If polls of National Front supporters at the elections of 2002 showed twice as much concern about the crime as about immigration, the fact was that the two were often merged in people's minds, and the first seemed more avowable than the second. A report to the United Nations Human Rights Commission depicted a country being shaken by 'a wave of xenophobia and racism'. Nearly two-thirds of those questioned in another survey acknowledged that they harboured racist attitudes. Anti-Arab jokes arouse chuckles rather than indignation around the dinner tables of bourgeois families. When a passing motorist from Montpellier came into a village café in the middle of France and announced that the head of an organisation of former settlers in Algeria had been murdered in the southern city, the universal reaction of the *pastis*-drinkers was: 'Must have been the wogs.' (In fact, the killing was done by three extreme right-wingers who regarded him as too moderate for their taste.) Some react with denial. A prominent university professor banned the use of the word 'immigration' among his students because it might encourage racism. A Christian group called on all public organisations to remove the word 'race' from official texts. A town outside Paris showed its solidarity with immigrants by installing the first-ever bust of a black Marianne.

Just before the 1997 legislative election, the minister responsible for urban affairs went on the radio to talk about immigrants. The President regarded the bluff Éric Raoult as one of his trump cards in the fight against the Front, a kind of Bernard Tapie of the right without the sleaze. Using a patronising collective term derived from the African name 'Amadou', Raoult said that, to be integrated, 'Mamadou, if he is here legally, must wear a suit and tie.' The correct attitude for immigrants should be to behave as children do at school. That was a bit like a British Home Office Minister going on television and telling 'Sambo' to get his hair cut if he wanted a job. It must have gone down a treat with the *beurs*.

An opinion poll published in *Le Monde* in May 2002 reported that 59 per cent of those questioned thought there were too many immigrants in France. 'We're not at home here,' said one of the women on the estate in Tourcoing. 'They say they are more French than we are; and they spit in our faces.' On the other side of the divide, a North African community worker in Khaled Kelkal's home town of Vaulx-en-Velin recalled how, a couple of decades ago, young Arabs wanted to become French. 'Today, it is exactly the opposite. Whatever we do to adapt, it will never be enough to get us accepted. White people can get out of the *banlieues* if they make the effort. We'd have to move the whole Earth to do that.'

When the government sought to show more recognition of immigrants in the public service by appointing a Muslim as the Prefect of an eastern department, his car was firebombed. Meanwhile, a particularly sensitive question of conformity to the rules of the Republic raised its head over the issue of Muslim girls wearing veils to state schools. For Islamists, legislation introduced in 2003 to ban the veil, along with the wearing of Jewish skullcaps and large Christian crosses, was an infringement of religious freedom and an affront to their beliefs. To the mass of French people, however, it was both in conformity with the secular nature of the state – and an attempt to discourage the growth of fundamentalism. The argument was heightened with reports of Muslim men refusing to let their wives or daughters be examined by male doctors. On the one side was the majority Republic with all its traditions that had been built up as the glue of France since the Revolution; on the other, an immigrant minority which risked becoming even more alienated from the country it inhabited.

In such a context of extremes, fuelled by the national anxiety about crime, mainstream politicians were found sadly lacking, reduced to averting their gaze, mouthing platitudes or focusing on the narrow issue of law and order without addressing the deeper ills behind it. Only one man could benefit, and, as the new century arrived, he made the most of the failures of integration and the tensions they gave birth to.

8

SPECTRE AT THE FEAST

The lights go out. The recording of Verdi's 'Chorus of the Slaves' rises to a deafening pitch. Two thousand people jump up on the rows of red plastic chairs set across the exhibition hall, craning their necks to catch a sight of the conquering hero. Surrounded by television cameras, Jean-Marie Le Pen marches towards the platform. The cheering drowns the music. Placards bob in the air – 'Vas-y Jean-Marie' and one held aloft by a touchingly solitary young woman, 'Jean-Marie, our only friend'. As the leader reaches the platform, the roar from the hall grows even louder. Plump and sleek in a dark-blue double-breasted suit, his one good eye glistening in the spotlight, his chest stuck out like a pigeon, the boss of France's National Front punches the air with both fists and waits for the din to subside. Then he tells a story.

He had arrived late that evening in Toulouse, and he apologised for keeping the good people of the south-west waiting. But it had not been his fault. On the way down from Paris the good French pilot had told him why the Airbus – made in the great city of Toulouse – was running behind schedule. It was all because control of French skies was now based – guess where? The crowd didn't have the faintest idea. So their friend Jean-Marie told them: French air space was controlled from Maastricht. That's right, Maastricht – he draws out the long first double vowel with a grimace and snarls the final 'icht'. Yes, Maastricht, the Dutch town where that terrible European Union treaty was signed which would wrench away national sovereignty and reduce the good people of the Hexagon of France to vassals of face-less bureaucrats of Brussels. And what had happened when the air control centre at Maastricht had been given authority over the skies above our country? Why, the French air-traffic controllers who worked there had been sacked. Their places had been taken by the Dutch, the Germans and the British who were delaying French aircraft on purpose to give their own national lines an unfair advantage. This was why Jean-Marie Le Pen's Airbus had been delayed on its way down to Toulouse that evening.

Before the crowd can quite digest this revelation, the man who speaks for all that is irrational, extremist and xenophobic in the nation of liberty, equality and fraternity is off and running. If the national madeleines are crumbling around them, the orator on the platform tells his audience why. For two hours, he paces from side to side of the wide stage, pausing occasionally to grin at one of his own jokes, halt-ing to stand to attention when he invokes the memory of those who died to preserve France over the centuries. In a horribly great stand-up act, he plumbs every depth of national insecurity. Immigration and law and order flow like poisoned streams, sometimes apart, sometimes intertwined. He tells of Arab families living on welfare who bring in their second and third cousins to squat in municipal housing estates: the bailiffs dare not evict them because they would be found later with their severed heads tucked under their arms. Three million immigrants sent home – three million jobs for the French – the social security system saved – public order restored – pensions safeguarded. How wonderfully simple. 'France is beautiful!' cries Le Pen. 'Let us show ourselves worthy of her. Defend her! Rebuild her!'

That was a week before the first round of the presidential election of 1995. Seven years later, in the middle of the battle for the Élysée with Jacques Chirac, Verdi's chorus sounds out again as up to 20,000 National Front supporters march in bright sunshine through the middle of Paris, from the Place du Châtelet past the gilded statue of Joan of Arc by the Louvre to the Place de l'Opéra. It is an annual procession held on the birthday of the Maid of Orleans, who Le Pen says is his political model – after all, she booted the foreigners out of the country, even if they were from across the Channel rather than from over the Mediterranean. This year's turnout is three times bigger than usual. There are a few thuggish looking young men, some wearing balaclavas, a group of Italian fascists, and an elderly woman who has fixed Front stickers on her dachshund. A man stripped to the waist carries a heavy crucifix. Anti-immigrant leaflets warn that France is about to be swamped by foreigners, not just Arabs and Africans, but also by Chinese who would, in time, take over the country. Patriotic badges are on sale, and a man in a dark suit carries a tray filled with far right periodicals heralding the imminent freeing of the nation from the 'anti-French'. But, as in the rally at Toulouse, most of those who turn out look like thoroughly ordinary French people. Despite huge counter-demonstrations in Paris and other cities, there is no serious trouble – police keep the two sides well apart and the main concern of the Front's security service is to prevent any electorally-unfriendly violence.

Looking out at the sea of tricolour flags, and placards proclaiming 'Proud to be French', Le Pen addresses his followers from a stand in front of the Opera House bearing the slogan 'France finds herself'. His second wife, in a white trouser suit, stands watching him – Le Pen says that the fact that she is partly Greek shows that 'love has no borders'. His image appears, vastly magnified on a screen behind him. All the old themes are there as he presents himself as the only politician who cares for the people of France, and will defend them against globalisation and the Europe of Maastricht. He alone, is a true patriot, a man whose favourite image is that of the national flag flying from the poop of a navy ship, who declares that 'France is our mother. She has given us a hundred thousand times more than we can ever give her back.'

He is as pugnacious as ever in denouncing Chirac as 'Quasimodo', 'SuperLiar', 'the prince of the moral swindle', and the 'godfather of the clans that carve up the country between them'. The President's crimes known no end – lax on crime, he has tried to change the nature of the French people by importing under-qualified workers, undermined the family with abortion laws, lowered the educational level, done the bidding of foreign leaders, and soiled the image of the nation. Equally, the Front's promises are limitless as its leader offers to recreate a nation-state secure within its borders, with a homogeneous population and a settled social order to protect French greatness and the French people from the perils that surround them. His party will renegotiate European treaties, guarantee law and order, control public spending, lower unemployment, recreate solidarity between generations, adopt a 'French first' social policy, defend children and nature, assure the independence of the judicial system, cooperate with other francophone countries, particularly in Africa, and annul the debts of developing nations. 'Dear compatriots,' he concludes 'open your eyes, do not let yourselves be blinded by lies and hysterical hate campaigns. Those of you who voted for the left, do not agree to vote [for Chirac] while holding your nose.' The establishment which Chirac personifies has occupied the nation – now, Le Pen booms to the crowd in the Place de l'Opéra, it is time for liberation. Then, having sung the national anthem, he goes off for lunch at the Hôtel Crillon, after being refused a table at the Ritz, which, presumably, feared his presence might disturb the peace of its dining room.

Le Pen had, of course, not the slightest chance of beating the man he describes as the 'gravedigger of the nation'. Merely getting to the second round had been triumph enough. His success brought the biggest united front seen in living memory to block him and make the run-off ballot into a referendum for the Republic against Le Pen – even if the slogan 'Better a crook than a fascist' reflected the lack of enthusiasm for Chirac felt by many who voted for him. Zinedine Zidane joined Gérard Depardieu in a television commercial urging voters to say 'Non'. May Day demonstrations against the Front attracted more than a million people. *Lycée* pupils staged protests, and the media lined up in a way that led one of Le Pen's lieutenants to complain of 'totalitarian brainwashing like a Pol Pot thought school'. The far right leader revelled in it all: he was one against the world, the only man who dared to tell the truth. He insisted that Chirac was lying when he said they had never met, and spread tales of being asked for his help by the President in the second round of the 1988 election. He challenged the incumbent to a televised debate, and chuckled knowingly when the idea was turned down. Chirac, he said – not without reason – was scared of being quizzed about the scandal allegations against him. Then he delivered his jibe that, if the debate had taken place, he would have taken a pair of handcuffs in the studio to be clamped on his opponent's wrists.

Suffering by far the heaviest defeat ever seen in the second round of a presidential election did not cramp his style, either. Though he got only 17.8 per cent of the poll on 5 May , he pulled in half-a-million more votes than at the first round. Just having got to the second round was achievement enough. When the result was announced, Le Pen called it 'a bitter defeat for hope' won by 'those in power uniting to defend their privileges'. But he was already looking ahead, to the National Assembly election in June. He knew that the electoral system made it virtually impossible to win any seats. But a survey published ten days before the first round of the legislative poll showed that 28 per cent of those questioned agreed with his ideas – a figure that shot up to 40 per cent on law-and-order and 35 per cent for the defence of traditional values. Though 70 per cent regarded it as a danger to democracy, the Front was France's third biggest political party, far outperforming the once powerful Communists, the Greens and even the centrist UDF. Once a marginalised group of squabbling extremists, the far right had become an organised movement catering for those who did not feel at home in the new France and were ready to place their faith in a 73-year-old ex-paratrooper who had been written off more times than any other politician in the country.

Other West European countries saw the rise of extreme right-wing politicians at the end of the twentieth century, but none has shown the durability of Le Pen. Nor has any got away with so much over the years – from allegations of torture to calling the Nazi gas chambers a 'detail of history'. His survival over the decades can be put down in part to his own unsinkability. But, again and again, he has been able to tap in to the insecurities of the country and to show up the shortcomings of mainstream politicians with all the skill of a boxer jabbing through his opponent's defences. His nostrums are based either on fear – immigration, crime, unemployment – or on a hankering for a supposedly golden past and the proclamation of the need to return to traditional values. His policies are often manifestly impractical – the abolition of income tax, France's withdrawal from the European Union. But that does not matter. Many who vote for him have no real wish for him to run the country. Their vote is, rather, the way they can protest at the condition in which they find themselves. They can be as incoherent as he is. Take the Alsatian wine growers who depend on immigrants to pick the grapes because the local French earn better money over the border in Germany. While profiting from using low-cost labour, the people of this traditionally conservative region resent the way the immigrants bring their customs and food with them, and do not conform to local habits. So, in the first round of presidential voting, Alsace put Le Pen five points ahead of Chirac, and gave him double Jospin's score – in some villages, where crime is low and the only immigrants are those brought in as pickers, Le Pen and the other far right candidate, Bruno Mégret, took 30 per cent of the poll.

After a roller coaster political career stretching back to the mid-1950s, the National Front leader must have thought that the gods were smiling on him as the 2002 elections approached. The 11 September attack enabled him to remind everybody that he had been warning for years about the dangers of Islamic fundamentalism. The slowing down of growth, factory closures and a rise in unemployment brought out basic economic worries that could only serve his purpose. Jacques Chirac's decision to make crime the main plank of his campaign moved the debate into solid Le Pen territory, helped by Jospin's fumbling approach to the issue, a rise in armed robberies, and the massacre of local councillors during a meeting in the Paris suburb of Nanterre by a gunman who subsequently killed himself by jumping out of the window at the capital's police headquarters. A steep increase in petty offences fanned a climate of insecurity. So did the stress put on crime reports by the media – notaby vivid television reports of the beating up by robbers of an old man in his provincial home. As the Front leader said, why go for 'Le Pen light' when you could vote for the real thing. Though lawlessness and immigration might be linked in the minds of many of his supporters, the issue gave him a resounding new drum to beat, as did concern about national identity. The polls taken after the presidential election showed the Front attracting most support for its policies on crime and traditional values, with its pledge to abolish income tax gathering as much backing as its views on immigrants.

In truth, Le Pen has few coherent answers to anything. He does not need to. All he has to do is to point to the failure of mainstream politicians to make France a safer place. As the Socialist Laurent Fabius had once said, Le Pen asked the right questions – the trouble was that the orthodox left and right did not have the right answers.

Fabius was criticised for that, but he was right. The establishment's disdain for the National Front and its leader all too easily translated into disdain for the people worried about the themes he exploited so ruthlessly. Since Le Pen was so obviously a visceral snake oil salesman, it was best to pretend that he did not really represent anything, that, if you put your head under the pillow, he would have gone away by the time you woke up. Engaging with him meant giving him a recognition that was better denied. So he was allowed to get away with it, as the establishment declined to dirty its hands dealing with him. Significantly, François Mitterrand chose his bit of rough trade, Bernard Tapie, to confront the far right – and he did better than anybody else before he fell from grace. In 2002, nobody was ready to mud-wrestle with the old terror, which left him to float free while Chirac and Jospin supporters tried to tear one another apart. The height of ridicule was reached in the week before the first round when the presenter of a fashionable television show, who had inter-viewed the candidates night by night, announced self-righteously that he refused to have Le Pen on his programme in the name of republican values. But the broadcasting commission insisted that the Front leader had the right to air time equal to that given to others. So the programme broadcast an interview conducted by one of his lieutenants in which no awkward questions were asked and Le Pen came across as an avuncular figure who had only the country's best interests at heart.

The son of a Breton fisherman who was killed in the Second World War when his boat hit a British mine, Le Pen was elected to the National Assembly in 1956 at the age of 27 from a constituency on the Left Bank in Paris during the populist right-wing Poujadist revolt against the Fourth Republic. He soon gave up his seat to join the paratroopers fighting to keep Algeria French. His involvement in the battle for Algiers has given rise to controversy which resurfaced between the presidential and legislative elections of 2002. The allega-tion is that Lieutenant Le Pen participated in the torture of Algerian suspects to get information about the FLN liberation movement. In 1962, he told a newspaper 'I have nothing to hide, I tortured because it had to be done'. But he sued detractors who described him as a torturer, and won several suits before losing two. A month after his defeat by Chirac, *Le Monde* published the recollections of four people who said they had been tortured by Le Pen or the squad he led in 1957. One, a retired teacher, said electric wires had been attached to his body, and that Le Pen sat on him as the shocks were transmitted, holding over the man's face a floor cloth on which one of his men poured dirty lavatory water. 'I can still hear him shouting "Go on, go on, don't stop",' the former teacher said. Another Algerian told of being taken to a French military centre where, he said, Le Pen administered electric shock torture, and forced water into his mouth till he suffocated. Le Pen immediately issued a denial, and said he would sue the newspaper.

Back in France, Le Pen founded the National Front in 1972, while running a small record company which included Third Reich marching songs among its repertoire. His main constituency at the time was among *pieds noirs* settlers who had left Algeria after independence. The far right was a murky, fragmented world of nostalgics for the Vichy years, neo-Nazis, would-be philosophical proponents of a new, racially pure Europe and heirs of a French tradition reaching back to the Dreyfus Affair. Le Pen has never shown much discrimination in those with whom he associates. He has flown to Moscow to express support for Russia's most extreme nationalists, and to Belgrade to meet Serbian ethnic-cleansers. He can see the good side of Saddam Hussein. One of the Front's candidates in the 1997 legislative election was a founder of the OAS terrorist group which was involved in an attempt to assassinate General de Gaulle. In that same election, Le Pen assaulted a woman Socialist candidate, bringing him a fine, a suspended prison sentence and the suspension of his civic rights which cost him his seat in the European Parliament. And then there is the matter of the Jews.

Le Pen denies he is anti-Semitic, inevitably saying that plenty of Jews vote for him. But, as usual, his words contradict the more acceptable image he has been trying to give to become less of an electoral scarecrow. He called the concentration camps a detail of history on the basis of a book on the Second World War that devoted only two pages to them. He made an awful pun on a Gaullist minister's name containing the syllable '*four*' – French for oven, as in the crematoriums in death camps. After the conviction of a Vichy-era civil servant, he put the trial down to 'Judeo-centrism' and said it was scandalous that Catholic bishops sought forgiveness from Jews for the church's passivity during the Second World War. He dismissed one leading television interviewer as 'a kosher butcher' and observed of the much admired centrist politician and concentration camp survivor, Simone Veil, that 'when I speak of genocide, I always say that, in any case, they missed old woman Veil'. In a speech one night in Corsica, he fell to musing in the masterly way in which he feints and dodges around a subject like a champion boxer before closing in for the kill. He wondered whether it wasn't unfair that he was criticised every time he attacked Veil. 'Where's our freedom of speech if I'm not allowed to criticise her because she's a woman [pause], or because she's [another pause] ugly, or because she's [after a longer and more pregnant pause] a Jew?' he asked in mock indignation. The audience laughed and clapped.

The Front once adopted a declared neo-Nazi as an election candidate. One of its representatives in the European Parliament referred to the 'invented' Holocaust. A Front figure in the south wore a swastika necklace and liked to sing Third Reich anthems. After one of Le Pen's long-standing companions-in-arms became mayor of the port city of Toulon, the authorities threatened to shut down the synagogue because its fire extinguishers were held to be below safety standards, and tried to stop Jewish students attending a Holocaust anniversary ceremony. A Jewish boy was suspended from a Toulon school for having punched another boy who praised the gas chambers, and a bookshop opened in the city centre specialising in works commemorating Nazi Germany. Another National Front mayor evoked an unfortunate historical echo when she told an interviewer from across the Rhine: 'You're German, so you must understand us.' Le Pen himself noted that 'big international groups, such as the Jewish International, play a not-negligible role in creating an anti-national spirit'. His proposal, during the 2002 campaign, of 'transit camps' for unauthorised immigrants brought back memories of the places where French Jews were kept before being taken to their deaths in the east.

From a man like Le Pen, none of this is surprising, For, if immigration and crime has given the Front its growth and aggression, anti-Semitism has provided an even deeper well of poison for the far right.

★

The plaque at the Gare d'Austerlitz in Paris is unobtrusive, set along a wall from a souvenir shop, a car rental office and a left-luggage office. Few of the train passengers hurrying by give even a glance to the only memorial to more than 11,000 Jews deported by French police from the station during the Nazi Occupation. The plaque was not put up by a post-war government or by the city authorities to atone for France's role in the deaths of so many innocents. It was placed there many years later by a Jewish students' association.

There is a phrase that some people like to bandy around when people talk about what happened in France between 1940 and 1944 – 'the right to forget'. It is a phrase which applies to many who would never vote for Le Pen, but who would prefer not to remember the Nazi Occupation – in particular the deportations of tens of thousands of Jews to their deaths from French soil. There is a good reason for this.

In the northern Paris suburb of Drancy, a drab housing estate was used as the main transit camp to which Jews were taken before being sent to the concentration camps in Eastern Europe. There were twenty water taps for up to 5,000 inmates. Many slept on the concrete floors. Meals sometimes consisted of bowls of warm water, with a daily ration of two lumps of sugar. The deportations started in March 1942 and speeded up to three convoys a week that summer. On arrival at the camp, mothers and children were forcibly separated. Some of the mothers went mad with despair, and some threw themselves to their deaths from the tops of buildings. A witness told of seeing one convoy which consisted entirely of children.

Today, an inscription on a marble plaque at Drancy reads:

IN THIS PLACE
which was a concentration camp
from 1941 to 1944
100,000 men, women and children
of Jewish religion or descendance
were interned by the Hitlerian occupiers
then
deported to Nazi extermination camps
where the immense majority
met their deaths

There is a nagging problem in those words 'interned by the Hitlerian occupiers'. True, Drancy came under the overall command of the SS officer who supervised all Jewish affairs in France. But for most of its existence as a transit camp for Auschwitz, only a few of its staff were German. The day-by-day running of the camp was the responsibility of the Paris police, following a decree signed by the Head of State of occupied France. French officers framed the rules governing the camp. For two years, all the guards were French. The files for the 2,000 children who passed through the camp were drawn up by French bureaucrats. Even after SS men moved in at Drancy during the summer of 1943, many local police remained. French gendarmes loaded Jews into the wagons on the 'sheep platform' at the nearby station. The French remained responsible for them until the trains crossed the frontier in the East, and the guards showed no compunction for those who passed through their hands.

Consider the case of a woman known to history as 'Mlle B.', who arrived at Drancy on 20 June 1944. She was 22 years old. The French police told her to bring her valuables with her when they arrested her. On arrival, the camp staff noted her possessions in their ledger – three gold bracelets, diamond rings, a strand of pearls, two watches, two diamond brooches, stock certificates, bonds, cash and a collection of seventy-five English books. Mlle B. died in Birkenau concentration camp on 27 January 1945. By then, her jewels had been stolen by the French staff at Drancy, and her stocks and bonds had been lodged with the French state in the official Caisse des Dépôts et Consignations.

Such matters were not mentioned in official memorials even half a century later. How could they be? The mythology of the Liberation needed to believe that, with a few wild exceptions, the French people had been anti-German during the Occupation. To say anything else until fairly recently was close to treason.

France has its tiny group of obdurate Second World War revisionists. A handful of would-be historians insist that the Holocaust never took place or, if it did, that the death toll of 6 million Jews is an exaggeration. A magazine editor was fined 30,000 francs for publishing articles denying that the only concentration camp on French territory, at Struthof in Alsace, was used to kills Jews. Putting aside such people, what is still striking, given the tragedy that gripped the nation between 1940 and 1944, is the proportions which more innocent insensitivity can reach.

It took a storm of last-minute protests to get France's synchronised-swimming team to drop a water ballet based on the concentration camps from its programme for the Olympic Games of 1996. A physics teacher in a town outside Paris set off an outcry by giving her teenage pupils a test to calculate the volume of carbon gas required to kill Jews in a death chamber, and a maths teacher in Normandy set a problem involving counting the number of people killed in the Dachau camp. At around the same time, it emerged that millions of dollars' worth of jewels, gold, stocks, bonds and cash confiscated from Jews like Mlle B. had ended up in a state-run financial institution. The newspaper *Libération* found that banks had still been selling plundered Jewish stocks two weeks after the Allied invasion of 1944. *Le Monde* reported that French banks had held on to the contents of Jewish accounts now worth a billion francs which had been blocked on Nazi orders, while nearly 2,000 works of art stolen from Jews during the Second World War were still housed in national museums, most of them in the Louvre.

For decades, the fate of the Jews during the Occupation was swept under the carpet. Simone Veil recalls how wounded she was when she returned from the Buchenwald concentration camp by the way nobody wanted to know what had happened to those who survived. 'Resistance fighters who came back from imprisonment in Germany were, quite legitimately, honoured, while Jewish deportees had the feeling of being rejected, that their return bothered people.' In the immediate post-war years, mention of anti-Semitism was virtually taboo – the historian, Léon Poliakov, had to wait until 1951 before publishing the first of his seminal works on the subject. Police archives were among official papers that were sealed for sixty years. The state television service sat for years on a groundbreaking documentary, *Le Chagrin et la Pitié*, that showed the extent of collaboration, and it took an American historian, Robert Paxton, to reveal how Vichy had done the Nazis' job for them. When the leading French historian of the Holocaust, Serge Klarsfeld, calculated that some 80,000 Jews had been deported from France, he was met with a mixture of indignation and disbelief. The feeling was that the French could not have participated in such an atrocity, and, if it turned out that they had, the less said the better. So Klarsfeld produced the names and birthplaces of 75,721 of the dead.

Symbolic of the ambivalence of the past half-century towards this substantial period of history were the stories of the only two Frenchmen to have been convicted of crimes against humanity for their wartime activities. Brought up in an extreme right-wing Catholic family, where it was taken for granted that twentieth-century Jews bore the responsibility for the death of Christ, Paul Touvier became head of the wartime collaborationist militia, the Milice, in Lyon. He may have been primarily a leg-man for Klaus Barbie, the Gestapo chief in the region, but he also undertook some freelance activities – kidnapping and killing an elderly Jewish couple; flinging grenades at Jews as they left a synagogue; murdering seven Jews on Nazi orders in retaliation for the Resistance's killing of a Vichy official (the eighth of his captives was allowed to escape because he was gentile).

So far, so bad. But the Touvier story becomes more than the story of an evil man making the most of his wartime opportunities because of what happened to him after the Nazis were driven from France. Summary execution as the Allied tanks rolled into Lyon? Arrest, trial and sentencing? None of it. By the time Touvier was sentenced to death in absentia, he had disappeared into the inner sanctums of a Catholic order which hid him from his pursuers. In 1947, Touvier ventured out, and was arrested – for armed robbery. He escaped before being tried, and went back into his high church refuge. Twenty years later the statute of limitations expired, and Touvier was able to move about more easily, portrayed by his supporters as an old man who deserved charity. In 1971, the President of the Republic granted him a pardon, declaring that 'the time has come to throw a veil over the period when the French people were caught up in hatred, civil strife and even murder'. As more evidence surfaced of Touvier's crimes, he fled back to his Catholic friends, but pressure rose to deal with him. In 1989, he was finally arrested at a Benedictine priory in the south-east, echoing Édith Piaf to tell the police: '*Je ne regrette rien.*' He was duly sentenced and died in a Paris prison in 1996, after going through a civil wedding to a woman he had married in church while in hiding half a century earlier. A Gaullist member of parliament raised eyebrows by attending his funeral.

The trial of Touvier was the trial of the Milice, of the Frenchmen who had actively co-operated in the attempt to liquidate democracy,

Gaullists and Jews for ever. The trial of Barbie, in 1987, had been the trial of the Nazi occupiers. Ten years later, after interminable delays, the third aspect of the Occupation years finally came to court, and it raised questions which reached beyond those evoked by Touvier or Barbie.

From 1942 to 1944, Maurice Papon had been a senior civil servant at the regional prefecture in Bordeaux. Later, he became chief of the Paris police under De Gaulle and a Cabinet minister under Giscard d'Estaing. For six months through the winter and spring of 1997–98, at the age of eighty-seven, he sat behind a protective screen in a courtroom in Bordeaux accused of complicity in the deportation to Drancy of more than 1,500 Jews, including 200 children, in his official functions between 1942 and 1944. As a stream of witnesses, some even older than him, told how relatives had been rounded up and sent to their deaths, Papon remained unrepentant, insisting that he had tried to save Jews and portraying himself as a scapegoat for a nation's guilt. His arrogance was astounding: in the apt description of Robert Graham of the *Financial Times*, he exuded 'the irritation of a self-important man interrupting a weekend in the country to attend an unwelcome business meeting'. Still, his cause was bolstered by the rambling proceedings with 764 separate charges, and by the counter-productive histrionics of a showy young lawyer representing the families of the dead. But, little by little, the truth emerged. Appropriately for the trial of a consummate bureaucrat like Papon, it was often the documents which delivered the most chilling evidence: when a round-up at a hospital ran into problems because one victim was too ill to move, a handwritten annotation on the order simply instructed: 'Must be dragged'.

On 2 April 1998, after deliberating for eighteen hours through the night, the jury found Maurice Papon guilty. The old man in the dock cupped his ear to hear the verdict better, and then covered his face with his hands. He looked totally alone: his wife of sixty-six years had died a few days earlier – Papon blamed her death on the prosecution. The sentence was ten years' imprisonment and payment of 4.6 million francs in damages and costs. The defence denounced the verdict as 'neither fish nor fowl' and Robert Paxton judged that, though the French had expected a black or white outcome, 'they've gotten shades of grey'. Instead of a racist monster, France had put a pedantic old civil servant in the dock. Clearly, Papon had done grievous wrong, and deserved punishment. But when he turned on his accusers to remind them of the time 'when we had bayonets in our backs', many people might reflect on how easy it was to be courageous fifty years on and wonder what they would have done in Papon's place.

The litany of revelations in the media that accompanied the trial was such that there seemed a danger of swinging from the old Gaullist fiction that all the French had been resistants to the belief that they had all collaborated with the Nazis. There were apologies from the Catholic Church and from associations of lawyers, the police and doctors for the discrimination against Jews by their professions between 1940 and 1944. A plan to put a portrait of the inventors of the cinema on the last 100-franc note was scuppered when it was pointed out that the Lumière brothers had sympathised with Vichy.

Despite all that had been written on the Occupation, an opinion poll carried out during the trial showed that 42 per cent of people still regarded Vichy as a period like any other in the nation's history. This was not, in fact, so surprising. Had not the towering figure of Charles de Gaulle declared the Vichy episode to be null and void? Some prominent wartime officials, including one who would become the General's Foreign Minister and Prime Minister, had pursued zigzag careers during the war. Having been among those who voted power to Pétain at Vichy in 1940 did not stop René Coty becoming President of the Fourth Republic in 1954. Successive Presidents sent wreaths to the tomb of Marshal Pétain on the anniversary of his death, as though his leadership in the First World War blotted out his record as head of the Vichy collaborationist administration. France's first President of the left, François Mitterrand, insisted half a century later that the state bore no responsibility for what happened to the Jews in France during the war. 'If the French nation had been involved in the unfortunate Vichy undertaking, then an apology would be due,' he said. 'But the French nation was never involved in that matter; nor was the French Republic.' It was not until 1995 that his successor acknowledged the debt that could never be repaid. Had the French been, in the title of a history of the period, *40 Millions de Pétainistes*, or was it simply, as Papon put it, that 'history is a fluid matter, and difficult to apprehend'?

But what happened to tens of thousands of people during the Occupation was, in reality, all too easy to understand. Take, for instance, the story of Sarah Yalibez. She grew up in the Marais district of Paris, a strange mixture of streets from the Middle Ages, pre-Revolutionary mansions and the place where the Jews from Central Europe settled. For Sarah Yalibez, it was the *pletzl* – the village square. Her parents had arrived there in 1922 from Poland. Her father ran an antiques shop. Twenty years later, under the Occupation, the Marais was classified as Zone 16. Marshal Pétain planned to raze it to the ground and build a new district for his senior bureaucrats. Jews were banned from owning property there. Sarah's father joined the Resistance, and was caught in 1944. He was deported to Auschwitz with his three sons. All died there. Two of the sons were teenager twins; they died in the wing where medical experiments were conducted at the camp. Sarah was also deported, but she survived. And she campaigned for fifty years to get a memorial put up to her father. 'I wrote to presidents, prime ministers, prefects and all the mayors of Paris. And I just kept doing it, even though no one replied.' Then, in 1995, she attended a ceremony at the memorial to the Unknown Jewish Martyr in Paris. Jacques Chirac was also there. 'I decided to stare at him,' she recalled. 'He asked what was wrong.' She told him. A couple of months later Chirac became the first President to admit the 'inescapable guilt' of the leaders of Vichy France. More personally, Sarah received an official letter which authorised her to put up a memorial plaque to her father and brothers. She has fastened it to the wall in the garden of her father's old antiques shop in the Marais. It says: 'Here lived Mr Elias Zajdner, who died for France at the age of 41. A resistance fighter, he was deported to Auschwitz by the Nazis in May 1944 with his three sons, Albert aged 21, and Salomon and Bernard aged 15 who died in the experiments wing. We shall never forget.'

In the chronicles of the persecution of the Jews in France, no event stirs more shame than the great round-up of 12,884 men, women and children on 16 July 1942. Some 4,000 of the children and 3,000 adults were held in stifling summer heat under the glass roof of a cycling stadium, the Vélodrome d'Hiver, generally known as the Vél d'Hiv, which gave the round-up its name for posterity. On that day, a French gentile from western France who was on holiday in Paris happened to go to pay a visit to the parents of a Jewish friend at their home in the north of Paris. That night, Roger Galéron wrote in his diary:

Go to the home of Jacques' parents, 38 rue Arthur-Rozier. Nobody there. Go opposite, 2B passage des Annelets, second floor. Knock at the door for five to ten minutes. No reply. However, I hear the sound of gas. Go up to the third floor. The neighbour questions me, and then takes me into the Schpeisers' place.

I had realised that they dared not open the door because of the round-ups going on since morning. Plain-clothes police inspectors arrive, give the unfortunates half an hour to put together their little bundles of possessions, and then cram them into a bus. Their destination? Forced labour in Germany or a concentration camp.

I will long remember the little drama that played itself out in front of me. Monsieur and Madame Schpeiser are there, with their daughter Fanny and the two little ones: a boy of nine and a girl of four – both very good-looking. They gave me tea and delicious cakes cooked by Madame Schpeiser. I had trouble eating. Fanny and her mother were crying.

Five times, there were knocks at the door. Minutes of anxiety. We had to keep quiet. The police? A friend? They checked, looking through the half-closed shutters, when the unknown person left. A stroke of luck in their unhappiness – the neighbour living below is humane and helps them as much as possible. For fear of being caught, they do not dare go outside, even to get milk for the little ones. Can this really be happening in our century and in France, blessed land of free spirits?

In any case, the reprobation is general, even among a number of anti-Semites. Children of a certain age are separated from their parents. Jacques' sister, Sarah, and her son of 11 were taken this morning. Only Fanny knows. Happily, Jacques is not aware of this drama.

I leave after embracing them and wishing them the strength to put up with their trials which, it must be hoped, will be halted one day by the victory of reason and humanity. The poor folk are convinced that they are victims of a new inquisition and that the extermination of the Jewish race is being planned. Fanny talks about suicide by gas. Facing this extreme ill fortune, I feel shameful, I who can move about freely and without fear.

I leave, upset, my heart full of sadness and bitterness. In the street, a
new warning (Bekanntmachung). Any person who harms the
German army will be shot, as well as his brothers, brothers-in-law,
cousins etc. (all the male members of the family over 17 or 18 years
of age). I have to read it twice to believe it.

There were many instances of French people saving Jews at the
risk of their lives. Luck could play its part; one concierge might keep
quiet while another tipped off the police or the Germans in the
hope of stealing the family silver as the Jews were led away. The
deputy Director of France's Institute of International Relations tells
how his mother was taken into hiding in a convent in the south-
west on the very day that his father, who had been decorated with
the military cross in 1940, was arrested by the Germans after having
been denounced as a Jew by a Frenchman. The tragedy was all the
greater because many of the adults who were deported to their
deaths had fled to France from Central and Eastern Europe in the
1920s and 1930s; some had been specifically encouraged to come
west to help make up for France's population losses during and after
the First World War. There is no doubt that they aroused the kind
of racial prejudice which new immigrants often suffer, with their
foreign ways, their difficulty in speaking French and a clannishness
born from generations of persecution. But they shared a general
feeling of trust in the Republic, and could be reassured by the
knowledge that many of their children were French citizens by dint
of having been born on French soil. Yet, in the great 1942 round-up
in Paris, it was French police who took thousands of those same
children from their parents and sent them off in cattle trucks to die
alone in the east.

Some of those involved in such oppression complained about the
job they were given to do, and they may have exercised their duty
with less than full rigour. As one eyewitness of the raids in Paris
noted of the French police, 'some did not push it; others kicked
down the doors'. A few families were tipped off by friends at police
headquarters. But there was only a handful of resignations in the Paris
police: at a similar round-up in Lyon, a local commander did refuse to
let his forces be used to detain Jews, and was obliged to retire by his
French superiors, not by the Nazis. At war-crimes trials, Germans noted

that the whole of the French police were at their disposal. The occupying forces drew up the plans; as loyal lackeys, the French executed them virtually without question. 'The French police have so far carried out a task worthy of praise,' a German security chief advised his masters one week after the Vél d'Hiv round-up. Sometimes, indeed, the Pétain administration in Vichy went further than the Germans demanded. Even veterans who had been decorated in the First World War fighting for France were not spared. The French produced a definition of Jewishness which was wider than the one the Nazis proposed, and it was the Vichy Prime Minister, Pierre Laval, who decided that children should be deported with adults. If he could not quite deliver Jews like goods in a shop, he declared, he would do his best.

Tens of thousands of Parisians visited an anti-Jewish exhibition which equalled anything staged in Germany. Frenchmen who signed up with the collaborationist militia, the Milice, swore to fight against Jewish leprosy as well as combating democracy and Gaullist insurrection. Associations of lawyers and doctors purged Jewish members. French people took 100 francs from the Germans for each Jew they denounced. Bishops and priests kept their silence when not actively celebrating the values of Vichy. Members of the French SS division 'Charlemagne' were among the last defenders of the Reichstag before the Russians took Berlin.

Though historians have found that bureaucrats who resigned rather than carry out German orders were not punished by the occupiers, many officials preferred to fall under what the historian Marc-Olivier Baruch has dubbed 'the anaesthesia of the conscience of civil servants'. Jewish goods and assets were painstakingly listed. At the Prefecture of Police in Paris, an archive of 600,000 record cards was put together, listing Jews by name, nationality, address and profession. There were censuses of Jewish ex-servicemen, of Jews who owned wireless sets, of Jews with bicycles. In 1942, a Prefect in Normandy forbade Jews to travel more than five kilometres from their home, and the Vichy regime then banned them from leaving their commune of residence. In Bordeaux, the prefecture paid a taxi firm 350 francs to drive two Jewish girls to a railway yard to make sure they did not miss the train to Drancy. Even after the Allied landings in Normandy in 1944, some Prefects were drawing up new lists of Jews in their areas, and one official was planning a ration card which would enable him to keep track of where Jews shopped.

And as a post scriptum to the fate of tens of thousands who were deported to their deaths between 1940 and 1944, there was the simple observation from Sarah Yalibez as she told her story fifty years later: 'I never saw a single German uniform when they took us away.'

Humans forget. Life moves on. Two generations have passed since the Occupation. And yet what is still striking about France is that a nation with so much on its conscience should, in the 1990s, give a sixth of its votes to a party on the wilder shores of racial extremism. Or perhaps the two are linked more closely than proper-thinking French people would like to believe.

By its nature, part of the appeal of the National Front harks back to the collaboration of the Second World War if only in the fear of the open society and the attachment to traditional patriotic and family values – even if they are imposed by force. A mythical France where everything is in order and strangers do not intrude is the mirage held up by Pétainists and Le Penists alike. 'Cosmopolitans' were as much a target of suspicion as 'globalisers' are today – both are out to ruin France in the service of non-national interests. It is no distance at all from fascists of the 1930s inveighing against Jews from East Europe undermining the purity of the French with the connivance of the Free Masons to Le Pen telling the crowd in Toulouse that ministries in Paris were trying to create a mongrel race by making it easier to adopt an African or South American baby than a French child, all backed up by the powers of international finance.

France has the largest Jewish community in Western Europe, numbering around half a million. Anti-Semitism has a long and often virulent history, stretching back through the abuse of the great Jewish politician Pierre Mendès-France when he led decolonisation in the 1950s, the 'better Hitler than Blum' motto of the 1930s and to the demonology of nineteenth-century anti-Semitism and the Dreyfus Affair – apart from the abominable treatment of the Captain himself, and the back-covering of the French establishment, there were anti-Semitic riots in Bordeaux, Rennes, Saint-Malo, Grenoble and towns and cities from Alsace to the Mediterranean. It was not until Jacques

Chirac became Head of State that a French president brought himself to admit the state's role in the persecution of the Jews during the Second World War and, as we will see, his predecessor in the Élysée adopted an evasive attitude to the past, including his own, maintaining a friendship with the police chief who had organised the round-up of Jews. Anti-Semitism still crops up in casual conversation in a way that would be rare outside racist circles in England or America. My son was warned by a hotel-owner in deepest France that he should not admit to being half-Jewish because of what might befall him. A Jewish dentist who has practised in the west of France for many years still does not mention his race for fear of losing patients. A poll in 2002 showed anti-Semitism to be in an often very small minority, but 22 per cent thought Jews had too much influence in business, finance and the media – and 9 to 10 per cent thought there was nothing wrong in joking about gas chambers or mocking somebody wearing a Star of David.

The 'Israelite conspiracy' always lurks around the corner, in particular for the National Front and its leader. After a Jewish cemetery at Carpentras in the south was profaned in 1990, the natural reaction was to view it as the act of members of the far right. Le Pen reacted angrily, seeing an attempt to smear him. Six years later, the perpetrators were finally identified as members of a neo-Nazi group, some of whose members had had links with the Front. Le Pen grew even more indignant, and insisted that it was nothing to do with his followers. And how did he phrase his counter-attack? It was, he insisted, all a matter of insinuations against him by 'Jewish extremists' like the former Education Minister, Jack Lang. So, when France suffered a rash of attacks on Jews and communal property starting in the autumn on 2000, the first reflex was to suspect the far right as synagogues were burned, and school buses attacked. Initially, public and official reaction was remarkably muted though the Interior Ministry reported more than two dozen attacks on Jewish property and 115 acts of intimidation during 2001. Israel accused France of being the worst Western country for anti-Semitism, and a Jewish body in Paris warned of the start of a campaign like the Nazi *Kristallnacht* 'with the government totally passive'. Three weeks before the first round of the presidential election, Chirac called on the government to provide better protection, and Jospin deployed a thousand special police to protect synagogues.

Well before then, it had become evident that many, if not all, the outrages were the work of young immigrants. In part, the attacks were blamed on 'delinquency' – after attacking one another, the police and other symbols of officialdom, they had chosen the Jews as a target. But the Israeli-Palestinians conflict undoubtedly also played a part, as young *beurs* viewed themselves as emulating the West Bank protestors they saw on the television. The Union of Jewish Students dated the rise in anti-Semitic incidents to the start of the latest *intifada* in September 2000, with 412 attacks in the next two years. In November, 2003, the burning of a Jewish school led Jacques Chirac to meet Jewish leaders to deny the charge that France was, at heart, an anti-Semitic nation. Three-quarters of racist attacks reported in 2003 were against Jews.

But the anti-Jewish feeling fuelled by hatred of Israel among young immigrants presented a dreadful conundrum, defying the notion of a rational, unified state organised by the graduates of l'ÉNA. Here were members of one minority community attacking those of another, egged on by events in another continent. Here were people who had long been the target of the extreme right being attacked by the immigrants about whom the establishment could not bring itself to say anything critical. Take, for example, the Duchère estate outside Lyon which had been built for settlers returning from Algeria and had originally housed five hundred Jewish families. Their numbers had fallen to a couple of hundred as they moved upwards or out, and Arabs had become the biggest group. The main wall of the *cité* was decorated with a mural of white, black and brown people dancing in a line, with the inscription that all would be wonderful if everybody put their heart into it. But others walls were covered with anti-Jewish graffiti, and the Minister for Towns was left in no doubt about the feelings of the congregation when he visited the synagogue that had been burned down. 'If you don't want to protect us, if you don't want us to stay, tell us – we're ready to leave for Israel,' he was told. 'They know how to defend themselves there.' The blame for the attack was put on Arab teenagers who had been watching television images of Palestinians fighting Israeli troops. At the local snack bar, the air was full of condemnations of Israel and the United States, expressions of 'solidarity with our humiliated Palestinian brothers – and the conspiracy theories that it was all a Jewish plot to win sympathy.

France had condemned other countries for falling prey to the far right. It approved the ostracisation of Austria when Jörg Haider's party entered government, and its Culture Minister had boycotted a book fair which honoured Italy because of the presence of remnant fascists in the government in Rome. But now it was in the front line.

As Denis Jeambar, the editor of the magazine, *L'Express,* put it: 'How many ignominies must France suffer to open its eyes, finally, on itself?' The vast majority of immigrants were not involved, but the attacks only underlined the question from which successive governments had shied. 'That such facts are, now, possible on our territory shows a real weakening of our republican defences against the unthinkable,' Jeambar wrote. The failure to integrate the *beurs* had become a central issue for the country, and played straight into the hands of the man whose supporters formed a whooping conga line at his headquarters as he eliminated Jospin from the presidential election and who shrugged off the allegations of torture all those years ago as the work of Algeria's secret service.

Wherever Le Pen goes, there is an element of menace. It comes partly from his bruising presence; he is no stranger to fights and lost one eye in an electoral brawl on his way to becoming France's youngest member of parliament in the 1950s. His mood can change in an instant from hail-fellow-well-met to a snarling pantomime of paranoia. His staff says he does not travel by train because he would require extra security protection. His followers are regularly involved in election punch-ups. In 1995, they shot an immigrant dead in one incident; others threw a North African to his death off a Paris bridge after one of their annual Joan of Arc rallies.

Interviewing him after he had failed to qualify for the presidential election of 1981, in the drawing room of the smart villa he inherited from an alcoholic supporter in Saint-Cloud outside Paris, I asked him if he had a dream of how he and his party could recover. Le Pen stroked his chin with his index finger as he reflected. Imagine, he replied, a fight between a group of Frenchmen and Algerian immigrants in which 'one of our compatriots' was killed. Then imagine that Algerian immigrants stage a protest march down the Champs-Élysées. Things get out of hand. Shop windows are broken, stores looted and policemen injured. That, said Le Pen, would give him the fuel he needed for electoral ascent, even to as much as 10 per cent of the vote. He grinned, downed a Chivas Regal, and drove off to a fund-raising dinner after kissing his first wife, who later sought to embarrass him by posing semi-nude for *Playboy* in a skimpy maid's pinafore,

The riot never happened, and Le Pen's political demise was forecast time and again in the next two decades, but he always bounced back. After his nadir of 1981–82, austerity nipped at the coat-tails of ordinary people, and the orthodox right descended into an unedifying fight between its rival chieftains. While the Communists lost ground, their working-class followers looked for another populist, anti-establishment movement to support. After the breakthrough in the Norman town Dreux, where a pact with the mainstream right got the local Front leader , Jean-Pierre Stirbois, on to the council, Le Pen took 11 per cent in a poor, melting-pot *arrondissement* in northern Paris. It then got the same score in European Parliament elections which provided an ideal ground for the Front's brand of bad-tempered revolt – the equivalent of a nationwide by-election at which a danger-free protest vote would not affect the way France was actually run. Then François Mitterrand handed Jean-Marie Le Pen a great gift by introducing proportional representation for the National Assembly election of 1986. This had the double effect of limiting a looming disaster for the Socialists, and ensuring that the Front's vote split the overall anti-left score, handing the Front 35 seats in parliament with 2.5 million votes.

As always, there were predictions that it was a flash in the pan. Indeed, some deputies elected under the Front's banner did soon revert to the more orthodox formations from which they had come. It was, however, not long before the Front's imminent decline and fall was again forecast when subsequent Assembly elections, held under the traditional constituency system, cut its parliamentary representation to a single deputy. Those who greeted the impending eclipse of the far right might have noted that it still took nearly 10 per cent of the overall national vote. At the 1995 presidential contest, Le Pen again confounded the predictions to take 14.4 per cent. He might have done even better. Another candidate from the far right, a viscount from western France with an earnest, gawky manner, had won 4.74 per cent – if he had heeded the Front's call to withdraw, Le Pen might have finished ahead of the incumbent Gaullist prime minister. Suffering, as usual, from the legislative election system at which the first past the post at the second round takes the constituency, the far right won only one seat at the Assembly elections of 1997, but kept 15 per cent slice of the vote, scoring well in the territory we visited in the last chapter, including 25 per cent in Tourcoing, 23 per cent in Saint-Etienne, and finishing only 1,500 votes behind the victorious Socialists in Khaled Kelkal's town of Vaulx-en-Velin. It decided to maintain candidates who got over 12.5 per cent of the first round vote and were therefore entitled to run in the second round, even if they had no chance of winning. The effect of this was to split the non-left, and thus to hand the Socialists and their allies some 40 seats which gave Lionel Jospin his majority. The system might exclude it from representation that reflected its support, but, though kept on the sidelines, the Front's ability to stir the pot was growing at each election.

From the primitive conspiratorial band of colonial die-hards and fascist sympathisers, the far right has developed into a real political party. Unlike the fascistic groups which sought to undermine the Third Republic in the 1930s, the Front is careful to stay within the law. It has built up a network of organisations to cater for women, pensioners, ex-servicemen and farmers. There is a National Front union for prison officers and it has done well in professional elections in the Paris police. The party holds summer teach-ins, and an annual 'Blue, White and Red' festival on the outskirts of Paris, which reaches its climax with a rant from the leader (at one event, effigies of Chirac and Juppé were put up as targets at the shooting gallery). It has the support of a clutch of magazines whose virulence was in inverse proportion to their limited circulations, and links with reactionary Catholics. After the 1988 election, its grassroots workers concentrated on the declining industrial areas of the north and east, and on recruiting young voters. Its development into more than a vehicle for floating protest voters was underlined by polls showing that, whereas many of those who backed it had said in the past that they felt close to the traditional right, by 1997 only 13 per cent expressed this view, and nearly 60 per cent declared that their prime loyalty lay with the Front. The rewards were shown in 2002 when the Front beat other parties among the working class, the unemployed and the young. In the traditional Socialist stronghold of the Nord-Pas de Calais, Le Pen came top of the first round poll with 19 per cent – two points ahead of Jospin. As well as drawing heavy support in the Mediterranean belt, he made a major breakthrough in the north and east, taking more than a fifth of the vote in ten departments.

The party's growing strength nationally had been underpinned by its expansion in local government during the 1990s, particularly in the south where it took control of Toulon and three sizeable towns. Its longest-lasting success was in Orange, a town in the southern Vaucluse department famous for its Roman amphitheatre and the summer festivals held there. Orange's 28,000 inhabitants include a high proportion of small shopkeepers, former settlers from Algeria and retired military families from nearby bases. In the local election of 1995, the Mayor's office was narrowly won by the departmental Front leader, a balding dentist called Jacques Bompard. The Mayor had graduated through far-right student groups and supported the *Algérie française* movement to hold on to France's last major colony before founding the Front's branch in the Vaucluse in 1975. Eleven years later, he was one of the party's candidates who won election to the National Assembly thanks to Mitterand's use of proportional representation.

As always, a reason could be found for his success in becoming Mayor of Orange – in this case, the familiar story of divisions among the squabbling mainstream right in the Vaucluse. But, in 2001, he showed there was more to his appeal than splits among his opponents on the right and weakness of the left in the town, scoring more than 60 per cent of the vote to win re-election. In 2002, Bompard was reckoned to represent the movement's best chance of winning a seat from department in the National Assembly. In the event, he fell short, being beaten by one of his fiercest opponents from the orthodox right, who could muster broader support outside Orange. But the Mayor still took 47 per cent of the second round vote, meaning that almost half the electorate had decided that, after seven years experience of living in a town run by the Front, they were ready to give him another vote of confidence.

Bompard is a good reflection of the two faces of the Front. As a populist, he is a tireless campaigner, tramping round apartment blocks and assuring voters he will deal with their everyday concerns, from taxes to fear of rising crime. As Mayor, he cleaned up the streets, beautified the town centre, created pedestrian zones, made sure complaints about public services were quickly dealt with, built free parking lots, gave banquets for the old folk, and cut the number of civil servants employed by the municipality. He blamed the crime rate on the failings of the national police, and insisted that, with him, the people of Orange could see where their local taxes were being spent. This meant he won votes from inhabitants who appreciated what he had done for the town, but are not, necessarily, National Front supporters, though Le Pen scored 33 per cent in Orange in the first round of the 2002 presidential election, more than Chirac and Jospin combined. But, just as many of those who voted for the Front leader in 1995 and 2002 did not really want him to become President, so many of those who kept Bompard in local office do not subscribe to the rhetoric he delivers on national issues, making a distinction in their minds between what he brings them as a local administrator, and his hard right beliefs.

At the same time, the Mayor is a ruthless political operator who brooks no dissent. He has forced out local officials of different political persuasions, isolating and downgrading them until they quit. He fights running battles with the regional council, and does not belong to the association of French mayors. His communications director, who is also a graduate for hard right student organisations, has drawn up a list of media to whom the Mayor refuses to speak during electoral periods. One of the proscribed publications, L'Express, described the Mayor as 'irascible, vindictive, authoritarian, crushing all opposition'. To shield the citizens from subversion, books which the Front disliked were removed from municipal libraries. Distribution of anti-Front pamphlets in the street was prohibited for a while before the order was overturned in the courts. The municipal theatre specialises in light comedies rather than more challenging fare. When a dance troupe of whom Bompard disapproved performed in a municipal building, the town council ordered those who wanted to attend to submit photocopies of their identity card with their address, their rent payment, plus documents showing they had paid local tax and two photographs. Funding of cultural groups for immigrants was stopped, and a theatrical farce was banned because its cast of characters included a lesbian, a gay couple and a priest with a child. Instead, a medieval festival is held and a statue has been moved to the town centre of a local ruler who conquered Jerusalem in 1109.

On the edge of Orange, the main immigrant estate, with its 5,000 inhabitants, has been left to rot. One of Bompard's first acts was to cut off funding for social groups there. Most of the native French who used to live there have moved out. A small group of *beur* troublemakers who ransack telephone cabins and burn bus shelters are, in the words of one local inhabitant, the Front's best recruiting agents. Critics may speak of ideological cleansing, and *Le Monde* write of 'Orange under the reign of hatred', but the voters evidently like what they are getting in local terms – the main danger to the Mayor comes from his voluntarily isolation from regional bodies which could provide funding, forcing him to raise the cash for his improvements from Orange's own resources.

In Toulon, where rivalries on the mainstream right gave the Front its first city of more than 100,000 inhabitants to run, the local front leader, Jean-Marie Le Chevalier, hit a folksy note by bringing back bicycle police patrols. He boasted that he refused all requests to allow immigrants to settle in the city, and pursued his party's cultural agenda by cutting off funding of an experimental dance theatre which had been declared a national institution in 1987: when a troupe of eminent figures took the train to Toulon to protest through the streets, the Mayor's wife stood on a balcony at city hall blowing them mock kisses, with a glass of champagne in her hand. Chevalier then quashed an award at a local book fair to an author descended from Polish Jews, Marek Halter, arguing that the writer had 'an internationalist vision whereas we are for family and nation'. 'I do not care that Mr Halter is Jewish,' he added. 'Jews are rarely unemployed and they come broadly from the same cultural framework. But in France we risk being overwhelmed by an Islamic invasion from North Africa. In France, bigamy is against the law. Yet we are importing bigamous, or even polygamous, unemployed foreigners and their children. The risk is that our country, a product of its heritage and its combined genes, will be transformed.' Again, the local citizens must have approved because the mayor was elected to the National Assembly in the 1990s. Unfortunately for Chevalier, irregularities were found in his campaign financing. After he was disqualified from running for re-election, his wife took his place, but was beaten by a Socialist, by 33 votes. However, internal feuding within the Front, the defection of some local figures and Chevalier's haphazard style of running the city made Toulon an exception among southern cities in 2002 – Le Pen's vote fell by 3 points and put him behind Chirac though he still racked up 27 per cent at the second round.

In 1997, the Front won another southern town when the wife of Le Pen's lieutenant, Bruno Mégret, was elected mayor of Vitrolles. Her husband had been ineligible to stand because of problems over his election spending, but there was no doubt who was in charge – a woman's role, she said was 'to bring up her children, run the house and support her husband'. Not that she was any shrinking violet when it came to her own views: soon after being elected she characterised immigrants as 'colonialists' and backed the notion of racial inequality – sentiments which earned her a fine and suspended prison sentence for racism, and which provoked accusations from her husband that France was like a police state where judges decided what politicians were allowed to say. One of the new municipal administration's first decisions was to double the number of police and to station them on immigrant housing estates. A popular cultural centre which featured rock and rap bands was closed down for encouraging 'uncivic behaviour'. Avenue Salvador Allende was renamed after the National Front pioneer in Dreux, Jean-Pierre Stirbois, and Place Nelson Mandela became simply Place de Provence.

Naturally, Le Pen celebrated the success in Vitrolles. But it contained the seeds of a split which was to bring fresh predictions that the Front was going to become a force of the past. Small and neat, Bruno Mégret is a good example of the way rejection by the elite can propel ambitious young men towards extremism. After graduating from the École Polytechnique and spending a year in California at Berkeley, where he is said to have smoked marijuana once, Mégret became a civil servant. In his spare time, he was a moving force in hard-right political discussion groups which put the accent on the preservation of the European way of life. By the time he was thirty, he was a member of the central committee of Chirac's RPR party. Self-contained and confident of his own intellectual powers, he sought to make a mark in the 1981 legislative elections by asking for an unwinnable constituency. He was granted his wish, running against the Socialist star, Michel Rocard, in his long-time fief west of Paris. In the first round of voting, Mégret took 26 per cent, forcing Rocard into a run-off ballot. At a time when the left was in the ascendancy, this was quite a success. But the RPR apparatus rejected him as a loser. His problem, Mégret later reflected, was that he was not an Énarque. That was why he had not been given due recognition for having grappled with Rocard. Although it took him five years to line up with the National Front, he had evidently already developed the persecution complex any genuine extremist needs.

Quitting the RPR, Mégret set up a group of his own, and, in 1986, was elected to the National Assembly in alliance with Le Pen's party. Two years later, he ran the National Front's successful presidential campaign. In 1989, he was elected to the European Parliament and, then, piloted his wife to become Mayor of Vitrolles. That victory, he said, was 'an emblem of what could happen tomorrow'. By the beginning of 1998, he was the undoubted number two in the party – in the headline of *L'Express* magazine, he was quite simply 'a dangerous man'. The paradox was that, in such a personalised movement as the Front, the dauphin should be so different from the king.

Le Pen, a veteran of street battles in 1956, is a visceral brawler; Mégret, twenty-one years younger, is all calculation, a man whose hobby is careful carpentry. One embarrasses even his own followers; the other is self-effacing. Le Pen has huge physical presence; Mégret is short and slim. It is hard to imagine the younger man singing rousing traditional songs as Le Pen likes to do. Equally, one cannot see the older man indulging in the intense, pursed-lipped ideological reasoning that Mégret indulges in buttressing his claims to be the prime intellectual of the far right. Le Pen has never wanted anything to do with other politicians who might cast a shadow over his domain. Mégret, on the other hand, preached entryism, believing that the Front could do deals with at least part of the orthodoxy right. One is a hustler, an Elmer Gantry who found his snake oil in colonial defeat, the failures of the political establishment over two decades and the spinning of policies nobody can believe in. The other is a true believer, in racial supremacy and health checks for foreigners, quotas on the number of immigrant children allowed into schools, the biological and genetic separation of human beings – and in dressing the police in Vitrolles in black commando uniforms.

In March 1998, Mégret's place as the coming man was strengthened when elections were held for the twenty-two regional councils of metropolitan France. The proportional representation system which was used meant that there were only two outright results. After horse-trading in the following days, the mainstream right got control of ten councils, and the left took seven councils. That left five undecided – all had previously been headed by the centre-right UDF party, but the balance of power was now in the hands of the National Front which had taken 15.5 per cent of the vote overall. At a tense meeting the morning after the election, Mégret convinced his leader that the time had come to drop the old go-it-alone approach, and to offer the orthodox right an alliance. That evening, Mégret appeared on the evening news programme of the main state television station. Sounding anything but an extremist, he insisted that the Front was a reasonable party which would not insist on the full adoption of its programme as the price of an understanding with the mainstream right.

As Chirac thundered against the 'racist and xenophobic party', his RPR held a firm anti-Front line – one of its dignitaries who talked enthusiastically about Mégret's offer was promptly expelled. The UDF leadership agreed to reject collaboration with the Front, but its provincial barons were less resolute than might have been expected from a loose coalition of not very ideological regional potentates. Charles Millon, president of the Rhône-Alpes regional council and a former Defence Minister, tried to build a majority without the Front, but ended up reaching an agreement with the far right's local boss. Jean-Pierre Soisson, president of the Burgundy council and a one-time Minister of State, met the Front's local representative in a restaurant in Dijon and gave him a lift back to the city centre after assuring him that the region would be run by a 'right wing that has finally been brought together'. Jacques Blanc, the long-time leader of the right in Languedoc-Roussillon, accepted the backing Mégret offered. Two lesser-known UDF figures did the same in Picardy and the Centre. The UDF's nominal leader, François Léotard, ordered all five men to be suspended from the party, but there was nothing he could do to change their minds. In another demonstration of the Front's power, Léotard had to throw his support behind a Socialist to head the regional council in the south-east to stop Le Pen getting the job.

'Hold on, we are coming,' Front posters proclaimed. 'Between us and the socialo-communists, there is only a back water which we have to dry out,' Le Pen declared. His party's role in denying seats to the orthodox right in 1997 had been enough of a success. Now Front members sat in regional councils, and the movement could claim to be a major political force. To progress further, it might be time to drop the pilot of the last three decades.

Le Pen's blustering style, unpredictability, age and domineering attitude all seemed to mark him down as a figure from the past. So, when his conviction for attacking a Socialist candidate meant he could not lead the Front's slate for the European elections the following year, the party's number two naturally thought that he should step in. Realising the danger this represented to his leadership, Le Pen blocked the move, even proposing, in a re-run of the Vitrolles scenario that the list should be headed by his wife – not a lady known for her political skills. The upshot was that the old man had Mégret and his sympathisers expelled from the party. They set up a group of their own, the National Front/National Movement and went to law over the use of the party's emblem and access to its treasury. Le Pen denounced his former deputy as a racist while the *polytechnicien* criticised the older man as 'an absolute monarch' running the Front like a family fief.

The very public nature of their feud was highly embarrassing for a movement which had always prided itself on marching in step behind its chief. The prospect of civil war between Le Pen and his former dauphin could only hit the morale of the far right and comfort the mainstream. Indeed, support for the Front did drop for a couple of years. But Le Pen showed his force and skill by marginalising Mégret, and key figures at the top of the movement remained loyal to their historical chieftain whose charisma overwhelmed the dry manner of his rival. 'Le Pen has been part of the scenery for thirty years,' as one of his aides noted. 'He is part of the French folklore.' To get himself into shape for 2002, he did exercises every morning, and took a week off on an island in the Indian Ocean. Then he launched into his fourth presidential campaign, adopting a less belligerent attitude in his public appearances. The loss of funds to the Mégret wing of the far right meant he held few big meetings like the one in Toulouse seven years earlier. Instead, he attended dinners in provincial cities, and gave interviews to regional newspapers. 'We're a group of pals, and we have a good time,' his campaign director said. A journalist for the magazine, *Le Point*, was reminded of 'a slightly bad-tempered old man who says things in bad taste.' A man well steeped in French literature, Le Pen could wax lyrical. 'When I was a seaman on long voyages, I saw thousands of galaxies around me and I knew that I was not a big thing,' he said as he began yet another electoral battle. 'I, too, aspire to do other things – to walk on the beach with my wife, to look after my grandchildren, but now I think I can pick the fruit of thirty years of work, so I'm in this.'

The opinion polls during the first four months of 2002 consistently under-estimated his votes. Le Pen said he thought it 'possible' that he could get to the second round because of the divisions on the left, but nobody took that seriously even when he raised his prediction to 'probable'. The media largely ignored him, until a few political correspondents realised at the last moment that the combination of voter alienation and the lacklustre campaigns of the two main con-tenders might help him. Even then, they wrote only that he could repeat his performance of seven years earlier. Hence, the sense of national shock at the result came in on 21 April. If the left had taken Le Pen more seriously, Jospin might have rallied enough voters to stop him taking second place. But, true to the habit of the past fifteen years, the political establishment chose to ignore the threat from the outsider, and the Socialists reaped the whirlwind of their self-absorp-tion.

Forty-six years after he had given up his parliamentary seat to fight in Algeria, Le Pen had confirmed himself as the principal candidate of the have-nots, of the French who felt left behind by progress and threatened by the modern world, and who hankered for a closed society in which everything would be as it had once been, even if it had never really been like that. He had also crushed the rebel Mégret who got only 2.3 per cent of the vote to his 16.9 per cent, and was later discomforted when it emerged that the neo-Nazi who tried to assassinate Jacques Chirac on Bastille Day had stood for his party in the local election.

Unlike the previous party of protest, the Communists, the Front appealed beyond the ranks of industrial workers to shopkeepers, small businessmen and the self-employed. As small farmers joined industrial workers and the unemployed in fearing what the future held, the Front built up support in agricultural areas from 11 per cent in 1995 to 21 per cent in 2002. The second round defeat was less important than the fact that Le Pen had been strong enough to provoke what was, in effect, a referendum that split France into two unequal portions.

Two years later, the National Front won 15 per cent of the vote in the first round of the regional elections of March, 2004; with Mégret's candidates gathering another 1.5 per cent. In the second round, when it had fewer candidates, its score dropped to 12.5 per cent. In a sign of the fear the far right aroused, the fact that it did not do better was greeted with relief by the French establishment. But, overall, this was still the best performance for the Front in a regional poll.

A bid by Le Pen to promote his daughter, Marine, as his eventual successor suffered a set-back when the party list in the Paris region, which she headed, did poorly. The Front's leader, himself, was barred from standing as a candidate in the south-east because he did not meet the require residence requirements – in typical tricky style, he may have welcomed not being allowed to run because he could pose as a victim of the system and would not be blamed for a three point drop in the votes for his party there. The Front also fell back a little in the south-west and was hurt by a regionalist party in Alsace. But that was more than balanced by its increased vote in 14 other regions, and the way it built up support in Brittany, the Limousin and the Loire where it had previously made hardly any impact. Though it did not come close to winning control of any of the regional councils, it got enough votes to be present in the second round of voting, and, once again, helped the left to do well by draining votes from the mainstream right.

While the bulk of the French were bound to reject Le Pen for his policies and record, he had come to play a key role in the nation's life, providing a means for many who felt left out of the system to make their voices heard. By offering an alternative to the conformism of the political and technocratic establishment, the National Front was, in effect, providing a democratic choice for those who rejected the way France was ruled. That it should be left to a man like him to do this is a sorry commentary on the performance of those who had run the country for so long.

9

'FOG OVER CHANNEL'

But what if Jean-Marie Le Pen has hit on a truth? Not in his overblown racist rhetoric, but in detecting deep reserves of Francophobia on this cosmopolitan planet. At first sight, such a proposition seems ridiculous, given the appeal France enjoys around the globe. But there is fuel enough for at least mild paranoia. At times, the world and France become caught in an irrational minuet of bad temper that brings out the worst on both sides. Take, for example the way the long-standing strain of anti-Americanism in France was mirrored by savage anti-French feeling in the USA and a surge of the always present anti-French across the Channel as Washington and London went to war against Iraq despite the sustained objections of Paris and its partners in the coalition of the unwilling.

As a survey showed the proportion of French people who took a favourable view of the United States dropping in half to 37 per cent, American was awash with attacks on France and its President. This was not simply a matter of differences over policy. It soon became much more personal, as regards both Jacques Chirac and the French people. The President's dalliance with Saddam Hussein during his first term as prime minister in the 1970s was raked over, and France's Foreign Minister, Dominique de Villepin, was depicted as a vainglorious double-dealer, equally suspect for his dashing good looks and his abilities as a poet.

Picking up a Homer Simpson phrase, America blasted the French as 'cheese-eating surrender monkeys' who were repeating the weak-kneed defeatism they had shown in the face of Hitler in 1940. Boycotts of French wine were organised, and French fries were renamed Freedom fries. Some American tourists decided to stay away from France. In the 2004 presidential election, the handlers of the Democrat candidate, John Kerry, found it best to hush up the fact that he had been educated at a French-speaking school and was a cousin of a former Green Party minister in Paris.

In Britain, where accusations that he was merely acting as George Bush's poodle rankled deeply, Tony Blair was reported to believe that Chirac was trying to use the split over Iraq to undermine the Prime Minister's position in Europe. The *Sun* baptised the President 'the worm' and stuck his head on top of a photograph of an invertebrate. It also distributed a translated edition of the paper in Paris with the same front page mock-up and a screaming headline *Le Ver*. When Chirac visited London, the paper declared that 'there are few more stomach-churning sights than Le Worm strutting brazenly along a line of Grenadier Guards.'

Some French commentators joined the attacks as a group of intellectuals emerged who sided with Washington. In a book published in 2003, journalists Romain Gubert and Emmanuel Saint-Martin, warned that 'with our sermons, our empty gestures and our poetic flights, we have pissed off the planet. Worse: we make them laugh.' While opposing the war in Iraq, the philosopher Bernard-Henri Lévy, called anti-Americanism 'one of the great sicknesses of the modern world'. A senior French diplomat acknowledged to me that his country had been driven in part by 'egotism', quickly adding with a smile 'but that is what is expected of us'. On the other side of the coin, Chirac became an unlikely hero to the left in Europe and elsewhere for standing up to Washington, even if he had no effect in preventing the war. Having been swept back to the Élysée Palace with the votes of his natural opponents to counter Jean-Marie Le Pen, the long-time enthusiast for national sovereignty and military power was now cast as the apostle of multilateralism and peace.

The rift over Iraq, in which German support was vital for France, can be seen as an extension of the disconnection between Paris and Washington that had run through the previous six decades. Though American troops and support would be vital for the liberation of his country, Charles de Gaulle never wavered in his suspicions of Franklin

Roosevelt. He could see all too clearly the implications for France's position in the world if America became the only counter-balance to the Soviet Union – and his fears were far from being unfounded.

While Churchill spoke of the need to restore French glory, Roosevelt retained an ambassador with the collaborationist Vichy regime until 1943, hatched plans to put France under an American military governor, and talked of detaching north-east France to form a new country of Wallonia with Belgium and Luxembourg. The independent nuclear force, the initial rejection of British membership of the Common Market, the construction of a new relationship with Germany, the use of France's permanent seat in the Security Council of the United Nations and the effort to act as a champion of the developing world were, apart from their specific merits, all part of a broader Gaullist design to buttress the position of France against the threat of American hegemony. The tone might be less harsh under the General's successors, but the template was set, and it was only natural that, seeing himself as the true heir of Gaullism, Jacques Chirac should stride out on the path set nearly half a century earlier. There was nothing new in this. At the beginning of his first presidential term, the President had already given a striking exhibition of his vision of how France should carve its own path, and had provoked reactions that said much about how other nations reacted to France's assertion of its special place in the world.

Nuclear weapons are special, and nowhere more so than in France. To a far greater degree than in Britain, possession of nuclear arms is a source of national pride. The nuclear force was closely associated with the revival of national prestige after Charles de Gaulle returned to save his country for the second time (though its development had, in fact, been decided under the Fourth Republic that preceded him). The name given to the nuclear arm is revealing. Elsewhere, governments speak of nuclear defence or deterrence as if these are weapons only to be used against offensive enemies. France, on the other hand, has a *force de frappe* – a means of hitting out. While other countries targeted their missiles at their opponents, the French reserved the right to point theirs anywhere they wished, and disdained any thought of graduated use of nuclear weapons in favour of an immediate, all-out big bang. In all this there is a strong historical strand. Defending his decision to resume testing, Jacques Chirac conjured up the country's lack of combativity in the face of Nazi Germany: 'You only have to look back at 1935. There were people then who were against France arming itself, and look what happened.'

Since Waterloo ended their most sweeping military expansion, the French have generally depended on outside help to bring wars to a satisfactory conclusion, and in the case of the two German wars of the twentieth century, to drive the invaders from their very soil. However great the heroism of the massed ranks of ordinary soldiers of the Flanders trenches and the Resistance fighters risking their lives against the Nazi occupiers, it was the force of American and British arms – plus the mighty pressure from the Eastern Front in the Second World War – which put France among the eventual victors. Counting on others is, however, not a palatable recipe for a nation which thinks as much of itself as France does.

So, as a supreme realist in the nuclear age, De Gaulle determined that France needed its own arms of mass destruction if it was to enjoy the independence in which he so ardently believed. When it came to the crunch, he reasoned, Washington would not actually get into a planet-destroying missile duel with Moscow to stop the Red Army crossing the Rhine. So the Gallic nuclear warriors had to be ready to fight on their own from submarines under the ocean or in bunkers and silos dug deep into some of the most beautiful scenery of south-eastern France.

Nuclear disarmers might march in Britain; opponents of missile deployment might demonstrate in Germany. In France, to oppose the nuclear force is tantamount to denying greatness to the nation. 'There are subjects, among them national defence and deterrence, which should receive the united support of the French political class,' declared one of Chirac's foreign affairs advisers. Spending on the nuclear force rose under the left as well as under the right. It took François Mitterrand a decade to suspend testing, and then only after the world had moved on from the Cold War. As the man who had set out to reclaim General de Gaulle's heritage after a 21-year gap, it was natural enough that Jacques Chirac should resume testing. The adrenaline rush was irresistible to a politician who has been spotted using a ball-point pen decorated in the national colours. So the blasts resumed at the bottom of a bore-hole below the South Seas atoll of Mururoa, and protest erupted around the world.

That summer was not an innocent time. Russian soldiers burned Chechens alive in their cellars, and reduced their capital to a second Stalingrad. Serbs slaughtered Bosnians. Algerian fundamentalists murdered at will – and were massacred in turn. Mass killings continued in Rwanda. Authoritarian regimes around the world went on jailing and persecuting opponents. But there were very few demonstrations about any of this. If international anger can only cope with one major issue at a time, the target that year was clear.

There were unprecedented demonstrations throughout Asia and the Pacific. In Polynesia, Tahiti airport was set on fire and squads of riot police had to be flown in to handle the protests. Boycotts of French goods sprouted, and business slumped at the Club Méditerranée holiday villages in the Pacific. Share prices of manufacturers of French luxury goods wobbled amid worries about sales in the Far East. Restaurants struck French dishes and wines from their menus. In Bangkok's huge weekend market, a bar gave pride of place to a wine-bottle labelled 'Château Nuke – Appellation Atomic Superieur Contrôlée'; in Japan, a store invited customers to come in and smash bottles of Beaujolais Nouveau. Visiting Bali, my French wife earned some peace and quiet by pretending she was Swiss.

If the tests were so safe, critics asked, why not conduct them in an isolated corner of metropolitan France? A Japanese minister suggested the Massif Central mountain range. What also became evident was that, for all the rhetoric about the togetherness of being part of the worldwide French network, the authorities in Paris did not demonstrate quite the same concern for the well-being of the local population as it did for its Bretons or Burgundians. A report by the medical organisation, Médecins Sans Frontières, showed that, despite its relatively young and generally healthy population, French Polynesia had cancer rates 20 per cent above those in metropolitan France. Blood and bone-marrow cancers, which are associated with radioactivity, appeared high. The report broke new ground for one simple reason: the French authorities had never bothered to study the possible effects of the 137 tests carried out at Mururoa on the local population, or even on the 10,000 manual workers employed at the atoll. This seemed all too typical of what boiled down to a faraway administration presiding over a colonial economy where the gap between rich and poor widens by the year, as the locals go unemployed and civil servants count the 'hardship allowances' paid to them for the pain of living in Gauguin-land.

There was another problem which does not seem to have been taken into account in Paris. It showed blind arrogance, or arrogant blindness. French generals wanted to get the tests over before Paris signed up to a general test-ban treaty. Mitterrand had procrastinated, but the military made the most of Chirac's gung-ho attitude. That meant the first explosion came hard on the heels of celebrations of the fiftieth anniversary of the defeat of Japan in 1945, and that brought with it two historical echoes which would have been picked up in advance by a country better attuned to sensitivities on the other side of the world.

The end of Japan's imperial adventure could have led to the independence of large swathes of East Asia; in fact, it only turned the clock back to the return of European imperialism in Indonesia, Malaysia and Indochina. In France's main Asian colony of Vietnam, the Japanese defeat brought a brief flowering of independence. The military soon blasted that away, and thus set off an epochal anti-colonial military struggle that would kill 35,000 French troops and perhaps half a million Vietnamese over the following nine years. For a European power to carry out a nuclear test just at the moment when Asia was remembering what might have been in 1945 was particularly ill-timed. But that was not all, since 1995 also marked the fiftieth anniversary of the dropping of atom bombs on Hiroshima and Nagasaki, with all the commemorations of devastation which that brought.

Nowhere was the anti-French mantra more virulent than in Australia. Schoolgirls in Adelaide came up with a new version of the 'Frère Jacques' nursery rhyme, which began: 'President Jacques, President Jacques, Vous êtes fou, Vous êtes fou.' An Australian mayor urged his fellow citizens to post stuffed cane toads to Paris; a senator wondered whether the French might be 'murdering their children, mincing them up and turning them into pet food'; and the press, never known for donning kid gloves, went into overdrive.

Australian prostitutes boycotted French sex equipment, and doubled charges for French clients. There were some snags in all this ire down under – a stripper in Canberra found that appearing as an Italian maid didn't get quite the same rise from her audience as portraying a French *soubrette*. Drinkers of Jacob's Creek had to order another bottle to make themselves forget that the wine firm was owned by Pernod Ricard of

France. And, for all its sound and fury, Australia went on exporting 300 tons of uranium to France a year, with no guarantee that it was not being used in the explosive charges being tested at Mururoa.

The French reaction to all this was as inept as Chirac's timing. The Minister of Agriculture banned kiwi fruit from his home, and a Gaullist waved 'this unhappy little green fruit' in the National Assembly as he called on patriots to buy home-grown produce instead. The government threatened to sue a French newspaper for suggesting that the explosions might damage the surrounding atoll. Within a week, another newspaper printed a photograph showing a three-metre crack which it said ran for several kilometres in the coral. The gala opening of a James Bond film in Paris was cancelled because the star made his opposition to the tests known after visiting Polynesia. The President put off summit meetings with Italy and Belgium after they dared to vote at the UN against nuclear testing. When the Secretary-General of Nato resigned, Paris employed all its diplomatic firepower to block the appointment of a Danish successor because of Copenhagen's opposition to the Mururoa explosions. Ignoring international criticism, a parliamentary report concluded that 'by its determination, France appears as a strong country and this image is undeniably positive'. Two and a half years later, France ratified the international treaty banning all forms of nuclear weapons testing.

Occasionally, the diplomats got it right. The ambassador to Australia complained that the impression had been spread of France as just a criminal country run by a criminal President and inhabited by criminal people. As the Consul-General in Hong Kong said, criticism of the tests was one thing, but it was quite another matter when the French were attacked simply for being French. A member of the Dutch government wrote that France was 'really great, but what a pity it's full of French people'. Reminiscent of an old joke: on the first day God created the coastline, on the second the mountains, on the third the rivers, on the fourth the fertile plains, on the fifth the vineyards and on the sixth the forests – and on the seventh day, He reflected that He had given too many good things to a single country, so he made up for it by creating the French. Around the world, a jab at the Hexagon and its people is as simple as falling off a log.

*

No people is more critically concerned with the French than the British. As the centenary of the Entente Cordiale between the two nations was celebrated with a royal visit to Paris, the distrust which flows south across the Channel was exacerbated by the fall-out from Iraq and divergences over Europe. Though they agreed to work on military co-operation, relations between Tony Blair and Jacques Chirac were, at best, distrustful and could explode into an open fight as when the President said nobody had ever treated him so rudely, and cancelled a planned summit with the Prime Minister. 'HOW MUCH DO YOU DISLIKE THE FRENCH?' asked a capitalised classified advertisement in *The Times* in the 1980s. 'With a book in view, Arthur Marshall would welcome accounts of unfortunate experiences or anything else you have to say about our closest neighbours.' In the next decade, the French polling organisation, Sofres, reported that only 35 per cent of the British had a 'largely favourable' view of the French, and 20 per cent expressed outright antipathy. Seven per cent saw honesty as a French characteristic and just 4 per cent thought the French were brave. As the historian of the Channel Tunnel put it: 'The British propensity for wading rivers, and the French for seeking out bridges, has long been scrutinised.'

The clichés are set in stone. The French are rude, dirty, shifty and obsessed with sex, preferably outside marriage. Start with hygiene. 'The otherwise sophisticated French have long had a reputation for a certain blithe disregard for personal cleanliness,' *The Economist* observed in 1998, with figures to back up its claim. But later that year, an annual survey of social trends in France reported the astounding news that the French bought almost exactly the same amount of soap each year as the British, and showered or bathed more often. They also purchased more deodorants than any other people in Europe.

The Economist also managed to establish a link between cleanliness and sex by asking: 'Does the disappearance of the bidet, used by philanderers for at least 250 years, mean that the French nation is abandoning its passion for *l'amour*?' Apparently not in the case of a ski instructor who appeared in court in Britain after he touched a woman's bottom in the street and gave it all away when he confessed that, being French, he had 'slightly different standards so far as these things are concerned'. François Mitterrand's varied love-life was never much of a secret, but the French may have been more surprised when a magazine reacted to Monica Lewinsky's allegations about Bill Clinton by disclosing a string of other presidential affairs, linking Giscard d'Estaing with the soft-porn actress Sylvia Kristel, and Jacques Chirac with Claudia Cardinale and a Soviet air hostess – and attributing an illegitimate son to Georges Pompidou. There was no puritanical shock, however, and the French reaction to the White House scandal appeared best summed-up by a woman in the street who told an American news agency reporter: 'So what? It was only about sex.' Some might see that as an eminently sensible point of view, but it didn't stop the French media going to town on '*l'affaire Monica*'.

As for rudeness, the *Daily Telegraph* left its readers in no doubt with an eight-column headline proclaiming that 'BEING HOSTILE AND RUDE IS LIKE BOULES TO THE FRENCH'. The accompanying article quoted a Japanese psychiatrist in Paris as defining a condition among foreigners caused in part from 'an impression of persecution by the French'. Nagging, as a columnist in a Sunday newspaper put it, is the only time a French wife will deign to speak to her English husband in his native tongue. A contribution to a debate in the letters column of the *Independent* on how offensive the French were to foreigners brought forth the observation that, 'During the summer, large numbers of French students obtain jobs as waiters in restaurants, with the intention of cheating customers out of as much money as possible, while amusing themselves by being as rude as possible.'

'As we proved at Agincourt and Waterloo, a good kicking on their Gallic *derrières* is the only language the greedy frogs understand,' thundered the *Daily Star*. What do you call Frenchmen with an IQ of 180, asked the *Sun*. Answer: A village. And why are there so many tree-lined streets in France? So the German army can march in the shade. As France beat England to take the rugby Grand Slam in 2004, a BBC commentator mentioned 'French resistance', and then added 'if that's not an oxymoron'. Or relish this from a star writer in the *Sunday Times*, using the humour the English adopt when having a dig at other races: 'French women are the opposite of English ones. With us the mystery is all on the inside; with them, it's plastered all over the outside. What's inside is rather dull and spiteful. But, if you're into appearances, then a French woman is for you. And if you like to spend a long time in the bath, she'll be perfect. They rarely go near water.' Calling a film/book/play 'very French' is condemnation enough. In 2002, the cinematic comedy, *Amélie*, was seen as epitomising the country's artistic poverty by critics who simply did not get the jokes. The poet and critic, Tom Paulin, spoke dismissively of France's moral void, and a writer in the *New Statesman* saw the French as being 'in thrall to cheap effects' which fuelled Jean-Marie Le Pen. Articles in the *Guardian* and *Observer* put down France as a cultural desert and categorised Paris as a fascist city, holding up the writer, Julian Barnes, and film director, Ken Loach, as suspect because the French like them.

The writer, John Mortimer, finds French taxi-drivers the nastiest people on earth and the south of France 'one of the worst places in the world.' When the Cotswold town of Stow-in-the-Wold rejected a proposal to twin itself with a town in the west of France, the local council chairman reflected that the inhabitants would rather have linked themselves with any other country. Margaret Thatcher never trusted the politicians in Paris; when the President tried to talk to her about cultural matters, she sensibly turned the conversation to the weather. In 2002, one of the younger royals was reported to have shouted anti-Gallic epithets as the French landlord ejected his drunken group from a pub. The rulers of France, according to the commentator Paul Johnson, 'hate the British, and our freedom-loving ways, because they consider us, and our example, as an insidious threat to their grip on the French masses'. As the unscrupulous Prime Minister Francis Urquhart of the *House of Cards* series remarked of a colleague, in words of fiction that have the ring of fact, 'He just can't stand Frenchmen, and who can blame him for that?' Not that there was anything new in all this. For Sir Philip Sidney in Tudor times, France was 'that sweet enemy', while George III wandered the grounds of Windsor Castle urging boys from Eton to hate the French.

Mrs Thatcher's adviser, Sir Charles Powell, has remarked on the way in which the British are far more obsessed with the French than vice-versa. He recounts the story of a young British diplomat seconded for a spell to the French Foreign Ministry. 'On her return to London, Foreign Office colleagues eagerly quizzed her as to where Britain figured in the master plan of French diplomacy. The answer was: nowhere. It seemed that the French simply did not spend time worrying about us.' The author, Pierre Daninos, produced a best-selling stereotypical Englishman, Major Marmaduke Thompson, but the portrait was affectionate satire at most. The French press can be roused to indignation by the way the English went on exporting animal feed suspected of causing BSE across the Channel long after its use was banned in Britain. In one outburst of press hostilities, a French writer described the slaughter of the French at the battle of Agincourt as a crime against humanity, and took the British to task for their obsession with 'knitting jumpers and breeding pet rabbits'. But, as a rule, the xenophobia so easily mined in Britain is not reflected in France. The Sofrès polling organisation found that half the French had a favourable opinion of the British, while the number of French people registering at the consulate in London has risen by 70 per cent since 1990. And when it comes to political models, the 1997 election saw French right-wingers, as well as born-again Socialists, proclaiming their ideological kinship with Tony Blair.

In a sense, the lack of French antipathy towards *les rosbifs* is surprising: there are plenty of historical reasons for the French to entertain a hearty dislike of the English, if not their auld allies in Scotland. For almost four centuries, the English either ruled large tracts of France, or simply claimed to be kings of the country across the water. Mercenary bands from the north raped and pillaged their way through the country – one can still find tunnels dug in the Middle Ages for local people to hide at their approach. South-west France is dotted with ruined castles where minor nobles from the Midlands held ruthless sway. One Anglo-Norman crusader chief had a simple recipe for dealing with heretical natives – 'kill them all, God will know his own'. The Burgundians sold Joan of Arc for £10,000, but it was the English who burned her. After the Reformation, the Channel gave a physical manifestation to Europe's great religious divide. England stood in defiant opposition to the Catholic kingdoms to the south, and the distinction was not only political and military. It is hard to imagine France producing a Shakespeare; he was far too unbuttoned a character, his freebooting genius and independence of mind lying light-years from the order of Corneille or Racine.

After some royal alliances across the Channel under the two Kings Charles, France and Britain fought seven major wars against one another between 1689 and 1815. It was not that they hated each other as such, just that the monarchs of Versailles and the Louvre could not give up the idea of ruling the continent while the politicians in London were intent on preventing any one power from dominating

Europe. Britain usually came out best. The Duke of Marlborough established the island's military credentials on the battlefield, and is remembered to this day in a French children's song but, given the usual outcome, there are not many other mementos of eighteenth-century Anglo-French conflicts around in France.

The British, on the other hand, anticipated Bonaparte's faithful soldier with their triumphalist chauvinism. Predating the mad-cow controversy by a couple of centuries, the French philosopher La Mettrie believed that the British contempt for other nations sprang from their excessive fondness for rare beef. As if to confirm his thesis, William Hogarth produced a striking depiction of the humbling of the French before a great side of beef from across the Channel in his painting *The Gate of Calais, or, The Roast Beef of Old England*. Being French, he declared, amounted to 'a farcical pomp of war, parade of religion and Bustle with very little business. In short, poverty, slavery and insolence with an affectation of politeness.' Or, as demonstrating artisans were reported to have shouted in the streets of Bristol in 1754: 'No French . . . No lowering of wages of labouring men to four pence a day and garlic.'

The last military landing on mainland Britain – by the Jacobites – was backed by the court of Versailles. Half a century later, Napoléon represented the greatest threat of invasion between the Armada and Hitler. But the cross-Channel antipathy went deeper once the Revolution had overthrown the old order. From 1789 on, the example of France stood in counterpoint to the essence of the English political system. Even after the first flush of revolution had passed, the jumped-up marshals and imperial parvenus of Napoleonic France posed a meritocratic menace to the Tory and Whig aristocracy. 'The prolonged success of French arms in Continental Europe did more than threaten British territorial autonomy,' observes the historian Linda Colley. 'It was also politically subversive, casting doubt on the belief that men of land and birth were inherently more suited to the exercise of author-ity than any other social group.' On top of which, the idea of a mass army headed by generals who had won their way to the top by merit rather than birth was truly disturbing, as was their leader's use of symbols – flags, decorations, recognition of individual regiments – to rally his men behind him and induce them to go the extra kilometre for his own greater glory.

The American ambassador to London might be astonished at the way in which English guests at an official dinner spoke to one another in French three years after Napoléon's final defeat, and Edmund Burke might note that France had 'always more or less influenced manners in England'. But British prejudices against the French were becoming ever more deeply rooted, with more than a tinge of sexual suspicion. As Ms Colley puts it: 'The British conceived of themselves as an essentially "masculine" culture – bluff, forthright, rational, down-to-earth to the extent of being Philistine – caught up in an eternal rivalry with an essentially "effeminate" France – subtle, intellectually devious, preoccupied with high fashion, fine cuisine and etiquette, and so obsessed with sex that boudoir politics were bound to direct it.' That contrast referred to the late eighteenth century: it could just as well have applied to John Major and François Mitterrand, or to the Eurosceptics' view from Westminster of the Euro-Énarques of Paris.

Perhaps Great Britain made a great mistake, as the West German Chancellor Konrad Adenauer once reflected, in so fearing the emergence of a new Napoléon that it extended Prussian power to the Rhine to block any future French expansion. In retrospect, France had less harmful potential for Europe than Germany. So try a what-if of history: if Britain had lined up militarily with the French in 1870, would Bismarck's Prussia have been contained, and the world spared two great wars? Maybe. But the French were continental, the British insular (Jane Austen managed to omit any mention of the Napoleonic Wars in her novels). France was a continental nation which felt a need to be among the top dogs on too many fronts – on land, at sea, in the Atlantic and the Mediterranean, and in the far-flung colonies. Having opted for the world maritime role, Britain was content to leave mainland Europe to its own devices, so long as no one power dominated. In each case, geography dictated the national destiny; in the historian Paul Kennedy's phrase, the two nations were like a whale and an elephant, each the largest creature in its own domain but neither able to master the other.

National differences grew as the nineteenth century progressed. Looking northwards, Balzac observed that, for his compatriots, 'Britain is either the Machiavellian Albion or the model we must all imitate. It is the Machiavellian Albion when French interests are at stake or when it comes to Napoléon. It is the model country when the opposition wants to lambaste the government.' For the British,

London was serious, industrious, the master of the industrial revolution. Paris was the capital of an unreliable race weakened by sexual license and over-eating. The French emperor might have had his brief moment in the sun after the Crimean War, but he had to be daubed with rouge to hide his pallor as his troops were routed by the Prussians at Sedan in 1870, and ended up seeking refuge at a Benedictine abbey built by his wife in Hampshire. As the century ended, a British flotilla steamed down the Nile to the outpost of Fashoda to force France to give up its colonial ambitions in East Africa with a mixture of whisky and brute force – a slight which entered the French language as an example of duplicitous behaviour. Britain's Crown Prince and some of his more sexually adventurous subjects-to-be slipped across the Channel to enjoy *fin de siècle* fruits in Paris, but the Third Republic's politics were the object of scorn: 'French ministries are as ephemeral house-flies,' wrote the *Financial Times* in 1886. As a contemporary joke went, the rise of Germany over France meant that Europe had lost a mistress and found a master.

It took the British rather too long to wake up to what Berlin's vision of mastery entailed, but all the Allied bloodletting in the trenches did not lay the ground for the deeper confidence between London and Paris needed to combat the rise of Hitler and the tricky matter of dealing with Mussolini. At times, Britain still seemed ready to prefer Berlin, even if this meant putting a distance between itself and Paris. In war and peace, cross-Channel relations continued on a switch-back course. The old view of France as a flighty female lay deep in the masculine British psyche. 'As a nation, France is like a pretty woman, who expects to be flattered, and is not always above being spiteful,' wrote one apparently typical English author, Philip Carr, in 1930. French schemes for alliances with Eastern Europe to contain Germany were dismissed as will-o'-the-wisps by insular officials in London, while governments in Paris grew alarmed by British cosying up to Hitler. When they returned from signing away Czechoslovakia at Munich, the British and French Prime Ministers were both acclaimed for having prevented war; the vital difference was in their minds. Neville Chamberlain had a clear conscience; Édouard Daladier feared he might be lynched when he got home, and the French took to pronouncing the British Prime Minister's name as *J'aime Berlin*.

Within two years, attitudes had swung round. In 1940, it was the

British War Cabinet which took the extraordinary step of offering France a Union between the two countries, and the French Cabinet which set its heart on suing for peace with Hitler instead. Soon afterwards, Churchill welcomed De Gaulle to Britain as the embodiment of France's involvement in the continuing fight, but, before long, he was describing the leader of the Free French as 'the cross I bear'. By the time of eventual victory, this had hardened to describing De Gaulle as 'this menacing and hostile man in our midst'. Not surprisingly, when De Gaulle took a leaf out of Churchill's 1940 book and offered an exclusive Franco-British alliance, London responded negatively for the sake of the warmer relationship across the Atlantic. If Britain was absolutely right to stage the Dunkirk evacuation and to refuse to throw more of its aircraft into fighting the Luftwaffe over France, the French could only see this as an act of desertion by *perfide Albion*. And when, sixteen years later, Britain was forced by the reaction of Washington to recognise the futility of the joint expedition to Suez, France saw itself as having been let down by an untrustworthy ally who was no better than an American vassal.

De Gaulle once told an aide: 'We're going to take back from the English all they stole from us: Quebec, which is in hand, then Mauritius, and then the Anglo-Norman islands.' By which he meant the Channel Isles. The idea of a Gaullist-led invasion of Guernsey and Sark would have spooked even the British tabloids – perhaps setting off page-one demands for a landing to seize back Henry II's kingdom in Aquitaine or William the Conqueror's Norman domains. But, with military conflict a matter of history, this touchy relationship and its attendant antipathies are now being played out on a different stage.

The French have become the main villains in Little England's disenchantment with the construction of Europe while, in Paris, as *The Times* put it, 'wise' British policies were seen as 'emasculating measures from perfidious Albion'. Hence, the glee with which British Eurosceptics greet disagreements between Paris and Berlin – though they might note that such debate does not bring into question the basic agreement to consolidate the European Union, and to talk about continental construction, not destruction. Franco-German differences deal with deeper themes than headline-grabbing clashes over the shape of cheese or keeping asylum seekers behind the fences on the Eurotunnel line.

France epitomises state power, Britain the rule of the market. The pragmatic British have never felt much empathy with France's long-term state planners. France signs up to agreements and then breaches them; the British see themselves as men of their word. Paris is stickily nationalistic in business, but Britain wakes up to find that its *laissez-faire* ways have enabled a French company to own fifty of its utility firms. The British spy a Franco-German plot behind the rhetoric of European union; French ministers shake their heads at London's lack of vision or European spirit. France does not need a tunnel to be physically connected with the rest of Europe, while the proverbial *Times* headline – 'FOG OVER CHANNEL, CONTINENT CUT OFF' – has always said more than it knew about Anglocentric attitudes, and, for most people in Britain, the Continent means France.

No matter that London dismissively refused to join the founding Common Market nations; when De Gaulle turned down Harold Macmillan's belated attempt to get into the club, the offence was deeply wounding to post-imperial Britain. By his own logic, De Gaulle was correct – the British would have been a disruptive pro-American force, and their economy was too weak to stand the pace The Six set themselves. But the General's way of going about it grated. He was grandeur personified, and the British found that rather ridiculous, and then downright insulting when he likened the supplicant Prime Minister to the man in the Édith Piaf song whom she urges: 'Go and have a cry, Milord.' In private, the Milord's reaction was equally forthright: Macmillan told John F. Kennedy that De Gaulle simply wanted 'to be the cock on a small dunghill instead of having two cocks on a larger one'. For his part, De Gaulle replied to a venerable French politician who objected to his treatment of Britain by sending him an empty envelope on the back of which he wrote, in his own hand: 'In case of absence, please forward to Agincourt (Somme) or to Waterloo (Belgium).'

Britain's entry into the Common Market in 1973 agreed by Edward Heath and De Gaulle's sensible successor, Georges Pompidou, might have put relations on track, but the next Labour government across the water threw everything into doubt with its referendum on Europe, and then the strident years of Margaret Thatcher descended on the European Community. Mrs Thatcher had a good point in wanting her just dues, but the way the campaign was fought and the desire to play to the gallery back home took its inevitable toll, and there was no easier target in all this than the French. 'We have by-elections to win, bugger France, bugger Europe,' as one of her principal aides told me at a European summit. He could have reflected that, had it not been for French help with information about the Exocet missiles sold to Argentina, the Falklands War might not have been such a vote-winner. When Jacques Delors moved from the Finance Ministry in Paris to the Presidency of the European Commission, Eurosceptics were presented with their perfect devil figure. Not only was he a former trade union official and a member of that strange (to the British) breed of Catholic Socialists – he was also a Frog, and could be told to hop off.

The French could usually find aspects of Britain to admire – and some of them found it a handy refuge, from the Huguenots fleeing the wars of religion and émigrés escaping the Terror to the Free French of 1940. But the mutual ambiguities were rarely far from the surface. The two peoples simply seemed to be set apart. 'The French,' wrote De Tocqueville after journeying through Britain and Ireland in the 1830s, 'want no one to be their superior. The English want inferiors. The Frenchman constantly raises his eyes above him with anxiety. The Englishman lowers his beneath him with satisfaction.' Through the centuries, some of the French may have wished that their fellow citizens had more of the commercial spirit that went with the Protestant work ethic, that their country was less influenced by its southern roots. Others were less impressed. Asked if God loved the English, Joan of Arc replied that He loved them best when they stayed at home. Later, they were linked in the French mind with the power of money. An eighteenth-century Foreign Minister concluded that they thought of nothing but money. Napoléon dubbed them a nation of shopkeepers and railed against the 'cowardly oligarchs of London' who bankrolled his enemies. Alexandre Dumas denounced 'impious England' as the 'executioner of all that France held divine'. More recently, a former adviser to President Mitterrand declared that the land across the Channel was on its way to becoming an underdeveloped nation, while a school textbook judged Britain to be so divided socially that it could not move forward economically. Fundamentally, General de Gaulle observed, France and Britain have always been at war. Or, as Hogarth put it in a template for tabloid leader-writers:

Let France grow proud, beneath the tyrant's lust
While the rack'd people crawl, and lick the dust:
The manly genius of this isle disdains
All tinsel slavery, or golden chains.

The extraordinary thing in all this is that no country engages the
British more than France, be it as a holiday destination, a source of
food and fashion, the home of their most frequently studied foreign
language or the land which has produced as many great works of
art and literature as any other place on Earth. The cross-Channel
currents reach from pre-history (did Bretons build Stonehenge?)
through legend (did King Arthur die in a forest in Normandy, or in
Brittany or in Cornwall?) to the National Anthem (adapted from a
tune originally written by the French composer Lully for Louis
XV's mistress) and on to the final building of the most logical
tunnel in the world nearly two centuries after Bonaparte first proposed it. The French owed the name of their pre-euro currency to
the ransom paid to the English for a medieval king which made
him *franc des Anglais*, while a gastronome assured me that the quintessentially French dish of *confit de canard* originated in the potting
of poultry left naked by the Black Prince's marauding soldiers after
they had ripped out their feathers for their arrows in the Hundred
Years War. Six centuries later, 225,000 French people lived in
Britain. Arsène Wenger managed Arsenal to the League and Cup
double of 2002 and subsequent successes, his team starring a clutch
of players from France who brought unaccustomed artistry to
Highbury – what were tabloid-reading Francophobe fans to make
of that?

In the last years of the twentieth century, as Tony Blair remarked
that, 'If you've ever lived in Paris, it's hard not to love France', the
French capital discovered British culture. BRITAIN'S CREATIVE BOOM
FINDS A HOME AWAY FROM HOME: FRANCE, declared a headline in the
International Herald Tribune. British designers, led by John Galliano,
Alexander McQueen and Stella McCartney, moved into august
fashion houses. English plays and films packed in audiences. The
Jeu de Paume gallery in the Tuileries in Paris displayed British
sculpture from Jacob Epstein to Damien Hirst, and young British

artists had a show of their own at the city's Museum of Modern Art.

After the novelist Smollett 'discovered' Nice in 1763, it was the nineteenth-century English who made the Riviera into a holiday resort for the rich and distinguished. A British clergyman laid lout the Promenade des Anglais in Nice, and Queen Victoria gave it the royal stamp of approval. As Prince of Wales, her son regularly took his mistress to Biarritz in the spring, while a friend of a more recent princely mistress has said that the peak of ambition for Charles and Camilla Parker Bowles would be to go painting in Provence. The 198 inhabitants of the southern village of Saint-Martin-d'Oydes were reported to have been thrilled to have Tony Blair and family staying with them as a summer guest. A local pensioner noted approvingly that Mr Blair even spoke decent French.

In which case, he would have come to see, as we have remarked earlier, how the two languages refract off one another. While the British take French leave, the French *filent à l'anglaise*. Males in Paris or Mulhouse don *capotes anglaises* while their counterparts in London or Doncaster slip on French letters (from 'let' in the sense of hinder rather than pertaining to mail). The House of Lords still uses old French when it amends a bill, and when the Queen gives her assent, the official notation is '*La reyne le veult*'. (On a different, but significant royal note, the Queen Mother decided to send one of her horses to be trained in France for the first time – and by a French trainer, to boot.) So is all this talk of an Anglo-French divide just *une tempête dans un verre d'eau* or a storm in a teacup? *Honni soit qui mal y pense* – except that it says *honi* in my British passport.

Regretfully, the answer remains in the negative, and a new form of cross-Channel difference opened up when Tony Blair addressed the National Assembly in March 1998. He may speak better French than any Prime Minister since Anthony Eden, but Blair's message was more of a hit with the right than with his Socialist hosts. He recalled his days as a young man working in a Paris bar, and remembered how after a few weeks he had noticed that he was the only member of staff putting his tips into the communal kitty – the Labour leader's subsequent joke about it being 'his first lesson in applied socialism' met with delight from the RPR and UDF benches. When asked about his reception, the visitor simply observed: 'If you get applause from both sides, that's just good politics.' Not exactly the approach of the still ideological French left.

Blairmanie might sweep the boulevards, but there is no denying the fratricidal sentiments which flow southwards across the Channel. As the critic Anthony Lane remarked, 'The English fondness for France is normally a sort of neutron love: take away the people and leave the buildings standing.' And, along the way, Francophobia has found a fresh twist: don't just accuse the French of being dirty and undemocratic – hit them in what are generally taken to be their strong suits, and do so in such a way that any objections can be dismissed as symptomatic of the absence of a sense of humour. (This is, remember, the country that regards Jerry Lewis as a comic genius.)

Food is a favourite field. British food writers can try to make a case that London has become a better place to eat than Paris, particularly after it became known that Jacques Chirac was so impressed by a pigeon served to him when lunching in London with Tony Blair that he asked for the chef's telephone number. Some people who know what they are talking about strike a different note – 'Anybody who believes that English cooking is better than French cooking can't be taken seriously,' as the British chef Marco Pierre White puts it. 'The French are the greatest cooks in the world.' But the jibes go on. 'I'm just back from a week in France,' a British journalist announces. 'Naturally, I took a case of non-French wine over on the ferry so as to have something decent to drink.' More subtly, the food writer Digby Anderson gets to the heart of the way the world likes to have its French cake and eat it. Every year, observes Mr Anderson, the culture across the Channel slips another notch, both in manners and food – but from such a high level that, whatever the decline, the level of its food is still way above that of England. And that is exactly what makes things so perfect. 'The upshot of this mixture – the mixture of the good and bad food – is that now is possibly the best point in the decline for eating in France. You can sit and eat the best food in the world while still being able to denounce the decadence evident immediately about you.'

So that's clear, then. Enjoy France, but criticise it and its people – if possible, for one and the same thing. As a Balzac character reflects of conduct she cannot understand: 'It's like an Englishman on holiday; you have to expect some strange behaviour, but there are limits!' Buy your house in the Dordogne and lament the lack of the delicacies you find in the boutique grocer in Islington; snap up a bargain holiday home in Gascony and complain that you can't understand the local accent. If the farmers shake your hand, they are too forward, if they don't, they are stand-offish. If they have video-cassette players in their homes, they have betrayed their roots at the altar of consumerism; if they don't, they are backward peasants who don't deserve their huge subsidies from Brussels. Contemplating the combined effect of France's popularity and of the large numbers of the French who like to vacation at home, even *The Economist* slumped into tabloid-speak to write of 'the hell of French holidays', while the Irish novelist Josephine Hart complained of how holidays at their Riviera villa were marred for her and her husband, Lord Saatchi, by the number of friends from London they bumped into when they went out for a walk.

Inevitably, one reaches the ultimate put-down – the French are lousy lovers. Take Napoléon: we all know about not tonight, Joséphine, and his remark on their honeymoon that they would have time to make love when the war was over, but he is now revealed as a premature ejaculator who liked to pour coffee over the clothes of the countless women he bedded, and who may have seen his first wife as an Oedipal reflection of his mother. Jabbing at French sexual performance in bed is even more rewarding than spitting in their soup. After all, as we have seen, the French and sex are synonymous – a British newspaper headline about one of the greatest writers of the century was content to describe André Malraux simply as 'PHILANDERING FRENCH MINISTER'. We all know that their men are actually one-minute wonders with hairy bodies who rarely wash and smoke while making love. Their women dream of lesbian affairs with film stars, or have to resort to perfumed bras to turn their menfolk on. Alternatively, they are, as one male British columnist put it, like French trains – 'the bodywork's great, they're comfortable, but, when you want to get on board, they're always on strike'. A poll in 1997 seemed to back up the charge as it reported that 44 per cent of men and 53 per cent of women in France acknowledged a flagging sex drive. But that was soon overtaken by an international survey by a maker of condoms which put France at the top of the sexual activity league. Twenty per cent of the French are reckoned to have love affairs on a regular basis. Even the elderly do not let the national reputation down: nearly half France's pensioners were reported to consider themselves sexually active, and 17.5 per cent of those over sixty said they had sex at least once a week.

So why are the British so anti-French, the former Prime Minister, Édouard Balladur, asked a lunch party in London after he had left office. He might have drawn his answer from a volume of reflections by the writer and journalist André Frossard, entitled *Pardon Me for Being French*. It was, Frossard noted, a bad habit he got into when he was born and 'had never succeeded in correcting'. Reading British commentaries and reports on France made it plain that he was 'ego-tistical, vain, servile, jingoistic, uncivil, hopeless in big business, peevish, undisciplined, garrulous, intemperate. I never go out except to chase glory which always escapes me . . . I devour frogs and I belong to the most beaten-up and oft-defeated people in the world. Forgive me, please.'

The question is not so much whether the attacks on France and the French are justified – any country and its people can be attacked on a variety of scores. But the natural reflex to all this may be for France to draw closer to those nations where Francophobia does not find fertile soil, to mainland European neighbours rather than to the island to the north which sees the French coast as the beginning of the foreign domain where people speak different languages and behave in different ways. The Germans, for instance, generally accept the French for what they are (they even go so far as to have a saying that happiness is like being 'God in France'). Though a cooling was evident between Jacques Chirac and Chancellor Schröder as Berlin grew less inclined to follow the political lead of Paris, an extraordinary act of reconciliation and recognition of mutual self-interest has under-lain the Franco-German relationship for half a century after three major wars and the Nazi occupation – not just at government level but in a host of exchange programmes, including one under which tens of thousands of young people go to live and work between the two countries each year. The importance of this, and of the progress of Western Europe from a theatre of persistent wars to a region of peace, is not something that has much interested or impressed the British, with their nostalgia for the Battle of Britain and the years of standing alone against Hitler in the last national glory days. Crude baiting of the Germans and the French reflects an attachment to a national comfort blanket which is bound to set the island apart. The very use of the word 'Europe' to mean the mainland part of a continent to which Britain belongs speaks volumes.

The 20th century saw Britain and France fighting on the same side in two world wars, though their very different performances in 1940 and experiences in the following four years would give them a very different historical perspective. They joined forces again in the disastrous Suez expedition of 1956, and were allies in the Cold War and the first Gulf war.

Yet cross-Channel history since the 1940s is a rocky one. That owes something to France's determined pursuit of its own objectives. But it is rooted more deeply in Britain's ambivalence about Europe, and how far it is ready to commit itself across the Channel if that conflicts with its links with the United States. Winston Churchill's up-and-down wartime relationship with Charles de Gaulle symbolised the conflicting pulls on Britain as the Prime Minister sought to buttress the importance of France but became exasperated with the General's vision of his importance and lived in dread of the Frenchman disrupting the more significant alliance with Washington. For his part, de Gaulle told an aide who urged him to try to get on better with Franklin Roosevelt that America was already too powerful and that, in the end, Britain would always accede to the wishes of Washington. It could have been Jacques Chirac speaking about Iraq.

The problem for those who drop so easily into Francophobia is that the French insist on remaining themselves. Their national personality is so clearly marked, so evidently stamped on them, that it unhinges many critics. At the same time, the British find the French so intriguing precisely because they are so different from them, because they resolutely refuse to listen to the plea of Professor Higgins and be more like us. What is certain is that France will remain France and the French will not stop behaving in a French manner, however many McDonald's outlets open and however many anglicisms creep into the language. While they must be central to the process of European unity, France's people are intent on remaining a proud nation-state of an old-fashioned kind, whatever the rest of the world thinks. That presents them with a difficult trick to pull off, but theirs is a country which has long been used to juggling with paradoxes. For a century or more, it has kept the balls in the air despite military defeat and occupation, the loss of empire and the rebirth of the mighty neighbour to the east. But now some of those balls are falling to the earth in another threat to the France we know and love, or hate.

10

DIVIDED WE STAND

It may be no accident that France was the Western country where the Manichaean heresy took deepest root, positing an absolute division between light and darkness, between the spirit and base matter, between an ultimate paradise for perfect followers of God and the irredeemably sinful world where the rest are damned. This is a people which lives on its divisions. A tradition of dualism courses through French life and history: the extended social structure of the south against the nuclear family of the north; the linguistic dichotomy between the *pays d'oïl* in the north and the *pays d'Oc* in the south; the old nutritional division between the dark bread and red plonk of the masses and the white bread and wine of the elite – peasants consumed food that came from the earth, while their lords feasted on the winged treasures of the air.

The land was torn by violent wars of competing faiths, by the St Bartholomew's Day massacre of the Protestants and Louis XIV's revocation of the Edict of Nantes which had granted toleration to the Huguenot dissenters, by the bloody eight-year war that ripped through the Cévennes at the beginning of the eighteenth century and the emigration of some 400,000 fleeing persecution – many of them artisans and businessmen whom France would sadly miss during its industrial revolution. Naturally, there were accommodations. Henri de Navarre thought Paris worth a mass and converted to Catholicism to become Henri IV. At the height of religious strife, Protestants and Catholics shared the nave of the fine sandstone church in Collonges-la-Rouge in the Corrèze, Protestants in the southern half, Catholics in the northern half. But it was not until 1764 that Protestants gained their religious freedom, and only during the Revolution that they became full citizens of France. Though religion is hardly a hot topic any more, the old divisions peep through at the summit of politics – if he had had a religious role, François Mitterrand would surely have been a calculating Cardinal of the Ancien Régime (didn't he call his illegitimate daughter after one?), whereas his chief rival in the Socialist Party, Michel Rocard, was the epitome of Protestant reason; equally, Jacques Chirac characterises cavalier Catholicism whereas Lionel Jospin radiated earnest Calvinism. The rotund, reassuring prime minister the President appointed after his re-election could have been a provincial bishop whereas the Socialist leader for the parliamentary elections came over as an earnest pastor.

Then came the struggle of enlightenment against obscurantism, revolution against monarchy, republic against reaction, state against church, anti-Semitism and the bitter rifts over the Dreyfus Affair, right-wing extremism of the 1930s against the Popular Front, and the traumatic divisions of the Occupation: resisters against collaborators, the General in London against the Marshal in Vichy, partisans against fascist militiamen – and the difference between those who deplored the wartime splits as a national tragedy and those who saw them as the chance to end the sickness of pre-war society. The court around the First World War hero at Vichy was rent with jockeying for power and favours, while the rivalries in the Resistance were accentuated by inevitable paranoia. Sixty years on, arguments still rage over whether orthodox Communists took the opportunity to shoot Trotskyites, and whether the first internal Resistance leader, Jean Moulin, was betrayed to the Gestapo by rival resisters. Much later, one man deeply involved in the shifting patterns of the times laid a blunt charge: 'De Gaulle did all he could to eliminate the leading figures in the internal Resistance, either by covering them with honours in London or perhaps, even, in some cases, by letting them be physically eliminated,' François Mitterrand alleged. 'He fought the internal Resistance more than he did the Germans.'

At a grass-roots level, take Saint-Amand in the middle of France as an illustration of the starkness of the Franco-French enmities of the war. The town contained both Resistance and fascist militia groups. Hearing of the Allied landings in Normandy, the Resistance partisans took control. They held some of their opponents hostage, together with the wife of a national leader of the militia. He responded by taking hostages of his own, threatening to kill them if his wife was not set free. As German troops moved in to re-establish control, the Resistance fighters killed thirteen of their captives. In retaliation, the militiamen turned on the local Jews. Thirty-eight were thrown down a well, and then had bags of cement and rocks dropped on them until they perished.

The Liberation of 1944 naturally brought a righteous settling of scores which perpetuated the divisions of wartime. Some 4,000 collaborators were sentenced to death, and 767 were executed. The Vichy Prime Minister, Pierre Laval, was shot after trying to poison himself while awaiting execution. There were less official revenge killings – some estimates put the number of those who perished in the settling of scores in the tens of thousands. Another 25,000 went to jail, and Marshal Pétain ended his days in lifelong detention on an island off the Atlantic coast. Sometimes the punishment of those who had been too close to the occupiers was ideological, but often the cause was more human. When accused of collaboration for her affair with a German officer, the actress Arletty could be bold enough to tell the court: 'My heart is French but my cunt is international' and get away with it. Many other less fortunate women who were never more than sexual collaborators had their heads shaved by kangaroo courts before being paraded in the streets in shame. As Vichyites tried to keep their heads down till the storm passed, the Liberation brought with it a regiment of latter-day converts to Resistance – one French literary historian remarked acidly of the country's most famous post-war couple: 'On 11 August 1944, Jean-Paul Sartre and Simone de Beauvoir entered the Resistance, at the same moment as the Paris police.'

The Fourth Republic brought new cleavages that went deeper than the everyday jockeying for positions by parties involved in the merry-go-round of Cabinet-making. Despite their electoral support, the Communists preached revolution from political purdah. The decolonisation in the 1950s and 1960s produced bitter divisions, exacerbated at a crucial phase by virulent anti-Semitism directed at the great Prime Minister, Pierre Mendès-France. The traumatic defeat by the Vietnamese at Dien Bien Phu now belongs to the history books, but the end of France's colonisation of Algeria is still a living memory to anybody over fifty-five: Jacques Chirac served there as a sub-lieutenant. As national traumas go, the withdrawal from France's last major possession was about as searing as you could get for a modern European nation. Apart from the bloodshed, the repression and the violent demonstrations in Algeria itself, it is easy for foreigners to forget that, as comparatively recently as 1958, France faced the very real prospect of an army coup. At a time when Dwight Eisenhower was presiding over bland Republican prosperity and Harold Macmillan was telling the British they'd never had it so good, generals in French Algeria were drawing up plans for Operation Resurrection, complete with the mobilisation of paratroopers and tanks in Paris to surround the National Assembly, City Hall, police headquarters, broadcasting stations and the Eiffel Tower. A detachment of paratroopers actually landed in Corsica on a self-proclaimed mission of revolt against the elected leaders of the nation. The President of the Republic and the Prime Minister held all-night crisis meetings, and, within two weeks, De Gaulle was back in power, using the menace of army action to carry out a political coup that incommoded only the resentful politicians of the old regime. The men who dreamed up Operation Resurrection insisted that their only aim was to bring the General to power, but there would have been all the world of difference between a new republic born out of a military coup, and the one which evolved through De Gaulle's masterly and ruthless handling of the situation. Outside the ranks of the displaced *pied noir* settlers and some revanchist National Front supporters, it would be hard to find even a handful of people today who think that military action in 1958 would have achieved anything positive. But, in considering the condition of modern-day France, it would be short-sighted to overlook the place in the national memory occupied by the events of 1958 – and the assassination attempts against De Gaulle by the ultras of Algérie Française that lasted until 1962.

For all his rhetoric about rallying the French into a single historic mass, De Gaulle's style was hardly calculated to avoid dispute. Having returned to power in the most dramatic circumstances of any post-war West European leader, he invited controversy from the start with France's politicians, its allies and the Algerian settlers who soon realised that he was no providential saviour. The Gaullist process injected France with the new life it so badly needed, but, once the threat of military action had been lifted, nobody could pretend that the President acted as a balm to the country's divisions. A decade after the barricades of Algiers, the nation was again split beyond the realms of orthodox politics by the biggest combination of urban strikes and street revolt of the century. That opened the way to thirteen years of rule by the centre-right, but, as we will see in detail in the next chapters, it was also a time for a different kind of political in-fighting to emerge, with long-running civil war among the once-impregnable conservatives and the phenomenon of Presidents of the Republic of one political camp having to appoint Prime Ministers from among their opponents.

Underscoring politics, old geographical traditions constantly assert themselves as regions stand aside from the mainstream. The medieval home of the non-conformist Manichaean heresy in the south-west became a hotbed for Protestants and then for the left before swinging towards the far right. The plateau around Chambon-sur-Lignon in the rugged Haute-Loire department, which was a major haven for Jews and others fleeing for their lives in the early 1940s, had been a Huguenot bastion during the wars of religion. The Resistance stronghold of the Limousin remained one of the last Communist bulwarks fifty years after the Liberation, and gave the party's hapless presidential candidate double his national result in the election of 2002. On the other side of the politics, the anti-Revolutionary Vendée in the west produced a family-values, anti-European party two hundred years after the republican army massacred its Chouan rebels in the 1790s, and then handed Jacques Chirac one of his best scores in each round of his re-election to the Elysée.

Take any element of French life and it will almost certainly contain rival factions. There are two national honours systems, for example: the Légion d'Honneur and the Ordre National du Mérite. The *cassoulet* stew may be the quintessential dish of the south-west, but don't expect regional solidarity as you sit down at the table. In the town of Castelnaudary it comes with pork, in Carcassonne with roast shoulder of mutton, and in Toulouse with the local sausage; and each version has its fervent disciples. To avoid becoming entangled in the gastronomic civil war, the writer Anatole France opted for an all-round spiritual benediction which hardly fits the temporal solidity of the dish – the *cassoulet* of Castelnaudary was God the Father, that of Carcassonne the Son and the Toulouse version the Holy Spirit.

There are competing associations of chess-players and authors, film-makers and anglers. The number of concierges may be falling by the year, but they still have no fewer than five unions to represent them. Even criminals might be said to be divided by the moral demarcation drawn between *crimes crapuleux* and *crimes passionnels*. Two centuries after the execution of Louis XVI, the old royal family is badly split: the pretender to the throne, the Comte de Paris, disinherited his eldest son and denounced four other children for trying to stop him selling off family treasures. Not to be outdone, the Bonaparte clan has recurrent rows about who is the rightful claimant to the imperial succession.

We have seen how Muslim immigrants are divided from mainstream society in counterpoint to the Catholicism which the French profess but practise little. Religious persecution may be long gone, but the 900,000 Protestants still remain, in many ways, a group apart, characterised by their seriousness and their perceived absence of social graces. Within the seemingly solid ranks of the middle class, a strain of anti-bourgeois thinking has been kept alive and kicking by critics from Gustave Flaubert to Claude Chabrol. In the country's top kitchens, civil war has broken out between defenders of traditional French gastronomy and those whom they branded as being guilty of 'globalisation'. There is always a good pretext to set up a new organisation whose chairman will revel in the title of 'Monsieur le Président' until his dying day. Thus, the National Union of Restaurant, Café and Hotel Owners might seem a pretty all-inclusive body to represent the catering trade. But no; it has a competitor, the French Confederation of Hotel, Restaurant, Café and Discotheque Owners. Ah yes, the disco owners must not be left without a voice.

Politics provides handy labels for divisions that reflect human differences and ambitions as much as real ideological divides. The main Islamic and Masonic organisations have each been upset by internal political rifts which overlie more basic battles for influence. There are rival organisations of hunters which put up competing lists at regional elections. Feelings in the world of former French settlers from Algeria grew so heated that the head of the main *pied noir* organisation was murdered in 1993 by three members of another group. In some places, one café is frequented by Socialists, another by conservatives, perpetuating an old tradition – in the mid-nineteenth century, Balzac noted that 'in the provinces, tradesmen had to profess a political opinion in order to attract customers'. Sometimes it pays to cover both sides of the field: in the 1980s the powerful newspaper-owning Baylet family of Toulouse had a son in the Socialist government in Paris while a daughter sat on the city council among the supporters of the centre-right mayor. Even family feuds can take on a political gloss: a long tussle for a very large provincial inheritance was recounted to me by one of the old lady protagonists in terms of 'my son is true to our radical tradition, but my sister's son has sold out to the right'; in fact, the only issue at stake was how to carve up the fortune.

The three main trade union federations carry on doctrinal disputes alongside the fight for members; each labour conflict is likely to produce a different line-up between them as they balance tactics and strategy. The *Quid* reference book lists 150 parties, movements and political clubs. With more than 8,400 candidates running for 577 seats in the National Assembly, the legislative election of 2002 set a record for dissention across the board – in the southwestern city of Rodez, no fewer than ten right-wingers competed in a single constituency; to the south, 101 would-be deputies ran for five seats in the Gard department. Splittism goes back to the start of the Fifth Republic. Leftish Gaullists fought waspish battles with the movement's mainstream through the 1960s, and ultra-orthodox disciples tried to block the ascension of the General's successor who was thought to lack devotion to the faith. The extreme right was stridently divided for years, and then saw the split between Jean-Marie Le Pen and Bruno Mégret in 1999. The once-monolithic Communists fell prey to discords which led to a champion of *glasnost* running against the official candidate in the 1988 presidential race. The presidential election of 2002 brought forth no fewer than three Trotskyite candidates. The Socialist Party is famously fractious – at one point, its nineteen-member national secretariat contained ten different groupings, one of which was generally believed to have gone out of existence. In 2001, the Interior Minister in the Jospin government walked out to pursue his own destiny. The following year, the formation of a movement to give Chirac a parliamentary majority was shot through with rivalries between its leaders, and the main centrist leader insisted on keeping apart.

In this galaxy, each side believes that it, and it alone, is right. That makes the kind of reasoned compromises which are commonplace elsewhere difficult to achieve in France. Consensus does not figure prominently in the French lexicon which was why the long period of enforced cohabitation between Jacques Chirac and Lionel Jospin from 1997 to 2002 aroused such interest. The system survived, but the rift at the top of the power structure was unmistakable as the two men acted with one eye on the presidential election to come.

By separating the functions of the executive President-Head of State and those of the Prime Minister-Head of Government, the constitution of the Fifth Republic provided for two power-centres, unequal to be sure but each with its separate mandate and source of legitimacy. The President in the Élysée is directly elected by the nation – until 2002, every seven years, thereafter, every five years; the Prime Minister in the Hôtel Matignon across the Seine is appointed by the Head of State, but can only be a man or woman who can command a majority in the National Assembly, whose election was only brought into line with that of the President in 2002. Under the first two Presidents of the Fifth Republic, the presidential and parliamentary majorities coincided. In his love-me-or-leave-me style, De Gaulle would no doubt have resigned if the opposition had won a parliamentary majority. His successors proved more supple. From 1974 to 1976, the President and Prime Minister came from different parties of the centre-right. More strikingly, from 1986 to 1988 and again from 1993 to 1995, the first President of the left was forced to appoint a Gaullist as his Prime Minister, making concrete the divisiveness at the very top of French life provided for in the constitution.

In 1997, it was the turn of Jacques Chirac to call on the Socialist Lionel Jospin to become Prime Minister, eleven years after he, him-self, had launched the cohabitation process as head of government under François Mitterrand. By then nobody found the idea of such fundamental division at the pinnacle of the nation strange. Indeed, the opinion polls showed that it was positively welcomed at the time; so much so that some saw a new form of Republic in the offing. But then the rivalry between Chirac and Jospin cast a shadow over the attractions of cohabitation, and the Socialists went into the presidential battle of 2002 decrying it – only to change tack again after Jospin's defeat.

For the first two decades of its existence, the Fifth Republic belonged to the right, under De Gaulle and Giscard d'Estaing. In the following decades, the Socialists emerged as a viable alternative – indeed, there were times when the fractious nature of the centre-right made them seem like the natural party of government. The vision of France as a country which belongs – with its heart – to the left and not – with its wallet – to the right is a seductive one. It is, after all, the land of the Revolution with a capital R, and with a national motto proclaiming Liberty, Equality, Fraternity. History, with its powerful political role, is seen as belonging to the left, resounding to the memory of the forces of liberal progress and modernity, the eighteenth-century writers who attacked royal absolutism and Catholic obscurantism, the rallying slogans of the Revolution and Zola's *J'Accuse* denunciation of the trial of Captain Alfred Dreyfus, the euphoria of the Popular Front governments in the 1930s, the questioning of shibboleths by post-war existentialists and the free-thinkers of the 1960s. Recognising the thread, De Gaulle responded to a suggestion that Sartre might be arrested for sedition with a historical dismissal: 'One does not put Voltaire in prison.'

In fact, modern France has hardly been a triumph of enlightenment. Most governments of the last two hundred years have come from the conservative side. The first Revolution ended in a dictatorship led by a man who advised his brother that the one thing to do in this world 'is to acquire money and more money, power and more power'. The Revolution of 1830 installed a bourgeois monarchy, and that of 1848 led to a second Bonapartist autocracy. The Paris Commune was followed by the wheeler-dealer politics of the Third Republic in which personal position took precedence over principle under the dominant – and misnamed – Radical Party. Vichy came five years after the Popular Front. The student revolt and general strike of 1968 were followed by an election in which the Prime Minister described as having 'one eye of a vicar, the other of a rascal' routed the left. The Mitterrand years turned from nationalisation to privatisation within half a decade, saw the election of right-wing governments in 1986 and 1993, and ended with a presidential election in which the only question was which Gaullist would win.

If conservatives keep their heads, they can usually be confident of returning to power and wealth. 'French society dreams of revolution but, in fact, is repelled by change,' as the late minister and historian, Michel Poniatowski, said. Even swings to the left may be motivated by

a far from revolutionary resistance to change. It can be argued that
the Socialist victory in 1981 was the last manifestation of post-war
economic and social conservatism, promising to keep life as it was
through massive intervention of the state just at the moment when
computers, the decline of Communism and the economic rise of
Asia were changing the balance of the world: rather than France
putting itself in shape to meet such fundamental shifts, it reacted with
outdated nostrums and flirted with isolationism. Equally, Jospin's
victory in 1997 was prompted by the rejection of Alain Juppé's public
sector reforms, by Socialist-promised resistance to privatisations and
by the party's sceptical approach to European monetary integration. In
each case, once in power, the left took on some of the right's clothes.
Mitterrand acknowledged that he found the trappings of the imperial
presidency, which he had once denounced as constituting a permanent
coup d'état, suited him pretty well. His government hacked away
at state enterprises, and saw unemployment rising to double digits.
A decade later, Jospin's government oversaw more privatisations than
its predecessors, and went along with the European common currency, accepting that central bankers in Frankfurt should set the
French interest rate and that the Maastricht Treaty should govern the
size of the budget deficit. In the first round of the 2002 presidential
election, the combined votes of the left lagged thirteen points behind
those of the right. When Jacques Chirac ends his second term in
2007, the right will have held the Élysée for 30 years compared to 14
for the left.

Naturally, influences from the left remain following the victories of
the right, as in educational reforms after 1968, the abolition of the
death penalty in 1981 or the 35-hour week implemented under Jospin.
France needs to be able to think of itself as the cradle of revolution, a
place of ideological innovation, a powerhouse of ideas – and these
have generally been seen as belonging to the left. Yet the fall-out from
the early Mitterrand experiment, and the long hangover that followed, has induced a lasting sense of caution and self-protection.
That moves politics away from ideology and towards normalcy. While
critics within his own party blamed Jospin for not being left-wing
enough, it is equally likely that voters were alienated by his attachment
to dogma, his desire to keep in with the Communists, and his inability to strike a modern pose free of inhibitions bred from old-style

Socialism. Instead, they found themselves with a re-elected Head of State who, for all his Gaullien poses, resembles nothing so much as a Radical Party boss of the Third Republic, a born pragmatist who can reassure the French that their future is in the hands of a man of the world not very dissimilar from themselves who cleaves to a traditional view of the nation.

That view introduces another paradox. The French like to think of themselves as individualists who believe in the power of independent ideas, but they also put great store on order and conformity. Hence the obeisance which this divisive people pays to the supposed source of the cohesion of the nation – the state. *L'État* is sacrosanct, the glue that holds everything together, and must receive its loyalty in return. *L'État* is la France; la France is *l'État*. While Britain and the United States embarked on free trade and economic liberalism in the nineteenth century, France opted for the state. Building on the Ancien Régime base of Colbertist protectionism, and buttressed by the centralisation of both revolutionaries and top-down Catholicism, the state was the guarantor of national order, providing a framework which could contain the occasional lurches to the left. The accidental course of history was to be eliminated by an all-seeing authority on high. France, in the process, evolved a unique mixture of conservatism and socialism, whatever the political colouring of the government in power. Its big state sector, an observer remarked, was the best example of an effective Soviet system. De Gaulle had no doubt that, as he put it, 'there can be no security, no freedom, no efficiency without the acceptance of great discipline under the guidance of a strong state and with the enthusiastic support of a people rallied in unity'. Asked for the keys to national identity, the historian, Emmanuel Le Roy Ladurie, put the state first. One of Mitterrand's chiefs of staff defined it to me as the guarantee against the law of the jungle, while Jacques Chirac declares: 'For a Frenchman, the notion of the public good is inseparable from that of the state.'

The state, for its part, has drawn on this lay faith to buttress its own position. In so doing, it has been powerfully helped by the relative weakness of organisations that act as counterbalancing forces in other countries. The Revolution abolished intermediate associations which stood between the state and the citizen. The First Emperor laid down his legal code to impose the values of the state as he perceived them on the nation. With it came the drive for linguistic unity, a uniform currency, a single system of weights and measures and the same educational process for all – as the historian Alistair Horne has observed, roads and bureaucracy radiated in tandem outward from the single centre of Paris to exert physical control over the furthest-flung regions of France. Later in the nineteenth century, the weakness of French capitalism and finance left a far greater economic role for the state than was the case in Britain or the United States, and its influence, in turn, dampened down the growth of financial and industrial enterprise. *L'État providence*, which ensures the well-being of citizens whether they want it or not, was a French concept long before the welfare state came into being.

So the state survives through thick and thin, and its servants exist to do its bidding without question, from the highest-placed Énarque to the gendarme on the beat. The tradition was set long ago, epitomised by the ever-adaptable Charles-Maurice de Talleyrand, successively Catholic Bishop of Autun in Burgundy, servant of the revolutionary church, Foreign Minister for Bonaparte and then for the restored Bourbon monarchy, and finally ambassador to London for their Orleanist successor. For those liable to pose moral questions about such survival shifts, this might cause some problems – Bonaparte called Talleyrand a 'shit in silk stockings'. So it is much easier all round if blind obedience to the state's commands is the order of the day. Marianne, or rather her living representatives, knows best. For two centuries, civil servants and lawyers have grown used to the ethical somersaults involved, from the religious school in the town of Vendôme which quickly slipped a fawning mention of Napoléon into its catechism when it saw the way the wind was blowing, to the judge at the trial of Philippe Pétain in 1945 who had sworn allegiance to the Marshal a few years earlier. Politicians get in the way; without them the functionary can exploit his personal identification with the state to the full. For some French civil servants, at least, the Occupation years were an unanticipated delight, in which they could erect a new model state free of politics in which a law professor became Minister for Justice, a leading academic ran the civil service and a well-trained official took over the Finance Ministry. It was just the kind of set-up to suit Maurice Papon, the civil servant who was eventually brought to trial over the deportation of Jews from Bordeaux and who, as much as any man, can be taken as a symbol of devoted service to the state – and, thus, to himself.

As a young man, Papon belonged to the moderate Radical Socialist party, the main political grouping of the declining Third Republic. In 1931, at the age of twenty, he joined the staff of the Air Minister, a senior member of the party. Five years later, he took a bigger job with another Radical Socialist member of the Popular Front government. At the end of 1940, he joined the Vichy administration, rising to become Secretary-General of the Prefecture of the Gironde department, based in Bordeaux. There were plenty of prefectorial jobs going since Vichy had sacked half the old staff to ensure loyalty to its order. In his new post, Papon was given responsibility for activities linked with the war and the Occupation, including Jewish affairs. Convoys of Jews left Bordeaux at regular intervals, and Papon earned high marks from the Germans for his 'quick and trustworthy' work. In May 1943, there was a disagreeable episode in which Gaullist graffiti was found scrawled in the toilets of the Prefecture; Papon had the toilets watched and a twenty-year-old employee was duly caught and sent off to forced labour in Germany.

At the end of 1943, as the Allies were landing in North Africa, Papon agreed to shelter a civil servant who had joined the Resistance after being sacked because he was Jewish. In January 1944, he turned down the offer of a prefecture of his own: at the same time he signed a warrant for 228 Jews which even told the police how to deal with the pets of those arrested – the servants of the state are sticklers for detail even in the worst of times. That spring, he made contact with a local Resistance leader and, when Bordeaux was liberated in August, became his chief of staff. After a post-war career as a prefect in France and its colonies, he worked as a senior official for the Socialist Interior Minister and was then appointed chief of the Paris police. Holding on to the job under the Fifth Republic, he was in charge of the forces of order who killed hundreds of Algerians in the capital in 1961. Elected to the National Assembly in 1968, he headed the parliamentary finance commission and became Minister for the Budget under Giscard d'Estaing. It was only in 1981 that, as a result of an electoral manoeuvre which we will hear more about later, the truth about his wartime career came into the spotlight.

Setting aside questions of morality, what is so striking about

Maurice Papon's career is how he worked for whoever was in power whatever their creed. It is one thing for a civil servant to regard himself as being above politics, but still quite a feat to have laboured for the Radical Socialists in the 1930s, Vichy in the 1940s, the Socialists in the 1950s, De Gaulle in the 1960s and Giscard in the 1970s. And it is equally amazing that his successive bosses did not seem to care about his past affiliations, so long as he did the job. For sixty years, Papon was the embodiment of the administrative continuity which that state prizes so highly. As he himself wrote: 'There are no crises of conscience when one obeys the orders of the government.' Or, as the war criminal Paul Touvier pleaded when he was finally brought to trial: 'All I ever did was to serve the French state.'

Article two of the 1958 constitution proclaims France to be an indivisible Republic. 'When the French are arguing with one another, one has to talk to them of France,' De Gaulle advised. The triumph of the Jacobin revolutionaries after 1789 imposed the idea of the nation on a heterogeneous people. To believe in the Revolution was to believe in the all-powerful unitary state, and vice-versa. Apart from scattered proponents of *le libéralisme avancé* who would entrust all to the market, the French are uncomfortable with any idea of the state withering away. Despite the continual grumbling about bureaucracy and taxes, there is not much indication that they seriously want it to re-think its role. 'The dominant political culture is to worship the cult of the nation state,' as the Gaullist deputy Patrick Devedjian puts it. 'We are an old country which has astonished the world by our influence, but we continue to doubt ourselves to the point at which we imagine that our future depends on the power of the state. A state to which we confide our soul and which we prefer to the rule of law.' Asked by pollsters what they most desired in the spring of 1995, the number-one answer of respondents was 'a strong state'. Only in France could there still be a General Commissariat of the Plan to chart the nation's path – though the Commissioner was replaced at the beginning of 1998 after expressing less than full enthusiasm for government policies. Significantly, the standard-bearer of market economics and a smaller state, Finance Minister Alain Madelin, was the first man to resign from the Chirac administration when his ideas threatened to disturb the status quo.

If the state is to hold the country together, it has to be present everywhere – whether in the extensive public transport network or in the incomprehensible official notices pinned up outside the *mairie* of every commune. It has to coddle teachers and allow them to rule their own roost because it has traditionally depended on them as its representatives to the youth of the nation. 'France is saved from death by education,' wrote Émile Zola in 1898, and there was never any doubt as to the strict republican form which that education should take. Teachers were more than mere educators; they represented the Republic and modernity. That strain in French life lives on a century after Zola's panegyric, or the warning from the Tiger of the Third Republic, Georges Clemenceau, that outlawing non-secular teaching would mean the tyranny of the state. So the idea of introducing more creativity into the classroom is deeply worrying just because of the way in which it could shake old certainties inherited from the nineteenth century. To withdraw the special pension privileges of teachers would be to betray their century-old republican mission on behalf of the state in classrooms throughout the land. Equally, to shut down hugely subsidised rural railway lines would be an abdication of responsibility to its people – even if the state employees at the SNCF account for 20 to 30 per cent of all days lost through strikes. Decentralisation has reduced the authority of prefects, but the existence of these emissaries from Paris has never been questioned. They represent the skein of *l'État* and a great in-bred domain for the graduates of the Grandes Écoles.

This state which cannot accept that any part of national life is beyond its reach is by far the biggest employer in the country. Its civil servants make up a quarter of the workforce – compared to 14–15 per cent in Britain and Germany. Their salaries take up almost one-sixth of the national income. As for the general belief that selfless civil servants are less well-paid than their peers in the private sector, an independent study in 1994 showed the reverse to be true in non-executive jobs. Despite the declining number of farmers, the Agriculture Ministry still employs as many functionaries as it did a decade ago. Long after the last big war, the Ex-Servicemen's Ministry costs 26 billion francs a year. Reform of other sectors of national life may be on the agenda, but not the sacred caste of the functionaries of the state. Whereas public-sector companies have been put under the spotlight, readied for privatisation or gone through painful slimming cures, the state has left its great administrative army alone. One investigation suggested that the number of hidden civil service scandals might exceed those that had come to light elsewhere – but no investigating magistrates have stuck their noses into the inner workings of the nation's administrative machinery. A list of white elephants spawned by bureaucratic incompetence drawn up by the magazine *Le Point* contained some of the following gems: the 880-million-franc high-speed train station at Lyon airport that handles only 500 passengers a day; the railway construction in Normandy where a new platform was built 300 metres away from the station; a 70-million-franc museum in Nice which was still empty ten years after being commissioned; a projected road tunnel in Toulon which collapsed and was abandoned after 1.4 billion francs had been spent on it; a planned conference centre in Paris which remained unbuilt despite the expenditure of 800 million francs; and a road bridge in Normandy with no road connected to it. No heads have rolled, or not to the knowledge of the taxpayers who footed the bill in each case. From teachers to mandarins, the civil service is unaccountable to anybody except itself. A damning report by an *Inspecteur des Finances* who had been close to the Socialists spoke of a looming disaster caused by the failure of successive governments of left and right to get to grips with the size and cost of the public-service sector.

In the nineteenth century, the state was at the vanguard of modernity, the guardian of the legacy of 1789. 'The English have William Shakespeare,' wrote the historian Jules Michelet, 'we have the French Revolution.' Having despatched their royal family, the French bowed the knee before the Nation and its representative on Earth. By the end of the twentieth century, however, the state has become a bulwark of conservative paternalism which the French find too comfortable to be questioned. Envious as they may be of Tony Blair's success, few politicians in Paris would dare to proclaim the New Labour doctrine that the issue is not what the state can do for you, but what it can enable you to do for yourself. For the French, what the state can do for them is a central plank of existence, and one which they will not readily give up.

That is not to say that they do not complain about its tentacles, particularly when this involves endless form-filling. In his 1995 presidential campaign, Jacques Chirac spoke stirringly about the need to make the state less grand and more impartial. But, while they may sometimes resent its encroachment on their individual lives, the French do not necessarily want any less pomp and circumstance, or any less of a buffer against the cold world outside. They would probably like the state to be more impartial, less political – at least, when their own interests are not being advanced. But they know that the chances are slim of any President loosening the grip of his men and women on the levers of power in the official apparatus, the state banks and companies, public utilities and a hundred other domains. In the republican ideal, the state should be not only the national glue, but also above reproach. In practice, it is the supreme power machine. No politician to date has shown any sign of taking a self-denying ordinance on pulling its levers, and the people whom *l'État* is meant to serve are caught in its vice, lacking the will or the nerve to free themselves and without leaders who would take them down such an adventurous path.

National unity has, in some ways, been bolstered by the standardisation of life. Local dialects and customs have been swamped by a television culture and by the mobility of modern transport. If regional media flourish, they are increasingly uniform: one group controls 36 per cent of the press with chains of local newspapers that share services and pages. More than a third of France's population live in suburban houses. The nuclear family of northern France has definitively won out over the extended family of the south. The nationwide Minitel computer service has made local telephone directories a thing of the past.

Despite this, France remains a country of many parts, and its regions prove a balance for the state to which they belong. The split dates back for more than 2,000 years – Julius Caesar famously found Gaul divided into three parts. In a highly imaginative declaration, François Mitterrand spoke of the Gauls as having forged the first manifestation of French unity. Sheer rubbish: the Gauls were split into dozens of warring tribes which made them effective guerrilla fighters, and it was only when they made the error of banding together into large armies that the Romans defeated them. But the conquerors still failed to impose unity on the land and then, under Charlemagne's empire, France itself was divided along the Loire. The Vikings found the country so permeable that they sailed three times down rivers to Clermont-Ferrand in the heart of the Massif Central. The dynastic conflicts of the Hundred Years War tore the land on lines of variable geography.

It is not surprising, therefore, that, since the unifying genius of Louis XI brought the modern nation together at the end of the fifteenth century, France has been obsessed by the idea of itself as a single entity bounded on three sides by the sea and on three others by its neighbours. It couldn't do anything about the sea, but, as the historian Fernand Braudel observed: 'Europe, by surrounding France, both traced and limited its destiny.' The search for patriotic balm after the loss of Alsace-Lorraine to Germany in 1870 led all the way back to the baptism of the late fifth-century Frankish king, Clovis, in the eastern city of Reims. This event, it was argued, marked the birth of France under the umbrella of the Church. The reality is that it took six more centuries for monarchs to call themselves kings of France, and historians date the first cries of '*Vive la France*' to 1580. But, though the date given for the baptism is probably wrong, the myth remains as strong as ever, and 1996 saw a succession of 1,500-year anniversary celebrations. The French unitary state, it seems, needs sources of reassurance as much as its people.

But, alongside this mantra, the legacy of regional power-players runs on down the ages. Some were mightier than the king sheltering in his small domain of the Île-de-France. A Duke of Normandy conquered England; and an Aquitainian marriage gave the English a great domain and the pretext for a hundred years of war on French soil. Normans and then the Counts of Anjou reigned over Sicily; other Normans set up as rulers in the Holy Land. Had they possessed greater will-power, the Counts of Toulouse might have established a separate kingdom in the south which, with neighbouring Provence, would have looked west and east along the Mediterranean coast, rather than northwards to Paris.

As France took shape, there was often a complex continental dimension which added an ingredient that the island nation to the north never experienced. Take, as an example, the story of the strikingly beautiful fortress on the hill of the town of Najac in the Aveyron department of the south-west. Probably a Roman oppidum in the first century after Christ, it gravitated into the orbit of the powerful Counts of Toulouse, but then passed to the English after Eléonore d'Aquitaine was repudiated by the King of France and married Henry II from across the water. The destinies of England, France, Toulouse and northern Spain collided there when Henry's son, Richard the

Lionheart, met the ruler of Aragon at the castle of Najac to forge a pact against the Count of Toulouse. But then the Count's son married one of Henry II's daughters, which put Najac back under the authority of Toulouse. Najac was strategically important because it towered over a vital river route through a lush and fruitful area where four powers jockeyed for influence. As the thirteenth century dawned, Anglo-Norman Crusaders swept down from the north to exterminate the followers of the Albigensian heresy in one of the most damnable expeditions of European history. After the Counts of Toulouse bent the knee to the invaders, the inhabitants of Najac were declared heretics and sentenced to build a large church atop the hill beside the castle. But when Count Raymond VII failed to produce a male heir, the fortress returned to the King of France, only to revert to the control of Toulouse five years later. Half a century after that, the English regained control of the region, but their rule provoked the people of Najac into a revolt in which they massacred the occupying garrison. Other English occupiers returned for a while, but Najac then became French for good. Such places show the complexities of history behind the façade of a single French identity. From the Rhine frontier to the Pyrenees, France is made up of a complex of characteristic regions, localities and characters which draw on different pasts, and need to be woven together rather than being taken as given parts of a uniform whole by the centralising heirs of the revolutionary Jacobins.

To add to the complexity, some regions, and their capital cities, look beyond France's frontiers to old links that confirm their wider identities. Thus, Montpellier and Toulouse shared southern roots with Barcelona and Catalonia; Bordeaux retains links with Britain, some of its best vineyards being called Montrose, Talbot or Lynch; Nice has a strong Italian streak; and the towns of Alsace could be Rhineland German. In the west, an organisation called the Atlantic Arc, with its headquarters in the Breton capital of Rennes, is trying to stitch together the old Gaelic world of Ireland, Wales, Cornwall, western France and northern Spain.

Within France, regional groupings reach into the heart of the capital. Hard-working men and women from the Auvergne and Aveyron dominate the café trade in Paris: a parish priest who runs a hostel for young men up from the Cantal department reckons he can find them a job as a waiter within twenty-four hours of their arrival. There has long been a Corsican bond in the Paris police and the civil service – a 'Corsican clan' whose members were called Tiberi, Dominati and Romani helped Jacques Chirac run the capital. Associations linked to rural communes in far-flung parts of the country attract hundreds of diners to their annual banquets. The area round the Gare Montparnasse, where trains from the west arrive, is stuffed with Breton restaurants – in one street alongside the station, there are restaurants and cafés named after the towns of Saint-Malo and Morlaix, plus L'Atlantique, L'Océan, and Le Cadran Breton, plus a branch of the Banque de Bretagne and a cinema multiplex bearing the region's name. Some of the best *choucroute* in town is to be found by the Gare de l'Est at the end of the tracks from Alsace. (In London terms, this would be like finding haggis restaurants around King's Cross, Yorkshire pudding joints at Euston and Dover sole specialists at Victoria.) As wise rulers have understood, the people of France want their regional diversity to be respected: they need to feel that they are Savoyards as they sip their *vin jaune* or Vendéens as they remember their ancestors' resistance to the pagan revolutionaries of 1789.

Long ago, De Tocqueville and Montesquieu admired England as a nation where local government flourished and the edicts of the centre were circumscribed by local power bases. Two centuries later, France had one elected local councillor to every 110 voters, compared to one to 1,800 in Britain. The layers of government enshrine the nation's diversity – the central administration in Paris, 22 regions, 96 departments and the 36,500 communes, each with its own mayor and council. In Paris, the twenty *arrondissements* have a mayor under the city's supreme boss. In the provinces, departments and regions of France, the local rulers have always been anxious to flex their muscles against the power of the capital and the mandarins in the ministries – and against one another, as seen in the long-running political contest between the power-brokers of individual departments and the politicians running the larger regions to which they belong.

When France rises against the central administration's proposed changes to public-sector working conditions, sociologists detect a strong element of revolt against Paris as the place which issues orders. Marches through the streets of the capital may catch the eye of foreign correspondents, but the real action is often in the provinces – in Marseille, in Brest or Nice, where mass demonstrations in 1996 became festive occasions harking back to 1968 and even to the Popular Front. As the old nation looks warily at the modern world, its regions become places where France is still France, the living symbols of freedom from the embrace of the central power, with its technocrats and its unsmiling modern logic. Beneath the unity imposed on the country over the last two centuries, there are still two nations, the old divisions fanned into new life by the social and economic changes of the late twentieth century. For mayors of big towns and cities from the opposition parties, these upsurges of anti-government local feeling can provide a useful means of buttressing their own authority. But, even in the absence of such rallying causes for resentment against the rule of the technocrats in the ministries in Paris, the strength of regionalism provides an essential and enduring counterpoint to the homogenisation of French life and the political power of the centre. Ironically, this applies even to the very seat of that power.

As well as being capital to the nation, Paris is also a great regional city whose people have a historic role in rising up to deliver judgement on the national authorities. The Revolution and the Commune have been succeeded by more peaceful manifestations of the popular will, but Paris was not allowed to have an elected mayor until 1976 because of the central government's fear of the authority he would wield. The surrounding region of the Île-de-France houses one-sixth of France's population. An official survey in 1998 placed it as West Europe's biggest economic region, accounting for 5 per cent of European Union production. It is a truism to note that Paris isn't France, but the way the city was run by Jacques Chirac for eighteen years did much to explain the earlier fears about creating his post. 'What we've done for Paris, we will do tomorrow for France,' he announced as he moved down the right bank of the Seine to the Élysée Palace in 1995. If his country was to be a beacon for the world, he had spent the previous years trying to make sure that its capital would light the way for the nation.

From the City Hall by the Seine, Chirac commanded a system of iron political control, efficient public services, gentrification and expansion helped along by the state. As shown by scandals which oozed out after his departure, the city fathers knew how to cut deals – and corners. But he kept the municipal debt low by the standards of

France's expansive city governments, though some experts warned that taxes would have to rise sharply as the true price of Chirac's spending finally came home to roost. Like its mayor, Paris is a proud place which wants to look good. It spends 20 per cent of its budget on keeping itself clean, and employs 4,200 gardeners to tend 6,425 acres of parks and gardens. The public buildings spawned by three Presidents of the Republic have given it a new allure, from the renovated Natural History museum in the Jardin des Plantes to the Science Park in the old slaughterhouse district of La Villette. The renovated Louvre, with its once-controversial glass pyramid in the courtyard, attracts twice as many visitors as it did when you had to search for its treasures through musty rooms and endless corridors. The Prince of the City works in the biggest office in the whole country. His City Hall, rebuilt after being burned during the Commune uprising in 1871, has 1,290 windows and 142 Baccarat crystal chandeliers. For a while after France's first defeat by the Germans, it was the seat of the national government. The index of the great French reference book, *Quid*, has a single entry for Hôtel de Ville: naturally it is for the one in Paris.

In the world's imagination, the city remains unique, a city of style, beauty and love with more familiar monuments and heart-stopping second-hand memories than anywhere else. This is where Americans fall in love, and Ted Hughes and Sylvia Plath honeymooned. But the French themselves say they would rather live in a dozen other cities elsewhere in the country. *Le Figaro* judges the capital to be a joyless, overcrowded metropolis where neighbourhoods have lost their individual character to bargain-basement conformity. Half a million dogs (nearly one for every four inhabitants) deposit 16 tonnes of excrement in the streets each day. Fundamentalist Islamic terrorism hit with murderous attacks on public transport and shops. That led to the lids on street litter-bins being temporarily sealed to prevent bombs being put inside, after which newspapers reported that the feast of rubbish on the pavements had produced a breed of super-rats up to a foot in length.

On the Left Bank of the Seine, the classic intellectual mecca of Saint-Germain-des-Prés has been declared dead by the intelligentsia as fashion outlets replace bookshops, philosophers vanish, jazz joints close and publishers move to cheaper areas. The district, meanwhile, merchandises itself with a vengeance. 'Limoges pillboxes with Jean-Paul Sartre's glasses on top of them: I mean, who the hell buys them?' wondered the American journalist Stanley Karnow as he recalled the village of Saint-Germain he had known in the late 1940s. 'And here is the Simone de Beauvoir ashtray.' Local residents, including the actress Catherine Deneuve and singers Juliette Gréco and Charles Aznavour, grew so worried that they formed an association called SOS Saint-Germain to save the district's soul. 'Little by little, Saint-Germain has turned into Monaco,' lamented the Goncourt prize-winning novelist and former presidential adviser Erik Orsenna. But Ms Gréco was still reported to have found time to help design a four-storey fashion and entertainment emporium for Giorgio Armani in the heart of the *quartier*, beside the venerable political eating-house of the Brasserie Lipp.

The popular spirit that was once an essential element in the city's lifeblood has not been wholly swamped by gentrification. Lightly-clad whores still throng the upper reaches of the Rue Saint-Denis, and bicycling police have been reintroduced to control the straight and transsexual prostitutes of the Bois de Boulogne. More than 10,000 concierges defy the onward march of the entry phone, and there are plenty of old courtyards to rouse nostalgia from one end of the city to the other. But the days of sparrow singers in the street, *bals populaires* and the great food market of Les Halles are long gone. The *petites gens* and the craftsmen who made the reputation of Paris as a bustling, irreverent people's city have moved to the suburbs. The city centre has become an upper-middle-class place to live; 'the world centre of nostalgia', in the words of *The Times Literary Supplement*. Paris gave France the idea of democracy being exercised in the streets, from the barricades and populist chaos of the nineteenth century to the marches against Alain Juppé in 1996. The boulevards can still be relied on to provide a touch of political psycho-drama for the nation, but for many of its inhabitants – and even more for the workers commuting from the ever-growing suburbs – the capital risks becoming 'a decor city', a splendid showplace from which the mass of people grow increasingly alienated.

For their part, not all foreigners are charmed when they reach the City of Light. A survey carried out by the Paris Chamber of Commerce reported that tourists found the inhabitants rude, aggressive, dirty, idle and disorganised. English visitors down the decades have taken the short manner in which the natives often deal with one another as a deliberate attempt to be obnoxious to visitors. 'Age cannot wither, nor custom stale, her infinite vulgarity,' was the verdict of the American writer William Gaddis after living in the city. A KGB agent recalled how, meeting a French contact, he found Montmartre nothing but a 'hell' of exhaust fumes from tourist buses – in 1997 the mayor's office recognised the extent of the problem by banning buses from driving up the hill to the Sacré Coeur.

Many of those who live in the twenty *arrondissements* have been hit where it hurts most, in their pockets: the value of old flats which Parisians bought with enthusiasm as investments in the early 1990s fell by more than a quarter in the following five years, while average property values slumped by 62 per cent in the six years to 1996. Nor are Parisians as rich or productive as might appear. A survey by the Swiss bank, UBS, put Paris ninth among world cities in the cost of living but eighteenth in net wages. Although it is Europe's biggest economic region, the Île-de-France ranks only fifth in productivity.

And when it comes to the sheen of art, the capital is hardly what it was. Zola wrote of the Belly of Paris, Hugo put Quasimodo up on Notre Dame, Proust wended his way through turn-of-the-century salons, the Impressionists immortalised the banks of the Seine, the boulevards and the Gare Saint-Lazare, while a string of entertainers and actors made the most of the *parigot* accent. The city will always have a unique face, with the Champs-Élysées, Eiffel Tower, Arc de Triomphe, Louvre museum, three-rosette restaurants, *bateaux-mouches* on the Seine, cafés under the chestnut trees and an enduring air of cosmopolitan life. But who writes great novels about the city or paints great pictures of it any more? The last moving song about waking up in the capital was written in the 1970s.

Politically, the city offered a model for any statist control freak for two decades after Chirac became master of the Hôtel de Ville. From the start, the mayor drew Giscard's supporters into his tent – and he certainly knew how to look after his citizens. Thirty-six per cent of city spending goes on social services and education, 16 per cent on the environment. Buses for the handicapped, hostels for Aids sufferers, help for the aged, sumptuous boxes of chocolates for pensioners at Christmas . . . there was no end to the largesse. Chirac operated through a select band of officials and a few trusted councillors with a kitchen Cabinet that was as notorious for its internal rivalries as for its loyalty to the boss. In 1993, the Gaullists and their allies won control of all twenty *arrondissements* of the capital. In Chirac's last year as mayor, his opponents occupied only 22 of the 163 seats on the City Council. They increased that to 61 in municipal elections in 1995, but the Gaullists and their allies still held a comfortable majority as they battened down the hatches against a storm of scandal allegations stretching all the way from the new mayor's family to the financing of the Gaullist machine. In 1997, however, Paris was hit by the national wave of rejection against Chirac and his former lieutenant at the Hôtel de Ville, Alain Juppé. Followers of the mayor-become-President lost seven of their National Assembly seats in the city to the Socialists who, with their allies, now held nine of the twenty-one Parisian parliamentary constituencies. Chirac's successor, Jean Tiberi, held on to his constituency by under 3,000 votes, but the former Minister of Justice and long-time Chirac companion in arms, Jacques Toubon, lost his. Worse, as we shall see, was to follow.

The political change owed something to the wearing effects of almost two decades in power. But it also reflected the sides of the city's evolution which Chirac didn't talk about too much. While the Île-de-France boomed in population and riches, the population of Paris itself has fallen by a fifth since the early 1960s. The city is increasingly dependent on the transitory service sector for employment. There are big problems with homelessness, drugs and Aids – not to mention unemployment only just below the national level. Crime has risen on the streets and under the ground, where late travellers on the Métro watch over their shoulders and hurry through the corridors. All the cars driving to its multiplying parking garages have sent air pollution to unprecedentedly dangerous levels. Nearly half of all emergency calls by doctors to children in Paris involve respiratory problems. How the pigeons survive in the traffic-clogged square in front of the Opéra or the Place de la Concorde is a miracle. One story about Chirac's pride in his city concerns a drive he made with the Minister of the Interior. Remarking on their uninterrupted progress, he congratulated himself on the success of his administration in getting the traffic moving so smoothly; the minister replied that it was more of a tribute to his own success in getting the police to make sure all the lights on their route went green as they approached.

Among the people of Paris, some paid the price for the Chirac vision of the capital as more and more traditional labouring areas turned into middle-class developments. 'Simple people have been made to leave, the very character of parts of Paris has been destroyed,' lamented one opposition leader. The old pattern of property ownership was broken by taxation and inheritance duties. In 1950, 68 per cent of Paris buildings were owned by individuals; now, that has shrunk to around 20 per cent. The gentrification of the city was matched by an office construction spree, which led to a glut of new commercial property and the descent of foreign 'vulture fund' investors out to buy empty buildings for half their original price. On the edges of town, rows of charming two-storey houses have been remorselessly torn down to make way for flats. The developers ruled, and the authorities made sure nobody got in their way. That pained lovers of old Paris, and gave rise to persistent allegations of kickbacks. But the sentimental folklore forgets the decaying dwellings, the shared lavatories on the landing, the insalubrious conditions which fuelled crossChannel jibes about French dirtiness. A walk through the Sentier district off the Grands Boulevards, with its crowded workshops, firehazard buildings, dim cobbled courtyards, illegal immigrants, creaking stairways, prostitutes, rats and zinc-bar cafés provides a quick shot of nostalgia. Not many people would like actually to live there.

If Paris is a region of France, it is, by its nature, a rather special kind of region. Local and national interest overlap, and its mayor of two decades was a master at exploiting the situation. Nearly 30 per cent of the city's revenue comes in grants from central government or the surrounding Île-de-France. Farmers in the Jura or Languedoc help to keep Paris Métro tickets cheap by subsidies paid with their taxes. They do not complain because, wherever they are, the French regard Paris as a city that represents their land: they may not want to live there, but they wish it to shine. Jacques Chirac knew how to exploit that feeling and the relationship with the sugar-daddy up the road in the Élysée to the full. When François Mitterrand unveiled his plans to renovate the Louvre, including the controversial pyramid in the courtyard designed by the Chinese–American architect, I. M. Pei, some Gaullists urged the mayor to denounce the project as a sacrilege. Chirac said nothing. The Louvre became a sparkling marvel, opening on to the restored Tuileries gardens and the spruced-up Place de la

Concorde, and then along one of the world's great perspectives of the Champs-Élysées to the Arc de Triomphe. The glory belonged to Paris, and Jacques Chirac was the prince of the city. But, of the whole stretch from the courtyard of the Louvre to the Place de l'Étoile, only the Champs-Élysées was his concern. The rest – like Notre Dame, the Pompidou Centre, Les Invalides or the Seine – belonged to the state. But who cared? The government paid for their upkeep; Chirac smiled and took the credit for his city and himself.

On a rung just below the Mayor of Paris, his peers in other cities are also real power-brokers in a way unknown in Britain since the beginning of this century. This country which has made a religion out of centralisation has also nurtured a multi-layered structure of regional authority whose influence was boosted by the decentralisation of the 1980s. But, in a Gallic twist, the provincial nabobs are not content with their weight back home; they also want a national stage. So they become ministers, run parties, even head governments, and all the while remain mayors of large cities and smaller towns, and preside over regional councils. Some leading politicians remain at the head of local government for an extraordinary length of time – a tradition set under earlier Republics when a figure like Édouard Daladier, the pre-war Prime Minister, held sway as mayor of the southern town of Carpentras from 1912 to 1958. The elder statesman of the post-war right, Antoine Pinay, outdid him in mayoral longevity, reigning in the town of Saint-Chamond in the middle of France from 1928 to 1977. A leading Gaullist of the Fourth and Fifth Republics, Jacques Chaban-Delmas, carried on the tradition as Mayor of Bordeaux for almost half a century, from 1947 to 1995.

There is a term for all this – *cumul des mandats*, or the accumulation of electoral mandates. The practice has diminished from the days when a provincial notable could hold half a dozen posts simultaneously. Members of the National Assembly are now permitted to occupy only one other significant elected post, and their total incomes have been capped. Lionel Jospin is committed to reducing the accumulation further. He is struggling against an entrenched tradition in which some 90 per cent of deputies also held a local government post. More than half were mayors. Eighteen ministers held local posts.

Governments in Paris come and go: provincial politics are for life.

Thus, Chaban-Delmas made sure he hung on to his fief in Bordeaux as he moved from the Defence Ministry to the Presidency of the National Assembly and eventually to the Hôtel Matignon for a not particularly happy spell as Prime Minister. Through it all, he never neglected the city, and it never forsook him. Eating the local speciality of oysters and sausages in a restaurant there, I was surprised when the other clients suddenly got to their feet and burst into applause: Chaban-Delmas was passing by, and they wanted to say hello. Another Gaullist, Alain Juppé, succeeded him in wine heaven when he, too, had just become Premier in Paris. In his national role, Juppé earned an unenviable reputation for his lack of anything like the common touch, but he left the Matignon every Friday to devote the weekend to getting to know the capital of Aquitaine, touring the city, opening trade fairs, cheering on the Girondins soccer team, dropping in at bars and jogging in the park. He ran for a parliamentary constituency from the city, and was there when the catastrophe of the 1997 election results began to filter through.

Other towns and cities were put on the national political map by their mayors. A slightly dotty defender of small businesses was emboldened by his record running Tours to mount a quixotic presidential bid. The moderate Mayor of La Rochelle became a symbol of the alliance of environmentalism and orthodox politics after turning his port into a green citadel. The undistinguished towns of Château-Chinon in the west of Burgundy and Conflans-Sainte-Honorine outside Paris acquired unwarranted fame through the presence of François Mitterrand and Michel Rocard as their mayors. In a different mode, Canon Félix Kir, Mayor of Dijon, became one of France's most celebrated names through his taste for mixing blackcurrant liquor and the local white wine.

Despite the media's concentration on national politics as played out in the republican palaces of Paris, political shifts in the regions often pre-figure national movements. One key to the left's victory in 1981 was the way it had expanded its control of electoral bastions across the country in the previous years. A sweep of twenty of France's twenty-two regional councils by the right in 1992 foreshadowed its subsequent parliamentary and presidential victories. The left's recovery in regional polls six years later was a key element in the Socialist strategy of retaining the presidency. A death-knell had sounded for the Communists when they began to lose their local government strongholds in the 1970s and 1980s – and were constrained by economics to close down the regional editions of their daily newspaper. Once they had got over the shock of defeat in 1981, the former President and Prime Minister each began their comeback bids in the middle of the country, not in national politics.

Like Richard Daley in Chicago or Willy Brandt in West Berlin, French big-city mayors can be the epitome of the place they run – Pierre Mauroy the bluff friend of the workers who takes coach trips to Portugal for his holiday; Chaban-Delmas and Juppé the suave representatives of their elegant city on the Gironde; the former Prime Minister Raymond Barre symbolising the sensible conservatism and gastronomic excellence of Lyon; or the disgraced Mayor of Nice, Jacques Médecin, as the raffish, high-living symbol of the Riviera. But, while underpinning the dichotomy between central and regional authority, the combination of powers which they exercise reinforces the closed political society in which the same limited circle of politicians have their hands on the levers in Paris and the provinces, guiding the state in their chosen direction. Ideally, the regional element should provide a countervailing influence to centralism. The snag is that, increasingly, both Parisian and provincial interests have been swallowed up by the same closely-knit group. With their range of social, economic, cultural and geographical differences, France's provinces might have come up with diverse answers to the problems facing the nation. But the system ties them to the centre, not only by the authority of *l'État* but also through the men and women who hang so determinedly to both their ministerial offices and their mayoral sashes. Just as politicians of different stripes swim in the same mainstream, so the interests of the regions end up in the lap of the central power. In the late 1980s, Jacques Chirac was Prime Minister, leader of the RPR party and Mayor of Paris at the same time; ten years on, the only difference for Alain Juppé was that his mayoral office was by the Gironde river rather than the Seine. In each case, whatever their concern for their cities, national destiny was bound to take first place. For an even longer-lived example of how the system works, and the perils it can contain, take a trip to the port city which regards itself as one of a kind.

★

For four decades, Gaston Defferre *was* Marseille. An afternoon with him at the height of his power was a living illustration of how a big boss operated – a clique of courtiers bowing to his every whim, a ward boss explaining what favours he needed to keep key voters happy, a businessman coming in to talk about planning regulations, a boat-builder submitting plans for the mayor's new yacht, and the editor of the main local newspaper ringing to read out the leading article of the night. Defferre had grabbed the paper at the Liberation in the summer of 1944 by the simple expedient of walking into the building with two pistols stuck in his belt and taking control from its collaborationist proprietors. Four decades later, he tried to convince his friend, the President of the Republic, that his wartime background would enable him to persuade the terrorist, Carlos, not to attack French targets if only they could meet and talk as one resistance fighter to another.

Such romanticism goes to the heart of Marseille, the city after which France's revolutionary national anthem is named. Defferre was the only French minister to have risked his life in a duel – not once but twice, with swords and pistols. That was the kind of exploit that his city loved, and that made France love his city. Marseille has a special place in French hearts, with its buccaneering tradition, its flamboyant gangsters, its *bouillabaisse* fish stew, and its equally pungent local accent. More than a century as the gateway to the colonies brought wealth from trade with overseas possessions. It was the door to adventure and fortune-seeking in Africa or the East, for the eventual return from exotic journey – the poet Rimbaud came home to die in a Marseille hospital with his leg amputated after a decade of travels in Africa – and, in the other direction, for deportation of political prisoners to exile in Algeria. The city thrived on melodrama and a belief in its special corner in southern folk wisdom. Its people like to think of themselves as being larger than life, personified by figures like the late *pastis* king, Paul Ricard, whose name appears each year on 90 million bottles of the world's third biggest-selling brand of spirits, and who, though not a Catholic, took his entire workforce to Rome to be blessed by the Pope. Throughout the twentieth century, Marseille provided a home for immigrants from all around the Mediterranean – Armenians fleeing Turkish massacres, Greeks from Asia Minor, Spanish Republicans, Jews and Christians expelled from

Nasser's Egypt, and then tens of thousands of *pied noir* settlers from former colonies in North Africa. The city was both outward-looking and self-regarding. The port was not unlike a stage. Its theatrical potential was not lost on one of the great dramatic figures of modern France: Charles de Gaulle once addressed a crowd from a boat moored opposite the main quayside to such effect that those standing at the front were pushed into the sea by the pressure of those behind. Music hall, operetta and popular theatre merged into everyday life and politics, epitomised in Marcel Pagnol's immortal fictional characters of Marius, Fanny and César in the Vieux Port. As played by the prodigious actor Raimu, César gave France an iconic father-figure, a dominating presence swinging from pathos to humour, an unschooled fountain of native wit and cunning. As the cinema historian Ginette Vincendeau has noted, the Pagnol trilogy was a paean to archaic values, spreading the notion of a specifically southern culture to the rest of the nation through the cinema. If Marseille already believed itself to be special, Pagnol and millions of cinema-goers confirmed it in that belief.

It was an amenable place, ready to offer anything the visitor wanted. During the First World War, a British troopship filled with Indian soldiers being sent to die on the Western Front hove into view and sent a request for 1,000 'girls' to be waiting for them; the mayor said he could summon up 300 young women immediately. The message was then corrected to call for 1,000 'goats'. If that's their pleasure, so be it, said the mayor. Even the underworld was painted in romantic colours, as in the hit film *Borsalino*, which brought Jean-Paul Belmondo and Alain Delon together in a tale of men who did what they had to do under cover of their broad-brimmed hats. The reality was less glamorous: the two gangsters on whom the starring roles were modelled formed a compact with quasi-fascist officials in the 1930s which allowed them to ply their trade unhindered and to get into the drugs business.

During the war, the city became the base for an extraordinary American Scarlet Pimpernel, Varian Fry, who arrived in 1940 with a dress suit bought in his last hours in New York, $3,000 taped to one leg and a list of 200 artists and writers he had come to spirit out of occupied France during what was meant to be a three-week mission. In the end, Fry, the son of a stockbroker with a red carnation in his buttonhole, stayed in Marseille for thirteen months. Working with false passports from the Czechoslovak consul and forged papers, he personally helped Marc Chagall, Hannah Arendt, Max Ernst, Wanda Landowska and 1,200 others to leave France for the safety of America. His wider operation, run from Marseille, is estimated to have saved 4,000 in all. Evidently, the local police were impressionable: when they took Chagall away from his hotel in one of the early round-ups, Fry telephoned to warn them that the arrest of such a famous artist would embarrass Vichy. If Chagall wasn't freed within half an hour, Fry threatened to inform the *New York Times*. Chagall was released, and, after bizarrely assuring himself that there were cows in America, crossed the Atlantic.

After the war, the hoods who had picked the winning side took control of France's biggest port. They helped the CIA by attacking the Communist dockers' union and, in return, got a free hand to export heroin across the Atlantic. Marseille became a major world narcotics centre. The heroin 'cooks' worked in remote houses in the countryside, in cellars, out-houses, garages and tenements. At the pinnacle of production in the mid-1960s, according to a historian of the opium trade, Martin Booth, there were about two dozen laboratories operating around the clock, producing high-grade heroin of a purity usually difficult to attain. The drugs went to America either direct or via France's overseas possessions in the Caribbean, where customs checks were minimal. In time, the American authorities hit back, arresting a top chemist involved and shutting down the main distribution point in New York – known as the Pleasant Avenue Connection. *The French Connection* told of the fight against the Marseille traffickers. And, as the exports to the USA became more difficult, some of the narcotics barons began selling heroin in their own country.

Through all this, the nominally Socialist Gaston Defferre held the city in the palm of his weather-beaten yachtsman's hand. He was invulnerable, and did not need to be too scrupulous in his choice of associates. A suppressed photograph showed the mayor at the head of a political procession arm-in-arm with a leading underworld figure. This man helped to organise his campaigns, had an office in the City Hall, and told police who had the audacity to try to arrest him: 'Let me go or I'll talk.'

Defferre was a fixture in the national parliament and served as a minister under the Fourth Republic. In 1969 he made an ill-advised bid for the presidency, netting just 5 per cent of the vote. That didn't dent his authority, however, for his passport to power was down on the Mediterranean, where he ruled from City Hall behind the Quai du Port or by remote-control from his large yachts. While nobody suggested that he had anything to hide personally, the fact was that Gaston could get away with just about anything he chose. The Socialist Party needed the Marseille electorate, and Defferre always delivered. It was an era when taxis were sent to pick up elderly voters who could be counted on to vote as he wished. This ensured that nobody on the non-Communist left in Paris would raise any questions about how he ran things back home, and would accord him proper deference when he travelled north. Successive governments of the centre-right saw him as a dependable anti-Communist bulwark, and did not object if their local chieftains allied themselves with City Hall. Defferre's system had room for every shade of opinion, so long as it wasn't Communist. He maintained a right-wing newspaper, *Le Méridional*, alongside his pale pink flagship, *Le Provençal*.

After thirty-five years in power, Defferre set off on a fresh crusade against the local Marxists, aiming to hit where it would hurt them most – in their party's pocket. That is to say, in the welfare system of the Bouches-du-Rhône department around his city, which was controlled by the Communist-led union federation, the CGT. The ensuing saga demonstrated the way in which regional and national politics merge into one another. An efficient civil servant from the Paris region, René Lucet, was brought south to do the job on the Communists. Lucet went to work with a will. He discovered how welfare funds had been diverted into party coffers, and began to take steps to put things right. The Communists were up in arms, but Lucet had the backing of both the mayor and the right-wing government up in the capital. So far so good. Then the left won power in 1981, and everything changed. Gaston Defferre became Interior Minister and the second-ranking member of the first Socialist government of the Fifth Republic. It was an honour which brought obligations with it. Some of Defferre's Cabinet colleagues were of a more ideological bent than him: a left-wing Socialist took charge of Social Security, and a Communist became Minister of Health.

Defferre saw the way the wind was blowing. The heat had to be taken off the CGT. René Lucet was abruptly sacked. In March 1982, he killed himself.

The outcry was deeply embarrassing for Defferre. It appeared to show him as a man who, in his new national functions, could not – or would not – stand up to the Communists or left-wing Socialists in Paris as he had done in his own city. The right-wing press gave the story additional spice by reporting two conflicting autopsy findings: one showed that Lucet had a single bullet in his skull, the other disclosed two. In a city where the police and the underworld traditionally drank at the same table, that went down as *suicide à la Marseillaise*. A string of municipal scandals which once would have been hushed up then broke into the open. A local police chief and five members of his family were murdered by three Gaullist toughs. Even the mayor's associate in the underworld with his office in City Hall wound up in jail. With the colonies gone and nothing much to replace it, local commerce slumped into the doldrums. Rising unemployment and a big immigrant population helped to raise social tension. Once a centre for drug traffickers who exported their poison, Marseille increasingly became a home for hard-core addicts, reckoned to number 5,000.

Defferre died in 1986. His successor, a local doctor without a solid political base, ruled in an increasingly solitary manner. The post-war coalition Defferre had headed fell apart in a jungle of feuds. His press empire was taken over by a businessman allied with the right. The city and surrounding department of the Bouches-du-Rhône became a breeding-ground for the National Front, while the left could find no better champion than Bernard Tapie, who then proceeded to besmirch the name of its sporting pride and joy. In National Assembly elections in 1993, the Socialists contrived to hold only two seats in the region, one fewer than the Communists. The mayor's office passed to the mainstream right, under the new conservative king of the city, Jean-Claude Gaudin, who showed a Defferre-like ability to meld local and national positions as a leader of the main non-Gaullist party of the right, minister, senator or deputy, mayor and president of the regional council – and still found time to put his name to three books.

At the turn of the century, the city launched a major programme to renew itself. An extension of the TGV high-speed train linked it to Paris and Lille – and to the Eurostar under the Channel to London. Its 300-hectare development and expansion scheme was said to be the biggest in France. The shabby area round the Saint-Charles station was cleaned up. Warehouses by the harbour were transformed into a business centre. There was to be a film and video city, and a cruise liner port. Marseille's old position as a trading entrepot between Europe and North Africa was seen as a trump card if the European Union carries through plans for a Mediterranean free trade zone. Bernard Tapie came back to star on the stage as an actor in the French version of *One Flew Over The Cuckoo's Nest*, and to cast his spell over Olympique de Marseille, but the football club became better known for the rapid turnover of players than for its success on the field. Yet, unemployment remained high, the stately nineteenth century buildings in the centre decayed, and the fear of crime rose. In the first round of the 2002 presidential election, the far right got 27.7 per cent of the vote compared to 18 per cent for Chirac and 15.5 per cent for the Socialists. For the ensuring parliamentary elections, the left was split by internal squabbles. The city which had always prided itself on being different looked like a mirror of France's problems.

Several chapters have passed without mention of food, so let us get back to that key subject, and look at its contribution to the diversity of the nation. Nothing embodies French regionalism so much as what people consume. 'Tell me what you eat, and I'll tell you what you are,' said the gastronomic writer Brillat-Savarin. He might have added, 'and where you come from.' We have noted the link which food provides to the countryside as a whole. Now focus this on the regions. Yes, sales of mass-processed food rise year by year. Yes, France likes to experiment with exotic fruit. And, yes, chic new restaurants in Paris offer tamales, Caesar salads and even English grub. Still, the essentials of eating are rooted in provincial diversity. Dishes may be available across the country, but each has its home. If you can get a perfectly fine *cassoulet* or *sandre au beurre blanc* in Paris, the dishes should truly eaten in restaurants in Toulouse or the Loire Valley. Tripe in Normandy is different from tripe in Nice or Lyon. How fish is treated in Brittany sets it apart from the Mediterranean. Wine from

different regions not only tastes different; it is also put into differently
shaped bottles – from the thin containers of Alsace and the elegance
of Champagne to the wine pots of Lyon, with their thick glass bot-
toms designed to keep them upright in the gravel of boulodromes.
Regional cuisine is a serious matter for the swelling ranks of food historians and academics. An ethnologist from the south has written a
treatise on 'The Influence of the Sardine on the Mediterranean
Imagination', while a conference in the eastern city of Nancy heard
papers dealing with subjects such as 'An Unusual Island of Stockfish-
Eating in Rouergue-Quercy', 'A Spatial Analysis of the Alimentary
Habits in Lozère: Oil, Soup and Pig Meat', and 'Pork as a Cultural
Determinant in the North-East of France'.

Less academically, the French simply relish the persistence of old
dishes from their region. Take some of them and realise why it is no
wonder France loves its provinces: Tourte de la Ville de Munster,
Choucroute Alsacienne, Kougelhopf, Galette Charentaise, Cul de Veau
à l'Angevine, Oie Farcie de Sègre, Boeuf aux Herbes de Massiac, Potée
Auvergnate, Toro de Saint-Jean-de-Luz, Sauce Béarnaise, Homard à la
Morbihannaise, Brochet Braisé au Champagne, Cou Farci du Quercy,
Pommes Sarladaises, Confit d'Oie du Gers, Tête de Veau à la
Parisienne, Poularde Demi-deuil de Lyon – not to mention such world
favourites as Boeuf Bourguignon, Gratin Dauphinois or Salade Niçoise.

The next course, cheese, has a whole set of regional and historical
cultures all its own. The Emperor Charlemagne developed a taste for
the unique ewe's milk cheese of Roquefort and had brie from the
town of Meaux sent to his court twice a year. Twelve hundred years
later, never confuse the Meaux brie with a rival variety from nearby
Melun: the head of a three-rosette restaurant in Paris completely lost
his customary cool at a lunch some years ago when he was caught out
mixing up the two. In another fading of a French icon, consumption
of Camembert is falling by 5 per cent a year, but Normans venerate
the memory of Marie Harel, the farmer's wife who gave the world the
cheese after learning a secret recipe from a priest she hid during the
Revolution – in 1928 the President of the Republic, no less, inaugurated a memorial to her in the village of Vimoutiers in the Orne
department.

For the traditional French, a full meal without cheese is like a kiss
without a moustache, to adopt an old phrase. It adds a key element to

the gastronomic occasion, which becomes essential within minutes of the main dish being cleared away and a new bottle of wine opened. As the food writer Peter Graham points out in his seminal book, *Classic Cheese Cookery*, its makers are true alchemists given the variables that go into their craft: '. . . the type of pasture where the cows are put to graze, the time of year they are milked, the breed of cow, the type of coagulation induced, the way the curd is cut and pressed, the technique of salting, the shaping of the cheese, the length of curing, and the very specific temperatures required at each stage of manufacture. The end product, not surprisingly, assumes a multitude of guises, sizes, textures and flavours that is quite stagger-ing given that most cheeses have but one ingredient: milk.' And nowhere is that staggering range more apparent than in France, with its 250-plus varieties. Criss-cross the country and taste a cheese that goes by the name of the old smelly man of Lille; delight in the deep pungency of Pont-l'Évêque; savour the depths of a mature Cantal cut from a huge chunk, and swallow a tiny goat's cheese in one mouthful; be bored by the blandness of Port-Salut and wolf down the *aligot* and *truffade* of the Auvergne, which mixes local cheese with potatoes in a manner that can only induce *gourmandise*. And pick the right regional wine to go with it – not always the traditional reds, either: those who can afford it hold that a glass of fine Sauternes or two is the perfect accompaniment for Roquefort as well as for *foie gras* and desserts, while the chef's wife at a highly-rated restaurant in Tours insisted that we accompany our goat's cheese with a Loire white, and she wasn't wrong.

For, like food, wine is a reflection of France's regional riches. In the restaurant of the Fagegaltier sisters at Belcastel, which we visited in Chapter 4, one of the delights is to sip the local 80-franc red wine while eating food that elevates the region beyond compare. Meursault is made to go with *suprême de volaille* and Aloxe-Corton with the red-meat dishes of the Côte d'Or; Alsatian wines partner *choucroute*; Muscadet washes down oysters; the rosés of Provence make a sunny fit with Mediterranean fish; and the reds of the south-west stand up to the robust cooking of the area. How could it be otherwise in a coun-try which boasts champagne, the great growths of Bordeaux and Burgundy, Anjou, Sancerre and the wines of the Loire, the ten *crus* of Beaujolais, the riches of the Côtes du Rhône, and the eastern delights of Riesling, Sylvaner and Gewürztraminer, not to mention Cahors and the flinty wines of Auvergne, or the better products of the Corbières, the Costières de Nîmes and the Minervois, tiny appellations like Bellet on the edge of the southern Alps or Condrieu on the Rhône, or the '-*ac*' vineyards from the south-west – Gaillac, Marcillac, Frontenac, Bergerac? Or take the regional aperitifs, sweet wines and liqueurs: *pastis* from Provence, Vermouth from Chambéry, Salers from the Auvergne, Pineau des Charentes, Banyuls, Rivesaltes and Muscat de Beaumes de Venise, Cognac and Armagnac, Marc from Burgundy or Champagne, Calvados from Normandy, Vieille Prune from the Lot or Framboise from Alsace. Each wine, *petit apéro* or *digestif* has a resonance of place, direct proof of the diversity and richness of the land.

For all the frozen pizzas, Dutch pork and German cold cuts on sale in mini-supermarkets throughout rural France, provincial cooking has never been better, and it belongs to the regional wealth of the land from ordinary kitchens to the establishments with three rosettes. France's perennial celebrity chef, Paul Bocuse, is resolutely Lyonnais even if he spends so much of his time trotting the globe; the ascetic star of the wild Aubrac region, Michel Bras, goes running in the morning to find new herbs in the hills around his home town of Laguiole; and to listen to the brothers and sons of the Troisgros restaurant in Roanne talk of the local produce brought to the back door in the morning is to be reminded of the importance of local roots in perhaps the world's greatest eating establishment.

So we have a nation which seeks unity but relishes division, which venerates the strong central state and the fruits it hands out to its people, which is becoming increasingly homogenised on urban, international lines but which craves older values and protection from the rigours of modernity. All this is taking place in a geographical context which appears stable, but which contains some illusions.

The French speak of their country as the Hexagon, clearly defined on all six sides. That has not spared it recurrent invasions – from the migratory movement of pre-history to the last great German attack. The Romans moved up from the south-east, the Arabs from the south-west, the Franks from the east and the English from the north. But today, most of those natural frontiers look pretty solid. Unless you count all those Brits buying up country houses as the heirs of Simon de Montfort, there is no problem with the Channel, while the long Atlantic coast has not seen a hostile force landing since the Duke of Buckingham was repulsed by Richelieu at La Rochelle in 1627. The last conquerors to come ashore in Provence in August 1944 were more than welcome – though Jean-Marie Le Pen would, of course, point to a rather different cross-Mediterranean invasion in recent years.

Internally, regional pride has bred separatist movements in various parts of the country, but, for the most part, their support has been small-scale, connected more to folklore and tradition than to any widespread desire to throw off the yoke of Paris. Brittany has its autonomists, but, apart from setting off a bomb or two, they appear to have been calmed by being given bilingual road-signs and Breton language classes in schools. Along the border with Spain, France's 250,000 Basques proudly guard their identity in far less militant or violent manner than their counterparts across the mountain frontier, and have considerably less say in running their own affairs. In 1996, 63 per cent of mayors in the region voted for the creation of a Basque department, but the central authorities refused to entertain the idea. As the Bordeaux newspaper *Sud-Ouest* noted, France has good reason not to be seen as an encourager of separatism in Quebec: just think of the problems that would be caused if such aspirations were transported to the Basque country. So the Pyrenees can be counted as forming another natural frontier, complete with the duty-free shopping haven of Andorra, whose joint princes are the President of France and the bishop of the nearby Spanish town of Urgel. Then, to the east of the junction of mountains and sea at the Spanish frontier, there stretches the long Mediterranean coast. Here students can learn Provençal, but there is no movement to re-create the great fiefdoms which ruled southern France in the Middle Ages. So the nation seems pretty secure on most sides, but then, 180 kilometres off its southern coast, there lies a cancerous growth on the state of France.

On 6 February 1998, the Republic's leading representative in Corsica set out to walk to a classical music concert in the island's capital of Ajaccio. Claude Érignac, a no-nonsense administrator, had been appointed Prefect of Corsica by the government of Alain Juppé in

January 1996, and kept in his post by the Socialists the following year. During his two years in the job, the sixty-year-old Érignac had not hesitated to use his authority to block a number of potentially lucrative projects backed by Corsican and Italian entrepreneurs, including a scheme to double the number of slot machines in the Ajaccio casino and another to turn the military barracks in the picturesque port of Bonifacio into a luxury hotel. He had launched probes into alleged fraud in the use of national and European subsidies, and into contracts for waste-disposal and public car-parks. He also had in his files a police report recommending investigations of local banks and racketeering by two well-known gangs – and, most explosive politically, of the island's agriculture which would involve some leading nationalists.

While Claude Érignac was engaged on his prefectoral house-cleaning, life went on as usual on the island justly known as the Île de Beauté. Lying in the Mediterranean between France and Italy, Corsica has a long tradition of violence, clan politics, racketeering, poverty – and a desire to affirm its own identity, if only it knew how. Although it has been under French rule since the eighteenth century, the island and its people are not really French at all.

If the sub-Sicilian gunmen who bomb for independence from the metropolitan government in Paris were not such B-movie hoods, they would have a smidgen of a point. Their homeland is, indeed, a separate place. It is much closer to the Italians who used to rule it than to the mainland. But Corsica faces some major problems in even thinking of divorcing itself from the Hexagon.

After centuries of rule by Genoa, the island did enjoy fourteen years of quasi-independence under Pascal Paoli, the 'father of the nation', in the middle of the eighteenth century. After Paris asserted control, the post-revolutionary wars encouraged Paoli to stage another rising. This ushered in two years of nominal rule by George III, who was proclaimed 'Anglo-Corsican King'. It cannot have been much of a consolation for having lost America. In 1796, Napoléon Bonaparte, who came from one of the island's many feuding clans, reasserted French control. He made no bones about his belief that Corsica should be French once and for all, and that the British-era nonsense about local democracy should be forgotten. He also introduced clan politics to the mainland at the highest levels – the first Bonaparte to become Emperor made sure, disastrously, that he looked after the family, a

Godfather before his time. The island is littered with his statues and mementos of his achievements, but his centralising zeal is rarely mentioned – a plaque in the Corsican capital of Ajaccio does, however, recall his role in developing Europe's beet industry. Even his memory is not always greatly respected: the sword on one of the main statues in his honour was bent for many years, and a developer was allowed to pull down his mother's mansion to put up an office block.

More to the current point, the home of the Foreign Legion is an economic basket-case which could not live in its accustomed style without cash from Paris now amounting to 7 billion francs a year. Most of its 250,000 people know that, and the depths of their devotion to their island's separateness is open to considerable doubt. Classes in the island's language have been introduced into the school curriculum, but three-quarters of pupils do not bother to go to them. Only 2 per cent of those sitting the *baccalauréat* take the examination in Corsican. France owes Corsica a blood debt; the island lost huge numbers of men in the trenches of the First World War, and became a land of widows and wounded veterans and sons and daughters without fathers. The dependence on state pensions bred a welfare habit which combined with the outlaw traditions of the maquis brushlands (that gave their name to the Resistance of the Second World War). Together, they created a hopeless culture of life. Today, less than 10 per cent of the population pays income tax, but this is not a poor place – car ownership is above the national average. The island has no industry to speak of and its gross domestic product is 30 per cent below that of France as a whole, but it contains four airports and six harbours built with subsidies. For generations, the young people have gone off in search of fortune elsewhere. Corsicans have long formed the backbone of the civil service on the mainland, and helped to bolster its mainland security forces, often on the edges of legality. The equivocal chief of the Paris police during the fascistic riots in the 1930s, Jean Chiappe, was a Corsican; so too was De Gaulle's faithful bodyguard Pierre Comiti, who, with his sunglasses, deeply bald head and pencil moustache, looked more like a small-time enforcer from a *film noir* than a man charged with protecting the President from assassination. (He had, it must be said, spent time as one of the leading heavies, or *gorilles*, who served the General so faithfully.)

There are a thousand associations of Corsicans in France and two hundred abroad. Corsicans pop up in Venezuela and Indochina, Canada and Hong Kong, in business and in the underworld. Corsicans ran the Marseille 'Connection'. During the wars in Indochina, Bonaventure 'Rock' Francisci headed an airline which flew morphine base from Laos to Saigon on its way to Europe and America. According to one former French anti-narcotics agent, an illiterate Corsican called Barthélémy Césari, who would have been heading for retirement in any other profession when he was nabbed, was one of the best heroin chemists the world has known, making the drug 'the way a French grandmother might make dinner – stirring, sniffing and tasting to perfection'. Another drug kingpin from the island arrived in New York in the guise of a priest from Brittany; the snag was that he had a distinctly Mediterranean complexion and spoke with a thick accent, and so was immediately marked down as somebody for the New York police to keep tabs on.

Keeping another connection on the other side of the world alive, Corsicans smuggled gold, gems, currency and narcotics to Marseille from Indochina long after the last French soldiers had left their former colonies. At one restaurant by the main cemetery of Saigon, which served excellent steak *au poivre*, I was assured in the mid-1960s that one was safe from Viet Cong attacks because '*le patron est Corse*'. Three decades later, Big Joseph Pantalacci sat shuffling a pack of cards at a table in his restaurant in the Laotian capital of Vientiane. He had arrived in Indochina on a troopship in 1937, became a timber trader, went into construction and married a seventeen-year-old French–Vietnamese. As the French empire collapsed around him, he watched his compatriots from Corsica trade in drugs and precious metals: 'They were not the Mafia, but they acted like the Mafia; some of them were wild men, crazy, too much wine and too many women.' Big Joseph went into the restaurant business instead.

Now, unemployment on the mainland and around the world keeps law-abiding young people of Corsica at home, but still jobless. Sixty per cent of the island's income comes from state aid. The national audit commission found that subsidies paid to Corsican agriculture were nearly two and a half times the amount budgeted, were ten times as large as those allocated to the average farm on the mainland, and supported 70 per cent of the island's full-time farmers. 'The practice,' the report added, 'sent many farmers deeper into debt as they

seem to have become used to requesting and obtaining fresh subsidies.'
Investors from the mainland show little interest in taking generous
subsidies to provide jobs: in four years in the mid-1990s, just two
companies signed up – and one of them lost its factory on the island
to a fire. Apart from wine and agriculture, tourism is the main revenue earner, but the militant separatists do their best to sabotage this
lifeline by bombing empty holiday villas. Corsica gave birth to the
vendetta tradition of mutual murder; its hoodlums love to pose for the
cameras in black masks waving guns. There are far too many hunting
rifles that can be used for other purposes. 'Everyone is armed in
Corsica,' an Interior Minister observed. The last two decades have
seen more than 8,000 attacks on property and people.

The island's politics are riddled with in-fighting between clans,
each defending its own territory and income. Fraud, both financial
and electoral, is endemic – regional elections in 1998 were annulled
after widespread irregularities. Corsicans are famed for their ability to
vote from beyond the grave and for the avalanche of postal votes that
may suddenly descend on selected constituencies – one village with
165 registered electors once recorded 5,998 ballots for a favoured
candidate. The clans distribute money and jobs to their followers, and
help them out of trouble. Their chieftains seem to live for ever, with
power being handed from father to son. In southern Corsica, the
Rocca-Serra family has held sway since the 1920s. When the father
fell into disgrace for wartime collaboration, his son – known as 'the
silver fox' for his cunning and his hair colouring – took up the reins.
Mayor of the beautiful coastal town of Porto-Vecchio for forty-seven
years and a member of the National Assembly for thirty-six until his
death in 1998, he paid for funerals, gave free consultations in his
medical practice and seemed to know everybody. Once, when a village mayor gambled away the communal funds, Rocca-Serra met the
loss from his own pocket and kept the police quiet.

There are compensations for such godfatherly behaviour. Though
Rocca-Serra was above such things, public works of the kind which
Claude Érignac was busy investigating just happen to facilitate access
to restaurants and hotels in which local potentates have an interest.
In another case which the Prefect promised to look into, the cost of
a water-treatment plant on the coast inexplicably went ten times
over budget. Links with Italy, as in the Bonifacio barracks-to-hotel

project which he vetoed, have led the President of the Republic to speak of Mafia-like interests on the island, and the nationalists have joined the game with a vengeance. One independence-seeker received a large grant to enable him to get into the pork processing business; in another case, a mayor was murdered by a nationalist gunman after failing to pick the designated firm for a garbage contract. A public prosecutor estimates that three-quarters of the so-called nationalist bomb attacks are in fact staged as part of private disputes.

Some parliamentarians in Paris have had enough. 'If the Corsicans aren't happy, forget about them,' said one conservative. An opinion poll on the mainland showed that no less than 42 per cent of voters would back independence for the island – just to get rid of it. For such a unitary state as France, that is a challenge and a half which the powers in Paris have no idea how to meet. The former Prime Minister, Raymond Barre, went straight to the point: 'If the Corsicans want their independence, let them take it.' But there is little sign that they really do. Polls show support for casting adrift from the mainland at between 7 and 10 per cent. A larger number would like some form of greater autonomy, which would let them feel more Corsican but not threaten the subsidies from across the water. From time to time, the central power tries to come to terms with the island, usually extending a nationalist carrot while waving the stick of a security clampdown. In the mid-1980s, François Mitterrand decided to give greater recognition to the island's language and specific identity. At the same time, he sent one of his top police officers – a tough man with an open mind – to deal with the terrorists. One sunny day, the Head of State, in person, alighted on the island and raced around in a flurry of security. It was all somewhat farcical. A sharp-shooting bodyguard was literally deafened when the bell began to ring in greeting at the top of the church tower where he was standing watch. Despite the worries about terrorist attacks, I had no problem wandering into an official candlelit garden party in Ajaccio through a back door, while, not far away, separatists daubed graffiti on the walls and waved a banner demanding 'decolonisation'. The Constitutional Council turned down the Mitterrand proposals as being counter to the unity of the nation; the bombers planted fresh explosive charges and the mess became even worse.

A dozen years later, the Gaullist Prime Minister flew to Ajaccio and warned that the island could not be allowed to escape from the law of the Republic. 'Corsica is part of the nation,' declared Alain Juppé. 'Corsica is French.' Still, he announced that more attention would be paid to teaching the Corsican language. National solidarity would be demonstrated by establishing a tax-free zone on the island. 'A tax-free zone is designed to resuscitate, not to save something which is already dead,' a local mayor remarked bitterly. The Corsican terrorists showed what they thought by bombing the Prime Minister's mayoral office in Bordeaux. A Magnum-packing anti-terrorist judge was put on the case, but blasts followed at half a dozen official buildings on the mainland as well as fifty in Corsica itself. A couple of months later, more than forty bombs went off in seventeen towns across the island, hitting businesses such as Air France and the telephone and electricity companies. Another series of attacks included the headquarters of ÉNA among its targets, while some historically-minded bombers planted three charges in the town of Vichy during the Maurice Papon trial, to mark 'the true nature of a state which is not well placed to give lessons on democracy'.

Don't look for logic in all this, or else for a logic which is nothing if not self-destructive. Corsica is a land where cash-dispensers are rare because they are routinely ripped open with explosives left over from attacks on tourist villas and official buildings. Or take the tale of 'Gulliver' and the golf club, at Sperone in the south of the island, which gives some idea of how things work in Corsica. One day at the end of 1996, a group of men paid a visit to the club and an adjoining resort village. They left a simple message: the club had been the target of three bomb attacks, and it was time for the owner to call a woman lawyer who was closely associated with the leader of one of the nationalist movements. She asked him to meet a go-between in Paris who would go by the codename of 'Gulliver'. The subterfuge was superfluous since the golf club owner recognised his visitor as the owner of a local restaurant in Corsica. 'Gulliver' asked for several million francs; otherwise, it would be too bad for the golf club. The owner refused to pay. The next day, the guard-house at the club was blown up. The owner went to the police. The woman lawyer was arrested. Her companion, who headed the legal arm of the nationalist movement, gave himself up as a point of honour. Everybody congratulated everybody else. The Prime Minister said that the episode might be a turning-point in the fight against nationalist extortion and violence. Within a month, the golf club received a demand to close, or face reprisals. It promptly shut down. 'We can't take risks with the golfers,' the owner told reporters.

The representatives of the state sheltered behind high walls and barbed wire. Repression did not work, but accommodation with the violent minority could make it seem that law could be taken for a fool. What, asked Alain Juppé, was left of the Republic if armed groups openly flouted it? When an Interior Minister visited the island, the Liberation Front stole headlines by inviting journalists to a night meeting with 600 armed members in the mountains. Gangsters paraded as nationalists, and the penalties they faced were hardly intimidating. Conviction for illegal possession of arms got the leader of one militant separatist group a twelve-month jail sentence, two-thirds of it suspended. The verdict was handed down *in absentia* since he had holed up in the brushlands with his bodyguards.

This was the kind of jungle with which the Prefect, Claude Érignac, was trying to come to grips. As he got down to work, nationalist commandos raided a police barracks in the southern town of Pietrosella, blowing up the building and temporarily taking two gendarmes hostage. Five weeks later a nationalist group called *Sampieru* issued a statement, proclaiming fidelity to 'legionnaire ideals' and swearing to wage an uncompromising struggle against the French state. Its leader was identified as a former paratrooper whose involvement in the cause stretched back to an incident in 1975, when two policemen were killed while dislodging nationalists from a wine cellar they had occupied in one of their early protests. In January 1998, some *Sampieru* members left the group, denouncing 'any action that may be undertaken against certain civil servants and leading representatives of the colonial state'. Evidently, they knew something was brewing.

A month later, two young men walked up to Claude Érignac as he made his way to the concert in Ajaccio. One was unshaven and fair-haired, the other dark and wearing a T-shirt. One of them shot the Prefect in the back of the head with the Beretta stolen at Pietrosella. He died immediately. The killer dropped the pistol and fled with his companion. Three days afterwards, a statement from *Sampieru* claimed responsibility for the murder.

Érignac's assassination shocked even the blasé Corsicans. Almost a sixth of the island's population joined in silent protest marches. Jacques Chirac and Lionel Jospin flew south to condemn the deed. A tough new Prefect, Bernard Bonnet, was sent in to restore law and order. Distrustful of the island's police, he established a parallel force of his own, with the approval of the authorities in Paris. A purge was launched on the financial front. Tonnes of documents involving nationalists were seized from a local bank, Corsica's development fund was audited, and doubtful loans amounting to a billion francs subjected to examination. Amid all his other concerns, Bonnet appears to have become obsessed with a beach-front restaurant frequented by nationalists which kept operating despite breaking environmental regulations. One night, a group of his men tried to burn it down, but were disturbed before they could complete the job. They left plenty of clues as to their identity as they fled, along with forged pamphlets which sought to make their attack seem like a criminal settling of scores with nationalist overtones. This farcical episode led to the arrest of the Prefect, who was subsequently sentenced to three years – two suspended – for having sanctioned the operation. It was the first significant prison sentence on a prefect.

By then, the methodical Lionel Jospin had decided to try reason after territorial elections in 1999 gave a quarter of the vote to the nationalists. Months of talks with leading figures on the island produced an offer of limited autonomy passed by parliament at the end of 2001, including some local legislative powers and greater Corsican language teaching in schools. The Interior Minister, Jean-Pierre Chevènement, resigned in protest at this affront to the integrity of the Republic. Violence continued as gang warfare took ten lives, and nationalist gunmen attacked official buildings. A bomb was deposited outside the Mayor of Bastia's flat. Nor did Jospin's attempts at dialogue do him much good electorally. In 2002, Corsica backed presidential candidates who opposed the new measures, putting the Prime Minister slightly behind Le Pen and far behind Chirac. In the second round, the National Front took 20 per cent of the island's vote and 24 per cent in Ajaccio. Soon after the presidential election, there was a fresh wave of bomb attacks and Corsicans in the crowd whistled at the *Marseillaise* before the Cup Final in which Bastia was playing, provoking a walk-out by Chirac until the club chairman apologised.

As Jacques Chirac, apostle of the unitary state, won re-election, a new attempt to get to grips with the problem of Corsica was inescapable. The Interior Minister, Nicolas Sarkozy, organised a referendum on proposals to give the island more autonomy while retaining it inside the Republic. But voters rejected the plan. Violence continued, as did the internal splits between the godfathers of Corsican politics. So the island remained a challenge to the Republic, a place which wanted special treatment but could not take on its own destiny, a morass of illegality and nationalism that defied the best minds of the administration in faraway Paris.

One of Louis XIV's ministers may have dreamed of 'Germanis Gallia clausa' (Gaul closed to the Germans), but the east is where France's identity is most porous, in land and people. Start in the south-east – and where better than Nice, which only became French in 1860 and which briefly reverted to Italian rule during the Second World War? Today, the people of the old port and the flower market and the sardine-codfish-and-tripe restaurants remain as much Italian as French in their way of life. Turn north and things become ever more murky as one moves from Italian-French, to Swiss-French, to German-French and then to Belgian-French. While the proximity to Italy has brought charm in food, architecture and living, and the Swiss border provides Alpine casinos with some of their highest rollers, it is the Rhine which counts for most in history. German possession of Alsace-Lorraine from 1871 to 1918 was the great territorial wound of modern French history. School children were made to conjugate a sentence about looking longingly over the Vosges hills to Alsace. Pledges to regain the 1.4 million hectares of lost lands to the east were a leitmotif of political speeches. The snag was that nobody in their right minds thought that France could actually wage war on Germany and win on its own – and not all the 1.6 million people of the region seemed too unhappy at finding themselves under Teutonic rule.

Setting aside the three German invasions of 1870, 1914 and 1940, the pressure which France has felt through these regions has not always been a bad thing – from Charlemagne and the commercial influences that flooded into Paris from the Low Countries and Germany in the late Middle Ages to the political refugees who brought new life, art and culture with them in the 1920s and 1930s. Still, understandably given the military history, French officials can sometimes worry about the immediate east in near-apocalyptic terms. In the 1980s, a Foreign Minister sat over breakfast in his office at the Quai d'Orsay and pondered his deepest concern. West (as it then was) Germany was an unstable nation, he said, a child beside France, a state only a century away from a galaxy of feuding princedoms. It could break apart again under the strain of Cold War rivalry, nuclear armaments and the Green movement. France had a historic obligation to hold its neighbour together, to give West Germany the backbone it lacked. So François Mitterrand flew to Bonn and made a speech backing the installation of new American nuclear missiles on German soil. The French, the minister believed, with the supreme assurance that hands France's critics so much ammunition, had saved the Germans from themselves. What he did not mention was that, as part of an unspoken deal, the Germans kept France from financial ruin by supporting the franc.

A decade and a half later, the French fear is different — that Germany may become too powerful as the central power of an increasingly united Europe, with a direct line to Washington and seeking a closer relationship with Britain. France would then be boxed in. It cannot isolate itself economically. Its north-eastern regions are bound up as closely with Germany as they are with the rest of France: the fortunes of Alsace and Lorraine rise and fall with German prosperity, and the best hope for the old industrial region round Lille is to stitch itself to the Ruhr. Politically, there can be no European vocation separate from Bonn or Berlin; but the relationship risks being that of Greece to Rome, London to Washington. This is a tough fate for any French President to accept after nearly four decades of playing an independent international role. The notion of the Gallic cock flapping along behind the German eagle is deeply unpalatable, particularly given the economic and political troubles afflicting the government in Bonn. But is there any other way?

The President and the Chancellor have regular programmed meetings, as do their ministers. Regular intercourse is good for the body, no doubt, but the French soul wants to soar free. The trouble is that it has nowhere to go. There is an in-built contradiction between the geographical position and foreign policies of Paris and Berlin. France, perched on the edge of Europe, has aspired to play a central role between East and West while Germany, though lying in the middle of the continent, has been tightly bound to the trans-Atlantic superpower. Now, seeing the choice that looms for their nation, the more apocalyptic of French observers imagine a renewed conflict between Paris, temple of the enlightened West, and Berlin, champion of the lands where Huns meet Slavs. 'We were happy when Germany meant Bonn,' one French diplomat says. 'Bonn is a Rhineland town, they grow wine there, it's only an hour over the border. But if we have to deal with Berlin, we will be in another world. With Bonn, we could feel equality; with Berlin, we will be ground under foot again.' And Washington, Paris knows, will be behind Berlin, if only to keep the uncertainties of the dismantled Soviet empire in some kind of check.

Does this mean that, once its neighbour's early twenty-first century economic blues fade, France is destined to become, in fact if not in name, a junior partner to united Germany? Despite his attempts to rewrite history in a mendacious book published posthumously, François Mitterrand saw the danger for his country and was lukewarm about German unity. As the writer François Mauriac remarked while the Berlin Wall still stood: 'I like Germany so much that I'm happy there are two of them.' Early in his presidency, Jacques Chirac back-tracked on agreements to open borders made by his predecessor. He cited the need to safeguard France from roaming Euro-criminals; the move could also be seen as a reflection of something much deeper. Kings, presidents and an emperor had built modern France behind these lines. Now, the Chancellor embraces the President; the power across the Rhine engulfs the Hexagon; and there is precious little Paris can do about it. Geography and the realities of politics and economics meet: the French can only shiver. They have no hinterland to the east or hot line to Washington. This may be the ultimate paradox to come: France as second string in a German-led Europe, but still telling herself that nothing has changed, that she can still be her proud old self – even though she is tied to German monetarism, the Ruhr and to other constraints so alien to what she would wish to be the case.

In a world where invasion is more likely to come from currency dealers' terminals than from marching feet, the Hexagon is as vulnerable as any other medium-sized country caught in the globalisation process. Equally, the nation is less united and the centralised state less omnipotent than republican theory imagines, but the people are still required to worship as loyal citizens at the traditional altars. The contrast between France's invigorating taste for individualism and the in-bred subservience to the state, between the diversity of its people and the heavy-handed vision of unity, between an international role that it assumes to be its by right and the clouds that swirl around it: all create a set of paradoxes and puzzles that call for strong but sensitive handling by the national leadership.

Like their ancestors, the Gauls, the French need chieftains who can meld the country together in their own person. Each of the myriad groups, units, associations and factions which make up the mainstream of the nation needs to be able to feel itself reflected in the man in the Élysée. The President should bind this disparate nation together, and incarnate its unity under the state, as Charles de Gaulle largely did in the early years of his presidency once opposition to his seizure of power had evaporated. Instead, France has found itself wounded by politicians who have fallen short of the task, invariably exceeding even the normal egotism of their profession. By exploiting either side of the paradoxes of French life, and failing to achieve the reconciliation they were elected to perform, they have contributed powerfully to the condition in which their country finds itself. For, if there is one divisive burden, from which France has suffered above all in the last quarter of the twentieth century, it has been the way that three men have conducted a combat for power that has no equal in any other major democratic nation. The overarching question after the earthquakes of 2002 was whether Jacques Chirac could put right the heritage they had left. It would have been a slightly less troublesome question had he not been one of them.

II

THREE MEN AND A COUNTRY

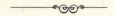

As political conflicts go, France's Thirty Years' War had its deadly aspects: two spectacular suicides and a lot of personal wounds, sometimes of a terminal nature. Many men and women saw their careers destroyed and their lives diverted to serve the ambitions of François Mitterrand, Valéry Giscard d'Estaing and Jacques Chirac. Between them, these three men have encapsulated France's political history since the decline of Charles de Gaulle. When hostilities opened, Lyndon Johnson was in the White House and Harold Wilson was in Downing Street, American troops were beginning their big build-up in Vietnam and the Soviet invasion of Czechoslovakia was still three years away. Other countries renew their leadership by whatever means. France works in impossibly long cycles as its politicians use the system to cling on to power. Victory is usually frittered away, and defeat is rarely final. The national play may move through fresh acts, but the same actors cling to the stage. Both the last two Presidents of the Republic were beaten twice before finally winning the job, and each of them plummeted to the bottom of the opinion polls within a few years of seizing the ultimate prize. In France, politics is the ultimate game, and the only losers are the people.

In the opening engagement of this war, the oldest of the three protagonists was in the north Burgundian town of which he was mayor when he learned that his first presidential bid had failed on 19 December 1965. With greater difficulty than expected, France's reigning monarch had repulsed the challenge to his throne from a collection of competing forces ranged against him from the far left of the battlefield to the far right. De Gaulle's final victory in France's first presidential election of the twentieth century by universal suffrage was no surprise, however, and François Mitterrand's 45 per cent of the vote was an honourable score which established him as the leader of the left ready to mount a fresh challenge when the ageing patriarch finally stepped down.

That became increasingly likely as the 1960s drew to a close. After a decade of Gaullist pre-eminence, the ground was shifting. The General and his country were growing out of touch with one another – while the king pursued grandeur from his castle, his people were becoming concerned about their standard of living. As a leading political commentator put it, France was getting bored. De Gaulle reflected that he should have ruled from the royal surround-ings of the Louvre rather than from a more modest palace in the 8th *arrondissement*: but voters were more interested in inflation and wages than in grandeur. It seemed that Mitterrand had only to wait patiently to claim his ultimate reward after more than twenty years in politics.

Three years later, everything fell to bits for the challenger. The General's hour of greatest danger, during the strikes and student riots of 1968, should have been a time of maximum opportunity for the opposition and its chief. But the upheaval caught the orthodox left as much by surprise as the Gaullist government. Mitterrand resorted to history, imagining himself on the barricades of 1848 or 1870, and proposing a Government of National Salvation. The Gaullists easily turned that into an attempted coup. Spectacular as the unrest was, most of the French soon came to want salvation from disorder. If they entertained doubts about De Gaulle, it was because they wondered if he really was in charge any more. So they rallied behind the reassur-ing Prime Minister, Georges Pompidou, who bought off the unions, made concessions to the students, and ended the revolt without a life lost on either side.

In the way of such things, the General sacked Pompidou as soon as victory over the strikers was in the bag. That only made De Gaulle's position untenable. At last, France had an alternative Head of State from the Gaullist ranks to whom it could turn; a man who, vitally, was now a free agent. Scheming against him by Gaullist diehards goaded the phlegmatic Pompidou into action. The former Rothschild banker had served the General loyally for years before becoming his Prime Minister, looking after his finances during the time in the wilderness and running a foundation dedicated to the memory of his invalid daughter. But, within months of Pompidou leaving office, Gaullist ultra-loyalists spread rumours that his wife was mixed up in a sex ring with Yugoslav hoodlums and French film stars. The former Premier was an easy-going man, but respect for his tall, ramrod-backed wife, Claude, was something he could not allow to be broached. There was a frosty dinner at the Élysée with the De Gaulles, which did no good. Pompidou went on television to warn that some boundaries should not be crossed. The General seemed unable, or unwilling, to rein in his zealots, who saw the prospect of a Pompidou presidency as the end of everything they believed in. On a visit to Rome, the former Prime Minister made it plain that he would stand for the presidency if De Gaulle left the Élysée. When the Head of State responded by asserting his intention to serve out his seven-year term, his former Premier spoke to a Swiss television interviewer of his own 'national destiny' – a phrase that could have only one meaning. That helped to propel the enfeebled founder of the Fifth Republic into a last bid to regain the initiative and restore the link between himself and the people. He opted for the old Bonapartist device of a plebiscite, but, unlike the first Emperor, he was not the kind of man who would arrange either for a farce in which he got more votes than there were voters, or to get himself elected for life. When he announced a referendum on regional reform and the composition of the Senate early in 1969, De Gaulle must have known in his heart that he was doomed. The subject was not one which excited the voters, the spectre of the May–June events was still alive in people's minds and, above all, the General could no longer play his favourite card of warning France that it faced a choice between him and chaos. Georges Pompidou was an all too solid bulwark against disorder.

After receiving secret polls by the police in the week before the referendum, De Gaulle gave orders for his personal files to be moved from the Élysée Palace. He recorded a broadcast to be transmitted in the event of defeat, and drove to his country home in Colombey-les-Deux-Églises in the Haute-Marne department of eastern France.

On Sunday, 27 April, the General went to mass in the morning, voted in the village and then shut himself away in his austere house. By 10 P.M., he had been told that the referendum had been lost by 47 per cent to 53. At ten minutes past midnight on 28 April 1969, the French news agency put out a terse statement from the Head of State: 'I am ceasing to exercise my functions as President of the Republic. This decision takes effect at noon today.'

Now it was time for treason. François Mitterrand decided not to stand in the 1969 presidential election that followed De Gaulle's departure; nobody asked him to, anyway. Pompidou won an over-whelming victory. Gaston Defferre and Pierre Mendès-France ran in tandem for the Socialists: they got just 5 per cent of the vote.

After the heroic founding epoch of the Fifth Republic, with its reassertion of national glory, the ending of the Algerian war and the development of the nuclear force, the Pompidou presidency ushered in a more businesslike era characterised by the construction of indus-trial empires rather than great international ambitions. It was one of those lulls which punctuate prolonged conflicts, a respite during which the left licked its wounds while the ambitious men of the centre and right planned their future. Things changed sooner than any of them had expected. Pompidou's face ballooned, and he increasingly had difficulty walking. It was generally believed that he was taking cortisone; was it for cancer and, if so, how bad was the illness? Speculation about his health became the leading subject of gossip, but the secret was well kept.

By the end of March 1974, however, the President was too ill to attend the annual dinner of the diplomatic corps in Paris, and had to cancel a trip to Bonn. On the last day of the month, he left Paris with his wife for a weekend at a country estate. His pain grew even more intense, and he was transported back to his personal apartment on the Quai Bourbon, overlooking the Seine. There, opposite Notre Dame, the second President of the Fifth Republic died of cancer on 2 April at the age of sixty-three. That night, the state television service ran a caption along the bottom of the screen on which a film starring the English actor Alan Bates was showing. It announced baldly: 'The President of the Republic is dead.' That was in keeping with Pompidou's image. He had been the Head of State France wanted, but he did not go down as a heroic figure. Sensible people rarely do.

Pompidou's death precipitated an era of treason, with a vicious three-cornered battle ensuing which established the pattern of French politics for a quarter of a century and has its repercussions even today. The dead ruler left no *dauphin* in the way that Pompidou had been De Gaulle's obvious heir. There was a leading Gaullist candidate in the person of Pompidou's Prime Minister, Jacques Chaban-Delmas. Chaban-Delmas had impeccable credentials and the status of a former head of government. He had been a hero of the Resistance in his twenties (and was incarnated by Alain Delon in the film *Is Paris Burning?*). A lieutenant of De Gaulle since the 1940s and Mayor of Bordeaux since 1947, Chaban was fit and attractive. An accomplished golfer and fine tennis-player, he ran up stairs four at a time at the age of sixty. He should have been a natural winner, but he was distrusted by many Gaullists on two counts.

The first was that he had swung too far to the left, listening to siren voices like that of his adviser on social affairs, Jacques Delors, as he sought to craft what he called a 'new society' for France. While Pompidou was preaching unadventurous corporatism, Chaban-Delmas promoted employees' involvement in running the companies they worked for. His second problem was more personal. He had run into difficulties over revelations about his tax affairs; he was a lacklustre campaigner with an unpleasantly metallic voice; and he seemed to many not to possess a true hunger for the job. In short, for the hard wing of the Gaullist party, Chaban-Delmas was not nearly tough enough to hold the most important post in France.

In contrast, meet two people who are virtually unknown outside France and rarely appeared in public at home. However, their influence on the country's politics was pivotal. Without them, the fortunes of the Gaullist party over the ensuing two decades would have been very different, the Socialists might not have come to power in 1981, and Jacques Chirac might never have been President. If Chaban-Delmas was judged insufficiently brutal, nobody thought Pierre Juillet and Marie-France Garaud came from anywhere but the hard Gaullist right. By the time of Pompidou's death, this duo from the provinces had achieved near-mythic status in political circles as the forces behind the throne, driven by an intense desire for the Gaullists to hold on to power at any cost and an equally visceral hatred of the left. Garaud was a lawyer from Poitiers, a Lady Macbeth with a dominating manner that seduced and subjugated the men around her; Juillet was a man of the shadows who walked with a cane and kept a sheep farm in the Limousin. In 1974, their main aim in life was to prevent the Socialists and their allies winning the presidency. To do that, they were convinced, they had to stop Chaban-Delmas being the Gaullist candidate.

There was no doubting the task that the centre-right faced in retaining power. In one of the extraordinary recoveries which marked his political career, François Mitterrand had established himself as the single candidate for the main parties of the opposition as he launched into his decade-long exercise of drawing the powerful Communist Party into his tent in order to strangle it. In 1969, the Communist presidential candidate had won 21 per cent of the vote – four times as much as the Socialist. Now, Mitterrand had got the whole of the left to line up behind him. Parliamentary elections saw big gains for the opposition and the loss of a hundred constituencies for the governing parties. The Gaullist crown was under serious threat. Showing the lack of scruples which marks consummate tacticians in politics or war, the powers behind the vacant throne sought a new alliance.

Valéry Giscard d'Estaing looks and acts like an aristocrat from the great days of the court at Versailles, though his family was actually only authorised to use the *d'* in 1922. Born four years later in Germany, where his father was a civil servant with the occupation forces after the First World War, Giscard was one of those brilliant individuals who shoot through the upper reaches of France's education system to run the country. He joined the Prime Minister's staff at the age of twenty-eight, won election to the National Assembly by the time he was thirty and was a junior member of the government at thirty-three. De Gaulle found the young man too clever by half, and there were doubts about the Algérie Française affiliations of some members of the right-wing political group he led. But nothing could stop Giscard. He became Finance Minister a month before his thirty-sixth birthday.

The post usually ranks just behind that of Prime Minister in terms of power, since its occupant controls so much of what his colleagues can afford to do. Giscard held the post for nine years, during which he and the job became synonymous. When I told a taxi-driver I wanted to go to the Finance Ministry one Saturday morning, he nodded and replied: '*Ah, chez Giscard.*'

The minister had style to spare. He spoke for hours in parliament without notes. Tall and self-assured, he looked perfect in formal dress, but he also met me that Saturday in his ornate office in the Louvre wearing a cardigan and no tie. Touching all the bases, he played the accordion and turned out for football in his native Auvergne – photographs taken in the changing-room showed that he carried not an ounce of surplus fat, in striking contrast to his well-padded Cabinet colleagues. Giscard had ambition by the kilometre. After a dozen years at the top of government, he was ready to make his bid for the summit in 1974, and the time was right. France was ready for a change from Gaullism. Giscard knew he could capture that national mood, without frightening the conservative middle classes. He was the thoroughly modern leader his country needed, a French Kennedy. And, in terms of personal ambition, he was well aware that, if he did not grab the opportunity in 1974, he might never have another chance: either Mitterrand would win, possibly going on to a second term, or a failure by the left would ensure Gaullist rule into the next century.

The snag was that, for all his attributes, the young man lacked one essential element – a mass political movement. However much De Gaulle may have despised parties and aspired to rule above them, the election of the President by universal suffrage which he introduced in 1962 means that the Head of State needed a big political organisation to get out the voters and maintain electoral discipline. Giscard had his followers, organised by a much more truly aristocratic friend, Prince Michel Poniatowski. But there were not enough of them; his Independent Republican party had only fifty-four seats in the National Assembly. Like their centrist allies, Giscard's followers tended to be local bigwigs, the notables who ran French country towns, men and women at home in upper bourgeois houses and small châteaux, where the food was excellent, the service discreet and money not mentioned as deals were made in a quiet corner of the salon after a day's shooting. However highly they might prize themselves, such folk were simply not numerous and well-organised enough to withstand Mitterrand's challenge. Rattling pearls at the peasants wasn't going to repel the populist hordes.

Giscard's problems found their mirror image across the Seine from his office in the Louvre. Pierre Juillet and Marie-France Garaud had no great liking for the Finance Minister: in many ways, he was the antithesis of their idea of a leader. Still, they needed him, as he needed them. Pompidou's death had come two years too early for the backroom pair. They were grooming their presidential candidate; but, like a classic racehorse being trained for the Derby or the Prix de l'Arc de Triomphe, timing was everything. If Pompidou had lived to the end of his term in 1976, it would have been a different matter. But this was 1974, and there was an inescapable symmetry. The anti-Chaban Gaullists had the troops to put into the field but no general to lead them; Giscard had few troops but was the ideal man to head the charge.

So a deal emerged. A breakaway group of Gaullist members of the National Assembly distanced themselves from Chaban-Delmas and lined up behind Giscard. In the first round of the two-stage presidential voting, Mitterrand easily topped the poll with 43 per cent. That had been expected. The vital thing was that he had fallen well short of the outright majority needed for election. The significant figures came next: Giscard took 32.6 per cent and Chaban-Delmas only 15.1. Although the left's man had finished first, the electoral arithmetic was stacked against him. A dozen candidates had run in the first round, and most of the votes for those who were eliminated would go to the right. Mitterrand could count on far smaller reserves of new support than Giscard. Even the Gaullists who had backed Chaban-Delmas reconciled themselves to the treason which had knocked their candidate out of the race.

At fifty-seven, Mitterrand looked decidedly dowdy compared to the cool young intelligence opposite him. He was still identified in many people's minds with the discredited Fourth Republic, in whose governments he had often served. He had been out of power for sixteen years whereas Giscard had run the Finance Ministry for most of the past decade. When his opponent asked him a direct question about international finance in France's first televised presidential debate, Mitterrand couldn't reply. Capitalising on his advantage, the young candidate told his ageing opponent that he did not have a monopoly on feelings of the heart. It was no shock when, on 19 May, Valéry Giscard d'Estaing became the third President of the Fifth Republic with 50.81 per cent of the vote. The only surprise was that the margin had not been larger. Much as Giscard wanted France, the electorate did not seem entirely convinced it wanted him.

Again, Mitterrand had not done badly. He had come much closer than in his first bid for the top job. But the seven-year length of the term in the Élysée Palace and the awesome power of the office make opposition a lonely, ill-defined job: France does not recognise a Leader of the Opposition as Britain does, which is sensible since there are nearly always several oppositions. As a man who knew the value of time, Mitterrand devoted the rest of the 1970s to building up a new Socialist Party and to his long-term campaign to snare the Communists in his web as he prepared for what would be a third tilt at the Élysée. For the moment, the field belonged to the new alliance which had defeated both the left and the old-style Gaullists. Giscard, the presiding general of the victorious forces, moved in to the Élysée on 27 May. His first action was to appoint as Prime Minister the man who had made victory possible.

Jacques Chirac was Georges Pompidou's political son. After a flirtation with the left during his late teens, when he sold the Communist newspaper *L'Humanité* in the street and signed a Moscow-inspired anti-nuclear petition, he had turned into a dyed-in-the-wool Gaullist. Pompidou had taken the young Énarque on to his staff while he was De Gaulle's Prime Minister. The product of a comfortable upper-middle-class family, Chirac had had a full life already: he had trained as a cavalry officer, had gone to sea and had spent a summer in America, where he studied at Harvard, won a certificate from a Howard Johnson ice-cream parlour for his skill in making banana splits, and gave a southern belle Latin lessons – and her first kiss, which she said she remembered forty years later.

To blood him politically, Pompidou sent the young man off to the Corrèze department in France's agricultural heartland to conquer it for the Gaullists: Chirac and his wife drove through the night from

Paris each Friday or took the train that arrived at 4:10 A.M. to campaign through the weekend in the markets and *charcuteries*. He became a municipal councillor, and, in 1967, went on to win the parliamentary constituency he still held when he became President two decades later. After Pompidou moved into the Élysée in 1969, he had promoted his protégé to be Minister for Relations with Parliament (where he was a disaster), then Agriculture Minister (where he ferociously defended French interests), and finally to the Interior Ministry (where he took office a month before Pompidou died). The President's death was a huge blow. 'I had the feeling of suddenly being an orphan,' he wrote. At the memorial mass for Pompidou on the Île Saint-Louis in Paris, he sobbed uncontrollably.

Had Pompidou lived through his presidential term and then been prevented by bad health from running for re-election, Chirac might well have been the Gaullist candidate in 1976. That was what Pierre Juillet and Marie-France Garaud had planned. They had taken Chirac to their bosom. On his way home in the evening from his various ministries, he would drop in to see them. If Pompidou was his political father, Pierre and Marie-France were his uncle and aunt. An only child, Chirac hides an unexpected need for mentors behind his straight-ahead style. It is as if he requires confirmatory approval from father (or mother) figures, whom he does not always choose with the greatest discrimination.

Since 1974 was too early for a presidential bid, Chirac and his closest advisers decided that if he could not be in the Élysée himself, he should at least become the power in another man's reign. As Interior Minister he organised the election, and Fifth Republic tradition did not require ministerial impartiality. Chirac had access to police polls which showed that Jacques Chaban-Delmas would lose to Mitterrand. With Juillet and Garaud orchestrating every move, forty-three eminent anti-Chaban Gaullists published a joint text saying that there should be just one representative of the governing majority in the coming election. The signatories included four members of the government, headed by the Interior Minister. Their message was clear: they would swing a significant section of Gaullist support away from Chaban-Delmas and behind the Minister of Finance and the Economy. 'Chirac is a falcon placed on the gloved fist of Marie-France,' Chaban-Delmas wrote later. 'From time to

time, Juillet slips the chain so that Chirac flies for an hour. And kills.'
Nine days after being elected President, Valéry Giscard d'Estaing
appointed the leader of the Gaullist *fronde* as the sixth Prime Minister
of the Fifth Republic.

The two men were strikingly young for a country which generally
liked its leaders to show their age. Giscard was forty-eight, Chirac
forty-one. They had first worked together when Chirac held a junior
post at the Finance Ministry. They had been in endless Cabinet meetings since then. They seemed the perfect team to move their country
to the forefront of the modern age. They may even have believed it
themselves: winning battles can provoke dangerous illusions. The
truth was that victory opened up a steadily-widening war between
two men pursuing the same prize.

Valéry Giscard d'Estaing set out to be a great President. He introduced
a flood of social reforms, with particular attention to women's rights.
His administration liberalised the abortion laws. He modernised
France's telecommunications and sought to free up the financial
system. With Helmut Schmidt, Germany's equally brainy Chancellor,
Giscard set up the European Monetary System. He mended fences
with the United States and pressed ahead with the construction of
Europe. But, as his presidency wore on, much of what he did could
be summed up by Marie-France Garaud's dismissive phrase – '*des
gadgets*'. Whether because he was, at heart, more conservative than he
seemed or because he was too removed from the realities of daily life,
Giscard's reforms changed things less than he thought. The President
was like one of those eighteenth-century aristocrats who played with
all the most advanced ideas about changing society, who set up model
farms and chatted with Voltaire and felt good envisaging a new
enlightenment – but who were never really ready to challenge the
society which had bred them.

There was another problem with Giscard. The exorbitant powers
of the presidency were irresistible. The opportunities to put his finger
in every pie could not be passed by. De Gaulle and Pompidou had
known that the President needed to limit the reach of his power, to
leave the Prime Minister room to breathe while the eyes of his boss
rested on loftier horizons: if France had been a business, the Fifth

Republic gave it a Chairman and a Chief Executive Officer. De Gaulle told the Americans to get out of Vietnam; his Prime Minister dealt with public-sector wage negotiations. Pompidou let Britain into the Common Market; his Prime Minister worried about workers' rights. Giscard relished the world horizon, but he also found it impossible to delegate at home. This was partly a personal trait. He wanted to be Chairman of the Board, Company President, CEO, CFO (he kept the Finance Ministry under close watch) and any other O around. He also had ambitions to replace Gaullism with Giscardianism, thus establishing his centre-right followers as France's main political movement. His anti-Gaullism was no new development – in 1967 he had spoken openly about preparing 'France for her future' and his party had discreetly advised its members to vote against the General in the 1969 referendum. Had he seized the moment in 1974 and called legislative elections, Giscard might have taken a big step towards his dream of a dominant centre-conservative party. Instead, with a Gaullist as Prime Minister, he made the mistake of contenting himself with the parliamentary majority bequeathed by Pompidou. Still, he kept a tight hand on the government, paying scant attention to the constitutional nicety that it should have been run by the man who had made his victory possible. Giscard had won the great prize, but would not take the distance necessary for a supreme leader, above the hurly-burly of everyday politics and administration. He telephoned ministers directly, endlessly by-passing Chirac. He appointed his close friend, Michel Poniatowski, as Interior Minister with the job of building up their Independent Republican party and cutting the ground from beneath Chirac's troops. But, as the President's men sought ways to change the face of French politics, the soldiers who had crossed the lines to win him victory in 1974 were preparing to move in a different direction.

For Marie-France Garaud and Pierre Juillet, Giscard's presidency was an unfortunate, if necessary, period whose only virtue was that it had stopped François Mitterrand becoming Head of State. France, they calculated, would tire of this hollow neo-aristocrat, and be ready for the return of dyed-in-the-wool Gaullism. Though Giscard would remain in office until 1981, preparations had to be made for the return of a true believer when the next election eventually came around. In the interim, the President could be reduced to a puppet by draining off his power towards his Prime Minister. So while Giscard sought to undermine the Gaullists, they were out to do exactly the same to him. It was a recipe for disaster, exacerbated by the basic differences of temperament between the men leading the two groups.

The new Head of State was desperately eager to find the common touch. He made regular television appearances to tell the nation what he was doing. He shared a barbecue at his Mediterranean presidential retreat with North African soldiers who had fought for the French, and invited dustmen to breakfast at the Élysée. He ventured out from time to time to dine with ordinary citizens – a lorry-driver, a picture-framer, a gamekeeper and a young couple in Garaud's home city of Poitiers. Sometimes, the President would abandon his official car and walk to official appointments through the streets of Paris. There were stories about him having crashed into the back of a milk delivery van while driving himself back to the Élysée in the early hours after a romantic assignation.

Away from the public-relations machine, Giscard had a strikingly lordly style for a supposedly modern man. He instructed his Prime Minister to walk three paces behind him on official occasions. His wife, Anne-Aymone Sauvage de Brantes, was said to have been flummoxed when a magazine photographer doing a feature on their home life asked her to put a pot on the stove. Even if the story wasn't true, it fitted their personalities so well that everybody believed it. After their initial honeymoon, life with Giscard became steadily less pleasant for Jacques Chirac. If he did not exactly condescend to the younger man, Giscard revelled in his own superiority. The President's broad intellectual approach sat ill with the hyperactive Chirac, who found himself frozen out of decision-making and reduced to jiggling his long legs beneath the Cabinet table in frustration. Their taste in food betrayed the essential gap between the two men. Chirac likes nothing better than large meals of solid country fare; his favourite dish has long been calf's head with a piquant sauce. Giscard prefers truffles – either with scrambled eggs or in a soup under a pastry shell created in his honour by Paul Bocuse. 'Tell me what you eat and I'll tell you what kind of man you are,' as the gastronome Brillat-Savarin observed.

Not that the President's sense of superiority could not be punctured, even if nobody dared to notice it. His reign included a prime example of *farce à la française*. When OPEC sent oil prices soaring,

Giscard produced a reassuring phrase. France might not have oil, he intoned, but it had ideas (an alternative was to call French agriculture 'green oil'). All very well, but when he was offered a revolutionary key to oil wealth and military security, the Head of State reacted like a child in a candy shop, and thereby became the most eminent figure in the cast of a farce that also involved two Gaullist bosses of the Elf oil company, the state Audit Court, intelligence agents, a vanishing Italian inventor, a Belgian count and the doyen of French conservatives, Antoine Pinay. Jacques Chirac was kept in the dark. He would have been furious had he known at the time. When the affair came to light seven years later, he must have blessed his stars that he could plead complete ignorance.

The self-styled inventor, Aldo Bonassoli, claimed to have two electronic devices, codenamed 'Delta' and 'Omega', which could shoot a newly-discovered particle into the earth. This particle would play back images or sound-waves revealing the existence of oil deposits. By mounting the equipment on aircraft known as 'sniffer planes', an oil company could avoid the high costs of exploratory drilling and would be able to buy leases in the precise sites where the miracle boxes housing the devices detected big reserves.

Bonassoli had an associate, a Belgian count who brought the invention to the attention of a well-connected French lawyer who also happened to be a reserve officer in France's counter-espionage service. The lawyer told Pinay, a former Premier who had reformed French finances for De Gaulle and become something of a political father-figure to Giscard. Pinay informed the President and the Chairman of Elf, Pierre Guillaumat, himself a former Gaullist intelligence chief. The President and the chairman leaped at the chance of giving France the jump on its rivals; Giscard also observed that the technique had military significance, since it could be used to detect deep-diving nuclear submarines.

The Head of State insisted that the project be developed in the utmost secrecy. When he gave Elf Aquitaine approval for a first investment in June 1976, the board of the oil group's holding company was not told anything. Nothing appeared in the accounts. Secret official clearance was given for the transfer of funds to the scheme's promoters in Switzerland. Not everybody involved appeared completely convinced: when a prominent Gaullist politician, Albin Chalandon, was appointed Chairman of Elf in 1977, he covered his back by asking for written official approval of the unorthodox way in which the project was being handled.

The Italian inventor and the Belgian count shared the obsession with secrecy. They told the French that they were investing large sums in the project, installing computers in their laboratory and equipping the sniffer planes with the necessary accessories, which included gold-plated ashtrays. Nobody at Elf was allowed to get a proper look at the equipment for safety reasons. The promoters of the scheme warned that the boxes were dangerously radioactive. Tests were held. Giscard attended one. Although the results were poor, Elf decided to buy the process. Soon afterwards, the Industry Ministry, which was on bad terms with the oil company, took an initiative which somebody might have thought of a bit earlier. An independent expert, Professor Jules Horowitz, was called in to sniff out the sniffers.

The professor went to see the Omega device, which was said to be able to show images from the other side of a wall on a screen as proof of the power of the miracle particle. On his first visit to the laboratory, Horowitz placed a test card behind a wall opposite the Omega box. Nothing happened. Then the machine minders gave him a metal ruler and suggested he take it behind the wall. When the professor did so, an image of a straight ruler appeared on Omega's screen. Good enough – except that, on his way to the back of the wall, the Professor had bent the ruler into a V-shape.

On a later visit, Professor Horowitz repeated the test-card experiment. This time two vertical bars came up on the screen. Excellent, except that they appeared before the professor had put his cards in place. When Omega was eventually dismantled, it was found to contain sheets of photocopied images and cheap components. Elf broke off the agreement. The Belgian count and the Italian inventor vanished. The whole affair remained secret. When the Audit Court looked into the oil company's accounts at the end of 1979, it was told that any mention of the oil-sniffing scheme should be kept confidential. Three copies of the report were sent to the government; the head of the Audit Court kept three others in his desk, and destroyed them when he stepped down from his job in 1982.

The story of the sniffer-plane project eventually surfaced the following summer in the whistle-blowing weekly *Le Canard Enchaîné*. Initially, it produced smiles but little reaction. Then, just before

Christmas 1983, the *Canard* reported that the Audit Court copies of the report had been destroyed. An indignant Giscard went on television to show that he had a copy and that it was still intact. He insisted that secrecy had been essential in view of the sensitive nature of the project. Elf's expenditure, estimated at up to 790 million francs, was, he argued, small by the standards of the oil industry.

The affair was soon submerged in the wider political battle, but it had produced the agreeable image of an omniscient Head of State slipping on a banana peel like any ordinary mortal. As Max Gallo, the Socialist writer and politician, observed, it was irresistibly reminiscent of the harebrained inventor of the Tintin comic strip, Professor Calculus. Not the kind of association the superior Giscard would relish.

A few months before he was told of the sniffer scheme, Giscard decided to reshuffle the government, which was nominally under the charge of the Prime Minister. The President drew up the list of new ministers himself; only then did he summon Jacques Chirac back from the country at a moment's notice on a Sunday morning to tell him whom he had chosen. That alone might have been grounds for resignation, but the Prime Minister bit his lip and soldiered on.

The Whitsun holiday of 1976 brought him a ray of hope. He and his wife were invited to spend the weekend at the presidential retreat at Brégançon on the Mediterranean coast. It was meant to be a simple occasion – Le Président and Madame Giscard d'Estaing invite Monsieur et Madame Chirac to a weekend by the sea. The Prime Minister, a man in whom hope springs eternal, thought this might be an opportunity to sort things out. It turned out to be a Weekend From Hell.

Chirac flew south expecting a meaningful *tête-à-tête* with the President. As soon as he arrived, he was disabused. One other guest was present – Giscard's ski instructor. That set the tone. As Chirac later recounted it, the President and his wife sat down for meals in armchairs while their guests were relegated to straight-backed seats. Things went from bad to worse. On a joint visit to review the fleet off Nice, Chirac became so annoyed with a television interview the

President was giving that he grabbed a pair of binoculars and scanned the sea as a diversion, not noticing in his rage that he was holding the glasses the wrong way round.

On 25 August, the Cabinet assembled at the Élysée following the summer holiday. After a ninety-minute trot through the agenda, Giscard regaled his ministers with a lengthy account of his recent trip to Gabon, where he enjoyed the big-game hunting laid on by the friendly dictator, Omar Bongo. Eventually, the President looked across the table at the man who had enabled him to win power two years earlier.

'Prime Minister,' he said, 'I believe you have something to say.'

'Mr President,' Chirac replied, 'I have the honour to present you with the resignation of my government.'

It was a first in the history of the Fifth Republic. Previously, Presidents had thanked Prime Ministers and sent them on their way. Now, Jacques Chirac was declaring his independence. This was the Gaullism of 1940 and 1958: fuck-you, in-your-face politics. Nobody was better suited to that than Jacques Chirac. A new civil war had erupted. Whatever his brilliance, Giscard was condemned to eventual ruin by the Faustian deal he had done in 1974, and by the nature of the partner he had chosen so mistakenly – the squire who ended up destroying his master.

Jacques Chirac's drive can be positively alarming, particularly for those who have crossed him. Four days after leaving government, he travelled to the Creuse department in the centre of France to spend the last Sunday in August at the country home of Pierre Juillet. Also present were Marie-France Garaud and two other Chirac loyalists. At lunch, Mme Juillet placed four-leaf clovers on each plate. By the time night fell on the calm countryside, the quintet had mapped out plans for a new political movement. It would be headed by the recently departed Prime Minister. It would be a mass party, an army of political militants based on the existing Gaullist movement but reaching out more widely with a message of national rebirth and dynamism.

The new party's strengths would be incarnated by its chief, personifying all that was strong and true about France, safeguarding the unity of the state and its leading role in the world, bringing together the disparate threads of the nation in a single great movement. The setting that day was symbolic: not a château or a Parisian apartment, but a farmhouse deep in the true heart of the land they would lift to new heights. The new party was to come from the real France, and the potency of the rural myth underpinned that day at the farm. Though its progenitors had actually spun their partisan webs on either side of the Seine for almost a decade, this was to be a movement which would stand above and beyond selfish, sectional Parisian concerns. The people around the table simply believed in the recurring Gaullist mantra: they, and they alone, knew what was best for France. A fly on the wall might have been a trifle concerned at the quasi-fascist superman tone that hung in the air.

That autumn, Chirac travelled to Égletons in his electoral home department of the Corrèze, a town celebrated for the excellence of its sausages. In a rousing speech in a gymnasium built with funds which he had arranged to be allocated to the region, the former Premier laid the groundwork for the new movement, calling on the nation to rally to its basic values. Such was the Chiracian surge that the existing Gaullist party agreed to be swallowed up: it helped that most of its barons were promised important posts in the new enterprise. In December 1976, at a great meeting in a Paris exhibition hall, the ex-Premier launched the Rassemblement Pour la République (Rally for the Republic) to take Gaullism into the next millennium and prove that ideologically-led populism had a future. The name had a vital historical echo: De Gaulle had called his post-war political movement the Rassemblement du Peuple Français.

From the start, the RPR had one over-riding aim – the election of Jacques Chirac as Head of State in 1981. That meant there were now two competing presidential candidates on the right, for an election where they would face a candidate of the left who was busy turning the Socialist Party into a vehicle to get him to power at long last. This intensely personal pattern, set in the mid-1970s, was to continue for two decades to the disadvantage of the nation caught in the hammer-lock of the three contenders.

The long wait until the next presidential election was no problem for the reigning Head of State. His opponent on the left needed the years ahead to consolidate and build his strength. For Jacques Chirac, on the other hand, no time could be wasted. Leading a big new party was a necessary platform for his ambitions. But he was also a man who had been in government for almost a decade and who was used to exerting authority: the idea of being bereft of power was unnatural. He did not have to wait long for a chance to get back from the wilderness.

Among the reforms Giscard cherished was the idea of giving Paris an elected mayor in place of the officials who ruled it at the behest of central government. As Prime Minister, Chirac had not been convinced; a real boss of the capital might become a thorn in the side of the national authorities, a countervailing challenge to the Jacobin centralism he had always practised. He was not alone in such thinking: it was why there had been no elected mayor of the city for so long. But Giscard had his way, and the poll was set for March 1977. The Head of State took personal charge. Ensuring that a friendly figure ran Paris would further enhance his own power. So, at a luncheon at the Élysée Palace in November 1976, Giscard picked one of his most faithful lieutenants, the Industry Minister Michel d'Ornano, as the Mayor of Paris to be. Two days later, Pierre Juillet and Marie-France Garaud had an idea: why didn't Chirac run against d'Ornano? Another front opened in the battle between the companions-in-arms of 1974.

Once the RPR leader had announced his candidacy, the idea seemed the most inevitable thing in the world. The Gaullists were strong in the city: a Chirac follower had just won a smashing by-election victory in the 5th *arrondissement*, while two Giscardians had lost seats elsewhere in the capital. A plump-cheeked Norman count, d'Ornano did not fit naturally into campaigning in the city streets; Chirac, on the other hand, relished the endless round of glad-handing and small talk in the shops, markets and cafés. It was said that his palms became so sore that he had to wrap them in soothing bandages at night. There was a challenge from the left to be fought as well, but the opponent who mattered for Chirac was not on the list of candidates. The RPR leader might be crossing swords with d'Ornano day by day: his real target was the man in the Élysée.

On 25 March 1977, seven months to the day since he had resigned as Prime Minister, Chirac was elected Mayor of Paris. He and his RPR were triumphant; Giscard was humiliated. The ex-Premier now had a mighty double power-base, made up of a mass party and control of France's greatest city, and he was ready for the ultimate challenge.

The presidential election of 1981 brought together themes which had run through French politics since 1965. In the left-hand corner, François Mitterrand was stronger than ever, with the solid backing of a resurgent Socialist Party plus the Communist regiments from the Red Belt suburbs and its provincial redoubts. The opposition had come close to winning parliamentary elections and was steadily extending its power in the regions. After a bout of internal feuding, Mitterrand had stitched together enough of the rival Socialist factions to ensure that he would face no internal challenge to his third presidential bid. On the right, in contrast, the two young allies of 1974 were fighting one another as much as they were combating the left.

For most of the previous five years, Chirac's RPR deputies had waged guerrilla warfare against the government in the National Assembly. Giscard's presidency was bogged down in low growth, rising unemployment, uncertainty about France's international standing and recurrent rumours that the President had accepted diamonds from the self-proclaimed Emperor Jean Bedel Bokassa in Central Africa. Social tension was rising: far from seeing their country becoming a fairer place, as Giscard had pledged, the French watched as inequalities rose and growth fell after the oil price crisis. The smoothly aloof man in the Élysée came to epitomise the haves to the growing ranks of the have-nots. When he attempted a reprise of his triumphal 1974 television debate with Mitterrand and asked about currency rates, the Socialist sat back and smiled: the next day, one of his staff told journalists that his boss had thought of asking whether Giscard knew the market rate for diamonds, but had held back out of respect for his office. The unspoken remark shot around town. Seven years of power had not been kind to Giscard; the unstoppably bright young man of 1974 had become the brittle autocrat of 1981. Eight months before the election, he held a 61–39 lead over Mitterrand in the polls. By the following March, the gap had narrowed to 51–49. Part of the reason was the challenge Giscard faced from his former Prime Minister.

Three years earlier, in the 1978 European elections, Chirac had shown his wild side with a Le Pen-like attack on the Giscardians as 'the party of the foreigners'. His only excuse was that he was in hospital after a car crash which may have affected his judgement. That kind of stridency cost the RPR dearly at the polls, but Chirac was unabashed. He was also more alone than he had ever been, having lost the counsel of his two original guides. It was said that his wife had issued an 'it's them or me' ultimatum, so Pierre Juillet went off to tend his sheep while Marie-France Garaud stood as an independent presidential candidate. Chirac's 1981 campaign made it plain that he was not fit to run the country. In the first round of voting, he won 18 per cent to Giscard's 28 and Mitterrand's 26 (Garaud scored 1.3 per cent). But the crude result was not the point. The RPR's leader was a killer force, a Clint Eastwood figure on a trail of bloody vengeance.

In public, Chirac had to say that he would vote for Giscard in the run-off fight with Mitterrand: as head of the biggest party of the right, he could not speak otherwise. But there was a deafening absence of any rallying call from Gaullist ranks. A minister recalled hearing Chirac say he would do all he could to ensure that Giscard was not re-elected. As for the RPR rank-and-file, five years of in-fighting had turned them against Giscard and his clan to the point at which some might let their hostility overcome their desire to keep Mitterrand out of the Élysée. The prospect of going fishing rather than voting on Sunday, 10 May 1981 held a large appeal for Chirac's supporters. The Communist leadership was equally ambivalent about backing Mitterrand, but their voters sensed a chance to install a government of the left at long last, and voted with their hearts.

As France's pre-eminent electoral strategist, François Mitterrand knew that he had to exploit the cancerous split between his two main opponents to the full. His best chance of winning lay in their ability to lose. Accordingly, he arranged a secret dinner for Chirac at the home of one of his most devoted supporters, Édith Cresson. As the evening ended, Mitterrand told the Mayor of Paris: 'If I am not elected President of the Republic this time, it will be a bore for me but, in the end, not too serious. I would go down as the man who took Socialism to 49 per cent of the vote. My place in history is already assured. I have left my mark. On the other hand, if Giscard wins again, you will have problems. I would not like to be in your shoes. He won't do you any favours, eh?'

It was vintage Mitterrand – setting his enemies against one another for his own good. The old fox knew who he was dealing with. Back in 1977, a guest at a dinner at the flat of a gadfly publisher, politician and short-lived Giscardian minister, Jean-Jacques Servan-Schreiber, had said: 'You may perhaps be surprised that I allow – or even cause – the election of Mitterrand, but it's the only way to get rid of Giscard. And we can't go on letting him sink France.' The speaker was Jacques Chirac. As for Mitterrand, before the first round of the election, he confided to a businessman friend: 'God save me from facing Jacques Chirac in the second round. If he is the candidate of the united right, I don't think I'll win.'

Mitterrand was spared that fight when Chirac was eliminated in the first round. But it was clearly going to be a very close battle with Giscard, and Mitterrand left no stone unturned. Among those he tipped over was the rock hiding the case of Michel Slitinsky, who, as a seventeen-year-old, had hidden in a cupboard and then escaped over the rooftops when two French policemen came to his family home in Bordeaux in the autumn of 1942 searching for Jews. After the Liberation, Slitinsky's sister, who had survived deportation, recognised the two policemen in the street. Slitinsky began legal proceedings against them, but they pleaded that they had been acting on orders from headquarters: they were never brought to trial. Researching into the complicity of the authorities with the genocide, Slitinsky found a sheaf of deportation orders signed by the head of the 'Jewish question' section in Bordeaux, Maurice Papon, who was now Giscard's Budget Minister. Slitinsky passed his documents to the investigative weekly, *Le Canard Enchaîné*, in the spring of 1981. According to Slitinsky, the journalist who wrote the documents up told him he had been in touch with Mitterrand before a front-page story appeared between the two rounds of the election under the headline, 'PAPON, AIDE DE CAMPS. When a minister of Giscard had Jews deported.' According to Slitinsky, the journalist, a former Socialist Party worker who now appears embarrassed and denies the tale, told him simply, 'Mitterrand agrees,' calculating that the revelation of Papon's role could swing 200,000 Jewish votes to him.

On a less public front, the champion of the united left sent a trusted friend, François de Grossouvre, to see the Mayor of Paris. De Grossouvre, an intriguer who spun schemes in the shadows for Mitterrand, had a special message to deliver. The left's electoral programme promised to introduce proportional representation to give smaller political groups seats in the National Assembly. This was acutely worrying for Chirac's RPR, which gained greatly from the winner-take-all system: in 1978, it had won one-third of the National Assembly with a quarter of the votes. De Grossouvre carried the message that, whatever his programme proclaimed, Mitterrand would keep the existing electoral system – if he said anything else in public, it was only to keep in with his Communist allies, who would benefit from a change in the voting method. Chirac appeared content. It was said that his visitor reminded him, pleasurably, of Pierre Juillet.

As the campaign reached its peak, François Mitterrand took to quoting the Paris mayor's public criticisms of Giscard in the late 1970s. Chirac did not rebut any of them. In a crucial television debate with the President, Mitterrand cited Chirac ten times. The Socialist and Gaullist might be on different sides of the political fence, but their mutual enmity towards Giscard brought them together. 'You have always been wrong,' Mitterrand told the Head of State in their television duel. He might have been speaking for Jacques Chirac. What role have the presence of the presidential ski instructor and straight-backed chairs at Brégançon played in the recent history of France? More, perhaps, than any policy debate in the National Assembly. Giscard's grandeur unwittingly hatched a complicity between the men to his left and right which was his undoing. Without it, Mitterrand would probably not have achieved 51.76 per cent of the vote, and France would not have spent the next fourteen years under his rule.

The first defeat of his life was traumatic for Valéry Giscard d'Estaing. President before he was fifty, he found himself rejected at fifty-five. In 1969, Charles de Gaulle resigned with a one-sentence communiqué and remained in seclusion in his country home. In 1974, Georges Pompidou died in office. In 1981, the third President of the Fifth

Republic delivered a farewell message to the nation through his favoured medium, television. When he had finished speaking, he rose from his seat and walked off the set while the camera stayed symbolically focused on the empty chair. The implication that France had a vacuum at the very pinnacle of the state was yet another sign of Giscard's self-regard, a maudlin exercise by a man whose main public-relations failure had been that, after their first honeymoon, he had related less and less to the public.

The ex-President suffered the indignity of an abusive Socialist demonstration as he drove out of the Élysée for the last time. He did not read newspapers for months to avoid hurtful criticism, and said he found it hard to look at his own reflection in a mirror. He had banked so much on his own brilliance that he could not duck personal blame for defeat and the sweeping Socialist gains in ensuing parliamentary elections. At a private dinner the following year, Mitterrand told Giscard that history had been unfair to him. 'You are the best,' the new President added. 'I am sure we will meet again.' Soothing words, but little balm. By then, Jacques Chirac was rising in the opinion polls and Giscard's second Prime Minister, Raymond Barre, had emerged as the true incarnation of reliable conservative values. In the new trinity of opposition, Giscard ranked only third to his two former heads of government. No wonder he spoke of wearing widow's weeds.

Three years later, the ex-President was driving a bright green Peugeot through the narrow, winding roads of the central Auvergne to modest meeting places where he chewed over the problems of milk prices with farmers, sipped an aperitif in country cafés and showed a remarkable ability to remember the names of the pettiest of rural dignitaries. He told me that he had seen 7,300 people in his by-election campaign for a rural constituency in his home department of the Puy-de-Dôme. Giscard had come out of purdah: he spoke to small groups in villages and town halls facing the official portrait of his successor. This was where he had entered politics at the age of twenty-nine, displacing a very old member of his mother's family back in 1956. The setting might be modest for a man who had founded the European Monetary System and sat at summits with superpower leaders, but Giscard showed an unexpected common touch as he discussed agricultural subsidies and the water supply. In one café, he sat at a Formica-topped table and recalled what he had done for the mountain farmers during his years in power. 'I'm no longer President,' he told the thirty people in the room. 'I'm picking up life again, and so should you. Your purchasing power is falling, so are your livestock prices. You haven't been defended.' To make the farmers feel important, he pulled rabbits from the hat. One morning, seeing me at the back of a quarter-filled village hall, he veered away from rural matters and told the assembled audience that the eyes of the world were upon them. 'How you vote will be noted in Great Britain, in the United States. *The Economist* is here, watching you,' he informed the old men in caps and clogs. Nobody but Giscard could bring such attention to a village lost among the volcanic peaks of central France.

The ex-President was relaxed that autumn day. He won the by-election easily, and later wrote a book expounding the notion that, if only the sectarian political barriers could be surmounted, two-thirds of the French could agree on a programme of national consensus – whose natural leader needed no identification. He had, he told me, drawn fresh inner strength from his reflections in the heart of the countryside. He was now involved with real life, real problems. 'I am taking the heartbeat of France,' he said as he piloted his green Peugeot on the upland roads. Then I asked him what he thought of the resurgent Jacques Chirac and the rising star of his other Prime Minister, Raymond Barre. Giscard replied with a pleasantry, but his gloved hands tightened sharply on the steering-wheel and the car almost lurched off the road. The war was not over.

12

FRIENDS OF FRANÇOIS

As the face of the new President of the Republic scrolled down on television screens across France at precisely 8 P.M. on 10 May 1981, the left erupted in joy. Crowds danced in the streets to celebrate the end of twenty-three years of rule from the right and centre. In the suburban Paris flat where I was having dinner, my host rushed into his kitchen and re-emerged with a bottle of champagne and a sheaf of Socialist red roses. Millions who had supported the left through decades of Gaullism and Giscardianism suddenly saw their impossible dream come true. François Mitterrand had proved that power at the summit could change hands. Driving home late that night to our flat near Socialist Party headquarters beside the Seine, I had to abandon the car far from home because of the crush of people celebrating in the street.

No presidential victory had ever been so fêted by the winners or feared by the losers. The Manichaean strain in French life was quickly apparent. While joyous crowds milled through the night on the site where the revolutionaries of 1789 had stormed the Bastille, alarmists on the right warned that political police would soon be knocking on doors. As businessmen smuggled their money over the Swiss border in suitcases, the head of the French Rothschilds went into exile in New York with the bitter phrase about being 'a traitor under Vichy, a pariah under Mitterrand'. A Socialist congress compared such people to the Royalist émigrés of 1789. A writer from the losing side reviled France for having the stupidest right wing in the world. Having shown that an alternance of power was possible, the left went on to win an absolute majority in parliamentary elections the following month. Four Communists joined the government. In their first year in office, the Socialists brought in changes which equalled Roosevelt's New Deal or the British Labour reforms of 1945. A dozen major firms were nationalised. The death penalty was abolished, the working week was cut to thirty-nine hours, and everybody got the right to a fifth week's annual holiday. There was a wealth tax and an increase in the minimum wage. Welfare payments rose substantially, and the regions were promised decentralisation.

When the Finance Minister, Jacques Delors, suggested after six months that it might be time for a pause in the pace of reform, nobody took any notice. But the intimations of reality soon rose to the surface. In the first thirteen months of François Mitterrand's presidency, the franc was devalued twice, and inflation rose to 18 per cent. Despite all the reflationary measures, unemployment hit 2 million. The boom in purchasing power sent imports spiralling upwards. France was forced to raise billions of dollars in international loans to cover its soaring debts. In June 1982, the first knockings of what came to be known as the policy of *rigueur* were introduced with an evident incoherence as ideology met necessity: state spending was cut but the minimum wage was raised again. Economics and politics had rarely made such uneasy bedfellows.

Amid all these great events, it was not surprising that few people paid any attention to the affairs of a shock-absorber company called Vibrachoc. The firm had an array of foreign subsidiaries and a murky web of cross-holdings through the financial haven of Liechtenstein. At the start of the 1980s, it was not in the best of health. One big industrial group which looked at it as a possible takeover target estimated that Vibrachoc was worth a maximum of 65 million francs, and warned that a purchaser would need to pump in capital to keep it afloat.

Three months later, that same industrial group and the subsidiaries of two large banks paid 110 million francs for the struggling shock-absorber manufacturer. Part of the payment went to Liechtenstein; part was transferred to a company operating under Luxembourg law from the capital of Liberia. It was just the kind of transaction which the new President denounced in his fulminations against 'money which corrupts, money which kills, which rots consciences'. This made it all the more striking that the man who had sold Vibrachoc to such personal advantage was the President's oldest friend – and that the sale would not have been possible had Mitterrand not been in the Élysée.

Tell me who you frequent, as a French proverb goes, and I will tell you who you are. By that measure, François Mitterrand does not emerge with flying colours. The Bernard Tapie saga and the string of scandals linked to his peers have already been set out. But the story of Roger-Patrice Pelat takes the tale of moral decay a step further. It shows how the rot set in from the start of the Mitterrand era, and was not – as the President's defenders would have it – simply a function of old age in the last years of his reign. And, in its way, it provides another illustration of how little those at the pinnacle of power are even aware of the gulf separating them from the proper standards of everyday life.

Pelat had fought for the Republicans in the International Brigade during the Spanish Civil War. He met François Mitterrand when they were prisoners of war of the Germans. Later, they were colleagues in the Resistance. It was in Pelat's flat in Paris that Mitterrand first saw a photograph of his wife to be. Half a century later, Danielle Mitterrand told an interviewer that the friends who had never disappointed her and the President were people they had met during the war, such as Roger-Patrice. He was certainly most helpful to the Mitterrands over the decades. One of the future President's brothers worked as a manager of Vibrachoc in its early years. Between 1972 and 1980, the firm paid the politician an annual fee for advice. After 1981, the payments were directed to one of Mitterrand's sons, a Socialist deputy in the National Assembly: asked what the firm got in return, Vibrachoc's finance director said that the payments were simply a means of assuring the younger Mitterrand of 'a friendly annuity'.

Pelat was one of the few people allowed to call Mitterrand '*tu*'. Danielle spoke of his 'intoxication' when he was with François. On one occasion in 1988, Pelat made out a cheque for 150,000 francs to Mitterrand: questioned about it later, the Élysée explained that the money was reimbursement for old books which the President had bought for his friend on his foreign travels. Although the Head of State had a perfectly good home in the narrow Rue de Bièvre on the Left Bank, Pelat contributed 300,000 francs to a fund established to help him buy a new flat in case a right-wing electoral victory deprived him of a second term in the Élysée. On a visit to Paris, Mikhail Gorbachev was surprised when a large man walked calmly into the salon at the Élysée where he was conferring with Mitterrand. As recounted by a French journalist, the Head of State smiled and said: 'Let me introduce Patrice Pelat. He's an old friend.' Some came to call the former maker of shock-absorbers France's Vice-President. He was said to keep a dinner jacket in the President's wardrobe.

Whatever Mitterrand might say in public about the awful power of money, his old pal liked getting it and spending it – and avoiding as many taxes as possible. He acquired a company yacht in the Mediterranean. He and his sons drove Rolls-Royces; he owned a hunting estate and racehorses. Vibrachoc was Pelat's biggest killing, and, though it was not publicised at the time, there was really no mystery about how he managed to get such a good price for his stumbling firm. The main buyer was the Alsthom industrial group, and Alsthom's parent company had just been nationalised by the Socialists. The two banks which bought smaller stakes were also under state control. At the same time, Pelat had also begun to build up a relationship with a couple of men he called the 'two Bs'. One was Alain Boublil, an adviser on industrial policy at the Élysée. The other was Pierre Bérégovoy, Mitterrand's chief of staff. With those cards in his hands, it was not surprising that Roger-Patrice had been able to push through such a sweet deal. At least one Mitterrand viewed the matter in a different way, however: 'When François became President,' said Danielle, 'Patrice relinquished his main business in order to be more available and closer to his friend.'

It is October 1982. One of the most senior members of the government is on the telephone. May I say, he breathes into the mouthpiece, that your funeral address today was one of the most brilliant speeches I have ever heard? A short silence. Then the minister humbly suggests that the speech might be reprinted and distributed to every school in France for the edification of the nation's youth. With that, he ends his conversation with the President of the Republic and turns to tell me about his plans to reform France's welfare system.

Pierre Bérégovoy had entered the government as Minister for Social Affairs at the end of June, two months after Pelat cashed in his Vibrachoc chips. Once the euphoria of 1981 dissipated, even François Mitterrand had to acknowledge that something needed to be done to

rein in the galloping welfare deficit, and Bérégovoy seemed just the
fellow for the job. The President had no more faithful servant than the
man who had been his Secretary-General at the Élysée. 'Béré' strutted like a bespectacled bantam cock behind his master. His devotion
was absolute; thanks to Mitterrand, he had risen to the uplands of
power, and he clearly intended to scale a few more peaks before he
was through, which he could only do with the help of the President.

While Pierre Bérégovoy was drawing up plans to cut billions from
the social security budget, Roger-Patrice Pelat went on trying to add
to his fortune. His closeness to Mitterrand got him a seat on the
board of Air France, meaning unlimited first-class travel to any destination he liked, including a home he had bought in the Caribbean. In
the summer of 1982, he had tried to muscle in on a deal to sell uranium to India, but was repulsed. Six months later, he invited a select
group of guests to spend Christmas with him at a luxury hotel in an
oasis in Morocco. Among the guests were Alain Boublil and Pierre
Bérégovoy, who had his fortune told by a local wizard.

Back in France, away from the delights of Yuletide in the desert,
the government was fast falling out of favour. It fared badly at municipal elections, and the economy needed another dose of strong
medicine. In March 1983, as pressure on the franc became unbearable,
Mitterrand spent a long weekend debating whether France should
remain a full member of the European Community or should sheer
off in pursuit of Socialism in one country. Jacques Delors negotiated
the European course in Brussels while left-wing Socialists in Paris
urged the President to go it alone. Mitterrand took the tough but
inevitable course. The franc was devalued again. Returning from
Brussels, the Finance Minister introduced a full austerity plan; France
got a huge European loan; and the Communists were forced to quit
the government. By the following spring, job cuts were being decreed
in the newly nationalised industries which, a couple of years before,
had been hailed as guarantors of employment and national prosperity.
Delors was the man of the moment, but when he was offered the premiership, he overstepped the mark by making it clear that he wanted
to retain control of the Finance Ministry, which would have made
him as powerful as the President. Instead, he went off to head the
European Commission. A Mitterrand loyalist became Prime Minister,
and Pierre Bérégovoy moved to the Finance Ministry.

Amid all this turmoil, the President found solace in long, reflective walks around Paris with Roger-Patrice. The two elderly men called at antiquarian bookshops and strolled by the Seine, Mitterrand wearing his characteristic big black hat, Pelat in a cap. When his friend turned back to affairs of state, Pelat devoted himself to seeking out fresh avenues of profit. France's economic policy might have gone austere, but that did not mean that a man could not use his contacts to good effect, even if it involved one of the more bizarre enterprises France has ever undertaken. The story was fully unveiled by the journalist Jean Montaldo in a book stuffed with revelations about doubtful members of Mitterrand's entourage.

Shortly before his election to the Élysée in 1981, the Socialist leader had paid a little-publicised visit to the Stalinist outpost of North Korea. After his victory, the North Koreans pressed for an improvement in relations with Paris, and the idea of France building a prestige hotel development in their country gradually emerged. A French company took up the idea, but wanted export credit guarantees from the government in case anything went wrong. Given the nature of the North Korean regime and the country's dubious attractions as a tourist centre, French ministers were wary – among them, the new chief of the nation's finances.

Pierre Bérégovoy advised the Prime Minister, Laurent Fabius, against the state underwriting the North Korean project. But the contract for a 46-storey hotel with 879 rooms and 123 suites was still signed in the autumn of 1984, with export credits guaranteed up to 95 per cent. Building work started a year later. It soon ran into difficulties when the Koreans withheld payment. The project was eventually completed, thanks to the intervention of Pelat. Despite the reticence of his friend at the Finance Ministry, he had used his influence at the highest levels to get the state guarantee. In return, Montaldo established, a subsidiary of the company involved showed its gratitude by carrying out work on Pelat's country estate to the precise value of 24,655,462 francs and 60 centimes.

Soon after he moved into the Finance Ministry, Pierre Bérégovoy invited three foreign journalists to lunch. His new seat of power was housed in part of the Louvre palace, where elegant salons and corridors stretched further than the eye could see. We sat with the minister at a round table in his ornate private dining-room and waited for him to lecture us about the economy.

Instead, Bérégovoy picked up the plate set before him – it was probably Sèvres porcelain. Who could have thought, he said, that the son of a Norman café-owner and a Ukrainian immigrant, a man who had gone from school to work in a textile factory at the age of sixteen, would now be sitting in the splendour of the Louvre eating off the finest of antique plates? And now could we three journalists give him, the newly-appointed Finance Minister of one of the world's major economies, some tips on how he should behave at a meeting with his peers in Washington the following week? In anybody else, it would have been sickeningly insincere. But Bérégovoy really meant it. Throughout his life, he was so genuinely and touchingly struck by what he had achieved that he found it impossible to hide his delight, and not to invite others to be equally impressed. But he also always seemed in need of a helping hand, a reassuring word.

The dining-room in the Louvre was indeed a long way from the world into which Pierre Bérégovoy had been born in Normandy two days before Christmas in 1925. His mother ran a small café-cum-grocery shop in a suburb of Rouen. The original Ukrainian family name meant 'down by the riverside', and Pierre was nicknamed '*le petit russe*' at school. The four children were brought up by their grandmother in the countryside. His family politics were of the left, and it was said that, as a child, Pierre made models of the Popular Front leader Léon Blum. According to a younger brother, he always had the last word in arguments: not even his grandmother dared to contradict him. As teenagers, he and his brothers played a game called Allies. Pierre allotted the roles, and was always Churchill.

Once he had earned his school proficiency certificate, Bérégovoy went to work as a fitter and turner. Then he moved to the railways and, while training to be an engine-driver at the age of seventeen, joined the Resistance, derailing German trains during the invasion of Normandy. After the Liberation, he joined the state gas board and took out membership of the main Socialist party of the time, the SFIO. He attended night-school classes and was promoted to increasingly important posts at the gas company. He quit the SFIO in protest at its support for repression in Algeria, allied himself with the patron saint of the French non-Communist left, Pierre Mendès-France, and then, in 1973, gravitated into the orbit of François Mitterrand, negotiating electoral agreements with the Communists and rising to the number-two position in the Socialist Party machine.

Bérégovoy's *modus operandi* was clear and honourable, unlike the ways of many around him. He got a foothold with a modest position in a company or political party and then, by dint of hard work and intelligence, rose steadily on his way to the ornate dining-room in the Louvre. Some of Mitterrand's more urbane companions sneered at his earnestly upward mobility. But he got things done. Just as Jacques Chirac had been Pompidou's bulldozer, so Pierre Bérégovoy was Mitterrand's earth-mover, and he readily shouldered responsibility for policies that won the government growing unpopularity at home but which made him a pin-up boy of international finance as French inflation dipped down to 5 per cent in 1985 – less than a third of its level in the left's go-go years.

There was one prize waiting to be won, but Mitterrand held back. In 1983, Bérégovoy was said to have believed that he had a chance of becoming Prime Minister, and was ready to follow whatever policy was needed to secure the top ministerial job. But, when the President decided in 1984 to replace his first Prime Minister, Pierre Mauroy, he promoted his young protégé, Laurent Fabius. Loyal retriever Bérégovoy was informed that, at fifty-eight, he was too old for the job.

The Finance Minister's tight policies contributed powerfully to the triumph of the right at National Assembly elections in 1986, and the opening of two years of uneasy *cohabitation* between François Mitterrand and his third Prime Minister, Jacques Chirac. During their months together, the President took sly pleasure in tripping up the eager Gaullist head of government. On one occasion, he set out for a summit in Japan on his own in the official aircraft, forcing Chirac to follow in a commercial airliner. The two men tussled over privatisations and legislation as they shaped up for their real clash – the 1988 presidential election. Powerfully helped by his opponent's abject campaign, Mitterrand won a decisive victory, with 54 per cent of the vote; he even beat Chirac in the Gaullist's adopted department of the Corrèze. After moderately successful National Assembly elections, the President was now free to pick a new Prime Minister from among his own followers again.

For the second time, Mitterrand told Bérégovoy he was too old. The man he was forced to appoint by the balance of power on the centre-left, Michel Rocard, was only five years younger and had been around since the mid-1960s. The President's visceral and well-known dislike for Rocard – 'he's just about good enough to be a junior minister for the Post Office' – must have made the appointment all the more galling for Bérégovoy. The Finance Minister received some consolation in being ranked as a Minister of State. The new Prime Minister, who had been Mitterrand's main challenger in the Socialist ranks for a decade, was a reasonable man who believed in dialogue and wanted to establish a broad Social Democratic party on West German lines. But few from outside the ranks of the left agreed to join the experiment, and France grew bored with Rocard's painstakingly sensible approach. The Socialists did very badly at European elections and tore themselves apart at a fratricidal party congress. And all the while, money stayed tight, unemployment rose, taxes remained high, the National Front stirred up rancour, and the President played favourites with his courtiers.

Still, France's state companies could cut a dash on the world stage. On 11 November 1988, after three months of negotiations, the big nationalised metals company, Péchiney, reached a $1.2 billion agreement to take over a US firm, American National Can. On 14 November, Péchiney informed the government of the deal, which was made public a week later amid official celebration that French enterprises were still international players. Within a few weeks, the takeover had set off one of the great scandals of the Mitterrand era, involving a rich cast: a Middle East arms-dealer, a senior Finance Ministry official, banks in Switzerland, Luxembourg and Anguilla, sharp-eyed investigators from the Securities and Exchange Commission in the United States – and some of the President's men.

The Securities and Exchange Commission was intrigued by the pattern of trading that had taken place in the shares of Triangle, the company which controlled American National Can, before the Péchiney deal was made public. The value of Triangle stock had increased significantly when the sale was made public. Anybody who bought Triangle shares in the weeks before the deal ended up considerably richer. The US investigation prodded the control commis- sion at the Paris Bourse into a similar probe. The joint inquiries revealed large buying of shares in Triangle by French and Middle Eastern investors, partly through Swiss banks. The purchases seemed to be linked to the progress of the secret talks: they had been particularly strong during the ten days between the deal being clinched in private and the public announcement in Paris.

As the scandal became known, Mitterrand went on television to denounce speculators, go-betweens and well-connected financiers. The snag was that the two main buyers of Triangle shares turned out to be his good friend, Roger-Patrice Pelat, and another businessman with close Socialist connections. Pelat was reported to have acquired 10,000 shares just one day after the government in Paris got its first confidential notice of the takeover agreement – and a full six days before the announcement. Then *Le Monde* revealed that Pelat or one of his sons had bought another 40,000 Triangle shares through a bank in Lausanne, giving them a total profit of $1.8 million.

The Péchiney affair was not the only such case of financial leger-demain: a group of businessmen linked to the government was alleged to have used insider information in a bid to take a strategic stake in a big bank during a takeover bid. There was also the matter of a sheaf of documents which various journalists were shown at the time. They indicated that France had tried to raise a $20 billion loan as the initial Socialist experiment went off the rails. It was never evident if the papers were real or forged; and, if genuine, whether they documented real negotiations or were an attempt to wring a large commission out of the government for a deal that never was. What made them tanta-lising was that one of those named in the documents was referred to as 'M. Patrick' – a name just one letter away from Patrice. Even if it was all a hoax, it was intriguing that the perpetrators had chosen to point in the direction of the President's best friend.

In the Péchiney case, there were no such uncertainties. Pelat had clearly indulged in insider dealing before the takeover was made public. The question was where he and his associates got their infor-mation. The answer led to the less illustrious of Pelat's 'two Bs', Alain Boublil. Short, tubby and cocky, Boublil was not a popular man. He exuded self-esteem and, as industrial adviser at the presidency in 1982, had contemptuously waved aside any suggestion that the subsidies and corporate engineering which the Socialists were implementing might not work. As losses in the state sector rose and jobs began to be cut, he showed not the slightest trace of self-doubt, switching seamlessly to the new orthodoxy like any good apparatchik. Moving to Bérégovoy's Finance Ministry, he strutted his stuff clear of the norms of mere mortals. He saw no problem, for instance, in accepting hospitality from a Lebanese wheeler-dealer, Samir Traboulsi, who was an intermediary between Péchiney and Triangle as well as being an investor in the ill-fated banking activities of Jean-Maxime Levêque and a man whose social life had gained him the nickname of the 'vizier of pleasures' – in 1998 he was named in a sensational Paris court case as having organised an evening with five or six high-class prostitutes for a Saudi Arabian prince, allegedly receiving $400,000 for his services. Boublil's defence was simple: he was being got at because he was 'neither a practising Jew, nor a freemason, nor a provincial, nor a member of the upper bourgeoisie, nor a member of the top civil service'.

When this inside-outsider and Traboulsi were sentenced to jail terms in connection with the Péchiney affair, nobody grieved. What was piquant, however, was that some of the insider information on which Pelat capitalised so avidly was divulged to him at Pierre Bérégovoy's fortieth wedding anniversary party, in a restaurant off the Champs-Élysées where the President's old crony sat at the top table. Boublil and Traboulsi were also present. Told about the guest-list at the party, Mitterrand was furious at Bérégovoy. 'He shouldn't have done it,' he exclaimed. 'He shouldn't have.' The Lebanese businessman was said to have put his private plane at Bérégovoy's disposal for election trips. A month before the anniversary party, the Finance Minister had presented Traboulsi with the Légion d'Honneur for his help in freeing French hostages in the Middle East: once again, Pelat had been present at the reception. Mitterrand had warned Bérégovoy against appearing in such company. But some things seemed to override even his master's voice for the minister who had found it so impressive to be eating off fine porcelain.

By the time Boublil went to jail for his involvement in the Péchiney affair, Roger-Patrice Pelat was dead. He had a weak heart, and died while awaiting trial. In conversation with his aide, Jacques Attali, François Mitterrand struck the self-pitying tone that he could affect when cornered. 'It's endless,' he said. 'Those people who are accused have no electoral mandate, no public job. They do not work with me. One cannot sanction them or sack them. I'm told I should do something, but I'm not going to put out a statement saying: "Tom is no longer my friend; I won't lunch with Dick any more; and I'm not going to go for walks with Harry." '

It was time for another change of Prime Minister. Yet again the President ignored the claims of Pierre Bérégovoy. He turned first to Jacques Delors, who spent a sleepless night considering whether to return to Paris but decided he preferred to continue running the European Commission. Rebuffed by France's most popular politician-in-exile, Mitterrand appointed France's first woman Premier, Édith Cresson. Bérégovoy promptly submitted his resignation from the Finance Ministry, where he had maintained the parity of the national currency through thick and thin. Mitterrand's reaction was typical. 'You'll get used to Cresson and you can hold the franc firm in the meantime,' he told his faithful servant, sweetening the pill by expanding Bérégovoy's empire to take in industry, trade and telecommunications. When asked how he was bearing up, the minister replied darkly: 'I just do what I'm told but I'm keeping my own records about everything.'

Powerful though he was, Bérégovoy showed signs of insecurity. He was always pulling opinion polls from his pocket to consult. The Finance Ministry moved to a huge new building down the Seine, where Bérégovoy delighted in showing foreign colleagues the extent of his domain. One caustic visitor remarked that it was typical of France to have a big new building but no new policies to run from it. The defender of the franc, whose notepaper was headed 'Former Mechanic, Minister of the Economy and Finance', grew shirty when it was suggested that he had known little about economics before 1981 and had been forced to take a quick lesson from the Governor of the Bank of France. He hated being the butt of the jokes which, as a politician, he should have learned to endure long before. The Interior Minister, Pierre Joxe – a superior fellow whose father had been a Gaullist luminary – once remarked that it was obvious Bérégovoy was an honest man because of the cheap red socks he wore. The story immediately did the Parisian rounds. It was said that his wife bought them at the low-cost Prisunic chain. Bérégovoy was furiously touchy about this: his staff was reported to have complained to *Le Monde* because its cartoonist, Plantu, always showed him with crumpled socks under baggy trousers.

When Cresson was sacked after a short and unhappy spell in power in 1992, it was obvious that whoever took over from her would be inheriting a rotten job. The National Assembly elections the following year were being written off in advance. It was lamb-to-the-slaughter time, and so the perfect moment to summon the final kamikaze. With Bérégovoy as Prime Minister at last, the Socialists slumped to 18 per cent in regional elections; unemployment rose to one-tenth of the labour force; and the Maastricht Treaty only barely scraped through a referendum despite being backed by almost the entire political establishment. On top of everything else, the spectre of Roger-Patrice Pelat fell across the Prime Minister's path from beyond the grave.

Bérégovoy was not a rich man, but his years in office had bred a taste for what the French, in one of their linguistic adoptions, call 'le standing'. In 1981, he had done all he could to get his hands on a fine official apartment in a historic building across the Seine from the Élysée. When he was given the job of bringing welfare spending under control, Bérégovoy insisted on having a private lift installed in his ministry. Later, he demanded a personal helicopter. He also bought a 100-square-metre flat in the smart 16th *arrondissement* of Paris. How was he going to pay for it? No problem: the President's pal stepped in. On 18 September 1986, a notary registered a loan for 1 million francs to Pierre Bérégovoy from Roger-Patrice Pelat. That covered nearly half the price of the apartment. And Pelat went even further – the loan was interest-free. Some doubted if it was ever meant to be repaid at all. And what would be the pay-back price for that, it might be wondered.

On 3 February 1993, seven weeks before the National Assembly elections, France's main investigative weekly reported the Pelat loan. Bérégovoy was immediately pursued by questions. Instead of coming clean, he gave ambiguous and halting replies. *Le Monde* recalled the existence of an anti-corruption code which insisted that officials must be clear and open about any loans they were granted; the code had been drawn up by a commission appointed by Pierre Bérégovoy. Such was the decline in the Prime Minister's status that even his parliamentary constituency in the city of Nevers – capital of the Nièvre department, and a political gift from Mitterrand – was thought to be under threat for a time.

When the election results were announced, the Socialists had lost 203 of their 258 seats in the National Assembly. Fifteen ministers were beaten. It was one of the greatest thrashings any major French political party had ever undergone, the price of sustained austerity, scandal and boredom with the same gang of men and women in government. If anybody carried responsibility for that, it was François Mitterrand, but, in his aloof way and with two more years of his term to run, he managed to position himself above the crude political battle. As a result, the blame went to the man who had begun hacking into the social security deficit a decade earlier and who had kept his shoulder to the wheel ever since.

With 242 Assembly seats – a gain of 115 – the Gaullists were the big winners, but Jacques Chirac did not want to become Prime Minister for a third time, so he passed the baton to his close colleague, Édouard Balladur, while he concentrated on the coming battle for the presidency. On a sunny afternoon on 30 March 1993, Balladur drove into his new official quarters at the Hôtel Matignon. After conferring inside, he and Bérégovoy emerged at the top of the steps in the courtyard. They smiled for the photographers, and walked down the steps, arm in arm. The staff crowded to the windows to clap their departing boss. Bérégovoy turned to raise his hand in a final greeting.

Watching the scene, Balladur's press secretary saw it as a perfect illustration of the continuity of the republican state as government swung from one party to another. 'On the two men's faces, one read something like mutual respect, a common faith in national institutions, and a quasi-certitude that the story would not stop there for these two men who recognised one another's mutual value, even if the fortunes of public life had placed them in opposing camps.' As he drove out into the Rue de Varenne, the outgoing Prime Minister looked remarkably serene.

Six weeks later, Pierre Bérégovoy bought flowers for his wife and went through routine duties as Mayor of Nevers. It was the ultimately symbolic left-wing day of 1 May, and Bérégovoy had a meeting with trade unionists as well as giving out prizes at a cycling race. He had not heard from the Head of State since the election, though at least a word of comfort from on high might have been appropriate. At the end of April, Bérégovoy had placed telephone calls to the President who had dictated so much of his life. But there was only silence from Paris. François Mitterrand had spoken publicly of his esteem for Roger-Patrice Pelat when his friend was caught insider dealing; in the spring of 1993, there was not a word for Bérégovoy.

So the son of a Norman café-owner, one-time gas-fitter, negotiator with the Communists, former chief of staff to the President, Social Affairs Minister, Finance Minister and Prime Minister of France got into his official car and told the driver to take him to a canal outside Nevers. When they arrived, he asked his driver and bodyguard to leave him alone. Unseen by them, he took his guard's pistol from the glove compartment of the car and walked to the side of the canal. There, he shot himself in the temple.

Bérégovoy was flown to Paris in a critical state. President Mitterrand and Prime Minister Balladur rushed to the hospital. Bérégovoy was dead on arrival.

In an interview recorded shortly before his death, the former Premier had spoken of the 'unpleasant political climate' and of his share of responsibility. As a loyal servant of the President, he gave no hint of the depths of his despair, though there were reports that he had written to another leading Socialist in terms that could have presaged suicide. For all his devotion, Pierre Bérégovoy never quite fitted into what one senior presidential aide described as 'a luxuriant jungle with some very beautiful aspects to it, but a jungle all the same'. He was always just a little too literal, a bit too ponderous on his feet, and never as amusing as the bright stars and con men who rose and fell at the Élysée, a victim of the system that enabled him to move from obscurity to the uplands of power but, in the end, left him with nowhere to go. It was entirely in character that Mitterrand should use his suicide for his own purposes, attacking the press for investigating the tide of scandals lapping around the regime. The President's voice choked when he lambasted the media as dogs who had hounded an honest man to his grave.

Bérégovoy would have sounded a similar note. Shortly before he killed himself, he told a group of journalists that he couldn't help feeling angry about the fuss over the Pelat loan. 'I'm sixty-seven and I cannot even have a 100-square-metre flat,' he said. 'You know in France, no one likes people who climb up the social ladder.' What neither he nor many of the others around the Élysée could recognise was that insider dealing, influence-peddling and interest-free loans from dubious sources are simply things that those in power should not indulge in. But then, despite all the rhetoric about the higher things of life, morality was not something which was much prized at the Élysée under François Mitterrand.

The Mitterrand presidency saw the emergence of a bright younger class of Socialists. Some, like Lionel Jospin, remained resolutely serious and middle-class, intent on improving themselves and the people they ruled over. Others – *la gauche caviar* – showed a taste for the high life, and were ready to make the most of their positions. But behind both these groups was a small cohort of men who had been with Mitterrand over the long years out of power, and who formed his praetorian guard. If Roger-Patrice Pelat was one of the more unusual of these, and Pierre Bérégovoy the most stoic, others fitted more readily into the traditional image of a political cabal. None more so than a man who combined a career as one of the smartest lawyers in town with a position as one of the key Mitterrandists.

On a snowy morning in 1956, Roland Dumas had taken the train from Limoges to Paris. A former Resistance fighter whose father had been shot by the Germans, Dumas had just been elected to the National Assembly as a deputy for the Democratic and Social Union of the Resistance for the Haute-Vienne department. He was met at the Gare d'Austerlitz by an emissary who took him to meet a leading figure of the soft centre-left of the Fourth Republic in a two-room office on the Champs-Élysées. 'Your election was a surprise,' François Mitterrand told the younger man. They soon became companions-in-arms, with the ultimate aim of winning power for the older man.

Away from politics, the elegant, silver-tongued and well-connected Dumas made a fair fortune as a lawyer for the Picasso estate, for Marc Chagall and Herbert von Karajan. From time to time, he showed that his heart was still in the right (that is to say, left) place by appearing in major political cases, including one involving Mitterrand. His legal office was in the narrow street off the Boulevard Saint-Germain where his leader had a duplex apartment. As a 'tenor' of the bar and part of the President's 'first circle', his standing was not diminished by not being included in the initial Socialist governments. Meeting him in the early 1980s, you knew that this was a man with a direct line to the presidency. When he did become Minister for European Affairs and government spokesman in 1984, one felt that the job was not quite up to him. Once, during lunch looking out over the Seine on the Quai d'Orsay, Dumas made clear his closeness to the Élysée, dropping references to what *le Président* was thinking into the conversation like truffles. When the Socialists returned to government in 1988, he became Foreign Minister.

Naturally, such a man liked to live high on the hog, and felt little need for the reserve which might have cramped a less confident fellow. He lamented how his income had dropped when he joined the government. But he also claimed another side to his character: explaining why he kept large amounts of cash in his office, he said that it was out of 'a peasant's mentality'. A renowned ladies' man, he entertained close relations with the daughter of the Defence Minister of Syria, and with the Frenchwoman employed as a social channel by the Elf oil firm whom we met in Chapter 6. She said her job was to use her influence with the Foreign Minister on the firm's behalf. Despite their friendship and the subsequent prison sentences passed on both of them for misusing the company's money, Dumas always denied having been swayed in any way in his ministerial judgments. In particular, he denied most vehemently having anything to do with a Mitterand-era scandal that stretched to the other side of the globe.

This arose from an industrial sector from which France has done well for decades, but which it prefers not to talk about too much – arms sales. At the end of the 1980s, the state-owned Thomson company launched a big sales drive for a new generation of high-technology frigates. Taiwan ordered six, worth a total of 16 billion francs. But the Foreign Ministry vetoed the sale for fear of a hostile reaction from mainland China. 'From start to finish, throughout the decision-making process, I gave an unfavourable opinion,' Dumas insisted later. Still, the sale went ahead.

As it turned out, Beijing did not react as strongly as might have been feared. That was just one of several puzzles surrounding the contract. Taiwan had originally been due to buy frigates from South Korea, but suddenly switched to the Thomson's ships though they were more expensive and bigger than the vessels called for in the island's defence plan. Stories of influence-peddling and corruption surfaced, centring on a ring of insiders from Elf who were said to have offered their connections in Taiwan to help swing the deal, using Dumas' lady friend to overcome any French resistance. In Taiwan, there was also the mysterious death of a naval captain who had investigated possible irregularities in the contract – his demise was classified as suicide although his head had been severely hit and wounds had been inflicted on his body while he was still alive.

When he came under investigation in the late 1990s for the way Elf's money had been spent by his mistress and himself, Roland Dumas lifted a corner of the veil. Though he insisted he had not been involved, his position at the court of François Mitterrand meant he was well informed about what had gone on. Now President of the Constitutional Council, Dumas spoke in a newspaper interview of a commission of $500 million, and added that Mitterrand had approved the sale with the agreement of the Prime Minister and Finance Ministry. In the autumn of 2001, a Swiss judge ordered the seizure of 5 billion francs in an account held in Zurich by a Taiwanese intermediary which was believed to constitute the commission. That set off a judicial inquiry in France, but the government refused to let the investigators see documents relating to the contract. Having failed to get at the papers, the magistrates put the head of Thomson at the time of the sale into custody for questioning in the spring of 2002. The scandal was given another twist by leaks from a report drawn up by an anti-corruption body in Taiwan. Citing official information from Paris, it said France had kept Beijing informed of what was going on all along. The man who had done so, on the instructions of the Prime Minister, was Roland Dumas. Like the wider Elf cases, the matter of the frigates for Taiwan was set to continue to illuminate some of the more murky corners of French officialdom for years to come.

Eighteen months after the left's triumph in 1981, a man in a grey wig entered the Élysée Palace by a side door. Led upstairs, the visitor noticed the Pretender to the French throne sitting patiently in the passageway. What, he asked his host, was the Comte de Paris doing waiting there? 'General de Gaulle promised him France. I am giving him Africa,' was the reply. It was not plain what that meant, but in the early days of Socialist rule just about anything seemed possible.

Inside a corner office, the man in the wig, which he had bought from a fashionable hairdresser as a disguise for the occasion, listened politely as his host explained that he no longer had anything to do with an illicit Socialist Party funding operation. To prove it, the President's aide reached inside his desk drawer to produce a document showing that he had resigned his positions with the organisations involved. On top of the folder containing the document lay a large revolver.

A decade later, if one was to believe officials who fed friendly journalists with information, the same aide was roaming the corridors of the palace like a madman. Those who dealt with him in his professional duties said they found him quite sane. But the official informants told another story. One colleague who met him in a corridor reported that he was suffering from some kind of hallucination, and believed he was being tailed. Another said he felt as though he was being treated like a dog. Once, it was said, he burst into the office of the Élysée chief of staff without knowing where he was. He was reported to have told the President that he was losing his mind. Clearly, the man was growing old and suffering from diminishing physical and psychological powers. It was a sad end for one who had served so well, they all agreed.

François de Grossouvre had been as close to Mitterrand's secrets as anybody over the years; even Roger-Patrice Pelat probably did not know as much. The two François were both educated by Catholics. Each participated in extreme right-wing groups in the 1930s and had relations with both the Vichy regime and the Resistance – each saying that their collaborationist links were undertaken at the behest of their Resistance bosses. In the early 1960s, however, they seemed to have nothing in common. Mitterrand was a politician with a long past and an uncertain future; De Grossouvre was a doctor, farmer, a former company chairman and Coca-Cola's bottler in Lyon. But when they met, the two men fell for one another.

Though never a man of the left, De Grossouvre helped to organise Mitterrand's campaign against De Gaulle, and took an interest in the Socialist Party's finances throughout the 1970s. Wherever Mitterrand went, De Grossouvre was there, an elegant figure with his beautifully-cut suits and spade beard: the master and his very *parfait* courtier could have stepped from a late Renaissance Italian picture. De Grossouvre hated to see his name in the newspapers, and carried over a love for secrecy and intrigue from his days in the Resistance. He maintained discreet contact with wartime buddies who had moved into the covert shadows of Gaullism. For a while, he worked for France's espionage service under the codename of 'Monsieur Leduc'. De Grossouvre saw himself as a man of hidden spheres who got on with business, whether settling his chief's financial problems, warding off trouble, establishing deniable contacts – or just making sure the leader's overcoat was ready for him when he left a meeting.

Like Mitterrand, De Grossouvre was fascinated by the mechanics of power and the manipulation of people. Each operated on a need-to-know basis towards the rest of the world, including those who put their trust in them. Neither saw any need to tell third parties what they were doing. As they aged, the two men also discussed ways of staying young: De Grossouvre favoured ginseng from the Far East while Mitterrand preferred borage. The politician did not share his friend's love of hunting and riding, but De Grossouvre turned his passion to other ends – he used hunting pavilions for secret meetings between Mitterrand and his opponents. So it was no surprise that, when the Socialists won ultimate power, François de Grossouvre moved in to his corner office at the Élysée with the duties of looking after the intelligence service 'and various matters'. Later, the man known to associates simply as 'the hunter' was put in charge of the extensive presidential game estates: how much of a demotion this represented was not clear, but then things were often opaque with De Grossouvre. 'A well-informed, silent and secret man of business,' a police report said of him.

He was also a man who knew the value of his position – Pelat was not the only friend of François to cash in on his contacts. In one case, De Grossouvre received more than 300,000 francs for his services as intermediary between a French company and Middle Eastern interests; the money was delivered in three instalments in cash to his country home and to the concierge of his Paris apartment. A former President of Lebanon was a close family friend. De Grossouvre was said to have been a go-between with African dictators who supplied funds for French political parties. He made secret trips to the Middle East while his discreet visit to Jacques Chirac on behalf of his master in 1981 was the kind of mission he was cut out to perform. It was all highly deniable: the fact that, from 1988, his salary was paid by the Dassault aircraft firm and not by the presidency was kept extremely confidential. If more is known about De Grossouvre after his death than during his life, it is because the man in the grey wig – journalist Jean Montaldo – met him regularly in the decade after 1982 and wrote up their conversations in a best-selling book.

This makes it clear that, by 1994, something had gone terribly wrong between the two François. Among other things, De Grossouvre claimed to be the only person to have slammed the door on a President of the Republic. He nurtured a hatred for Pelat and Tapie, and warned Mitterrand that he was surrounded by bandits.

'You cannot say that,' was the reply.

'Not only can I say it, but I can prove it.'

'I forbid you,' the President commanded.

So, said De Grossouvre, 'I slammed the door on him.'

To go with his Élysée office, De Grossouvre secured for himself an apartment on the Quai Branly by the Seine which Pierre Bérégovoy had coveted in 1981. It was a floor above the premises officially allocated to a loyal Mitterrandist senator, but De Grossouvre said its real occupant was the mother of the President's illegitimate daughter, who kept a bicycle parked on the first-floor landing. As well as anybody, De Grossouvre knew the extent of bugging employed by the French state – in their telephone calls, he and Jean Montaldo used codewords. But this man of the shadows felt able to talk openly in his apartment about Mitterrand and his mistress, despite the probable presence of microphones in the building. And, in Montaldo's account, De Grossouvre implied the existence of a corrupt financial network reaching up to Mitterrand himself.

It was an extraordinary indiscretion, but imagine that De Grossouvre knew that his conversations with Montaldo were being recorded by the buggers from the Élysée. He would also know that the transcripts of the recordings would be delivered to his former friend, the President, who would no longer talk to him. What better way, then, for a jilted devotee to speak to the one-time object of his fealty than through the microphones hidden in the Quai Branly? Mitterrand would have to read them. One François could speak to another.

'If something terrible happens to me, it will be that they have killed me,' De Grossouvre told Montaldo. 'They'll get me.' The former head of Mitterrand's secret 'black box' cell at the Élysée, Paul Barril, recalls him saying in 1993: 'They're going to gun me down. I know every-thing now. They're afraid.' Either De Grossouvre was becoming paranoid, or he had good reason to feel a net tightening around him. Certainly, his health was giving him problems. At seventy-six, age was catching up on this always active man. His sight was fading – a painful handicap for somebody devoted to hunting – and the detonation of so many rifles over the years had given him ear trouble. Unknown to him, Mitterrand had asked his personal doctor to examine De Grossouvre and arrange for him to be treated in a Paris hospital.

On 7 April 1994, François de Grossouvre lunched with one of his sons, put in a spot of hunting outside Paris and then drove to his office. He took with him a heavy revolver from the collection of almost 200 guns he kept in his official apartment. At around 6 P.M., he had a visit from his doctor. Seemingly mentally and physically dis-turbed, De Grossouvre turned the conversation to suicide and firearms, and referred to the buzzing in his ears. His doctor, an old friend, spoke of God and of the importance of keeping up one's spirits. De Grossouvre produced a small hunting badge and gave it to his guest, saying, 'Keep this in memory of me.' Then they talked of other things.

At 6:30 P.M., according to Captain Barril, De Grossouvre sent flow-ers to a former African Prime Minister with whom he was due to dine, saying that he would arrive at 8:30. He let his secretary leave, and spent half an hour alone. His doctor, meanwhile, had sent a mes-sage to Mitterrand warning him of De Grossouvre's state of mind. By then, however, the President's once-faithful servant had put the .357 Magnum pistol to his head and pulled the trigger. Blood splattered the walls, but the thick doors muffled the sound of the shot. His chauffeur discovered the body an hour later.

Paul Barril declared himself unconvinced by the official account. The message that had gone out with the 6:30 flowers hardly indicated a man who was about to end his life, he observed. There was no sui-cide letter. 'If he had, indeed, killed himself, the man I knew would have left a delayed-action bomb, files, the hundreds of notes he had sent to the President,' the Captain added in an interview given as he promoted his own memoirs. The dead man's archives would be 'not just a scandal, but Hiroshima!'. That might have been said of several other friends of François Mitterrand who had met untimely ends. De Grossouvre's archives, if they existed, remained well concealed, just as

Pierre Bérégovoy's widow never managed to get back the black Hermès diary her husband was carrying when he killed himself. In the halls of mirrors of the late Mitterrand era, it is impossible to separate truth from conjecture, book promotion from genuine questions. One thing was certain, however. In the last year of the previous century, a Head of State had died on the premises after over-exerting himself with his mistress, but François de Grossouvre went down in history as the first suicide at the Élysée.

It was raining on the morning of 11 April as the President of the Republic arrived at the church of Saint-Pierre in Moulins, capital of the agricultural Allier department in central France. A couple of Socialist former ministers were waiting for him. An ex-President of Lebanon stood to one side. Four hundred people filled the church for the funeral mass. After the service, a cortège of thirty vehicles drove with the coffin to the village of Lusigny, fifteen kilometres away, where François Mitterrand had sometimes stayed in the dead man's manor house set in a large estate. At the cemetery on top of a small hill, the coffin was carried down a sandy path to the family tomb. There, François de Grossouvre was laid to rest under the gaze of his former friend who stood holding an umbrella. For a brief moment, his eyes met those of the widow, standing surrounded by her children and grandchildren. Not a word was spoken. Accompanied by one of his ex-ministers, Mitterrand turned and walked away.

His closest friend gone from a heart attack in the midst of scandal, a former head of government committing suicide, an associate of three decades shooting himself in his corner office at the presidential palace; flying too close to Mitterrand's flame was a dangerous business. Particularly so because of the emotional power which the man was able to exercise over even strong-minded, successful individuals. The self-interest of a Bernard Tapie was understandable, but the depths of feeling which rejection by Mitterrand evoked in De Grossouvre or Bérégovoy was out of the ordinary. Politicians who came across him in his early provincial campaigns in the 1940s remembered his powers of seduction fifty years later. As his actor brother-in-law observed: 'Mitterrand aroused even more loving feeling among men than among women.' Which, given his sexual conquests, was saying quite something.

13

A FRENCH LIFE

The French were intrigued rather than shocked when the existence of François Mitterrand's mistress and illegitimate daughter became public knowledge late in his second term. His wife had known about them for a long time, but accepted the situation. 'So, yes, I was married to a seducer. I had to make do,' Danielle Mitterrand said later. 'She's his daughter, and François loved her enormously. They resemble one another like two peas in a pod.' Asked about the young Mazarine towards the end of his life, Mitterrand shrugged the matter off. His widow was philosophical. 'We must accept that a human being is capable of loving, passionately loving somebody – and then, as the years go by, he loves in a different way, perhaps more deeply, and then he can fall in love with someone else. It is absolute hypocrisy to want to pass judgement on that.'

Such honesty spoke volumes about France. It was fitting from the widow of a man who, in so many things, personified his nation's history over more than half a century. By the time he became President, Mitterrand had already spent nearly four decades in politics. He was Europe's last ruler who had been in office in pre-nuclear days, and held his first government job when Truman, Attlee and Stalin were meeting to fix the shape of the post-war world. For most of his presidency he was known affectionately as 'Tonton' ('Uncle'). By the end, some followers had taken to calling him 'Dieu' ('God') if only for his seeming immortality. In everything from his childhood to the secrecy about his health, from his private life to the equivocations about his wartime years, from the twists of his career to his last New Year's dinner, François Mitterrand's odyssey was a parable of modern France. Beginning as a true Catholic believer, he ended up, in the words of one of his Prime Ministers, as a pure cynic. The man and his country moved in parallel from traditional roots to end-of-century malaise.

'My childhood, which was happy, has illuminated my life. When one is a child, when one arrives on this planet of which one knows nothing, everything is to be learnt, everything to be felt. The first sensations are so strong and dominant. They make their mark on a virgin canvas. I draw the largest part of my reserves of strength from my childhood. I have the impression that what I had at that moment and the little of it I have preserved (and I have kept some of it) represents the purest and cleanest part of my personality.'

Jarnac is an ordinary town of some 5,000 inhabitants surrounded by open countryside and rivers in the Charente department of western France. Before its association with François Mitterrand, it was best known for having given its name to the expression for a stab in the back, *'un coup de Jarnac'*, from a sixteenth-century incident in which one nobleman did the dirty on another. The future President was born there on 26 October 1916. His father was a station-master who later changed profession and became head of the vinegar-makers of the region. With four sons and four daughters, the Mitterrands were a close-knit family into which, François recalled, 'guests entered as if they were burglars'. They were austere and devout Catholics, who distrusted money-making and rarely displayed emotion.

François was sent to boarding school in the nearby big town of Angoulême. A withdrawn child, he had trouble communicating with others and made few friends. One lifelong character trait was established at an early age. 'I have never tended to confide in others,' Mitterrand remarked much later. 'In a big family, one has to develop zones of solitude.'

As a loner, the young Mitterrand enjoyed going for long country walks. He nurtured a taste for strolls along riverbanks, and wrote poems about their waters, starting with the Charente and the Gironde of his native region and going on to take the Rhine, the Rhône, the Nile and the Niger as inspiration. Seventy years later, he recalled with pleasure the sound of the wind blowing at night through the riverside trees. On his walks, the shy boy from the Catholic school spoke to imaginary crowds, haranguing them with rhetoric inspired by the revolutionaries of 1789 and 1848. Back at home, he climbed up to the attic, littered with maize husks, and launched vibrant speeches through the window overlooking the garden, 'changing the course of history according to my choices'.

'I think that there is only one role to play: to bring the directives and principles of our faith to the political groups to which it is necessary to belong and which are approved by the Church. The National Volunteers want a clean and strong France.'

If François Mitterrand always looked back with happy nostalgia to his childhood in the Charente, he was less forthcoming for many years about his early life in Paris. Arriving by train from Angoulême just before his eighteenth birthday to study politics and law, he felt lost and small in the big city – 'at the foot of a mountain that was to be climbed. I was without an identity.'

As the product of a Catholic education, it was natural for the youth from the provinces to seek a haven in a religious pension in the Rue de Vaugirard on the Left Bank. He quickly gravitated into reactionary politics, which was not surprising for somebody of his background in the fevered climate of the mid-1930s, when some dreamed of a Socialist–Communist revolution and others looked at Mussolini and Hitler as role models. He joined a group called the National Volunteers, the youth wing of a big extremist movement, the Croix-de-Feu. Mitterrand said he was 'seduced' by the Croix-de-Feu's leader, Colonel de la Rocque, but insisted that the Colonel was neither a fascist nor an anti-Semite – an opinion not shared by many. Above all, Mitterrand was influenced by his religion. He was put off the main extreme-right movement, Action Française, not by its political stance but because the Pope had declared an anathema on it.

Within a month of arriving in Paris he took part in his first demonstration. A photograph taken in February 1935 shows Mitterrand at a march against foreign students: a banner beside him proclaims, 'Go on strike against the wogs.' The future leader of the left wrote for a newspaper which admired Mussolini. He travelled to Belgium to visit the pretender to the throne of France, gave 500 francs to a campaign against the Socialist leader Léon Blum, and became head of a right-wing student group. At the age of twenty-one, he also fell in love.

'*One Saturday, I had the blues. I went back to my room. On the table, I came across an invitation I had forgotten about. It was to a dance at the teachers' training college. I went. I saw a blonde with her back to me. She turned towards me. My feet were riveted to the ground . . . Then I asked her to dance . . . I was mad about her.*'

Women were always important to François Mitterrand. Over the years there was as much speculation about his love-life as about his real political beliefs. He was said to have had a string of celebrated journalists as mistresses and a love-nest in Venice. He was reported to take particular pleasure in caressing the insteps of his lady friends. 'He was fascinated by Casanova,' according to a journalist whom Mitterrand picked to chronicle his last days. 'He couldn't go into a bar or a restaurant without seeking out the face of a woman, and giving his famous wink.' When he met the actress Juliette Binoche by chance in a bookshop, he asked her to give him a call. With undue modesty, she found the prospect too intimidating: 'How does one call the President of the Republic?' she wondered. 'It's like picking up the phone and asking for Father Christmas.' Others were not so reticent. Any attractive woman who rose to a high position in the Socialist ranks was suspected of having slept with him on the way up: when he told one of them that she might become a party secretary as a reward, she is said to have replied on the pillow that she didn't know how to type. A roman-à-clef in the 1980s suggested that Mitterrand had an illegitimate child as well as the sons born to his wife. The rumours were confirmed in 1994 when *Paris-Match* magazine printed photographs of the President stepping out to a twentieth-birthday lunch at a celebrated fish restaurant with his daughter, Mazarine, who had been conceived as he embarked on his second unsuccessful presidential campaign and who bore a striking resemblance to her father. Her mother was an archivist whom Mitterrand had met near his home on the south-western Atlantic coast. In *Premier Roman*, a thin novel that was scoured for autobiographical fragments when it became a best-seller in 1998, Mazarine wrote of her heroine's parents as 'long-time lovers, unmarried, leading their own lives, even while loving each other more than anything. They taught her that love was the only tie that triumphs over looks and judgements, convention and taboos.'

There was never any secret about Mitterrand's first love, even if the blonde Marie-Louise Terrasse had not been as struck by him as he was by her when his eye fell on her at the student ball. She did not give him her name because her mother forbade her to identify herself to unknown young men. In his mind, Mitterrand dubbed her 'Béatrice', as in Dante. He spoke incessantly about her to friends and watched her as she travelled between home and school. Finally, he accosted her. Defying her mother's command, she joined him at a café table and they shared a pancake. In the spring of 1940, when Mitterrand was called up to the army, they got engaged. In his letters to her from his army post, he referred to Marie-Louise as VM, for '*visage merveilleux*' (marvellous face).

As a sergeant during the Phoney War before the Nazis attacked, Mitterrand must have found the time slow. So, when not writing to VM, he turned his hand to a spot of fiction, with a short story entitled 'First Chord' about a young couple, Philippe and Elsa. She was 'supple and gay, sparkling as she awoke, a Persian at the sword, her pink curves like a jar of hair cream'. The prose slurped on. 'Every day of their brief love, she leaped from bed. As he lay about, she walked round the room dressed in her blue dream [*sic*]. She loved this hour of daydreams . . . Elsa never dared to parade naked in their room, for Philippe had a curious degree of modesty for a flirtatious man: odd habits, delights that remained ever elusive.' He was, after all, only twenty-three years old and, if only he had known it, was following in the footsteps of Charles de Gaulle, who had penned romantic fiction (equally unpublished) while convalescing from a war wound in 1914.

After France's defeat, the sergeant was taken prisoner of war together with thousands of French soldiers. As the months dragged by in his Stalag, VM's letters became rarer and rarer. Friends attributed Mitterrand's three escape attempts to his desire to get back to her. Again, there was a parallel with De Gaulle, who repeatedly escaped from German prison camps in the First World War, only to be recaptured each time. Mitterrand was more successful; his third break-out succeeded and he returned to France. But he found that the girl with the marvellous face no longer fancied the idea of marrying him. Early in 1942, the engagement was broken off. Many years later, as Catherine Langeais, Marie-Louise became more famous for a time than her former fiancé as an early television announcer. Some amateur psychologists believe that rejection hardened the young man's character and contributed to the growth of his pervasive cynicism. At the time, he spoke of the 'dryness of my feelings'. Decades later, he still sent Langeais flowers on her birthday.

Two years after being dropped by Marie-Louise, Mitterrand was in love again, this time with a photograph. In March 1944, when he headed a Resistance network, Mitterrand attended a party at the Paris home of his friend, Roger-Patrice Pelat. On the piano in the flat was a photograph of the sister of Pelat's partner at the time. 'I want to meet her, I will marry her,' Mitterrand said. A blind date was duly arranged at a restaurant on the Boulevard Saint-Germain. As with Marie-Louise, Mitterrand was not an immediate hit. Wearing an off-white raincoat and the large hat which became his trademark in later years, he also sported a pencil moustache. The overall effect made him look like a caricature of a tango dancer.

The young woman, Danielle Gouze, was in her last year at school. She found his acid tone irritating: Mitterrand only fell more deeply in love with her. He deployed to the full his powers of persuasion and seduction, and, within a couple of months, she agreed to marry him. There then followed a series of wartime adventures, including a train trip to her native Burgundy during which a friendly German soldier unknowingly ushered the young man through a police control that had him on its wanted list. They married in October 1944, after the Liberation of France (during which Mitterrand claimed to have saved De Gaulle's life by grabbing his legs as the General was about to be swept out of a window by an enthusiastic crowd in Paris). Over the wedding lunch, the groom announced that he was going off to a political meeting with former prisoners of war. The bride said she would accompany him. If you want to, Mitterrand replied. That was the moment at which she discovered her 'first and main rival: politics'.

Nobody outside the couple knows how much Danielle influenced her husband. Her own reflections on the subject indicate that she was content to watch him go his own way while she dedicated herself to good works and Third World causes. What she thought of her husband's decision to maintain close relations with some of Africa's worst dictators can be imagined; she, herself, showed lasting concern for human rights and stayed true to her old beliefs. She organised demonstrations for prisoners of conscience and remained a fan of Fidel Castro to the end, urging her husband to invite him on a state visit to France which earned them all a degree of mockery. She persuaded the shyster businessman, Armand Hammer, to agree to contribute $300,000 to her good works, though she never got her hands on the money. Danielle Mitterrand could have become an object of pity; instead, she remained dignified. After his death, she wrote: 'I see now how my husband excelled in the art of seduction towards the young girls who passed by. He was François the seducer.' That was part of life. A striking photograph taken at the Cannes film festival in 1956 shows a dark-suited Mitterrand gazing with more than passing interest at Brigitte Bardot while Danielle, in matelot jersey and sunglasses with her hands clasped behind her back, stares at the 22-year-old starlet as though at an anthropological specimen. 'Which woman can say, "I've never been cheated on" or that she never cheated in her own love-life?' Danielle Mitterrand once reflected. 'I stayed with him because he was different. With him life was never boring.' It was the matter-of-fact voice of the woman who, as a high-school girl, had hidden Resistance fighters at ultimate risk to herself. When warned by a friend that she should flee Paris because her photograph had been seized in a Gestapo raid on a Resistance hide-out, Danielle had replied: 'But what about my exams?'

'I could have devoted my life to reflection, to have lived in the country in the company of trees, animals and a few loved ones. Perhaps that is a bucolic dream; still, I think I could have done it. But the stimulus of action was doubtless stronger than that of reflection, so in the end I launched myself into politics.'

In October 1946, after an unsuccessful attempt to get elected in the Paris region, the thirty-year-old Mitterrand set off for the rural Nièvre department in central France to seek a seat in the National Assembly of the Fourth Republic. His first campaign in the department which was to become his electoral base for the next thirty-five years had its share of ironies given what was to happen three and a half decades later. The politician who would lead the Socialists and their Communist allies to the greatest power they have ever enjoyed in modern France first won his way to the National Assembly with the active backing of a network of conservative local notables. His speeches denounced the tripartite government of the left and moderate Catholics ruling France. Above all, the man who was to give the Communists their only taste of ministerial power under the Fifth Republic preached hard-line anti-Communism to rapt audiences in country halls.

The Nièvre, where the faithful Bérégovoy was to kill himself half a century later, went on electing Mitterrand throughout the Fourth Republic as he moved smoothly between ministerial posts – from ex-servicemen's affairs to the Information Ministry, then on to superintend France's Overseas Territories before taking the powerful post of Interior Minister in 1954–55 and ending up as Justice Minister in 1956–57, at the time of the Suez expedition and France's war to hold on to its last big overseas possession across the Mediterranean. As a politician who knew the importance of patriotism, Mitterrand left no public doubt of his belief that Algeria must remain French. Heading a series of small parties and political combinations, he never had a strong popular following, eclipsed in intellectual ability by Pierre Mendès-France and in machine clout by the Socialist boss, Guy Mollet. In 1957, one of his associates told a Soviet agent that Mitterrand was likely to become Prime Minister and would bring Mendès-France and Gaston Defferre into his government, wind up the war in Algeria, and strengthen the nation's finances.

If he never achieved the premier role he sought, Mitterrand still proved to be one of the most skilful exponents of the Fourth Republic game of ministerial musical chairs. The ever-shifting, unideological back-room world of French politics in the 1940s and 1950s suited him to perfection and shaped his style. Still, not everybody was impressed. I remember sitting at a dinner party of once-powerful provincial newspaper figures from the Fourth Republic who expressed universal distrust of the man. And the American ambassador to France, Douglas Dillon, wrote of the Interior Minister of the time in a classified despatch in 1954: 'My principal impression was his extreme cruelty. This man is very competent but dangerous.' The failure of the

Fourth Republic was, above all, a failure of its politicians rather than of its institutions, and François Mitterrand epitomised those for whom politics counted more than the nation.

When De Gaulle swept away the Fourth Republic in 1958, the shock was terrible. Mitterrand voted against the General's investiture. In the first parliamentary elections of the new Republic, he was defeated, and was said to have broken down in tears. But, as Douglas Dillon also noted, 'he is intensely ambitious and will do anything to reach his goals'.

After his defeat, Mitterrand wrote an article in his tame local news-paper, putting himself forward as a true republican standing up to De Gaulle's military coup. At the same time, as a supreme realist, he knew the need to try to dissociate himself from the system which had served him so well. 'For a long time, I have said "no" to complicated party combinations, to immobility, to colonial wars,' this archetype of the Fourth Republic and defender of French Algeria suddenly declared. If one constant ran through Mitterrand's long career, it was the ability to disown his beliefs of yesterday.

Such a man did not stay politically unemployed for long and, in 1959, the Senate – a body whose members are picked by local digni-taries – beckoned. Mitterrand dramatically announced that he had been the target of an assassination attempt, which appeared to have been a put-up job engineered to win sympathy. The episode earned him ridicule and reinforced the widespread belief that he was a man without scruples who would stop at nothing to advance his political career. He stayed in the Senate for three years, writing biting anti-Gaullist tracts before winning his way back to the more important National Assembly. At the same time, the one-time provincial boy strengthened his roots in the Nièvre by becoming Mayor of Château-Chinon in the hilly, wooded Morvan area of the department. On election days, he put up at the old-fashioned Hôtel du Morvan in the middle of the town to await the results. He would frequently eat lunch with the hotel's owners and always slept in the same room on the first floor. Lit by a single weak light-bulb, it was sparsely furnished with a lumpy bed, a straight-backed chair and a plastic-topped table on which Mitterrand wrote late into the night. There was a wash basin, but the lavatory was on the landing. A window looked out on to the surrounding hills – the latter-day equivalent of the attic window from which Mitterrand had once imagined himself addressing the nation as a boy.

'So what?'

During the long years of waiting for supreme power while the right fought its fratricidal battles, François Mitterrand collected an odd bunch of friends and associates, some of whom we met in the last chapter. But there was one acquaintance who would stand out as an especially strange man for the first President of the left to have entertained. A jovial rogue like Roger-Patrice Pelat might be explained away on the basis of wartime comradeship. René Bousquet was a different matter, and Mitterrand's relationship with him over more than three decades reflected another aspect of France which still stirs deep emotions half a century after the 1940 parliament voted full powers to Pétain, and Vichy agreed to collaborate with the Nazis.

The question of collaboration and complicity in genocide has, as we have seen, been an uncomfortable one which France has often preferred to ignore. Few of those who went along with Vichy and the German occupiers could have imagined the existence of extermination camps as such: they preferred vague formulae about work camps in Eastern Europe. Yet, even if they did not know of the extermination camps, anybody with eyes in their head could see that Jews were being forced to wear yellow stars on the streets of France before being rounded up and taken away. Later, even those who owned up to working for Vichy or the Germans denied that they had known about the more unpleasant things going on around them. A fair number insisted that their collaboration had, in fact, been a cover for clandestine Resistance work, leading the press baron Robert Hersant, who made no bones about his collaborationist record, to call himself 'the only Frenchman of my generation not to have been a hero of the Resistance'.

In much later years, nobody's war record was more subject to debate than that of François Mitterrand. Not only did he seem to have played a double game, but he also appeared unable to shake off the negative elements of the past, or even to admit that there might be anything questionable about them. Sometimes he grew indignant that anybody should presume to raise the subject, or else he put on a poker-face and muttered a dismissive 'So what?' If France preferred to blot out the memory of its equivocations about the years between 1940 and 1944, François Mitterrand stood as an example for the nation.

His role during those years reflected both sides of the country under occupation. There was no doubt that the future President had faced great personal danger as a member of the Resistance. He helped to organise underground networks among ex-servicemen, travelled to England for a frosty meeting with General de Gaulle, and was on the wanted list under his pseudonym of Morland. At the same time, he worked for the Vichy government as a civil servant, dealing with prisoners of war, which enabled him to save some French servicemen from concentration camps. Mitterrand said later that he did this with the blessing of the Resistance, which certainly found it useful to keep some of its people as moles inside the collaborationist regime. 'I was not part of the Vichy system,' he said in his posthumously-published memoirs. 'I was not a functionary but a contract worker.' He used the word 'press-ganged' to describe his employment, and added, as if it had some relevance, that he had filled a high-level post for less than today's minimum wage. The young man must have been good at his job because he was awarded the Francisque, one of the regime's top decorations, and was presented to the Vichy leader, Philippe Pétain. As President, Mitterrand continued the tradition of sending a wreath to Pétain's grave each Armistice Day in honour of his military leadership in the First World War.

If he was to be believed, Mitterrand, who prided himself on being a great humanist, managed to keep his eyes shut to some of the things going on around him. 'I didn't think about anti-Semitism at Vichy,' he once insisted. 'I knew that, unfortunately, there were anti-Semites who filled senior positions around Marshal Pétain, but I didn't follow the laws of the time and the measures that were being taken.' The 'unfortunately' jars, and Mitterrand's memoirs struck a somewhat different tone. 'Vichy was a weak regime, shapeless and lacking in soul, inspired by fascists, anti-Semites and determined ideologues,' he told a journalist who worked with him on his last reburnishing of history.

Still, as Head of State, he steadfastly refused to accept that there was anything amiss in his long relationship with a man who had signed the agreement with the Germans pledging the French police to round up foreign Jews, and who was the main organiser of the Vél d'Hiv atrocity in Paris in 1942. When it came to René Bousquet, Mitterrand said simply that he found the man to be a brilliant individual with whom he had interesting conversations. The President went on meeting the former police chief until 1986, five years into his rule and after well-publicised moves were made to get Bousquet tried for crimes against humanity. Despite having access to the full panoply of official French records, Mitterrand insisted that he had not been aware of Bousquet's wartime activities.

This was simply unbelievable. It was no secret that from April 1942 to December 1943 Bousquet had been Secretary-General of the police. As such, he was in charge of the national police, of economic policing and of 'supplementary police', which meant the anti-Jewish, anti-Masonic and anti-Communist crusade. He, too, claimed to have been involved with the Resistance, and was indeed arrested by the Germans in 1944, by which time any sensible collaborator would have sought a lifeline on the other side. After the Liberation, Bousquet was sentenced to five years of 'national degradation', but was later amnestied. Whatever his Resistance activities may or may not have been, there was no doubting Bousquet's key role in rounding up Jews. It was not as if Mitterrand needed access to official papers to know what Bousquet had been up to during the Occupation. His responsibilities had been outlined at the Nuremberg war-crimes trials in 1946 by the lawyer and politician, Edgar Faure, another friend of Mitterrand.

Every time the President denied that there was anything wrong in his links with Bousquet, new information emerged. There is no evidence that the two men actually met while serving Vichy, but Mitterrand's evasions inevitably fuelled speculation. It was widely believed that his Resistance group, based on ex-prisoners of war, had unofficial contacts with the Vichy Ministry of the Interior and the police – and his membership of a far-right organisation was only a decade behind him. Whether Mitterrand found Vichy ideologically objectionable is a question which is unlikely ever to be answered, just as the true extent of his commitment to Socialism will always remain uncertain. No doubt he deplored Vichy's treatment of those it persecuted; but as a cool-eyed realist, his engagement in the Resistance may have been as much a matter of pragmatism as of political conviction, just as he could see clearly from 1965 onwards that the only way to win the presidency was to come at it from the left.

The links with the collaborationist right continued after the Liberation. When Mitterrand found himself briefly out of a job, he was taken under the wing of a cosmetics group founded by a tycoon who had financed pre-war terrorists of the far right, and who gave him a job running a beauty-care magazine. Back in politics after winning his place in parliament from the Nièvre, Mitterrand pushed an amnesty bill for collaborators which was said to have weighed on the judges' decision not to punish Bousquet more severely for his wartime activities. At that time, the former policeman was on the board of the Banque d'Indochine, which later merged into the Indosuez Bank. The bank financed anti-Gaullist politicians after the General's return to power in 1958. That year, Bousquet ran unsuccessfully for parliament – with the backing of a small political party headed by Mitterrand. Another of his associates was Robert Hersant, who had also been found guilty of collaborationist crimes.

During Mitterrand's first presidential bid in 1965, the Toulouse newspaper *La Dépêche du Midi* printed his leaflets for free, contributed half a million francs to his campaign funds, and ran an appeal by former Petainists and extreme right-wingers to vote for the anti-Gaullist candidate. Bousquet was on the board of the newspaper. The two men met again during Mitterrand's second presidential campaign in 1974. A magazine photographer snapped a lunch party at the candidate's country home in the south-west. Bousquet and his wife sat opposite Mitterrand: the caption did not identify the guests.

Research by a tenacious British journalist, Paul Webster, uncovered other links. Around the time Bousquet was being tried by the High Court of Justice, the rising politician named one of the former police chief's wartime staff as his press officer. At the Interior Ministry in 1954, with access to all the files, Mitterrand appointed three members of Bousquet's old entourage to his team. In 1965, he engaged as his parliamentary aide another of Bousquet's former subordinates – a man called Pierre Saury, who had worked on the deportation of Jews from Paris. Saury also acted as Mitterrand's link with former Petainists. When he died in 1973, his wartime and peacetime employers both attended his funeral. As President, Mitterrand did not break off contact with Bousquet until 1988. That was five years after France's leading hunter of Nazis and collaborators, Serge Klarsfeld, had published documents detailing Bousquet's eagerness to deport Jews. But still, the Head of State was unable to snap the link completely. After being booed by young Jews at a commemoration of the 1942 round-up in Paris, Mitterrand appointed his own lawyer, Georges Kiejman, whose father died in Auschwitz, as junior Justice Minister. Kiejman blocked legal proceedings against Bousquet in the name of national unity.

Towards the end of Mitterrand's rule, the Nobel Prize-winner, Elie Wiesel, was commissioned to write up a series of conversations with him. It was to be the President's philosophical apotheosis. When Wiesel, a Jew and a great admirer of Mitterrand at the time, raised the matter of Bousquet, the Head of State replied that he felt he had made no mistake.

'None?' Wiesel asked.

'None,' Mitterrand insisted.

'So,' wrote Wiesel some years later, 'there was no remorse, nor regrets. The anti-Jewish laws of Vichy? He didn't know.'

Trying to delve more deeply, Wiesel fired off faxes about Vichy and Pétain, the wreath sent to the Marshal's tomb, Bousquet and Mitterrand's Vichy medal. The President did not deign to reply, and then, unbelievably, insisted that he had been the one who had wanted to deal with the subject of Bousquet. All Wiesel could say was: 'I feel bad about that man.' He was not alone.

It was not even as if Bousquet was an isolated example. His wartime deputy was charged, but was never brought to trial and died in peace in 1989. Another senior official who oversaw all the prefects in the Vichy zone ended his days untroubled at his Riviera villa in 1992. And when it came to Maurice Papon, irony was added to neglect on the President's part. If the story told by the Jew who escaped death by hiding in a cupboard in Bordeaux in 1942 is true, Mitterrand owed part of his election against Giscard in 1981 to the revelation of Papon's wartime role. But, when the case came up in Cabinet, the President made it plain on several occasions that he was not in favour of reopening the case against a man he described as being 'of outstanding stature'. After Le Canard Enchaîné had broken the Papon story in 1981, Michel Slitinsky recalls that the journalist who wrote it told him that Mitterrand would certainly invite him to visit his country home, south of Bordeaux. Slitinsky never received an invitation, but René Bousquet did.

The fact that Mitterrand felt so little compunction about befriending Bousquet and protecting Papon was both a reminder of the extent of his own self-centred amorality and – once again – a sign of how accurately he reflected the inner feelings of so many of his compatriots. There was also an obvious personal parallel between these two Vichy-Resistants and his own wartime career. When Bousquet was murdered in 1993, conspiracy theories flared up, but the truth seemed to be that the killer was simply deranged. As he was sentenced to ten years in jail for the shooting, he said he sought pardon from God for breaking the commitment not to kill, from the Jews for having prevented Bousquet appearing in court, and from the dead man's family for having removed their father. A crazy gunman had also deprived France of a chance to purge part of a dark stain on its history, and the first elected President of the left ended his rule under the shadow of the collaboration his country longed to put behind it without going through the pain of exorcism.

'I think I'm going to mess up my exit by a couple of months.'

It was a sunny day in September 1994, and the President of the Republic was talking to a guest at his home among the pine trees of the Landes department on the south-western coast, where he felt 'the ocean in the forest'. They ate *foie gras*, lobster and grapes and drank white wine. Mitterrand was in aphoristic mood, speaking of 'Nationalism, the opium of imbeciles' or producing the none-too-profound observation that 'Socialism and Communism are branches of the same tree – like Christianity and Islam'. He felt free to criticise his opponents and his successor as leader of the Socialist Party with impunity as birds whirled above and a bluebottle swooped on to his forehead.

Three months later, the man whom some referred to as God was asked what he expected the Father in Heaven to say to him when he reached paradise. Terminally ill, Mitterrand sat stiffly in his chair as he pondered his response. He had difficulty speaking; from time to time, his right hand darted to the pocket of his jacket as if he needed to touch a talisman. A confirmed agnostic who had rejected his Catholic upbringing, he showed a shaft of wit as he answered the question. 'Now you know,' God would say. 'And I hope that He would add – "Welcome."'

By then, the President had been living under the shadow of death for more than a dozen years. In his 1981 election campaign, he had pledged 'transparency' on the state of his health. There would be none of the secrecy which had surrounded the last months of Georges Pompidou's life, he promised. His doctor, Claude Gubler, issued two bulletins a year, giving his patient a good bill of health. They were, to say the least, highly economical with the truth. Every day for eleven years, the Head of State received secret medical attention. When he travelled abroad, he had treatment at night wherever he was: the needles and bottles of liquid were sealed in special suitcases and sent back to France in diplomatic bags for destruction. On trips to Communist countries, the injections were conducted in total silence for fear that the room might be bugged.

In 1992, the President was operated on for a decade-old cancer of the prostate, and the secret was out – or rather, in true Mitterrand fashion, part of it. Gubler had diagnosed the illness eleven years earlier. As the doctor recounted it, his patient's immediate reaction when told the news six months after moving into the Élysée had been that it must remain a state secret. After the first diagnosis, Mitterrand asked how long he had to live. The prognosis was three years; the President muttered under his breath: 'I'm done for.' But the treatment appeared to be working, and Mitterrand began to believe he had beaten the cancer. He did not consult Gubler before announcing that he would stand for re-election in 1988. France duly gave another seven years in power to a cancer patient in his seventies. Only he and his doctor knew the truth; the government and the electorate were kept in the dark. If it had known, would France have voted differently? Jacques Chirac ran a terrible campaign, but the facts about Mitterrand's state of health might have swung the balance or, even worse from the President's viewpoint, have encouraged the centre-left to throw its support behind his long-time antagonist, Michel Rocard. That could have shifted the course of history. But Mitterrand played the sphinx; he did not even tell his wife of his condition until 1991. In her usual understanding fashion, she said she did not regard this as untoward: 'He simply preserved our tranquillity of spirit.'

Even when the operation in 1992 destroyed the secrecy, the fact that the cancer had already spread was still kept quiet from the public. But radiotherapy, chemotherapy and a second operation diminished the man physically. In a book published immediately after Mitterrand's death, which was later banned and earned him a four-month suspended prison sentence, Dr Gubler reported that Mitterrand was so weakened that he was incapable of doing the job for the last six months of his time in the Élysée. His Gaullist Prime Minister of the time did not object since he was left to get on with running the country. The President apparently went straight to bed when he arrived at the Palace from his private home on the Left Bank at 9:30 A.M., and rested for most of the day. Nothing interested him except his illness and some of his grand projects, particularly the controversial new national library in Paris which was on its way to running six times over budget.

François Mitterrand spent the 237 days that would remain to him after he left the Élysée revisiting what he had most enjoyed in life – Venice and the booksellers of Paris, the countryside of Burgundy and political gossip with his old associates. Dying, he stayed in control. He saw out 1995 at separate Christmas and New Year celebrations with his wife and his mistress and their respective offspring. On his return from a trip to the Nile Valley with his second family, he told Danielle that he had decided to end his life by stopping eating. He asked his doctor what would happen if he ceased his medication. He would die three days later, he was told. Before that, he took a last delight in food. At a dinner over New Year, he started by consuming thirty oysters. He then ate an ortolan. This rare small bird is an officially protected species, but it is still caught while flying over the south-west and fattened on grain in a darkened barn for three weeks before being killed by a big shot of Armagnac liqueur. By tradition, the ortolan is eaten whole – wings, beak, innards and all. To ensure that not a whiff of the bird's unique aroma is lost, it should be consumed under a large napkin. At the end of the main course of the New Year dinner, one ortolan remained on the platter. Mitterrand took it and disappeared beneath his napkin for the second time that evening. After chewing the little bird, he lay back in his chair, beaming in ecstasy.

Then the man who had fought a solitary combat for half a century got ready to perish. He wrote out the instructions for his funeral –

one grand state affair in Paris and a simpler ceremony in his native Charente department. He completed his memoirs. He wrote a letter to a long-time crony. And then, on 9 January 1996, at the age of seventy-nine, François Mitterrand died. A joke which did the rounds a few months later had the President arriving at the gates of heaven. You can't come in, says God, you are an adulterer – even worse than that, you think you are God and in this kingdom there is only one God. To which Mitterrand replies: 'When's the next election?'

His death was the occasion for a great outpouring of national reverence. A monument had gone; the Fifth Republic had lost its second great figure. His home town of Jarnac became a pilgrimage centre (though local tradespeople were disappointed when they tried to cash in on the Mitterrand legacy – a confectioner sold only 40 of 1,000 boxes of chocolates with the President's face stamped on them). Even a strident anti-Socialist like the former Gaullist minister, Alain Peyrefitte, opined that it was no time for polemics since Mitterrand had been France for fourteen years. There were bizarre touches; in Bulgaria, Mitterrand was hailed as the first foreign leader to draw attention to that country, and in China, it was recalled that the transliteration of his name was said by the supreme leader, Deng Xiaoping, to mean 'Enigma, all is clear'. Two months after his death, five of the ten best-selling books in France were about the late President: in all, at least four million books about him are reckoned to have been sold. One was by his widow; two were spoof memoirs in the name of his black Labrador dog, Baltique. A Swedish journalist wrote a book about her 'loving friendship' with the late President and their conversations on the Middle East, but she drew a veil over whether he was the father of her son. A woman who helped people to die peacefully told how she had eased the President through the last stage of his life, and how he had asked her to place a small stone for him near a Celtic cross below her house in the South of France. A former head of the secret service went into print to show that Mitterrand had personally approved the project to stop the Greenpeace boat, *Rainbow Warrior*, from sailing to protest against French nuclear tests in 1985, leading to an operation by French agents which cost a Portuguese photographer his life. A member of his intimate court unveiled Mitterrand's views on the great and the good: Margaret Thatcher had the lips of Marilyn Monroe and the eyes of the Roman Emperor Caligula, while Ronald Reagan 'has only a few records going round and round in his head'. In keeping with the paranormal tenor of the times, France's leading popular astrologer revealed that the late President had consulted her before making important decisions, greeting her with the query: 'How am I doing, and how is France doing?' and then asking where Helmut Kohl, Saddam Hussein and his own Prime Minister stood with the stars. When the French edition of *Penthouse* ran photographs of the astrologer from a pornographic film in which she had appeared in 1971, some wondered if the President's interest in her had ranged more widely than horoscopes.

Mitterrand's gooey wartime short story about Philippe and Elsa fetched 38,000 francs at auction. His family successfully sued Dr Gubler over the revelations about the President's illness, though they got less than half the damages they asked for. In December 1996, Jacques Chirac inaugurated the huge new national library building by the Seine. When he had been asked if he wanted the building to be named after him, Mitterrand had replied: 'If you had to take the decision and you asked me to take that decision, I would say "no".' Which most people took for a yes. So the huge 30-billion-franc building was duly named the Bibliothèque François Mitterrand. A poll carried out for *Le Figaro* at the same time showed that he was the second most popular President of the Fifth Republic. Despite all the woes and stress they had suffered under him, 65 per cent now said they had good memories of the Mitterrand years. As the newspaper remarked, 'He is greater dead than alive.'

Nobody had reflected the contradictions of the people he ruled more clearly. Nobody had done more to turn the Socialist movement into a party of government. Nobody had been more removed from the everyday world but more intimately involved in human affairs – Vichyite and Resister; the visceral enemy of the Fifth Republic who became its longest-serving Head of State and pronounced its presidential vestments greatly to his liking; intellectual and base schemer; a seemingly unworldly figure who never carried money but who presided over a scandal-ridden administration; a chronically unpunctual being who was also one of the greatest experts on the minutiae of French electoral geography. A man who liked to present himself as a great humanist and champion of freedom in the Third World, he had presided over a government which armed the genocide in Rwanda and propped up crude dictators in its former colonies. A driving force in the construction of Europe, he had proved unable to craft a role for Paris beyond the shadow of Bonn. A man who prided himself on his grasp of history, he had failed to visualise the break-up of Yugoslavia or the unification of Germany. In the end, François Mitterrand was everything and, at the same time, nothing: his own greatest promoter and his own worst enemy, a solitary figure whose self-esteem and contempt for those around him seemed to know no limits. He was, he told his aide Jacques Attali, surrounded by dwarfs.

In the end, two things were plain: France's longest-serving President was not nearly as clever as he thought he was, and he had sacrificed the good of his country at his own altar. Commentators and those who had been seduced and abandoned by François Mitterrand wondered at his lack of any ethical dimension. In opposition, his amorality could be excused as necessary in the pursuit of power. But once he had reached the summit, it got even worse. He simply did not seem to care about any real values. His ultimate cynicism in power may have had a very simple root: from the end of 1981 onwards he knew that every additional day was a medical miracle. He was on the way out physically from virtually the moment he finally achieved supreme power. Life, in existential terms, held no promise, and so he would amuse himself by playing with power until the end came. The sadness for France as a nation was that the game lasted so long.

To the very end, there were two sides to the man.

Asked late in life if he had any regrets, Mitterrand was characteristically self-assured. 'None,' he replied. 'Not everything was perfect in my life; who can claim that it was? But everything I did, I can be proud of. I mean to say, as a man. I never bowed the knee in front of anything or anybody.'

But there was also another side.

A traveller comes across a group of men in his path.

'What are you doing?' he asks them.

'We are piling up stones,' they reply.

Further on, he meets another group, doing the same thing.

'What are you doing?' he asks them.

'We are building a cathedral,' comes the response.

'Well,' added François Mitterrand as he recounted the story to visitors before his death, 'I ought to have, and could have, built cathedrals. Often, all I did was to make piles of stones.'

14

THE JAWS OF VICTORY

La Rochelle, in the Charente-Maritime department of western France, is a pleasant place, with excellent fish restaurants, pedestrian zones and a fine yachting harbour. An English expedition sailed there in 1627 in a vain attempt to relieve the siege of the Protestant Huguenots, an episode immortalised by Alexandre Dumas and his musketeers. Three and a half centuries later, two of France's leading politicians flew to La Rochelle for a party congress to confirm who would become the next President of the Republic. The meeting was meant to be another step towards an effortless Gaullist restoration after François Mitterrand's fourteen years in the Élysée Palace. As things turned out, the weekend on the Atlantic coast set off the final battle in the Thirty Years' War of French politics.

The period since the left won power in 1981 had been a frustrating, unsettled time for the Gaullists under Jacques Chirac and the centre–conservative coalition headed by Valéry Giscard d'Estaing. Frustrating, because the right was not accustomed to being out of power – its leaders had been brought up to assume that the Fifth Republic belonged to them and, though they had won two major parliamentary elections in 1986 and 1993, they had been unable to best the man in the Élysée. Unsettled, because it was never quite clear who was in charge of the opposition to the so-called Socialist presiding over France.

After 1981, Jacques Chirac had rushed into the vacuum on his side of politics. Alone of Mitterrand's opponents, he had a real power-base as Mayor of Paris. Then the man who had succeeded him as Prime Minister back in 1976, the professorial Raymond Barre, emerged as the incarnation of true French values, too. Watching him tucking into a meal at Paul Bocuse's celebrated restaurant outside Lyon one stormy night in the mid-1980s gave one the impression that this was a man made to lead the traditional forces of France. On the menu that night was the truffle soup which Bocuse had named in honour of Giscard. The coolness that had set in since one man lost the presidency and the other the premiership did not affect Barre's appetite. As always, he acted as though he had time on his side. During the dinner, he mentioned a piece I had written in *The Economist* which contrasted his deliberate style with the livewire Chirac. He appeared quite content to have been portrayed as the tortoise moving at his own pace behind the Gaullist hare. Once described by Giscard as the best economist in France, his conservative manner disguises a sharp appreciation of the realities of modern finance. The portly Barre is never in a hurry; he doesn't feel the need to run, confident that he will get there in the end. He is certainly not a man lacking in self-assurance. Once, when a journalist queried the rightness of one of his policies, he simply told the man not to be so silly.

That approach struck a chord in the increasingly rudderless right of the mid-1980s, and the notion of both his former Prime Ministers moving to the front of the opposition ranks was enough to spur the deposed Head of State into action. Giscard thought he could outflank the impetuous Chirac without difficulty. But the idea that Raymond Barre might become President was a goad that could not be tolerated. Stirring the pot, Mitterrand promoted the idea that Giscard might agree to become his Prime Minister. A short time afterwards, he spoke approvingly of Barre as the kind of man he could easily work with. The right was in a mess, and Mitterrand knew how to make the most of it.

In the event, it was Chirac who was appointed to run the government after the left lost its parliamentary majority in 1986. In the presidential election two years later, Raymond Barre insisted on running and proved the emptiness of Charles de Gaulle's tirades against political parties. This most De Gaulle-like candidate had no organised movement behind him. Although he was clearly the best man in the race, he lacked an electoral machine to get the votes out, and so was eliminated with only 16.5 per cent in the first round. As one of his aides later said with a sigh, 'In France, the best never win.' When it came to the run-off ballot, Mitterrand beat Chirac by a handsome 54–46 per cent margin. It was a triumph for the old fox in the Élysée and a disaster for his opponent's shoot-from-the-hip style. Equally, it was fresh evidence of the right's continuing ability to auto-destruct through internal rivalries. Some drew the inevitable conclusion that Chirac was not the man to wrest power back at the summit of the state. For others, it was time to leave the battlefield. Raymond Barre moved to the sidelines to become a sage and happy Mayor of Lyon. As he put it to me, having operated at a national and international level, it was good to get down to earth. He seemed that rare animal, a one-time Prime Minister who was actually content with his born-again role in the centre of France, and chuckled with genuine pleasure as we talked in a Hong Kong hotel of *quenelles de brochet* and *poularde demi-deuil*.

So the war narrowed to the two companions-in-arms of 1974. It was an unequal conflict. Giscard's day was clearly passing: his ambitious younger followers paid him lip-service, but feuded for the succession. Recovering from a period of depression after his presidential defeat, Chirac consolidated his power by building up the Gaullist party. By the time of the left's collapse at the 1993 parliamentary election, the one-time protégé of Georges Pompidou was king of the heap. He had wobbled from time to time, notably during France's referendum on the Maastricht Treaty, but he and his cohorts were now on a roll, and the future seemed assured. No more internal wars, no Giscard, no Barre, no worries about the National Front. Having twice suffered as Prime Minister, Jacques Chirac was only too happy to leave his good friend and former Finance Minister, Édouard Balladur, to head the government while he concentrated on the apparently easy campaign to get to the Élysée. Two decades after knifing Chaban-Delmas in the back, life seemed to be simple at last. Blood simple, as it turned out.

Chirac and Balladur had met when the first was Pompidou's dashing lieutenant and the second the President's chief of staff. They stayed together through the years. From 1986 to 1988, Finance Minister Balladur implemented privatisations and financial liberalisation for Prime Minister Chirac. The Gaullist leader regularly sent drafts of his speeches to his friend for comment and approval. Just as he had taken guidance from Pierre Juillet and Marie-France Garaud in the 1970s, so, two decades on, Jacques Chirac sought another source of benediction. For a man who lived for the roar of the crowd and who washed down his favourite dish of calf's head with Mexican beer, his choice was a strange one. Pierre and Marie-France spoke from the roots of France; Édouard floated free of terrestrial attachments.

Son of a rich trading family living in the Turkish city of Smyrna, he had pursued a career as discreet as that of his Gaullist friend had been public. Balladur was a born-again chamberlain of the Ancien Régime, a man of silk and velvet who could glide across a gravel courtyard without leaving the trace of a footstep. The Prime Minister hated loud noise and liked the company of soft-voiced noble ladies. He ate steamed sole and answered his telephone with a strange, fluting '*alloooo*'. As Finance Minister, Balladur had insisted on moving his offices from a modern building down the Seine back to the Louvre, where major-domos walked backwards in front of him. The flashier members of the Mitterrand entourage were known as the 'caviar left'; there was no doubt that Édouard Balladur belonged firmly in the ranks of the caviar right. As President-in-waiting from 1993 onwards, Jacques Chirac waded through a hundred banquets, pumping hands, promising everything under the sun, a man seemingly with no aim in life except to campaign. As Prime Minister, meanwhile, Balladur lulled the nation into a comatose sense of peace, and watched with hooded eyes while his popularity soared. Everybody knew Chirac's latest opinion before his brain had fully formulated it; nobody had much idea of what went on behind the Premier's opaque exterior.

After the Gaullist triumph at the general election of March 1993, the deal had been clear: Balladur for Prime Minister, Chirac for President. Apart from freeing Chirac from the day-to-day business of government which he was convinced had harmed his previous presidential bid, the arrangement gave the Gaullist leader time to tour the country, to think and to seek his campaign themes. Balladur's reassuringly good links with big business would also be a help, counteracting the nervousness which Chirac aroused in that quarter. The two men might be very different, particularly in their public personae. But, if each kept to his appointed role, they could make a perfect team.

When he spoke to his Gaullist party congress at La Rochelle six months later, Chirac referred to their pact. As his eyes swept the hall, he saw Balladur looking up at the ceiling, avoiding his gaze. From a man as subtle as the Prime Minister, it was more than a signal. So the two companions-in-arms decided to take a stroll around the harbour. After that, Chirac later recalled, he 'understood that the presidential election might well not turn out as planned'. Balladur flew off in his official jet while the man who had headed his party for twenty years was left standing on the tarmac, waiting for his hired plane. At that moment, Jacques Chirac could be in no doubt that power had gone to his friend's head.

This was hardly surprising. Anybody with a surer strategic sense would have seen the danger coming: most French Prime Ministers nurture presidential ambitions at one time or another. Still, the rise and rise of Édouard Balladur had something unreal about it, as if he was touched by divine providence. Platitudinous and self-satisfied, the Prime Minister rose from peak to peak in the polls. He gave in to the threat of strikes and won more plaudits. He avoided decisions and became a hero. The *Financial Times* made him its man of the year. With Balladur, it was time to look forward to the past. Like his first patron, Georges Pompidou, two decades earlier, he epitomised a settled national existence. After the tremors of the Socialist years, his deliberate, courtly style struck a reassuring note. He seemed within reach of forging a new conservative consensus which would go beyond Gaullism and give France a single big centre-right party as a rampart against the Socialists. The Prime Minister personified the rule of the state, with pre-revolution echoes: *Le Monde*'s cartoonist showed him being carried in a sedan chair. Let them eat cake, he might have said as he sought to keep the populace happy by taking the easy way out. Adopting a phrase invented by Marie-France Garaud, satirists altered the last syllable of his name to dub him 'Ballamou' (*Balla-dur* = Balla-hard; *Balla-mou* = Balla-soft). But his hauteur created an illusion of living on a thoroughly superior plane, in which the nation could share – at least for a while.

As the Prime Minister soared in the polls, ambitious young conservatives also looked back at recent history. If Balladur was a second Pompidou, they could not help calculating, his presidency might spawn a bright young successor from outside the Gaullist ranks. So they lined up to be a second Giscard d'Estaing. Not to be outdone, some sharp young Gaullists deserted their party leader and joined the rush to the side of '*cher Édouard*'. It was, after all, only what Jacques Chirac had done in 1974. More surprisingly, the Interior Minister, Charles Pasqua, switched camps. In his ministerial job, Pasqua had access to political intelligence reports from around the country; so, some reasoned, if he had jumped ship, Chirac must really be done for. The Prime Minister's people began to talk of '*pauvre*' Chirac and the lost people around him.

This was a battle between two strands of politics, between straight-on, no-nonsense populism and genteel conservatism – calf's head versus caviar. While Chirac championed republican values, Balladur once told a lunch party that, overall, he thought that 1789 had been a bad thing for France. However great his airs and graces, President Balladur would run the government; however populist his appeal, President Chirac would leave day-to-day domestic business to his Prime Minister. Had there been a serious chance of the left winning, Balladur's ecumenical appeal might well have been irresistible. His base was broader, and he could easily have painted Chirac into a corner, accusing him of opening the door to another seven years of Socialism in a repeat of his performance in 1981. But once the only heavyweight figure from the opposite corner, Jacques Delors, decided not to run, the way was open for Chirac to stamp around the ring, facing Balladur with an impossible task in broadening his coalition.

There were plenty of precedents for this kind of fight on the right: the tussle between Giscard and Chirac; the struggle of Gaullists of the early 1960s against conservatives trying to hang on after the demise of the Fourth Republic; even, in its way, the contrast between the silent majority of the Second World War and the men of the right who actively engaged themselves on one side or the other. But there was also a new twist. From 1976 to 1981, the fight had been between Valéry Giscard d'Estaing and Jacques Chirac. In the 1980s, the battle had widened to take in Raymond Barre. Through all those years, Chirac's RPR party had always been a monolith behind its leader. Now, the Giscard–Barre camp had fled the field, and it was the great Gaullist army which was shockingly rent by internal strife on the verge of victory. In the past, whatever their differences, the General's followers had usually managed to weave together their different wings. But now, it was as if the imminence of the return to supreme power had infected the movement with the old French virus of division. The Socialists appeared terminally discredited; the centrists would not field a candidate; the Gaullists had only to push the door and the Élysée was theirs – with all the symbolism which that entailed for the party of the man who had founded the regime. But they nearly blew it. Another strange tale of the ways of the men who presume to run France.

As the election came over the political horizon, Balladur was the clear favourite, ready to move from his official residence at the Hôtel Matignon to a much grander residence across the Seine, where he could have as many major-domos as he wished waiting on him morning, noon and night. International finance and the French establishment knew who they backed. 'Chirac's fun, but Balladur's serious,' one major fund manager told me. 'Chirac's time has passed; we're ready for a time of real management,' echoed a French business tycoon. 'It's simple,' said an international businessman. 'Chirac's mad.' Given the later disclosures about Mitterrand's parlous state of health and preoccupation with day-to-day survival, the Prime Minister's authority was even greater than it appeared at the time. So much so that Chirac showed uncharacteristic signs of hesitation about declaring his own candidacy – and, by one account, had to be encouraged into making the announcement by none other than the old man in the Élysée, who may have calculated that a wild performance from the right could be the only faint hope left to the Socialists.

In fact, Chirac enjoyed strengths of which Balladur could not even dream. He controlled France's strongest political party machine, and had a thousand debts to call in. His praetorian guard was loyal, and he had Paris. The Prime Minister might be the darling of the establishment, but elections are decided by voters – and, when it came to the hustings, there was only one show in France in the spring of 1995.

Jacques Chirac hurled himself into his third presidential campaign with all the *brio* of a man who knew that this was his last chance to win the prize he had sought all his adult life. Incoherence incarnate, he promised both wage rises and a decline in inflation. One day, he swore his European fidelity; then he talked of a fresh referendum on the Maastricht Treaty. He pledged tax cuts, but predicted an increase in the value-added levy. He was for modern business, but sent an emissary to ensure the latter-day support of the leader of the rioting small shop-keepers of the 1950s, Pierre Poujade. It was great theatre, with policy made on the hoof, arms in the air, rictus smiles freezing his face, a hundred hands pumped every hour. In contrast, Balladur was an also-ran, and some key figures read the way the wind was really blowing.

France's greatest political proponent of free-market economics, the Minister for Business, Alain Madelin, stayed loyal to Chirac: as an exponent of *libéralisme avancé*, he could see that Balladur was the re-incarnation of a consensus-corporatist spirit which even the born-again left rejected. The government's best cutting-edge, Foreign Minister Alain Juppé, also remained true to the man he had first served in 1983 in the Paris city government. And the main Gaullist Eurosceptic, the bloodhound-faced President of the National Assembly, Philippe Séguin, decided that, whatever their differences, Chirac was the man who should win the election. This trio, and the party machine, con-stituted such a formidable force that Balladur's chances ought to have been discounted as the election campaign got under way. But his bro-mide appeal was such that the media went on promoting him as the next Head of State – which only spurred the Mayor of Paris to greater activity.

As the election battle moved into top gear, one of the main protag-onists of the Thirty Years' War considered his options from the sidelines. The last non-Socialist President had every reason to hate Chirac for his tepid attitude in the 1981 presidential poll. But Mr Ex, as Valéry Giscard d'Estaing had come to be known, still had hopes for the future: if the European Union ever had a real President, who was better suited to fill the post than himself? At the same time, he wanted to preserve a domestic power-base, and he knew that Balladur was going right for his natural constituency, for the local notables who had kept him at the forefront of French politics through good times and bad. If the Premier won the election, Giscard might as well retire to his memoirs. Under Chirac, there might still be a role for him. So it was time to put aside old rancours for the sake of mutual survival.

As spring blossomed on the hillside behind his elegant country home in the Massif Central, Valéry Giscard d'Estaing announced his support for the man whose rivalry had cost him the presidency fourteen years earlier. His hopes for the future were not to be fulfilled, however. He failed in a bid to become mayor of the Auvergnat capital of Clermont-Ferrand, up the road from one of his châteaux; and family pride was dented when a nephew was fined for involvement in a corruption scandal. Eventually, in a meeting-hall in Lyon, the seventy-year-old wunderkind of the 1960s and 1970s was forced to pass the leadership of the UDF to a former Defence Minister, François Léotard. He was not the successor Giscard would have chosen; the two men had long crossed swords. But the ex-President's days of party political influence were waning. He could settle old scores by influencing the choice of ministers on the right, entertain dreams of becoming Europe's world spokesman and turn his hand to a volume of soapy romantic fiction. He could rouse himself to indignation at the design of the British architect, Norman Foster, for a great motorway viaduct over the Tarn river, caress a project for a volcanic theme park in his native Auvergne, and speculate about the benefits of devaluing the franc. But Giscard's time as a front-line general had passed: the war on the right had narrowed down to the Gaullist ranks.

On the hustings, the Prime Minister cut an increasingly poor figure. But who could have asked for anything more? Whatever one might think of Édouard Balladur, he was always true to himself, and his self did not include being at ease with the people. So when he accosted teenagers in the street and tried to talk to them about basketball, he clearly didn't have a clue what their replies meant. Electioneering in a café, he was visibly ill at ease if he had to touch anybody. Down in the Rouergue, a lamb peed on his jacket and the farmers laughed among themselves. A satirical television show which shaped public perceptions had great fun with skits in which His Smugness the Prime Minister washed his hands after each electoral handshake and told his wife that he had discovered some charming new words – '*tu*' and '*le peuple*'. Such invention went down so well because everybody believed it to be true, and the Prime Minister's behaviour seemed to confirm it each and every day. As his press secretary put it later, Balladur had a problem with 'those French who are called ordinary when one doesn't want to have too much to do with them but who are the real people of France, those whose virtues one praises as a group but whom one ignores as individuals'.

Suddenly, the man who had done so well in the polls seemed incapable of getting anything right. When low cloud forced his helicopter to land in southern France, the newspapers were fed a folksy story about how the Prime Minister had been picked up by a passing motorist, with two big dogs on the back seat, and how he had shown the common touch by chatting to the driver as she took him to the next stage of his trip. Some even reported the unlikely spectacle of Balladur standing by the road with his thumb in the air, hitching a lift from the lady. A couple of days later, he sent her a bunch of roses and a visiting card with his hand-written thanks. Unfortunately, it later turned out that the woman was the cousin by marriage of a Balladur adviser who was on the trip – and that he had telephoned to ask her to come to pick up the Premier. When the press learned of the spin that had been put on the tale, it reacted with a belly-laugh and a fresh dose of satire about the hitch-hike that never was. Things got even worse when it emerged that the supposedly ordinary motorist had been driving a large white Mercedes. (Coincidentally, Giscard d'Estaing had just published a romantic novel in which a man of a certain age gives a lift to a young hitch-hiker and embarks on an affair with her.)

The first round of the election duly propelled Jacques Chirac into the decisive second round and eliminated Balladur from the two-man run-off. Lionel Jospin, the last-minute candidate of the supposedly down-and-out Socialists, got the nomination after Jacques Delors ruled himself out of the running – as Mitterrand once said, Delors 'would like to be President without being a candidate'. Jospin showed how mistaken St Jacques had been by winning 23.3 per cent of the vote, to 20.8 for Chirac and 18.5 for Balladur. In part, that was not so surprising: Chirac and Balladur had, after all, split their party, and Jospin had managed to rally the Socialist faithful. If the orthodox right's scores at the first round were put together, and some of Le Pen's 15 per cent were added in, Chirac was well ahead for the run-off. But the Mayor of Paris could only be disappointed to have received just one-fifth of the overall poll. The combined scores of the two Gaullists still fell well short of the 50 per cent needed for eventual victory.

'This is the ultimate combat of his whole life, and he will not let himself fail,' one of Chirac's advisers said as we sat at a pavement café between the two rounds of voting. 'Anyway, the country wants a change. But it will be a hollow victory. We should have blown both Balladur and the left out of the water; we should have humbled Le

Pen. We have the best candidate, the man to lead the nation, but we have to struggle to win over voters. They don't believe in us. They don't believe in anybody any more.'

As the second-round campaign unfurled, Chirac became somewhat more presidential; he even relaxed from time to time. His press office disclosed that in the afternoon of the Saturday before the final voting he went into the garden of the Paris City Hall to read a volume of Japanese poetry. Not everybody believed the tale, but it was a sign of how his staff were trying to spin an image of a mature, thoughtful politician with wide horizons. Balladur rallied more loyally to the flag than Chirac had done to the colours of Giscard in 1981. Some 85 per cent of the Prime Minister's first-round voters backed Chirac in the second round. So did a few from the left. As for the National Front, its leader told his supporters they might as well go hunting snails as vote; and 60 per cent of them did not support Chirac in the run-off. However one analysed the figures, there were a lot of non-Socialists who felt disassociated from the new President. Once again, Le Pen seemed to have his finger on the national pulse. Twenty per cent of the electorate abstained, and another 6 per cent cast blank or spoiled ballots. Snail-hunting might well seem more attractive than politics as practised by France's leaders over the past three decades.

If France is still a chauvinist nation when it comes to the sexes, imagine it as a woman in an old-fashioned tale. In 1974, she fell for the undeniable seduction of a brilliant, tall and slim young semi-aristocrat who promised so much but delivered a lot less, and ended up spending too much time away on safari. In 1981, she collapsed into the arms of an old roué who offered to lift her to better and brighter horizons. Despite his broken promises and self-absorption, she found herself unable to turn her back on him when the occasion came in 1988. Seven years on, she had become terminally disenchanted with the decaying and dying man and wanted a complete change of partner. For a while, she was seduced by the notion of a platonic, pursed-lip relationship with an unctuous eater of steamed sole. But, in her heart, she still believed that each advent of the seven-year itch should bring a fresh outburst of passion. The prospect of slipping into bed with Édouard Balladur was hardly calculated to give her a new lease of life.

After a long, lingering sigh for a wise and decent elder cousin from Brussels who decided she'd be too much trouble to handle, she finally went for a former cavalry officer who had been trying to sweep her off her feet for fourteen years. He was hardly the dashing new figure she dreamed of. But consider the alternatives. The professorial Socialist would give her lectures, and was hardly calculated to stir the juices. She might engage in a quick flirtation with the one-eyed rascal on her far right-hand side, give a quick smile to the engaging and stout Communist garden gnome, and even proffer a sisterly caress to a woman bank clerk who preached Trotskyite revolution in an endless presidential quest. But, in the end, she let her most assiduous suitor have his way with her at last, though not with any great joy. The groom grimaced in crazed excitement as he fought his way through the crowd to the wedding party on the Avenue d'Iéna on election night: a kilometre away, a clutch of political experts gathered round an early-morning dinner table in a restaurant off the Champs-Élysées and gave the marriage two months before it would begin to run into the ground.

The political experts were right. After an initial honeymoon, troubles mounted. Nuclear fury abroad was followed by the wave of protests at home against proposed reforms in the welfare system. The concentration on beating Balladur had been so intense that Chirac's men and women came to office without having been able to give sufficient time or thought to the job ahead. As the political editor of *Le Monde* put it, Chirac's only real election programme had been 'no to Balladur'. His campaign had aroused expectations of a new start, but, with a couple of exceptions, nobody around the Cabinet table had anything concrete to offer. Legislation which enshrined proposals made by candidate Chirac took a year or more to see the light, while other major policy changes had not been mentioned during the campaign. 'Now our difficulties start,' Alain Juppé told his staff encouragingly at their first meeting with the new Prime Minister.

The government made it known that the budget deficit was some 50 billion francs greater than it had been led to believe (a charge indignantly denied by Balladur). Privatisation revenue was a good deal less than expected. 'Our economy is good and healthy, our inflation is one of the lowest in the world, and our foreign trade is in strong surplus,' the new President declared. 'What is not working is our public finances.' Alain Madelin was sacked from the Finance Ministry after a running fight with the Prime Minister. Other ministries were all over the place. The President's ideas man, Emmanuel Todd, rounded on Chirac at the Élysée one day and accused him of having slammed the door on his electorate. As if to confirm Todd's suspicions, Juppé drew up his programme to reform welfare and state spending without any of the traditional consultations with bodies representing those who would be affected. After seeing 2 million demonstrators take to the streets and crippling strikes spread across the nation, even Super Énarque had to step back.

What was a month of strikes when the administration had seven years ahead of it to reform the country, mused Chirac. But the administration's unpopularity made it difficult to get anything done, let alone push through the deep reforms it had in mind. The President's standing in the polls dropped well under 50 per cent within a year as he alternately scolded the French for falling short of his expectations and then told them how wonderful they really were. His one-time companion-in-arms, Charles Pasqua, compared him to 'an unstable husband who beats his wife one day, then apologises the next day by showering her with compliments'. Such unions, Pasqua noted, usually go off the rails – 'the wife gets fed up, finds a lover and the marriage collapses'. Or else, the husband turns his weary eyes from problems at home and thinks about a trip abroad.

Not that Chirac's incessant international journeys weren't hard work: he threw himself into his role as France's top travelling salesman with all his usual energy. He also made some sensible decisions to set relations on a more realistic basis for the post-Cold War world. France even brought itself to admit 'without acrimony' that the United States was the sole superpower and that Paris now only ranked as one of the seven or eight most influential capitals. A closer relationship with Nato was developed. Missiles aimed at Russia were dismantled. The nuclear site at Mururoa was run down. Plans to reduce the overall strength of the military forces by more than 20 per cent were announced, with an end to conscription and army numbers cut by more than a third. Most of France's troops would be withdrawn from Germany, and the nuclear missile base on the Plateau d'Albion in the south-east shut. Surveying the cutbacks, a Gaullist deputy with strong military links mused that the losses were worse than at Waterloo. The army chief of staff, Philippe Mercier, revealed that, to help France meet the Maastricht criteria, spending on the army in 1998 was to be cut by 11 per cent. If such cuts continued, he warned, France would either have under-equipped forces, or would have to 'redefine a new defence tool' – whatever that meant.

By the end of his reign, Europe had become François Mitterrand's over-riding concern. That meant keeping in with Germany, and reciting the mantra of Maastricht. Jacques Chirac set out to re-assert a broader and specifically Gaullist and French approach to international affairs, aspiring to rekindle the glory years of the 1960s. But the over-arching question which he studiously avoided was whether France could – or should – play its old role in a post-Cold War world. By balancing membership of the Western alliance with independence from Washington, Charles de Gaulle had been able to carve out a national niche in a bi-polar world. Now the globe was a much more fractured place and there was only one superpower. Chirac wanted to build up stronger relations with Washington; at the same time, he could not resist the temptation to try to ape the old Gaullist pretensions. But, with united Germany the dominant continental power, any attempt to run a freelance foreign policy on behalf of Europe could only irritate France's partners, and make a less than convincing impression in Washington. Economic policy was shaped in Germany, and world policy across the Atlantic: where did that leave France? As the second most important member of the European Union, certainly. But on a wider world scale, as little more than a power which might or might not decide to join *ad hoc* alliances, and might be welcomed or barracked according to its decisions.

The key relationship, with Germany and Europe, might, in theory at least, offer a sphere for a resumption of classic Gaullism. With Britain having disqualified itself from being taken seriously by its behaviour in the later years of Conservative rule, the French President was the only leader in the Union who could realistically challenge the German Chancellor on whether what is right for Germany is necessarily right for its partners. As an American economist, Robert Levine, has pointed out, there is a parallel between the potential French role in present-day Europe and De Gaulle's questioning of American influence in the 1960s. When differences briefly flicked between Paris and Bonn over monetary policy, some saw a glimmer of such an approach. After the Jospin government took office, one of the first questions was whether it would establish an alternative to Teutonic orthodoxy within the Community. There are, after all, fundamental differences in the outlook of the two nations. France is Eurocentric; Germany has looked across the Atlantic since 1945. The Bundesbank's heart and soul are rooted in the need to contain inflation for deep historical reasons; the politicians on the Seine, whatever their pride in having kept the economy in line for a decade, are temperamentally more ready to flirt with greater flexibility.

But it is also inconceivable that France should not be one of the two key players in the future of Europe – which was the basic reason why Jacques Chirac could not have joined the anti-Maastricht campaign in 1992 whatever short-term advantage he might have gained from its victory. This means that Paris has to be viscerally tied to Bonn, the Banque de France to the Bundesbank, the President to the Chancellor. And, while Marianne may bare her breast with a smile, Germania rarely relaxes.

So, while the economic criteria of the Maastricht Treaty snapped at France's heels, the vicious circle of economic policy remained as tight as ever, and took its political toll. The price of continuing low inflation and Euro-orthodoxy was low growth. But this kept down government revenue, made the deficit reduction required by Maastricht that much more difficult to achieve, and turned the promised tax cuts into a chimera. To try to boost its income, the Juppé government put up the sales tax, which hit the poor and the unemployed whom Chirac had promised to defend. The number of firms going bust rose, with almost 6,000 businesses shutting down each month. Only a third of bosses of small businesses expressed any optimism about the future, as unemployment edged up again to the record levels of the worst days of the Mitterrand era. The President went on television with a marathon programme whose audience dropped embarrassingly low as viewers turned to a sexy film on the other channel. 'The truth is that we live in a profoundly conservative country and that it is very difficult to change things,' he lamented. Perfectly true, but he was in a fix of his own making. He had won the presidency by promising a new economic and social deal at home, and he wasn't delivering. Or, rather, what he was serving up through his Prime Minister was not the dish the nation had ordered. It had asked for a rich stew; Chirac and Juppé were giving it gruel. No wonder that a lot of people saw attractions in *l'autre politique*, a code-word for reflation. Senior officials might speak proudly of the strong franc and sneer at the floating pound, but the economic situation across the Channel could look quite attractive to a long-term unemployed steel-worker or a former Félix Potin manager searching for bargains at the local discount store.

Through it all, Alain Juppé kept an iron grip on the business of government. The political editor of *Le Monde* compared the President of the Republic to an unidentified flying object – 'one no longer knows quite who he is, where he is, what he wants'. But his Prime Minister was always there. He put his imprint on anything and everything. Given the ministerial chaos around him, he had little choice, but he went that mile further. In the midst of the national strikes of 1995, Juppé personally put in an urgent telephone call to the head of the Communist trade union federation – to ask about the staff situation on one Paris Métro line. He did not admit to the slightest fault in anything. Even when his grace-and-favour housing in a municipal flat on the Left Bank cast a stain on his squeaky-clean technocratic image, he waxed indignant at the fuss. A trusted aide moved across the Seine to become chief of staff at the Élysée; other acolytes were put in to run ministries, often showing more loyalty to the Juppé machine than to their nominal bosses. The Minister of Justice, Jacques Toubon, was moved to remark that there was a difference between a conductor and a one-man band. All this might have been fine if the government was doing well, but Juppé had achieved the double feat of getting very little done and breaking records for unpopularity. Visibly, the Prime Minister didn't know what to do about it except to call another meeting of experts. Some of those around him wondered if he was losing his way. Even his boss sensed that it was time to do something about the mess.

Chirac is a Bonapartist, a man who puts his trust in his direct link with the people, in his ability to incarnate the nation. Like the First Emperor, he believes in moving fast, living off the land, using concentrated force to achieve his ends. And, like the First Emperor, none of his victories has led to lasting peace. But that did not stop either of them having another go. So what Jacques did next should have surprised nobody. Like a general who has finally won his battle but finds peace hard to deal with, he went back to war.

Some of his advisers thought he should have done this two years earlier to finish off the job. The presidential victory had left Chirac with a dilemma: did he co-opt the supporters of Édouard Balladur by bringing them into the government or did he banish them from the regained Gaullist paradise? Sensible as the first option would have been in producing a dominant Gaullist-conservative bloc, the winners of 1995 were not in a forgive-and-forget mood: Chirac's wife was said to be unremittingly bitter about former supporters who had deserted their camp, and it was known that politicians who fell foul of the former Bernadette Chodron de Courcel had a short life-expectancy with her husband. But there was still a large Balladurian block in the National Assembly who were saying that the new President hadn't won, it had been they who had lost. This was not simply crying over spilt milk for, as Patrick Jarreau of *Le Monde* wrote, 'they had in their hands a deck of cards that appeared to be solid gold, with a large majority of deputies of the right in their camp, plus the most watched television channel in France, etc. . . . Given the result they arrived at, one has to conclude that they were really lousy players.'

So the logical course for Chirac in 1995 would have been to have called legislative elections immediately to clear out these traitors. Some of his top advisers pressed him to go to the country to finish off the anti-Balladurian job. The conjunction of presidential and parliamentary elections was well established: the Socialists had gone to the country after Mitterrand's victories of 1981 and 1988. But, like the allies in the Gulf War hesitating to invade Iraq to finish off Saddam Hussein, Chirac held back – in part because he had tied his own hands during the fight for the presidency. Balladur had pledged to call legislative elections if he won. That had been enough to produce a negative knee-jerk from Chirac, who brushed the idea aside and then, once in the Élysée, compounded his refusal with a high-minded observation about not using elections as a means of governing France.

Two years later, it was all he could think of. The government had fallen into impossibly deep discredit with the public. The task it had set itself was eminently necessary – to lift France from its late Mitterrandist

gloom, to give it a new national and international élan, and to prepare
it for the single European currency. That last objective was a suitably
long-term goal for a seven-year presidency, but the imminence of the
Maastricht Treaty deadline meant that Chirac and Juppé did not have
much time to play with. On top of that, their bossy, elitist style was
completely wrong for the times. As so often, it ain't what you do, it's
the way that you do it. But the men at the top ploughed on in ever-
decreasing circles. To make sure there was no weakening of resolve, the
President established a four-man 'crisis cell' at the Élysée, consisting of
himself, the Prime Minister and their two closest officials. 'Act without talking,' was their watchword.

They might act, but senior politicians warned Chirac that the long
grind of reform risked undermining the administration and encouraging anti-European sentiment. Gloomy forecasts were piling up about
unemployment, tax rises and spending cuts. Chirac's loyalty to Juppé
ruled out the traditional presidential escape route of sacking the Prime
Minister. His hostility to the Balladurians led him to veto Juppé's proposal to replace his lacklustre Finance Minister with a bright spark who
had gone over to the other side in 1995. The chief of staff at the
Élysée, Dominique de Villepin, proposed the old Gaullist recipe of a
referendum. De Villepin, a member of the crisis cell who was known
for having an iron first in an iron glove, was the ultimate Juppé–Chirac
loyalist, having served the first when he was Foreign Minister and
organised the presidential campaign of the second. When a journalist
sourced a story on the President's circle, De Villepin told him curtly, 'I
am the circle.' His referendum wheeze was, however, rejected since it
entailed the risk of provoking a hostile line-up ranging from the left to
the National Front, and taking in a fair number of Eurosceptic Gaullists
along the way. So was the idea of a crisis government of the great and
good, to include such luminaries as Giscard d'Estaing and Raymond
Barre. Instead, at noon on 17 April 1997, Chirac called half a dozen
advisers to a room beside his office at the Élysée. Among those present
was his younger daughter, Claude, who passed for an expert in public
relations. The meeting agreed that the time had come for decisive
action. Four days later, the President announced the dissolution of the
National Assembly and two-round elections for 25 May and 1 June to
give France 'a fresh impetus' for the challenges that lay ahead. On a
visit to Beijing soon afterwards, he told the Prime Minister, Li Peng,

that he had called the election because his majority was too large and uncontrollable. 'I will lose a hundred deputies, but they will be easier to handle,' he added. 'And Juppé will put everything in order.'

There was no denying the problem which Chirac and his men faced. But the way they attacked it was like the old joke – How do you get to the Eiffel Tower, asks a tourist. If I were you I wouldn't start from here, responds the Parisian. As often happens with politicians who hunker in the bunker, the men in the crisis cell were starting from the wrong point in several ways. They assumed that France was still set in the political environment of 1993–95, in the crushing defeat for the left at the last parliamentary election and the pre-eminent position of the Gaullists at the presidential poll. The débâcle of the late Mitterrand years seemed too close for the French to be ready to put their faith in the left under the leadership of the well-meaning but uninspiring Lionel Jospin. If the President and his men had lifted their eyes from their dossiers, they might have noticed how Mitterrand was not faring so badly in posthumous opinion polls, recalled how Jospin had revived the spirits of the left in 1995, and even recognised how his shadow team looked a good deal more attractive than the apparatchiks of the right. And some fearless aide might have pointed to a poll which showed that 59 per cent of those who had voted for Chirac two years earlier now thought that he talked a lot but that nothing concrete followed.

Another problem was not so much that the President was blatantly going back on his word about holding the election – the French were well used to being lied to by their leaders. It was rather that he and his head of government had nothing new to offer except fresh spoonfuls of Dr Juppé's purge. So why was he holding an election at all? If he won, it was more of the same. The only logical conclusion was that he was offering voters a chance to change policies. There was a fault here which the country was not slow to latch on to.

And then there was a difficulty which went to the heart of the political system. However low his popularity, a President of France has to appear to be in charge. At the depths of his fortunes, François Mitterrand always seemed capable of manipulating events. As for Chirac, his whole career had been based on leading from the front. But now he appeared to be in thrall to his Prime Minister. Even worse, Chirac looked like a man who was running scared on behalf of his

government. And of what? Surely not the schoolmasterish Lionel
Jospin: the Prime Minister had summed up the administration's con-
temptuous view of him when, a cigarillo between his lips, he asked a
group of journalists at the start of the campaign what they thought of
the Socialist chief and, before they could reply, supplied his own
answer: 'He's really very bad, isn't he?' No, the demon at Chirac's back
was the French people. He had won their highly conditional love in
1995, but now it was seeping away by the day. He had to regain it,
haunted by a terrible frustration at having been unable to capitalise on
winning the greatest prize of his life and by the fear of what might lie
down the road. For the ultimate macho performer of French politics,
this could only be a sign of failure foretold.

Now pause for a paragraph of what the French call *la psychologie de
concierge*. Throughout his career, as we have seen, Chirac has sought
guidance from others. Having won the supreme prize, he should have
been his own man. But he still felt the need for a bond, and he chose
Alain Juppé as the mast for his ship of state. The two men had worked
together for more than a decade at the Hôtel de Ville in Paris.
According to one account, they had another bond. Chirac's elder
daughter was prey to suicidal depression. Reports of her death swept
Paris from time to time: on one occasion, the Chiracs received thousands of condolence messages for a death which had not taken place.
Juppé's youngest daughter fell prey to the same illness, and Chirac
moved in to comfort and give advice. She survived in much better
shape than Chirac's daughter. That gave a depth to their relationship
which went beyond politics, and contained an echo of the way in
which Georges Pompidou had run a foundation in memory of De
Gaulle's Down's syndrome daughter. In a sense, the policies which
Chirac and Juppé were jointly defending could be seen as being irrel-
evant. This intensely fragile President had put faith in his Prime
Minister in a way that went beyond the usual relationship between the
Élysée and the Hôtel Matignon. In human terms, it was admirable.
Politically, it paved the way for ruin.

The worst duly came to pass. The Socialists mounted a campaign
which made some of their more thoughtful leaders blush in private –
a little, at least. Under the slogan 'Dare to return to the left', they
pledged to create hundreds of thousands of jobs without upsetting
public finances, to cut the working week to thirty-five hours without

any reduction in pay, to stop privatisations and to meet the requirements of the Communists, the Greens and any other allies they could
find. Lionel Jospin emerged as the man France had been looking for –
modest, determined, approachable and honest. Though an Énarque
himself, he struck a welcome contrast to the superior technocracy of
Juppé, De Villepin and their ilk.

As a power in the land under Mitterrand, Jospin had been as obnox-
iously full of himself as the average French minister, a man who had
undergone a charisma bypass somewhere along the path from his first
career as a diplomat to the heights of the Socialist Party. I recall meeting him once at a 'summer university' outside Bordeaux and being
taken aback by his condescension towards those he was introduced to.
When the Prime Minister of the time, Michel Rocard, suggested that
they might call one another '*tu*', Jospin was reported to have replied
that the head of the government should remember that he was speaking to *Monsieur le Ministre de l'Éducation Nationale*, and ought to address
him as such or by his even grander title of *Ministre d'État*. But a new
marriage, and his unexpectedly good showing in the presidential poll,
produced a definite change. His smarter colleagues complained that
Jospin still dressed badly; however, he made the effort of buying some
glad rags and a dinner suit from Armani – apparently he had a model
figure, because the only alterations that had to be made were to the
length of the trousers. He also learned how to smile. The nickname of
'Yo-Yo' given to him by a satirical television programme became
rather endearing. He bought new glasses and a car with a convertible
roof. Pictures of him smiling behind the wheel made Jospin look like
a man who had discovered pleasure in life somewhat late in the day.

Showing the requisite degree of steel, he sidelined the political
dinosaurs of the Mitterrand era and brought forward a new team,
including Jacques Delors' tough and able daughter whose job would be
to get to grips with unemployment. He kept the usual voluble
Socialists quiet and disciplined during the month-long campaign, calculating correctly that their best chance of success lay in creating as few
waves as possible and leaving their opponents to lose. Shedding their
downbeat image of the early 1990s, the Socialists held out the comfort
blanket of promises which the French wanted to hear, but they also
radiated an impression of managerial competence. In keeping with the
times, Jospin declared himself to be a man of ideas, not ideology. Even

if those ideas sometimes looked less than realistic, and the move to a 35-hour week by the dawn of the twenty-first century seemed distinctly ideological, they were sold by men and women in sharp suits who spoke the language of modernity. And, unlike their opponents, at least they had some dreams to sell.

However well the Socialists fought, this was an election waiting to be lost by men who appeared to have acquired a death-wish. A saying from the 1980s that France had the stupidest right wing in the world suddenly came back into vogue. Travelling through France during the campaign that spring, I was struck by how many of those who rejected Alain Juppé retained a degree of respect for his fortitude, and how even those who backed the left raised their eyebrows when the talk turned to its economic programme. What people couldn't fathom was why those in power had given the country the chance to reject them. That questioning became even more pointed when Juppé proclaimed that he would unveil his programme for the future within forty days of the poll if he won. Why not do it straight away without needing an election? There was only one answer: what the Gaullists had up their sleeve must be so dreadful that they did not dare to reveal it before the voters went to the polls. In such circumstances, the prospect of flopping down at an oasis with Lionel Jospin rather than undertaking another forced march across the desert behind the unrelenting Juppé was all too alluring. So, at the first round of voting on Sunday, 25 May, the orthodox right got its lowest score under the Fifth Republic, abstentions soared, the National Front scored another triumph, and only one minister won an outright majority.

It was the greatest political shock Alain Juppé had ever suffered, his first major defeat. What made the awakening even worse was that he had ignored the storm signals. Such was the blindness at the top that, as France voted, the chief of staff at the Hôtel Matignon had been working on the inauguration speech for the Prime Minister's second government. The normally imperturbable Juppé was reported to have been unable to string more than a couple of sentences together when he met right-wing leaders on the Sunday evening. Later, he drove to the Élysée and mentioned the possibility of resignation: Chirac brushed aside the suggestion with a gesture of his hand. The following morning, the climate changed. Jacques Pilhan, the President's adviser on public relations, and Chirac's daughter, Claude, insisted that Juppé had to go. The Prime Minister's champion at the palace, Dominique de Villepin, was powerless to protect his man. Within ninety minutes the decision was taken. Some of the Prime Minister's faithful technocrats burst into tears when they learned the news. On Monday night, Juppé went on television to announce that, whatever happened at the decisive second round six days later, he would step down. Not for the first time, Claude Chirac's judgement was a matter of debate: for two years, the Prime Minister had taken the flak, but now her father was alone in the front line. As the Tiger of the First World War, Georges Clemenceau, said of his chief of staff: 'I fart; he smells.' Now nobody could deflect the odour from the President.

The following Sunday, 1 June, the left duly won its majority. The Socialists doubled their representation in almost half the departments of France. Rejected in his constituency near Toulouse in 1993, Lionel Jospin was returned this time with 63 per cent of the vote. In Bordeaux, Juppé, who later acknowledged how mistaken he had been not to have called a legislative election in 1995, won his seat – but with just 54 per cent of the vote in a constituency held by his predecessor in 1993 with 75 per cent. Ministers hurriedly removed their files from their offices; Jospin became the new head of government; and France entered a new era in its politics with a humiliated Head of State who still had five years of his term to run. On the other side of the world, the Chinese Prime Minister might have reflected on the strange ways of Western democracy.

The Socialists had staged a stunning comeback, but the reality behind the voting was somewhat more complex than it appeared – thanks to the genie in the National Front bottle. If the mainstream right had been humiliated, the combined forces of the left still fell short of a majority of votes, with 48.2 per cent in the second round. Without the ballots for Le Pen's men and women, Jospin would have had a significantly less convincing majority in the new Assembly. Once more, the splits on the right had opened the door to the left. In the past, the division had been in the mainstream; now the wrecker came from the far bank.

It was not surprising that reports swiftly spread of Chirac sitting in his palace sunk in the kind of gloom that had enveloped him after his

1988 defeat by Mitterrand. *Le Canard Enchaîné* quoted a friend of the President as saying: 'He's doing what he always does when things go against him. He's eating a lot of *charcuterie*, drinking a lot of beer and watching a lot of television.' When the Head of State asked the former Finance Minister what his followers were saying about him, Alain Madelin was reported to have replied: 'They say that you always lead us to failure, Jacques. They believe you bring bad luck.' Sympathising with a defeated Gaullist, Chirac remarked: 'You have had a slap in the face. I know something about that: it's often happened to me.'

The President used the traditional television interview on Bastille Day to tick off the government on subjects ranging from immigration to the need not to tie down industry with 'obsolete and absurd regulations'. But the Socialists were making the running, and the national mood was hugely boosted by the World Cup victory of 1998 which was widely portrayed as the advent of a new and more inclusive France epitomised by the black-*blanc-beur* team and by Zidane's position as a national hero. While Mitterrand had brought Communists into his early government, Jospin went a step further to forge what was known as la *gauche plurielle*. The Socialists were in the driving seat, with main ministries as well as the Hôtel Matignon, but the Green party leader, Dominique Voynet, was appointed Environment Minister and the Communists took their old bailiwick of transport. Positioned on the edge of the Socialist group with his own party, the Citizens' Movement, the old warrior of the left, Jean-Pierre Chevènement, became Interior Minister and preached an increasingly tough line on law and order which did not always go down well with his more liberal-minded colleagues. Sceptics in the smaller parties saw this as a re-run of the old Mitterrandist tactic of inviting allies inside the fold in order to smother them, and to steal their votes at subsequent elections. But Jospin proclaimed the plural strategy as the big tent politics which would enable the left to complete its grip on power by taking the Élysée in 2002.

The tide was certainly running in its favour. The international boom flowing out of the United States sent French growth up above 3 per cent, as the economic restructuring of the 1990s enabled French companies to profit to the full. Unemployment fell at long last, dropping by a million over four years, helped by government schemes to create jobs. The Labour Minister, Martine Aubry, introduced a 35-hour working week, initially for big companies which found that they could negotiate more flexible shift patterns in the process. Welfare cover was extended. Jospin launched his effort to work out a solution for Corsica. The constitution was amended to cut the presidential term to five years. In future, elections for the Élysée and the National Assembly would take place within two months of one another, which Jospin hoped would enhance his chances of taking the top job and of the left getting a renewed parliamentary majority to avoid fresh *cohabitation*. So confident was he that he insisted on the contest for the Élysée being held first, to create an unstoppable electoral dynamic for the left.

Despite the election campaign slogans, privatisation continued at an even greater rate than before, though the Socialists preferred to talk about 'opening' the capital of state enterprises, rather than using the P word. French companies marched into the United States, Asia and the rest of Europe, and the talk rose of France outstripping Germany economically. In foreign affairs, the Socialist foreign minister, Hubert Védrine, struck the independent note that French diplomacy prizes, waving his finger at American 'hyperpower' while the Prime Minister and his more left-wing colleagues expressed their reservations towards globalisation. Though he did not show any great Euro-enthusiasm and relations with Germany lost their earlier warmth, Jospin kept to France's commitments under the Maastricht Treaty, and the budgetary deficit was steadily reduced. By 2001, the government was able to announce a programme of income tax cuts.

There were some personal hiccups along the way. Chevènement resigned in protest at the threat to the unity of the Republic represented by the agreement to grant Corsica limited autonomy. Jospin felt obliged to drop his close friend, the scientist Claude Allègre, from the education ministry when proposed reforms aroused mass protests from the teachers who make up one of the solidest Socialist voting groups – he was replaced by the Mitterrand-era shooting star, Jack Lang, who immediately made clear that he was going to be the teacher's pet. Legislation to make it harder for employers to sack workers was regarded as insufficiently tough, so Jospin had it strengthened – giving the impression that he might be a bit too keen on keeping the declining Communist Party happy, and further alienating company bosses who were already up in arms about rising charges and taxes, increased regulation epitomised by the 35-hour week, and a government which they saw as being motivated more by ideology than by a knowledge of how modern business works.

The Prime Minister ran into a spot of personal bother over revelations about his Trotskyite past – the main embarrassment being over how he had denied them for so long. More seriously, the impressive finance minister, Dominique Strauss-Kahn became embroiled in yet another outbreak of scandal allegations. In a strange coincidence, he decided to lower a tax demand on a leading couturier, Karl Lagerfeld, shortly after the designer's lawyer had passed him a video-cassette containing sleaze allegations against Chirac by a now-dead property developer. The minister shrugged that off, insisting he had never watched the recording. But he then found himself under investigation over his payment for work as a lawyer for a student insurance fund. On top of which, he was called in by the magistrates in the Elf affair to be questioned about the way his secretary's salary had allegedly been met by the oil company. At the end of 1999, Strauss-Kahn felt obliged to resign over the student fund issue, though he was subsequently cleared and returned to play a prominent role in the election campaigns of 2002. His successor at the finance ministry suffered Allègre's fate when he tried to reduce the number of civil servants, and he was replaced by another party heavyweight, the Mitterrand-era Prime Minister, Laurent Fabius, a man who was seen as a rival to Jospin, and who certainly did not regard his future as being behind him.

From the moment their *cohabitation* began in 1997, there was a clear target at the end of the road for both Chirac and Jospin – the presidential contest that would come five years later. In one sense, the regime fitted France pretty well. Chirac had been given his chance in 1995, and had blown it – elected on the promise to heal the 'social fracture', he had only made it worse. Although the government contained more than its quota of Énarques, it managed to present a more human face, from the smooth modernisers like Strauss-Kahn and Fabius to Martine Aubry as the standard bearer of the left. Despite conscious attempts to unbend, the Prime Minister could not be anything other than his schoolmasterish self, but he radiated honesty and reason compared to the scandal-tinged resident of the Élysée. He was said to have benefitted from the influence of his second wife, a philosopher who did her best to keep to herself until the advent of the 2002 election brought her into the magazine limelight. Plural as it was, the left maintained its shape whereas the right was riven by continued squabbles. With economic growth powering ahead, and the majority of the population apparently ready to forget about those who were not sharing in increasing wealth and happiness, it was little wonder that the Socialists began to show an arrogance born from an assumption of lasting success.

That could only be encouraged by the disarray on the right, exacerbated by rows over whether to accept National Front support in local government. A pro-European former education minister, François Bayrou, took charge of Giscard d'Estaing's old UDF party, making plain that he wanted to remain independent of Chirac. The free market champion, Alain Madelin, had his own group, and one of the regional barons who had treated with Le Pen, former defence minister Charles Millon, launched a new movement called simply La Droite ('The Right'), which he said would bring together everybody from 'nationalists to Europeans, centralists to regionalists, traditionalists to reformers'. The President's own party even came under the sway of the only man in France who would refuse to take Chirac's telephone calls.

A photograph taken in the Paris Hôtel de Ville on the evening of 7 May 1995, as the second-round results of the presidential election were awaited, shows the candidate, tieless and in shirtsleeves, looking anxiously up from his desk flanked by four men. The dominant figure is a heavy-set figure with pouched eyes and the air of a mournful bloodhound, leaning forward, his hands on the desk as he makes a point. Born in Tunisia into a family of teachers, the Gitane-smoking Philippe Séguin had been a key actor in Chirac's electoral strategy. His demeanour and quick temper, his high intelligence and fine sense of strategy, had long marked him as one of the more individualistic French politicians. He claimed to be a true bearer of the Gaullist faith, but was not the most loyal of Chirac's followers, having followed his own path several times, notably in leading the campaign against the Maastricht Treaty on monetary union. When in a bad mood, he refused to come to the telephone when Chirac called.

After the 1997 defeat, Séguin proclaimed that it was time for a 'knife fight' in the RPR, and emerged as the party's secretary-general, advocating leftist social policies and Euroscepticism. This was a disaster – the party got 12 per cent of the vote in the European election of 1999 compared to 22 per cent for the Socialists, and one point behind a new anti-Europe movement set up by the President's former crony, Charles Pasqua. Séguin resigned in mid-campaign, replaced temporarily by one of Chirac's adversaries from the 1995 presidential battle, and then by the RPR's first female secretary-general who won the job against the Head of State's own candidate. The President appeared in imminent danger of losing control over his own troops. 'The RPR is dead,' Pasqua declared. At the end of its sixth decade, Gaullism faced an existential choice – was it just a machine to get its leader to the Élysée or did it need a deeper ideological purpose if it was to survive and be meaningful to a majority of voters? For the man who had finally got to the very top in 1995 the first had to be the only way he could claw his way back – deep ideology could wait for another day.

In fact, the left's self confidence was not as justified as it appeared. The 1998 elections for regional councils had shown the abiding strength of the centre-right at local level. Though the left took 39.6 per cent of the vote to the centre-right's 35.6, the Socialists won only seven of the councils while their opponents took ten outright, and then acquired five more after the deals with the National Front described in Chapter 8. The European elections the following year had, indeed, been a disaster for the RPR but could be attributed, in part, to the party's internal troubles, Séguin's behaviour and the way in which voters tend to take such elections as the occasion for a protest vote.

The major test before the presidential and legislative battles of 2002 came in nationwide municipal elections in March 2001. The left grabbed the immediate headlines by winning control of Paris and Lyon. The conquest of the President's one-time citadel was particularly satisfying since the victor, the diligent Jospinist, Bernard Delanoë, headed a plural left coalition that stayed together while the right split asunder, with the orthodox Gaullists finally running Philippe Séguin against the scandal-tarred incumbent. As the openly gay Delanoë promised a thorough house-cleaning, the outcome in the capital could only be seen as a severe personal rebuff for the man in the Élysée. The capture of Lyon was helped by local division on the right, but was still another big feather in the Socialist cap.

When the results were looked at more closely, however, the left had less reason to celebrate. Of 583 towns and cities with more than 15,000 inhabitants, the right held 318, an increase of 40. Even the victory in

Paris was not all it seemed – the right actually won more votes in the capital but was deprived of a majority on the city council by running three competing slates and by the arrangement of the constituency system. In Lyon, too, the left won a minority of votes. Some of ministers failed embarrassingly to conquer provincial bastions, and Jack Lang lost his mayoral office in Blois.

At a municipal level, France had, clearly, not been swept by enthusiasm for the plural majority, and, in several key races, had preferred new and younger faces from the right. At the same time, what the *Financial Times* dubbed 'the virtuous circle of business confidence, investment and job creation' started to evaporate. The government declined to rewrite the budget to take account of the downturn after the 11 September attack in a mood that reminded some of the confident prediction that the nuclear cloud from Chernobyl would not enter French air space, as if the Hexagon could insulate itself from the world. Sticking to a growth forecast of 2.25 per cent though analysts put the likely figure at just under 2 per cent, Fabius sought to boost demand by handing out credits to 8 million low income households and promising tax cuts, and showed how far the anti-privatisation rhetoric of 1997 had been forgotten by arranging to sell off part of a motorway network in the south.

Most worryingly for the left was the lack of enthusiasm it was able to arouse despite its voter-pleasing measures. Jospin simply could not pull ahead of Chirac in the polls. Increasingly, he showed his frustration. To his mind, his accession to the Élysée was the natural continuation of the process he had launched when he revived the Socialist Party after the Mitterrand era had finally ended. In a television interview, he remarked that the French people 'do not always have the sense of perspective and of time'. That was quite true, but it was something with which he had to deal if he wanted to become President. He needed to hit a resounding public chord, to make big speeches, and to explain why he would be good for France, and a second Chirac presidency would be bad. He was, personally, so convinced that he held the keys to the future that he spoke of the dangers of a new period of *cohabitation*, even allowing his chief of staff to publish a book on how awful it had been to work with Chirac. Though everybody knew he was going to run, he held back the formal announcement of his candidacy as long as possible, believing that he would be best served by a short, sharp campaign in which he could charge out from behind the battlement of the Hôtel Matignon to rout the old warrior on the other side of the Seine. When the time came, instead of launching himself into the fight with a rousing speech, Jospin sent a terse fax to the French news agency.

His whole approach grated. It seemed as if the Prime Minister was pre-empting the verdict of the voters, as though he regarded his election to the presidency as a bureaucratic formality, and the campaign as a unwelcome process that had to be gone through. At the same time, his position as Prime Minister meant he was immersed in the recurrent challenges and details of day-to-day government. This opened him up to attack from all sides while preventing him from elaborating a new strategy. Instead of resigning to free himself for his presidential run, he clung on to office as if afraid to give up his old power base in search of a new one. As the economic downturn brought factory closures, he became identified as an administrator removed from the common people who would not make the concessions needed to ensure his own election – an honest man, certainly, but one who could all too easily come to be seen as a loser in the making.

Despite his rebuff in 1997, that was not an image which clung to Jacques Chirac any more as the 2002 deadline approached. He had precious little to show for his seven-year presidency; he was surrounded by allegations of scandal; he was 69, and had a political history that began before under-40 voters were born. Nor did he come up with any striking vision for the future, falling back on two tried and tested campaign themes of law and order and tax cuts much bigger than anything Fabius proposed. But, for all his difficulties, the President held up well in the polls – even when he and Jospin ran neck-and-neck, a majority predicted that he would be re-elected. Winning a second term would, however, mean putting the right's house in order, and Chirac got down to that task as soon as the municipal elections showed the breadth of support on which he might call.

After nearly a year's work on that front, he was ready to announce his candidacy. He kept his cards close to his chest – only a few close advisers were told before he made the speech on a trip to Avignon on the new high-speed train link to the south. From the start, there was to be no doubt that he would run the campaign as he wanted. But the President needed a broad church movement of the right to make sure that there was no repeat of the 1995 rivalry between him and Edouard Balladur. The last time around, he had run against the Gaullist party establishment. This time, he would use it as the base for the big centre-right movement France had always lacked. The centrist, François Bayrou, and the free marketeer, Alain Madelin, remained outside the tent, knowing that if they were absorbed by Chirac, their parties would lose their identity. But some members of their groups went over to the President, bringing provincial power bases with them. The Balladurians of 1995 signed up en masse, including the aggressive and ultra-ambitious Mayor of the smart Paris suburb of Neuilly, Nicolas Sarkozy, whom Chirac's wife was said to have sworn never to allow in the house. Alain Juppé returned to centre-stage as the mastermind of the embryonic presidential majority party – and was already spoken of as a successor in the Élysée in 2007. Despite belonging to Madelin's party, Jean-Pierre Raffarin, President of the Poitou-Charente region in the west, emerged as a likely Prime Minsiter after joining Chirac's movement.

Although there had been talk after the 1997 election of the presidency retreating to its ceremonial role of the Fourth Republic as far as domestic affairs were concerned, Chirac was in a better position for his great comeback than his detractors realised. He could watch and wait, and time his interventions for maximum effect, as in a stinging attack on the government in his Bastille Day interview in 2001. Jospin and the Socialists faced an awkward puzzle in attacking Chirac without appearing to demean the presidency – the party leadership distanced itself from a Socialist member of the National Assembly who pressed for a change in the law to enable an incumbent president to be prosecuted. When the Prime Minister made disobliging remarks to journalists about his opponent being old and worn out, public reaction was that he had delivered an unseemly blow below the belt, particularly as the 69-year-old Head of State seemed as active as ever, even if he appeared to have put on some weight. Jospin, after all, was hardly a spring chicken at 64, with two decades at the head of the Socialist Party behind him.

The need to stay above the fray for much of the time before the campaign actually began was, admittedly, not behaviour that came naturally to the hyper-active Chirac, but could always use ceremonial occasions and provincial trips to press the flesh. Visitors reported that he was more relaxed than he had ever been – he even went to the theatre for the first time for two years, and had sumo wrestling videos flown in from Japan to keep up with his favourite sport. His standing in the opinion polls rose steadily, particularly when he asserted France's independence from Washington by leading allied opposition to the bombing of Iraq. He saw that the decision to hold the presidential election before the National Assembly was chosen gave him a chance of seizing the initiative. He played on his status anad even had a museum in his name opened in the village of Sarran where he has his country château in the Corrèze. A wood, glass and brick building was put up by the village pond to house the 2,500 gifts Chirac has received in seven years as Head of State – cowboy boots from Bill Clinton, enough fine porcelain for several banquets, a Chinese gong from 1200 BC, an African fly whisk and a gold falcon from Saudi Arabia embedded with rubies, emeralds and sapphires.

In contrast, Jospin and his ministers were on the battlements every day, framing legislation, handling demonstrations by angry lorry drivers or farmers, assuaging laid-off workers and dealing with the sinking of oil tankers or disasters in the tunnel through Mont Blanc. For all their activity, there was a growing tendency to take the better times France had enjoyed under their rule for granted. As Dominique Strauss-Kahn said on the night of the parliamentary defeat in June 2002, he had been surprised during the campaign by the number of people who asked him what the government had done. Take, for instance, the 35-hour week. When introduced, it had been widely welcomed by workers as a benefit. By 2002, it was seen increasingly as a piece of regulation which did not take account of the way ordinary people wanted to live and work. Giving employees extra time off might seem an unalloyed benefit to Martine Aubry and her lieutenants, but the accompanying effects on pay were less welcome to workers who would have preferred to put in more time to earn more. The benefits were felt most by the better-off, many of whom would vote for the centre-right in any case. The extension of the system to small firms threatened to boost their costs in a serious way while public sector unions made it plain that they would press for more staff when it hit the civil service, the health service and education. Shops and restaurants closed for an extra day to meet the requirements of the legislation, reducing their takings and annoying customers instead of boosting employment.

Chirac's genius for grabbing the limelight, whether at France's sporting victories or at disaster scenes, wrong-footed the more plodding Prime Minister. In more relaxed surroundings, he took *mon ami Bill* and Hillary Clinton to the highly traditional, and enormously expensive, Paris restaurant, l'Ami Louis, where they munched through smoked ham and goose liver, roast baby lamb, potatoes and wild mushrooms, followed by red fruits, all helped down by a white Graves and a Saint Julien claret. He asserted national sovereignty by insisting on a veto power over air attacks on Kosovo in which French planes were involved. The French politician who flew across the Atlantic to be George W. Bush's first foreign visitor after the 11 September attack was, naturally, Jacques Chirac.

So, by the early spring of 2002, five years of the plural left had introduced considerable changes in France, but had not altered the political topography of the country as Jospin had expected. Unable to rally the broad left behind him, the Prime Minister became the impotent victim of the fragementation of those who preferred to vote at the first round for the myriad minor candidates. He looked increasingly remote, and Chirac increasingly confident, both of them underestimating the way the third man would upset the second round scenario they had established between themselves five years earlier. Personal factors aside, Jospin's great error had been to perpetuate the left-wing strategy invented in the 1970s by François Mitterrand of an alliance centred round the Socialist Party. That had provided the votes in 1997, but had then held the main grouping of the left from forging a new character of its own, without having to worry about what the Communists or the Greens or Jean-Pierre Chevènement thought. The Prime Minister had not had the vision to adapt his party, and had only been able to offer extensions of the old medicine to a country which wanted something fresh. By the time France voted on 21 April , he had come to appear as an old-fashioned figure, part of the establishment France increasingly rejected. The irony was that the man who beat him was even more a figure from the past, promising 'action' after seven years of inaction. In that sense, at least, the elections of 2002 admirably served their purpose of reflecting the nation – a desire for change, but a reluctance to give up on the past; a readiness to walk along the brink without knowing which side to come down on.

15

ON THE BRINK

There is, of course, another way of looking at France. The lure of the country remains as strong as ever. Foreign holidaymakers flock to the Côte d'Azur, the Loire Valley, Paris and the long western coast. The British colonise the Dordogne and Provence, not to mention the Channel Tunnel hinterland of the Pas de Calais, and can now take a direct train to Avignon. Rock stars and Asian tycoons buy Riviera homes. A village in the Drôme has become a corner of Belgium, and reports of prehistoric beings emerging at the foot of the gorges of the Ardèche turned out to be Dutch nudists cavorting in the river. The success of Peter Mayle's books shows the pull of southern country life, and where did the last governor of Hong Kong go to write his Asian memoirs but in a village by the Gorges de l'Aveyron? So where's the worry? *Tout va très bien*, and a tribe of official spokespeople will always tell you how the nation has pulled itself out of its difficulties and is set to lead Europe. To ask too many questions may be seen as an annoying Anglo-Saxon attempt to shoot holes in the glorious Gallic balloon. When I mentioned the uncertainties of the 35-hour working week during a dinner one night at the turn of the century, an official told me curtly that I should look on the bright side and not deliver below-the-belt blows. A later reference to the roller coaster of the 2002 elections brought a weary look from a French diplomat who insisted that such things did not matter any more since France's future was in the hands of Brussels and multinational companies – though this was surely not a sentiment with which the re-elected President would have agreed.

That is in keeping with the rosy side of France, which may have been too obscured in the previous chapters. Whatever its travails, the Hexagon always has a rosy side, and one would be a fool not to make the most of it. Moving away from the famous attractions, take a trip to the big heart of the country from which only the most committed Francophobe could remain immune. The high-speed train from the Gare Montparnasse whisks us to a station outside Tours on the Loire. There is champagne before a family dinner in a sixteenth-century château overlooking a small lake where dozens of fish have just been caught. The last bottles of 1982 Lynch-Bages claret from the cellar in the limestone cliffs are brought across the courtyard in a plastic milk-bottle carrier by the château-owner, to accompany jellied chicken, roast lamb and goat's cheese. Strangely, he serves his wine in small tumblers, like shot glasses, rather than the usual expansive *verres à vin*. As we eat, he recalls how, as a teenager in the Resistance, he had helped in the first assassination of a Gestapo officer and rose to command a unit alongside André Malraux in 1944. He had helped people escape across the demarcation line not far from where we sat, and still keeps his *nom de guerre*. Many years later, having turned down offers of a political or journalistic career and established himself as a successful businessman, he took clients shooting in the Loire Valley and saw this small château. He asked about buying it, but was told that the path of a planned motorway would go through its grounds. The owner wanted to sell, but who in their right mind would buy? From time to time he talked about the place to friends from wartime days. One day, one of them, an official in a position to know, telephoned to say that the motorway had been moved. Our host drove round that afternoon, and bought the château in cash for a knock-down price. Corruption? Or a reward for risks taken so long ago? A dyed-in-the-wool capitalist, he is a close friend of a Communist Resistance leader who lives down the valley.

Then comes an easy drive through the verdant hills of Indre-et-Loire and the Haute-Vienne to a country hotel in a converted mill, with ducks on the pond, a gentle path through the woods and two excellent meals from the wellsprings of French gastronomy. After that, a touch of grim history at the martyr town of Ouradour-sur-Glane, where the retreating Reich Division massacred 642 inhabitants, including 500 women and children, in 1944. And then, in a more sunny mood, a visit to the beautiful red sandstone village of Collonges-la-Rouge before driving gently down the highland roads to the town of Figeac, home of the great Egyptologist, Champollion. Finally, the journey ends at a small village where the hardy Auvergne meets the softer Rouergue for five days of French country life, walking, eating, drinking, trying to soak up some of that old-time country wisdom, and marathon sessions of the archetypal French card game of *belote*. Pigs roam free by the woods; mushrooms sprout beneath the trees; the calves have never had a mad mother. We wake one morning to the rich smell of *foie gras* cooking below our bedroom, and our host presents us with a huge terrine to be consumed at a single lunch. In contrast to the château in Touraine, the wine from the cellar below us is poured into glasses large enough to take a whole bottle. In the nearby small town of Maurs-la-Jolie, market day brings out more than two hundred stalls. Two elderly couples – one man with a beret, the other with an old straw hat, one stout woman in a floral dress, the other wearing her apron – sit outside a café sipping *pastis* and soft drinks as if posing for a postcard. An elderly woman sells punnets of wild mushrooms. A grizzled farmer weighs his vegetables on a hand-held scale. A young woman stands behind a table covered with jars of snail pâté. The smell of melons is in the air. The only thing missing is the tourists.

At the start of the trip back to England, the shrine of Rocamadour is as beautifully impressive as ever on its cliff-face; nearby a fairy-tale château rises above our hotel and the *carpaccio de canard aux truffes* served in a gravelled courtyard by a river could not be bettered. The train to the north from Brive-la-Gaillarde is on time at both ends. In Paris, under the summer sun, the Natural History museum in the Jardin des Plantes is a wonder to visit. Friends and relations are fit and happy on their return from holidays in Brittany. There is even some good news in the air: the Health Ministry reports that new Aids cases and deaths have dropped by more than half in a year. A French pair reach the final of the world ping-pong championship. Wine exports are booming. For the umpteenth time, politicians say that they can even see a decline in unemployment not too far around the corner.

At the Café Croissant behind the Bourse, where the Socialist hero Jean Jaurès was assassinated in 1914, the Père Duval *andouillette* tripe sausage is, as they say, grilled to perfection. Badoit mineral water is served in its proper light-green glass bottle instead of the more usual plastic. The political gossip over lunch is as lively as ever, and there is yet another project to start the newspaper France really needs. Then comes a lingering walk through the Marché Saint-Honoré, where the revolutionary Jacobins of 1790 planned the modernist centralisation of the nation in the library of a convent. Down the street, past the Rubis bar with its tasty Loire wines, stands the dimly-lit church of Notre-Dame-de-l'Assomption, which was given to the Polish community of Paris in 1850 and to which we used to take aid bundles to be sent to Solidarity in Poland. Three people worship in the gloom inside, and a pigeon flies in and out with me. Along the Rue Saint-Honoré lie the fashion shops of Christian Lacroix, Guerlain, Grès before one reaches the Rue Royale. Maxim's, the epitome of outmoded style, lies to the left, just before the Place de la Concorde where Louis XVI and Marie-Antoinette, Robespierre and Danton lost their heads. In the other direction is the neo-classical pillared temple of the Madeleine and the ornate *boiseries* and 230-euro meals of Lucas-Carton. An old-fashioned glazier in blue overalls crosses the road with the glass slotted into a wooden frame on his back. The cars hoot, but he moves at his own pace.

The street becomes the Faubourg Saint-Honoré, and, clustered all along it stand the shops of the great fashion names – Hermès, Lanvin, Dior to start with, and then Givenchy, Guy Laroche, Yves Saint-Laurent, Cartier, Gianfranco Ferré, Versace, and Valentino. The chauffeurs waiting outside the smart Cercle Interallié club have parked their cars on the pavement while their employers exchange polite conversation over drinks in the garden at the back. Diplomacy puts in an appearance with the Japanese and British embassies behind the walls of their ancien régime palaces – the latter the scene of a garden party on the royal birthday for which invitations are among the hottest tickets in town. A little further on, you can peer through the high metal gates into the gravel courtyard of the Élysée Palace, perhaps glimpsing a presidential visitor coming out through the glass doors at the top of the steps or officials hurrying about their business. Across the narrow street, you look up at the whitewashed buildings and wonder if there is a Jackal-check on their occupants.

Just up the road, across the Place Beauvau with its Pierre Cardin outlet on the corner, sits another formidable centre of French politics, the Interior Ministry, housed behind its own impressive set of gates in a fine old aristocratic town-house. This is where the police get their orders, elections are organised and the inter-ministerial telephone system is centralised. The walk ends a hundred yards further on, at perhaps the most soberly stylish of Parisian hotels, the Bristol, where some bathrooms are as big as the bedrooms, where a Rothschild strangled himself, and where a German Defence Minister left a sheaf of secret Nato papers in the bar after a long night of drinking.

There are a hundred other excursions through Paris, each with its own character. The capital's compact size and variety make it a great place for urban walking. To take any one part of the city is to taste only part of its essence, just as to take Paris as representative of the nation is to miss most of what makes France the country it is. Personally, as you may have guessed, I prefer to flee high fashion – *dîner au champagne* is not my cup of tea, as it were. I'd rather wander through the market in Maurs-la-Jolie, drink a *pastis* in Calvinet or eat *truffade* in the kitchen. But, when it comes to visible signs of style on the street, a stroll down this stretch of the middle of Paris gives more than a clue to why, for all its present vicissitudes, France still has a special face to show the world.

So, is everything really all right, Madame la Marquise? Has France just become a national incarnation of Molière's *Malade Imaginaire* which was actually much better off than it thought? When he first reached the Élysée in 1995, Jacques Chirac had no doubt about the depths of the sickness. France, he said, was suffering from 'an illness that goes deeper than the political class, economic leaders, fashionable intellectuals or the media stars realise. The people have lost confidence. Their feeling of helplessness inclines them towards resignation; it also risks arousing their anger.'

As that anger was vented, first at his own government in 1997 and then at the whole political establishment on 21 April 2002, the President acknowledged that 'as the years pass, indifference, resignation and fatalism have advanced at the same time as radical protest and extremism'. He traced the roots to disappointment at what governments had actually achieved, to a failure by the state to exercise its powers and to a growing feeling of public powerlessnesss. The end of *cohabitation* had, he went on, proved the strength of the institutions of the Fifth Republic, though this begged the question of why the power-sharing had come about in the first place. The true answer to the country's problems, Chirac declared, lay in decentralisation to the regions – it was no accident that the man he had chosen as Prime Minister had made his mark as a provincial political baron in the western Poitou-Charente area. Centralisation had been necessary as France was forged as a nation, but had now become a handicap.

On a less elevated level, he proposed the strengthening of the police, the establishment of local courts to deal quickly with minor offences, detention centres for young repeat offenders while they awaited trial, and special squads to cope with gangs on housing estates and lawless inner city areas. The 35-hour week was to be made more flexible, taxes and social security contributions cut, and measures introduced to help young people to find jobs. A million new companies were to bloom with state help. The Prime Minister promised to listen to those 'down below', and insisted that he would not govern in the interests merely of the right.

So far, so good. The danger was that, as so often before, the promises and rhetoric would run out of stream when they came up against the entrenched nature of a deeply cynical population that considered the united front against the National Front on 5 June to have been the limit of its duty. The ability of politicians to bring about fundamental change was restricted by the nature of the system, by the alienation of voters and by the desire of those who had held privileges to retain them, regardless of the claims of those 'down below'. The soaring abstention rate had shown dramatically the extent to which voters no longer put their faith in politicians. As the Gaullist, Philippe Séguin, once remarked, the French 'find, facing them, men and women elected from the right, the left, the centre who are like little green birds that have less and less grip on things. Politics cannot improve people's lives. Our democratic system is operating in a complete void.' Or, in the words of the man set to inhabit the Élysée for twelve years: 'The gap is widening dangerously between the man in the street and a political class which offers the French people the spectacle of an interminable costume ball at which the waltzers parade in front of the cameras before going off to foment their little plots.'

In 1995, Jacques Chirac had been well aware of the state of the nation. His diagnostic spoke of a country in which 'more than half the population is neither listened to nor defended . . . the poor get poorer, those on low salaries stagnate. Shopkeepers, artisans, professionals, small business people face growing problems. More and more households have trouble meeting the rent or repaying loans; more and more small firms, with little or no support from the banks, are forced to declare themselves bankrupt or to cut staff. In some rundown suburbs of big cities, whole districts are outside the law . . . too many of the French feel that they are not understood, and are looked down upon. They, too, are afraid. Fear of unemployment which a return of growth will not be enough to conquer. Fear of losing their social benefits, their retirement rights, the possibility of giving their children a better future. Fear of feeling like orphans in a world without moral standards, and fear of being passive spectators of the decline of France.'

As he also noted, the leaders of France too often operated on the basis of statistics, not real life. Thus, the Socialists had been able to comfort themselves by noting that the crime rate in France was not the highest in Europe – and ignore the fact that this meant nothing to a mother worried about the safety of her daughter walking home at night or the irritation of somebody who had just had a mobile telephone snatched in the street. Jospin's discomfort when faced with real people expressing their real concerns was palpable; they did not fit into the scenarios elaborated in his campaign workshop where the jockeying between factions in the Socialist Party took priority. The major party of the left had become, above all, the representative of public service employees who were increasingly middle-class and removed from those in need of help – at one point, the former Prime Minister, Pierre Mauroy, caused something akin to a shock at an electoral strategy meeting when he remarked at the way in which the word 'worker' was absent from the party's language.

For all Chirac's stirring rhetoric of 1995 and measures like the 35-hour week, the social fracture persisted, and the establishment did not know what to do about it. Take a trip back to Les Tartarets, the housing estate on the hill of Corbeil-Essonne described in Chapter 7. When I went there in 1998 it was run-down, but the local mayor and National Assembly deputy, a good friend of Chirac, promised improvement. When I returned for a new edition of this book, it was worse. The place stood as a symbol of that part of France which the elite had abandoned to its fate. A signboard had been set up on the road leading to the estate to list shops at the new commercial centre.

More than half the slots on it were empty. Sons of Arab and African immigrants sat listlessly on the pavements. A group of drug dealers huddled in a doorway. The commercial centre had one functioning outlet – a chemist's. Otherwise, the shops had been abandoned, and were either boarded up or burned and filled with litter, stinking of urine. Even the pharmacy had a broken window, and a sign that its opening hours were being reduced 'due to the departure of a member of staff and the 35 hours'. The graffiti still spelled out death to the police, and to gangs from other estates. The minutes of a meeting between parents and teachers at the school down the hill were mainly about playground violence. Election posters for the mayor and his Socialist opponent were covered with sprayed-on slogans and geometric designs. A vivid wall painting showed two black/brown youths with two Rottweilers snarling beside them. Another depicted the inhabitants of the 'Tarte Zoo' with wording declaring 'Go towards your life' and 'If man can make life hell, he can also make it a paradise.' The bus driver at the station looked incredulous when I said I wanted to go to Les Tartarets. On the train from Paris, three policemen stood with their *flashball* pellet-firing pistols. They were happy to show them to me. When I asked when they thought they might use them, they said they had no idea – but they hoped that the publicity given to their new arms would deter trouble-makers. Maybe, but the troubles up the hill seemed unlikely to be cured by rubber bullets. Nine years on from Chirac's warnings of 1995, large parts of France remained as disconnected from the nation's idea of itself as they had ever been.

France and its people will not change their nature. Why on earth should they do so? They will remain both charming and superior, patriotic and cynical, grandiose and petty, witty and yet strangely lacking in a sense of humour. Still, the shift in the reality within which they live is undeniable. They are not an introspective people like the Germans, nor are they given to Slav melancholia or to the insularity of the British. But, like their fictional national templates from the musketeers onwards, they are self-regarding. How they see themselves is important, and what they have glimpsed in the national mirror has given them pause for thought.

When the first edition of this book was published in 1998, there appeared some room for cautious hope that, after decades of confrontational politics, cohabitation between right and left after the previous year's election could offer the opportunity for a cooperative attempt to grapple with France's problems – though any such hope had to be tempered by the depths of division in the political system. Indeed, those old cleavages and rivalries prevailed, particularly as Jacques Chirac and Lionel Jospin moved towards the presidential contest of 2002. The overwhelming victory of the centre-right giving it control of the National Assembly as well as the Élysée Palace opened the door for a process of structural reform by an administration that should have been able to shoulder the unpopularity that such changes inevitably bring. But Chirac and Raffarin proved timid reformers, the President influenced by his awareness of how thin his level support had been in the first round of voting and the memory of how abrupt change had brought the defeat for his followers in 1997.

Two years after his freak landslide, the electorate made plain that it rejected even the prudent programme followed by the President and his Prime Minister as it swung against the administration and cast a massive vote in regional elections for the left it had thrown out in 2002. As a result, the country found itself in a paradoxical situation. Despite the big vote against it across the country, the right still held the presidency and parliament. Despite the big vote for it and its control of all but two of France's regions, the left had no way of translating that popular discontent into national policy.

This raises one immediate question. Having repeatedly switched from right to left and back again over the past two decades, do the French know what they want? Has the country become gripped by rejectionism, turning against governments as a matter of course rather than allowing them to pursue programmes that need a long time frame to implement? The results of elections since 1981, together with the regular upsurges of street protests, certainly point to a yo-yo pattern in which whoever is up today can expect to be down tomorrow. It is not even as if policies matter much any more – the left's triumph in the 2004 election was not on the basis of any new platform: merely giving those in office a good kicking appears to be enough in itself.

This is not simply a matter of fickle behaviour by the French. It also reflects repeated failure by the political class to offer solutions and policies that carry conviction. Too often over the two decades, politicians have not delivered or, even more striking, have done the opposite of what they promised.

In 1983, only two years after being elected on a sweeping left-wing programme, François Mitterrand changed gear and began to apply an austerity programme that backtracked on all the heady pledges that had taken him to the Élysée. In 1995, Jacques Chirac proclaimed his determination to heal the 'social fracture' and then appointed Alain Juppé to implement measures that appeared to the French to go in the opposite direction. Lionel Jospin brought in the 35-hour week and job-creation schemes, but, having campaigned on an anti-privatisation platform, his government presided over the biggest sell-off of public assets France had ever seen. In 2002, Jean-Pierre Raffarin pledged that his government would show a caring face and would be closer to the people while appointing expert non-politicians to the Finance, Health and Education ministries. That was soon undermined by the rise in unemployment, the way that ministers went on issuing decrees without consultation, and the lack of concern dramatically demonstrated by the failure to act to save the lives of the 15,000 old people who died in the summer heat wave of 2003.

Not that failure to live up to electoral pledges, defeat or scandal is a cause for sanction within the political class. French politicians, even more than those elsewhere, cling on to their positions, in or out of office – the extreme example being Valéry Giscard d'Estaing who, having lost the presidency in 1981, was still crafting the European Union constitution 22 years later and ran (unsuccessfully) at the head of the centre-right list in his native Auvergne region in 2004.

The line-up on the main television programme on the night of the second round of voting in March, 2004, was symbolic. The chief spokesman for the Socialists was Laurent Fabius who had gone down to defeat 18 years earlier after two years as Mitterrand's second prime minister. For the Chirac side, the cameras focussed on Alain Juppé, who had been rejected by voters in 1997 and who had just been found guilty of political corruption. While acknowledging that voters had registered a strong negative vote, Chirac re-appointed Raffarin, dropped the ministers who had been brought in from outside the political world and shifted the remaining cast as if rejection at the polls carried no price for them.

France, as I have sought to show in this book, is a complex nation, perhaps uniquely so. Its self confident, revolutionary heritage, buttressed by the Republican state tradition and its brilliant Gaullist ability to punch above its weight, leads it to see itself as a prime force for enlightenment, and, thus, for modernity. Its Foreign Minister explains its policy over the war in Iraq in terms of France evolving a new concept of 'soft power' which offers an answer to the problems of the 21st century world. At the same time, however, it is a deeply conservative nation, often in the best sense of the term. Its regions, its people, its culture retain an identity which has enormous value. It values its republican traditions as a guide to modern life. But the outcome is also what the sociologist, Alain Touraine, terms a corporatists resistance to change, in which high rhetoric about solidarity becomes a mask for selfish defence of privileges, in which the state retains an unhealthy weight and in which those who do not fit the mould are left by the wayside.

The need is for France to be guided by its leaders into paths that bring the varied strains in national life together. Too often, however, instead of seeking ways of binding the nation together, the self-centred political class, abetted by the civil service elite, has concentrated on its own games. The result has been a broad and deep alienation of the people from orthodox politics which poses a real threat that France could become, in reality if not in theory, ungovernable.

This raises fundamental issues for the future of a country which has always assumed that its republican inheritance means that it does not have to go in for national soul-searching and that the 'French model' sets it apart from the troubles of other nations. The Fifth Republic founded by Charles de Gaulle in 1958 has been, as described by the historian, François Furet, an artful combination of the quasi-monarchical authority of the *Ancien Régime* with the recognition of the freedoms and unity of the Revolution under the umbrella of the state. Now the danger is that the state has become too powerful for the modern world, constricting the development of the nation as it labours under what the commentator, Alain Duhamel, castigates as 'the culture of power'. Talk of a more flexible Sixth Republic surfaces from time to time, but nobody has much idea of how it might be constituted. Meanwhile, warns Duhamel, 'democracy, the political balance and even the nation's personality are at risk'. Equally alarming, he adds, France's 'exceptional nature' may turn out to be a handicap not a trump card.

'When people ask the reason for my journey, I usually reply that I know what I'm getting away from, but not what I am looking for,' wrote the sixteenth-century sage, Michel de Montaigne. The same might be said of many of the French today, and of their leaders. Too often, progress is seen in terms of sudden, sharp steps – a dramatic anti-crime policy or the leaking of plans for a Franco-German union – which either peter out or contain less substance than style. The long haul is not something French leaders much relish as is shown by the permanence of high unemployment and the failure to integrate the immigrants of the last three decades. As a result, a country which has always set great store by its unity risks becoming two nations – on the one hand, the comfortable urban elite; on the other those who have been left on one side of modernity and see no way of getting back on board.

Such a threat deserves the sustained attention of those chosen to lead France. Yet, all too easily, those in power – political, economic and social – become insulated from those they rule, 21st century equivalents of monarchs in their palaces. If this applies to rulers in other countries to varying degrees, the hermetic and self-perpetuating nature of the French elite makes it particularly prone to live in a world of its own, removed from the surrounding reality. When Jacques Chirac was spotted wearing a hearing aid in 2003, there were jokes about whether he would turn it on to listen to the concerns of his fellow citizens. But, for all their intelligence and savoir-faire, too many of the men and women running France have tin ears, and lack continuing concern for what matters to the nation as a whole. In good times, that may not matter too much. But, when the economy is sluggish, alienation sets in and fear of the future stalks the land, the danger rises of a breakdown of the system by which France operates.

But, if the mirror in which France looks at itself is cracked, it can be repaired if the will is there. There has to be both a recognition of how the world has changed, in everything from economic flows to the effects of 11 September and its aftermath. The future of France in Europe needs to be viewed in a broad, lucid context, not as a matter of defending entrenched national privileges. The state and the politicians have to free themselves from the grasp of lobbies, and to be ready to face down sectorial interests in the name of the people as a whole. Dialogue has to triumph over confrontation as Jacques Chirac remarked somewhat wistfully after his government's electoral drubbing in 2004. Public morality has to triumph over corruption, requiring higher standards from those in power and restoring the notion of fraternity to the land of the Revolution. *L'État* has to relax its grip and become, in an expression of the economist Alain Minc, 'less of a shield and more of a sword of justice', a less dominating and more liberating force in French society. The political class has to take on a new life; business leaders have to move beyond cost-cutting and personal aggrandisement; mainstream politicians have to find the way to bring extremism to its knees by showing that they listen to the electorate instead of talking down to it. The fabric of life has to be reconstituted, and the lessons of recent elections absorbed as the elite grows less domineering and society becomes more truly egalitarian.

Above all, France has to become more open internally, seeing the unexpected events of the early years of the new century as a chance to move forward, rather than dwelling on the outburst of extremism and the spectre of Le Pen. For, despite the uncertainties crowding in on it, this nation does remain special, and special places need to be able to rise to special heights to remain exceptional. It is time for a fresh revolution following a non-violent but sharply determined path which embraces the modern world while preserving the best of the past. Otherwise, the beacon from this lighthouse nation will grow dim as France implodes on the problems it cannot bring itself to face – and Europe and the world will be poorer places as a result.

BIBLIOGRAPHY

Alexandre, Philippe, *L'Élysée en péril* (Paris: Fayard, 1969)

——, *Le Duel De Gaulle–Pompidou* (Paris: Grasset, 1970)

Alexandre, Philippe, with Priouret, Roger, *Marianne et le pot au lait* (Paris: Grasset, 1983)

——, *Paysages de campagne* (Paris: Grasset, 1988)

Ardagh, John, *The New France* (London: Penguin, 1977 and later editions)

Attali, Jacques, *Verbatim* (Paris: Fayard, two volumes, 1993–96)

Bacqué, Raphaëlle, and Saverot, Denis, *Seul comme Chirac* (Paris: Grasset, 1997)

Baverez, Nicolas, *La France Qui Tombe* (Paris: Perrin, 2003)

Benamou, Georges, *Le Dernier Mitterrand* (Paris: Plon, 1997)

Booth, Martin, *Opium* (London: Simon & Schuster, 1996)

Bredin, Jean-Denis, *L'Affaire* (Paris: Julliard, 1983)

Brigouleix, Bernard, *Histoire indiscrète des années Balladur* (Paris: Albin Michel, 1995)

Brogan, Denis, *The Development of Modern France* (London: Hamish Hamilton, 1940)

Chirac, Jacques, *La France pour tous* (Paris: Nil, 1994)

Colombani, Jean-Marie, *La France sans Mitterrand* (Paris: Flammarion, 1992)

——, *Le Résident de la République* (Paris: Stock, 1998)

Dallas, Gregor, *At the Heart of a Tiger* (London: Macmillan, 1993)

de Gaulle, Charles, *Le Fil de l'épée* (Paris: Berger-Levrault, 1932)

——, *Mémoires d'espoir* (Paris: Plon, two volumes, 1970–71)

Domenach, Nicolas, and Szafran, Maurice, *Le Roman d'un Président* (Paris: Plon, 1997)

Dubief, Henri, *Le Déclin de la IIIe République* (Paris: Seuil, 1976)

Duhamel, Alain, *La République giscardienne* (Paris: Gallimard, 1980)

——, *La République de Monsieur Mitterrand* (Paris: Gallimard, 1982)

——, *Le Complexe d'Astérix* (Paris: Gallimard, 1985)

L'État de la France (Paris: La Découverte, 1992)

Ferniot, Jean, *De Gaulle et le 13 mai* (Paris: Plon, 1965)

Forrester, Viviane, *L'Horreur économique* (Paris: Fayard, 1996)

Giesbert, Franz-Olivier, *François Mitterrand, ou La Tentation de l'histoire* (Paris: Seuil, 1987)

——, *Jacques Chirac* (Paris: Seuil, 1987)

——, *Le Président* (Paris: Seuil, 1990)

——, *François Mitterrand: Une Vie* (Paris: Seuil, 1997)

Giscard d'Estaing, Valéry, *Démocratie française* (Paris: Fayard, 1976)

——, *Deux Français sur trois* (Paris: Flammarion, 1984)

——, *Le Pouvoir et la Vie* (Paris: Interforum, 1988)

Gubler, Claude, *Le Grand Secret* (Paris: Plon, 1996)

Hayward, Susan, and Vincendeau, Ginette, *French Film* (London: Routledge & Kegan Paul, 1990)

Hobsbawm, E. J., *The Age of Capital* (London: Weidenfeld & Nicolson, 1975)

——, *The Age of Empire* (London: Weidenfeld & Nicolson, 1987)

Horne, Alistair, *To Lose a Battle: France, 1940* (London: Macmillan, 1969)

——, *A Savage War of Peace* (London: Macmillan, 1977)

Imbert, Claude, and Julliard, Jacques, *La Droite et la Gauche* (Paris: Laffont/Grasset, 1995)

James, Colin, *France* (Cambridge: CUP, 1994)

Jamet, Dominique, *Demain le Front?* (Paris: Bartillat, 1995)

Jarreau, Patrick, *La France de Chirac* (Paris: Flammarion, 1995)

——, *Chirac: La malédiction* (Paris: Stock, 1997)

Jarreau, Patrick, with Kergoat, Jacques, *François Mitterrand: 14 ans de pouvoir* (Paris: Éditions Le Monde, 1995)

Jeanneney, Jean-Noël, *L'Argent caché* (Paris: Fayard, 1981)

Johnson, Michael, *French Resistance* (London: Cassell, 1996)

Julliard, Jacques, *La Cinquième République* (Paris: Seuil, 1976)

Klein, Richard, *Cigarettes are Sublime* (London: Picador, 1995)

Lacouture, Jean, *De Gaulle* (Paris: Seuil, three volumes, 1984–86)

Lavigne family, *Cousins d'Auvergne* (Aurillac: Association Cousins d'Auvergne, 1995)

Lévy, Claude, and Tillard, Paul, *La Grande Rafle du Vél d'Hiv* (Paris: Laffont, 1992)

Maîtres Cuisiniers de France, *Les Recettes du terroir* (Paris: Laffont, 1984)

Maspero, François, *Les Passagers du Roissy-Express* (Paris: Seuil, 1990)

Mauriac, François, *De Gaulle* (Paris: Grasset, 1964)

McLynn, Frank, *Napoleon* (London: Jonathan Cape, 1998)

Mermet, Gérard, *Francoscopie* (Paris: Larousse, 1994 and later editions)

Minc, Alain, *Le Nouveau moyen âge* (Paris: Gallimard, 1993)

Minc, Alain, and the Commissariat Général du Plan, *La France de l'an 2000* (Paris: Odile Jacob, 1994)

Mitterrand, Danielle, *En toutes libertés* (Paris: Ramsay, 1996)

Mitterrand, François, *Le Coup d'État permanent* (Paris: Plon, 1964)

——, *Ma Part de vérité* (Paris: Fayard, 1969)

——, *La Rose au poing* (Paris: Flammarion, 1973)

Mitterrand, François, *La Paille et le Grain* (Paris: Flammarion, 1975)

Moïsi, Dominique, 'The Trouble With France' in *Foreign Affairs* (New York, May/June 1998)

Montaldo, Jean, *Mitterrand et les 40 voleurs* (Paris: Albin Michel, 1994)

Monnet, Jean, *Mémoires* (Paris: Fayard, 1976)

Nay, Catherine, *Le Double Mépris* (Paris: Grasset, 1980)

———, *Le Noir et le Rouge* (Paris: Grasset, 1984)

Ottenheimer, Ghislaine, *Les Intouchables* (Paris: Albin Michel, 2004)

Paxton, Robert, *Vichy France* (New York: Columbia University Press, 1972)

Péan, Pierre, *Une Jeunesse française: François Mitterrand, 1934–47* (Paris: Fayard, 1994)

Peyrefitte, Alain, *Le Mal français* (Paris: Plon, 1977)

———, *Quand la Rose se fanera* (Paris: Plon, 1983)

Pingeot, Mazarine, *Premier Roman* (Paris: Julliard, 1998)

Pompidou, Georges, *Pour Rétablir une vérité* (Paris: Flammarion, 1982)

Rol-Tanguy and Bourderon, Roger, *Libération de Paris* (Paris: Hachette, 1994)

Ross, George; Hoffmann, Stanley; and Malzacher, Sylvia, *The Mitterrand Experiment* (Oxford: Polity, 1987)

Tournoux, Jean-Raymond, *Pétain et De Gaulle* (Paris: Plon, 1964)

———, *La Tragédie du Général* (Paris: Plon, 1967)

Viansson-Ponté, Pierre, *Histoire de la République gaullienne* (Paris: Fayard, two volumes, 1970–71)

Weber, Eugen, *Peasants into Frenchmen* (Stanford, CA: Stanford University Press, 1976)

Werth, Alexander, *De Gaulle* (London: Penguin, 1965)

Willard, Claude, *La France ouvrière* (Paris: Editions Ouvrières, 1995)

Williams, Charles, *The Last Great Frenchman* (London: Little, Brown, 1993)

Williams, Philip, and Harrison, Martin, *Politics and Society in De Gaulle's Republic* (London: Longman, 1971)

Winock, Michel, *Histoire de l'extrême droite en France* (Paris: Seuil, 1993)

———, *Parlez-moi de la France* (Paris: Plon, 1995)

Zeldin, Theodore, *France, 1848–1914* (Oxford: Clarendon Press, two volumes, 1973–77)

———, *The French* (London: Collins Harvill, 1983)

I have also drawn extensively on the French press. Apart from the daily recording of events by *Le Monde*, *Libération* and *Le Figaro*, various passages in this book owe a particular debt to the reporting by *L'Express* during 1997–98 and 2000-2002. The annual *Quid* almanac is a unique reference book. It has been invaluable to me in a hundred or more ways. I remain astonished by the way that a country whose books rarely contain even the most cursory of indexes can have created such a treasure. But then, this is a land of paradoxes.

INDEX